Lecture Notes in Computer Sci

Commenced Publication in 1973
Founding and Former Series Editors:
Gerhard Goos, Juris Hartmanis, and Jan van Leeuwen

Victor Larios   Félix F. Ramos
Herwig Unger (Eds.)

Advanced Distributed Systems

Third International School and Symposium, ISSADS 2004
Guadalajara, Mexico, January 24-30, 2004
Revised Selected Papers

 Springer

Volume Editors

Victor Larios
Universidad de Guadalajara
CUCEA, Dept. Sistemas de Informacion
799, Periferico Norte, Edif.L-308, Zappam, Jal., 45100, Mexico
E-mail: vlarios@acm.org

Félix F. Ramos
CINVESTAN
Prol. López Mateos Sur 590 Guadalajara, J 45090 A.P. 31-438, Mexico
E-mail: framos@gdl.cinvestav.mx

Herwig Unger
Universität Rostock
Fachbereich Informatik, Albert-Einstein-Str.23, 18051 Rostock, Germany
E-mail: hunger@informatik.uni-rostock.de

Library of Congress Control Number: 2004107500

CR Subject Classification (1998): C.2.4, I.2.11, D.2.12, D.1.3, D.4, H.3, H.4

ISSN 0302-9743
ISBN 3-540-22172-7 Springer-Verlag Berlin Heidelberg New York

Springer-Verlag is a part of Springer Science+Business Media

springeronline.com

© Springer-Verlag Berlin Heidelberg 2004
Printed in Germany

Typesetting: Camera-ready by author, data conversion by DA-TeX Gerd Blumenstein
Printed on acid-free paper   SPIN: 11011446   06/3142   5 4 3 2 1 0

Preface

This volume contains the accepted papers from the 3rd International School and Symposium on Advanced Distributed Systems held in Guadalajara, Mexico, January 24–30, 2004. This event was organized by the teams made up of members of CINVESTAV Guadalajara, CUCEI, the Computer Science Department of the Centre of Research and Advances Studies at the CUCEA campus of the University of Guadalajara, Mexico, the University of Rostock, Germany and ITESO, Guadalajara. The ISSADS symposium provides a forum for scientists and people from industry to discuss the progress of applications and theory of distributed systems. This year there were over 300 participants from 3 continents, among which about 20 percent came from industry.

The conference program consisted of 25 accepted papers out of 46 submissions and covered several aspects of distributed systems from hardware and system level up to different applications. These papers were selected by a peer review process, in which each paper was evaluated by at least three members of the international program committee.

In addition, the three invited speakers, Adolfo Guzman Arenas, Yakup Parker and Joaquin Vila, presented interesting overviews to current development and research directions in distributed systems. Furthermore, eight tutorials and four industrial forums from IBM, INTEL, HP and SUN enabled the participants to extend their knowledge in selected areas. A panel, which was organized by a team composed of researchers from the Universidad de Guadalajara and focused on traffic control and simulation, also demonstrated the practical application of recent research in distributed systems to the problems of Guadalajara.

At this moment, we would like to say thank you to all the members of the program and organizing committees as well as their teams, and we would like to show our particular gratitude to all those who submitted their papers to ISSADS 2004. Furthermore, we would like to acknowledge the local support from the Council of Science and Research of Jalisco, Mexico and the Jalisco Software Industry. Special thanks are also given to Yuniva Gonzalez and Cynthia Guerrero for their organizational support. We hope that all the participants enjoyed their stay in Mexico and benefited from fruitful discussions and a good time. We look forward to more new participants at the next ISSADS conference to be held again in Guadalajara, Mexico, in January 2005.

May 2004

Félix F. Ramos C.
Herwig Unger
Victor Larios

Program Committee

Chair Félix Francisco Ramos Corchado, CINVESTAV Guadalajara
Co-chair Victor Manuel Larios Rosillo, CUCEA, Universidad de Guadalajara
Editorial chair Herwig Unger, Rostock University, Germany

Scientific Committee

Anbulagan	A. Gelbukh	P. de Saqui Sannes
F. Arbad	A.A. Guzmán	R.M. Pires
G. Babin	G. Juanole	R. Rajkumar
H.R. Barradas	H. Kihl	F. Ren
J.P. Barthés	J.-L. Koning	G. Román
N. Bennani	P. Kropf	E.E. Scalabrin
T. Böhme	S. Lecomte	S. Tazi
P. Boulanger	A. López	H. Unger
M. Bui	R. Mandiau	J. Vila
L. Chen	E. Moreira	T. Villemur
M. Diaz	S. Murugesan	P. Young-Hwan
D. Donsez	A. N Tchernykh	A. Zekl
K. Drira	Y. Paker	
C.V. Estivill	E.P. Cortéz	

Organization

Public Relations Carolina Mata, CINVESTAV Guadalajara
Logistics Cynthia Guerrero, CINVESTAV Guadalajara
Logistics Jorge Hernández, CINVESTAV Guadalajara
Logistics Yuniva González, CINVESTAV Guadalajara

Table of Contents

International School and Symposium on Advanced Distributed Systems

Myths, Beliefs and Superstitions about the Quality of Software
and of Its Teaching
Adolfo Guzman Arenas 1

Enhancing a Telerobotics Java Tool with Augmented Reality
Nancy Rodriguez, Luis Jose Pulido, and Jean-Pierre Jessel 9

VIBES: Bringing Autonomy to Virtual Characters
Stéphane Sanchez, Hervé Luga, Yves Duthen, and Olivier Balet............ 19

An Overview of the VIRTUOSI Toolkit
Alcides Calsavara, Agnaldo K. Noda, and Juarez da Costa Cesar Filho..... 31

Assessing the Impact of Rapid Serial Visual Presentation (RSVP):
A Reading Technique
Barbara Beccue and Joaquin Vila 42

An Open Multiagent Architecture to Improve Reliability
and Adaptability of Systems
Edson Scalabrin, Deborah Carvalho, Elaini Angelotti, Hilton de Azevedo,
and Milton Ramos... 54

Toward a Generic MAS Test Bed
Juan Salvador Gómez Álvarez, Gerardo Chavarín Rodríguez,
and Victor Hugo Zaldivar Carrillo.. 67

State Controlled Execution for Agent-Object Hybrid Languages
Ivan Romero Hernandez and Jean-Luc Koning 78

Cognitive Agents and Paraconsistent Logic
Elaini Simoni Angelotti and Edson Emílio Scalabrin 91

A Multiagent Infrastructure for Self-organized Physical Embodied Systems:
An Application to Wireless Communication Management
Jean-Paul Jamont and Michel Occello 105

Tlachtli: A Framework for Soccer Agents Based on GeDa-3D
Francisco Ocegueda, Roberto Sánchez, and Félix Ramos.................. 118

Evaluating Location Dependent Queries Using ISLANDS
Marie Thilliez and Thierry Delot 125

Conceptual Information Retrieval
Emerson L. dos Santos, Fabiano M. Hasegawa, Bráulio C. Ávila,
and Fabrício Enembreck 137

Semantic Search Engines
Alcides Calsavara and Glauco Schmidt................................. 145

The Internal-Local-Remote Dependency Model for Generic Coordination
in Distributed Collaboration Sessions
José Martin Molina Espinosa, Jean Fanchon, and Khalil Drira 158

About the Value of Virtual Communities in P2P Networks
German Sakaryan, Herwig Unger, and Ulrike Lechner 170

Search in Communities: An Approach Derived from the Physic Analogue
of Thermal Fields
Herwig Unger and Markus Wulff 186

A Component-Based Design Approach
for Collaborative Distributed Systems
Francisco Moo-Mena and Khalil Drira 197

Architecture for Locating Mobile CORBA Objects
in Wireless Mobile Environment
Mayank Mishra.. 207

Integration of Load Balancing into a Parallel Evolutionary Algorithm
Miguel Castro, Graciela Román, Jorge Buenabad, Alma Martínez,
and John Goddard... 219

Random Distributed Self-stabilizing Structures Maintenance
Thibault Bernard, Alain Bui, and Olivier Flauzac....................... 231

A New On-Line Scheduling Algorithm for Distributed Real-Time System
Mourad Hakem and Franck Butelle.................................... 241

Facing Combinatory Explosion in NAC Networks
Jérôme Leboeuf Pasquier 252

Multiple Correspondences and Log-linear Adjustment in E-commerce
María Beatriz Bernábe Loranca and Luis Antonio Olsina Santos 261

A Distributed Digital Text Accessing and Acquisition System
Adolfo Guzmán Arenas and Victor-Polo de Gyves 274

Author Index 285

Myths, Beliefs and Superstitions about the Quality of Software and of Its Teaching

Adolfo Guzman Arenas

Centro de Investigacion en Computacion (CIC)
Instituto Politecnico Nacional, Mexico
a.guzman@acm.org

Abstract. It is a surprise to see how, as years go by, two activities so germane to our discipline, (1) the creation of quality software, and (2) the quality teaching of software construction, and more generally of Computer Science, are surrounded or covered, little by little, by beliefs, attitudes, "schools of thought," superstitions and fetishes rarely seen in a scientific endeavor. Each day, more people question them less frequently, so that they become "everyday truths" or "standards to observe and demand." I have the feeling that I am minority in this wave of believers and beliefs, and that my viewpoints are highly unpopular. I dare to express them because I fail to see enough faults in my reasoning and reasons, and because perhaps there exist other "believers" not so convinced about these viewpoints, so that, perhaps, we will discover that "the imperator had no clothes, he was naked."

1 Myths and Beliefs about the Production of Quality Software

This section lists several "general truths," labeled A, B..., G concerning quality of software, and tries to ascertain whether they are reasonable assertions ("facts," sustainable opinions) or myths.

1.1 About Measuring Software Quality

A. It Is Possible to Measure the Main Attributes that Characterize Good Quality Software. The idea here is that software quality can be characterized by certain attributes: reliability, flexibility, robustness, comprehension, adaptability, modularity, complexity, portability, usability, reuse, efficiency... and that it is possible to measure each of these, and therefore, characterize or measure the quality of the software under examination. To ascertain whether point A is a fact or a myth, let us analyze three facets of it.

1) *It is possible to measure above attributes subjectively*, asking their opinion to people who have used the software in question.

Comment 1. Opinions by Experienced Users Are Reliable. That is, (1) is not a myth, but something real. It is easy to agree that a program can be characterized by above attributes (or similar list). Also, it is convincing that the opinions of a group of

F. F. Ramos, H. Unger, V. Larios (Eds.): ISSADS 2004, LNCS 3061, pp. 1-8, 2004.
© Springer-Verlag Berlin Heidelberg 2004

qualified users respect to the quality, ergonomics, portability… of a given software are reliable and worth to be taken into account (subjective, but reliable opinions).

2) Another practice is to try to measure above attributes *objectively,* by measuring surrogate attributes if the real attribute is difficult to measure [Myth B below].

Comment 2. Measuring Surrogate Attributes. To measure the height of a water tank when one wishes to measure its volume, is risky. Objective (accurate) measurements of surrogate attributes may be possible, but to think that these measures are proportional to the real attribute, is risky. "If you can not measure beauty of a face, measure the length of the nose, the color of eyes…" If you can not measure the complexity of a program, measure the degree of nesting in its formulas and equations, and say that they are directly related. More in my comments to Myth B.

3) Finally, instead of measuring the quality of a piece of software, go ahead and measure the quality of the *manufacturing process* of such software: if the building process has quality, no doubt the resulting software should have quality, too (Discussed below as Myth C).

Comment 3. To Measure the Process, instead of Measuring the Product. In old disciplines (manufacturing of steel hinges, leather production, wine production, cooking…) where there are hundred of years of experience, and which are based in established disciplines (Physics, Chemistry…), it is possible to design a process that guarantees the quality of the product. A process to produce good leather, let us say. And it is also possible to (objectively) measure the quality of the resulting product. And to *adapt* the process, modifying it to fix errors (deviations) in the product quality: for instance, to obtain a more elastic leather. Our problem is that *it is not possible* to do that with software. We do not know what processes are good to produce good quality software. We do not know what part of the process to change in order, let us say, to produce software with less complexity, or with greater portability. More in my comments to Myth C.

B. There Exists a Reliable Measurement for Each Attribute. *For each attribute to be measured, there exists a reliable, objective measurement* that can be carried out. The idea is that, if the original attribute is difficult to measure,[1] measure another attribute, correlated to the first, and report the (second) measurement as proportional or a substitute for the measure of the original attribute.

1. Reliability (reliable software, few errors): measure instead the number of error messages in the code. The more, the less errors that software has.
2. Flexibility (malleability to different usage, to different environments) or adaptability: measure instead the number of standards to which that software adheres.
3. Robustness (few drastic failures, the system rarely goes down): measure through tests and long use (Subjective measurement).
4. Comprehension (ability to understand what the system does): measure instead the extent of comments in source code, and the size of its manuals.

---

[1] Or we do not know how to measure it.

5. The size of a program is measured in bytes, the space it occupies in memory (This measurement has no objection, we measure what we want to measure).
6. Speed of execution is measured in seconds (This measurement has no objection, we measure what we want to measure).
7. Modularity: count the number of source modules forming it.
8. Program complexity (how difficult it is to understand the code): measure instead the level of nesting in expressions and commands ("cyclomatic complexity").
9. Portability (how easy it is to port a software to a different operating system): ask users that have done these portings (Subjective measurement).
10. Program usability (it is high when the program brings large added value to our work. "It is essential to have it."): measure the percentage of our needs that this program covers (Subjective measurement).
11. Program reuse: measure how many times (parts of) this program have been used in other software development projects. (Objective measurement, but only obtained in hindsight).
12. Ease of use (ergonomics) characterizes programs that are easy to learn, tailored to our intuitive ways to carry out certain tasks. Measure instead the quantity of screens that interact with the user, and their sophistication.

Comment 4. Measuring Surrogate Attributes. These "surrogate measurements" can produce irrelevant figures for the quality that we are really trying to measure. For instance, the complexity of a program will be difficult to measure using point 8, for languages that use no parenthesis for nesting. For instance, it is not clear that a software with long manuals is easier to comprehend (point 4). To measure the temperature of a body when one wants to measure the amount of heat (calories) in it, is incorrect and will produce false results. A very hot needle has less heat that a lukewarm anvil.

Comment 5. It is true that in the production of other goods, say iron hinges, is easy to list the qualities that a good hinge must possess: hardness, resistance to corrosion... And it is also easy to objectively measure those qualities. Why is it difficult, then, to measure the equivalent quantities about software? Because hinges have been produced before Pharaohnic times, humankind has accumulated experience on this, and because its manufacture is based on Physics, which is a consolidated science more than 2,000 years old. Physics has defined units (mass, hardness, tensile strength...) capable of objective measurement. More over, Physics often gives us equations ($f = ma$) that these measurements need to obey. In contrast, Computer Science has existed only for 60 years, and thus almost all its dimensions (reliability, ease of use...) are not susceptible (yet) of objective measurements. Computer Science is not a science yet, it is an art or a craft.[2] Nevertheless, it is tempting to apply to software characterization (about its quality, say), methods that belong and are useful in these more mature disciplines, but that are not (yet) applicable in our emerging science. We are not aware that methods that work in leather production, do not work

---

[2] Remember the title of the book "The Art of Computer Programming" of Donald C. Knuth. In addition, we should not be afraid that our science begins as an art or a craft. Visualize Medicine when it was only 60 years old: properties of lemon tea were just being discovered. And physicians talked for a long time of fluids, effluvia, bad air, and witchcraft. With time, our discipline will become a science.

in software creation. Indeed, it is useful at times to talk of software *creation,* not of software production, to emphasize the fact that software building is an art, dominated by inspiration, good luck… (see Comment 7).

1.2 Measuring the Process instead of Measuring the Product

An indirect manner to ascertain the quality of a piece of software, is to review the quality of the process producing it.

C. Measuring the Quality of the Process, Not the Product Quality. Instead of measuring the quality of the software product, let us measure the quality of its construction process. To have a good process implies to produce quality software.

Comment 6. It is tempting to claim that a "good" process produces good quality software, and therefore, deviations of programmers with respect to the given process should be measured and corrected. The problem here is that it is not possible to say which process will produce good quality software. For instance, if I want to produce portable software, what process should I introduce, versus if what I want to emphasize is ease of use? Thus, the definition of the process becomes very subjective, an act of faith. Processes are used that sound and look reasonable, or that have been used in other places with some success. Or that are given by some standard or international committee. "If so many people use them, they must be good." We need to recognize that our discipline is not (yet) a science nor an Engineering discipline, where one can design a process that guarantees certain properties in the resulting product, much in the same manner that the time and temperature of an oven can be selected to produce hinges of certain strength. Instead, our discipline is more of an art or a craft, where inspiration counts, "to see how others do it," "to follow the school of Prof. Wirth," to follow certain rites and traditions or tics that a programmer copied (perhaps unconsciously) from his teacher.

Comment 7. A more contrasting manner to see that certain measurement processes are not applicable to certain areas, is to examine an art, such as Painting or Symphony Composition. Following the rules of the hard disciplines (manufacturing of hinges), we would first characterize the quality symphonies as those having sonority, cadence, rhythm… Here, measuring those qualities becomes (as in software) subjective. Then, we would establish the rules that govern the *process* of fabrication of symphonies (by observing or asking notable composers, say Sergei Prokoffiev): the pen needs to have enough ink, use thick point; the paper must have a brightness no less than x, its thickness must be at least z; it must be placed on the desk forming an angle not bigger than 35 degrees. Light shall come from the left shoulder. Certainly, these rules will not hurt. But there is no guarantee that anybody that follows them will produce great quality symphonies, even if the very same rules in hands of Prokoffiev produce excellent results, over and over.

D. If You Have a Controlled Process, You Will Produce Good Quality Software. It is easy to know when you have a "good" (reasonable) process. It is easy to design a "good" process to produce software.

Comment 8. On the other hand, it is not really known which processes will produce easy-to-use software, which other processes will produce portable software, or software with good real-time properties, etc. The "process design" bears thus little relation to the goal: to produce a software product with this and that features. The problem resembles that of hospital surgeons in the pre-Pasteurian period, when bacteria were not yet discovered. Many people who underwent surgery died, full of infection and pus, without anybody knowing why. Of course, it was easy to measure the quality of a product of a surgery process: "birth-giving woman died of septicemia." Therefore, processes were designed to make sure that patients with surgery would not die: when coming to work, surgeons should pray to Saint Diego. Then, hang from your neck a chain of garlic bulbs. Then, wash your hands. You shall not commit surgery during days with nights having full moon… These rules certainly did not hurt (did not produce worse results), but they were not very related to the quality of the final results. Once bacteria were discovered, the rules were simplified, fine tuned and complemented with others: "wash your knives," "disinfect your hands." It is my impression that, in software creation, we are in a pre-Luis Pasteur epoch, and that we invent rules and processes "to have one at hand," but that the results (the quality of the resulting software) of these processes have little to do with the invented process, and with its fulfillment or lack thereof.

E. It Is Necessary to Create "Quality Champions," Quality Committees, and other human organizations whose goal is "to promote quality (of software)." Generally, a committee of this type (1) generates norms and rules saying how the construction of software is to be handled (regulations about the process; they *define* the process), including formats that certain intermediate and final documents (manuals, say) shall have, and (2) it observes if the programming team follows the rules (1), seeking to correct deviations.

Comment 9. These committees, since they do not know for sure neither how to measure the quality of the product (Myths A and B) nor how to alter the fabrication process if certain output attributes are unacceptable (Myth D), end up becoming hindrances and stereotyped bureaucracies. What they can demand (and they do) from the programming and design team is adherence to the process invented by said committee (or copied from an international organization). If they adhere and follow the process, "that is good," and (by faith) "good quality software shall be the result." If the team deviates, that is bad; offenders should be punished and be blamed for the bad quality of the results. This is equivalent to have, in a pre-Pasteurian hospital (see Comment 8) a committee that, watching that this week more patients died of general infection than in the previous week, strengthens its efforts and detects surgeons that did not pray to Saint Diego, while others hanged from their necks garlic bulbs that were not fresh. Let us reprehend these offenders, and less patients shall die.

F. Attitude Matters. The right mind-set towards quality shall permeate and impregnate each coder. The designer or programmer must be constantly thinking about quality, must have faith in that he will produce good quality software; he shall watch that the quality of his works be above a (high) minimum.

Comment 10. This is an act of faith, that certainly will not hurt. But it helps little. Software confection should not be based on faith or beliefs. Certainly, it helps somewhat that a programmer says each morning "today I am going to produce high quality software, I am sure of that," much in the same manner as a pre-Pasteurian surgeon said "Today, no one of my patients undergoing surgery will die; today, no one of my patients undergoing surgery will die." With respect to the idea that a programmer "shall watch the quality of his production," this is commendable, but it is certainly difficult, since *it is difficult to measure software quality,* even if the person measuring is the software builder.

1.3 The Myth of Standards

G. Adhesion to Standards Means High Quality Software. "If we do software construction following the rules dictated by a standards organization, we will be producing good quality software." "Following software construction standards ensures the quality of the process and the quality of the resulting software." That is to say, of the many processes that we could follow when creating software, let us use one that is part of a norm or standard (preferably, an international one), or let us follow the process used by a company that produces good quality software (Oracle, say).

Comment 11. Nothing wrong can be perceived in this practice. It is as if the surgeons of a low quality hospital (of Comment 8) decide to copy the surgery process of The Hospital of the Holy Virgin Mary, which has low post-surgery mortality. Or if I want to use Prokoffiev's "rules for composing good symphonies" (Comment 7). No evil will come out of this. Nevertheless, subjectivity and the scanty relation between these "preferred" procedures and the quality of the resulting software must be clear, as Comment 8 explains.

2   Myths and Beliefs about the Quality of Teaching in Computer Science

We now examine how quality in Computer Science schools is measured.

2.1 It Is Enough to Measure the Product

It seems very reasonable and obvious (but let us examine it) to measure the quality of the product, in order to ascertain its quality.

H. Measure the Product and See if It Is of Good Quality. If I make a test or examination to two young undergraduate alumni of different Computer Science schools, and one of then knows more computer science than the other, certainly the person knowing more is of better quality. Example: the organism "Ceneval" in Mexico, who does just that.

Comment 12. This measurement is "almost right," except that it does not measure the great *obsolescence* in our field. I estimate that the mean half-life[3] of a computer science concept is about 5 years. That is, every five years, half of what we know becomes useless; not because we forget concepts or because they were inadequately learnt. Just because these concepts are no longer useful, they are obsolete: bubble memories, remote job entry, punch tape... The measurement of point H simply measures the *today* quality, the quality *as measured today.* What will happen in five or ten years with alumnus 1 versus alumnus 2? May be alumnus 1 still displays useful knowledge, while alumnus 2 (the more knowledgeable today) no longer has. One rusted faster than the other. That is, alumni formation (specially in high obsolescence fields, such as ours –this is due to its youth, scantly 60 years old) depends on two factors: (a) the basic, theoretical knowledge, which will enable our alumni to *keep acquiring knowledge* through his productive life, outside College; and (b) the "today" knowledge, the knowledge that is "fashion today" (in 2004, objects, UML, Java, say) that will allow them to become immediately productive. "To go out into the sugar cane field and start cutting cane." Knowledge acquired in College is like the quality of a machete, which depends on two attributes: its *temper,* that permits it several resharpenings along its productive life (and we need to prepare alumni capably of a productive life of 40 years), and the *sharpness* of the cutting edge (which allows immediate productivity, "to go out and start cutting cane." My problem with procedure H is that only measures the *sharpness* of the edge, the "today usefulness." Add measurements every five years (longitudinal studies), or add measurements (today) about the degree of theory and basic subjects (those that can hardly change in 50 years, say) that the alumnus has; this knowledge is what renders him resistant to obsolescence.

I. Quality of a College Is Measured by the Quality of Its Alumni.

Comment 13. Again, this is "almost true." Certainly, we tend to give high quality to those Colleges that produce high-quality alumni. But often these schools require the entering students *to have already high quality.* At entrance time. High entrance requirements. I only accept the best. Obviously, these people will exit school better prepared than students at another College who, due to incoming deficiencies, finish their studies less well prepared. To be fair, the quality of a school should be measured by the *added value.* That is, measure the student at entrance and exit times, and perform a subtraction.

2.2 To Measure Quality of the Alumni, It Is Sufficient to Measure Quality of the Process

The certification process of a College implies measuring the teaching process that it carries. There is a thought that good (certified) colleges produce high quality alumni.

---

[3] The half-life of a radioactive substance is the time taken by that substance's mass to decay to half its original mass.

J. Good Teaching Processes Will Produce Good Alumni. To know the quality of an alumnus, it is enough to measure the quality of the teaching process.

Comment 14. This looks like §1.2, "let us measure the process instead of measuring the product." Again, the idea here is that it is possible to design a teaching process that guarantees the quality of the alumni. "He shall have laboratory practices." "Exams should be designed by a Department commission." "Every student shall have his own computer." Nevertheless, unlike §1.2 (which is just a belief, called Myth C), point J is true, it is a truth (not a myth).. This is due to the many centuries that humankind has devoted to education, which shines much light on how to design good educational processes. And also tells us what part of the process to modify if, say, students are not acquiring enough knowledge in Experimental Chemistry. I will only add that in educational processes (as in cooking) two things are also important: (a) the *ingredients,* the books, the available software, the transmitted knowledge, the syllabus, and (b) the *artisans,* the cookers, that is, the teachers, the instructors.

References

These works are not referred in the text.

[1]   Roger S. Pressman. *Software Engineering, a practical approach.* McGraw Hill. A standard textbook on software engineering, with many methods for software construction, and software metrics.

[2]   I. Sommerville. *Software Engineering.* Addison-Wesley. Idem.

Enhancing a Telerobotics Java Tool with Augmented Reality

Nancy Rodriguez, Luis Jose Pulido, and Jean-Pierre Jessel

IRIT - Institut de Recherche en Informatique de Toulouse
Equipe Synthèse d'Images et Réalité Virtuelle
118 Route de Narbonne, 31062 Toulouse, France
{rodri,pulido,jessel}@irit.fr

Abstract. This paper describes the integration of an Augmented Reality service into our telerobotics system ASSET. ASSET is a teleoperation tool written in Java offering the services of simulation, 3D visualization, devices management and Java3D/VRML2.0 models loading. ASSET allows the definition of behaviors for each simulation object, and hence, entities sharing the same environment can have different degrees of autonomy. The Augmented Reality service that we have integrated uses the Java binding of the ARToolkit in order to allow operators and autonomous robots to gather information about the mission. Information points are represented in the real world by visual patterns, which trigger actions to be executed by the robot or activate virtual objects display when recognized by the Augmented Reality Service.

1 Introduction

Teleoperation is especially useful in manipulating in dangerous or unreachable work sites, e.g. toxic substances treatment or spatial exploration. However, as the teleoperated robot is far from the control site, delays in transmission of commands and feedback appear. This latency could be reduced by using a virtual representation of the robot that can be manipulated in real time [14]. The virtual robot is generally implemented using augmented or virtual reality. In Augmented reality environments, real images are overlaid with computer generated images. In Virtual reality, users interact with a virtual world representing the real work site. By using virtual robots it is possible to compensate communication delays because abstract control is less sensitive to latency than direct control [18]. Based on this statement, different projects [15] have shown that virtual reality interfaces can improve mission knowledge by providing tools to analyse and understand the remote environment.

In our system ASSET (Architecture for systems of Simulation and Training in Teleoperation), we use virtual reality techniques for the design and the implementation of an environment for teleoperation systems development. This tool allows flexible customizing and can be used as a testbed for evaluating interaction techniques, devices, simulation models and autonomous agent behaviors. Augmented reality mechanisms have been added to ASSET to provide mission information in a different manner. The video images from the real robot viewpoint are overlaid with virtual objects in order to guide the user or to signal that an action must be executed.

F. F. Ramos, H. Unger, V. Larios (Eds.): ISSADS 2004, LNCS 3061, pp. 9-18, 2004.
© Springer-Verlag Berlin Heidelberg 2004

This Augmented Reality service reinforces the overall teleoperation system by allowing users to discover and resolve problems, which are not detected by the simulation module.

This paper is organized as follows: in section 2 we review related work in augmented reality and its application to teleoperation systems. In section 3, we provide a description of the tools used in our work: ASSET, ARToolkit and JARToolkit. Section 4 covers the Augmented Reality Service implementation. Finally, some conclusions and directions for future research are presented.

2   Background

In Augmented Reality (AR) environments, virtual and real elements coexist. AR enriches real images by superimposing virtual elements that the user cannot directly perceive: task instructions, world information (e.g. distance, temperature), etc. AR has been successfully applied in several domains as manufacturing, medicine, training and entertainment. It is widely used to add information about the environment being displayed (Figure 1). In medicine, for example, datasets collected from medical tests are rendered and combined with a view of the real patient to give access to useful data simultaneously and hence facilitate the diagnostic [12, 23]. In augmented prototyping, the real product prototype is enriched by adding textual annotations or by "virtually" changing the prototype characteristics such as material or color [20,24]. In touring applications, a user - wearing special equipment- can walk outdoors and visualize graphical objects that provide information about the environment [4]. This idea has been extended to entertainment applications. For instance, the ARQuake system allows users to play Quake game in the real physical world and experience computer-generated graphical monsters and objects [16,17].

As we have stated, in telerobotics, virtual robots compensate communication delays and increase efficiency. The system ARGOS shows that path planning is an easier and more accurate process when augmented reality is used [3,14]. The user can plan the mission and specify the robot's actions by manipulating the local virtual version and the results are directly displayed on the real world images. Once the plan is finished and evaluated, it can be executed by the real robot. Furthermore, as Azuma states: "the virtual versions can also predict the effects of manipulating the environment, thus serving as a planning and previewing tool to help the user in performing the desired task". Other approaches used a simulated environment augmented with virtual fixtures to assist programming of teleoperation tasks[22]. In Lloyd's system [13], the operator interacts with a simulated environment, which models each object as a polyhedron and implements full 3D contact dynamics. This system simplifies the place and the manipulation of objects using inputs from a simple 2D mouse. It allows robotic programming for untrained users.

Fig. 1. Annotations in an Augmented Reality Application (Image courtesy of W. Piekarski and B. Thomas, Wearable Computer Laboratory, University of South Australia [25])

In Augmented Reality, data from the real world is provided by video cameras and tracking systems. Collected data are then processed to calculate the transformation to be applied to the virtual objects. Finally, the transformed virtual objects are combined with the real image and visualized. The most important aspect to consider in an augmented reality application is the proper overlay of virtual objects onto the real scene. That means a precise calculation of the camera's viewpoint in real time to allow virtual objects to be located at the correct location in the image [7,9].

Several technologies such as video see-through, optical see-through and monitor are available to enable AR applications. A see-through Head Mounted Display (HMD) allows tracking of user's head and combines real and virtual sources using video or optical technologies. In optical see-through HMDs, the user can see the real world through the optical combiners located in front of his eyes. Video see-through HMDs do not allow a direct view: images from the real world are provided by one or two head-mounted video cameras, and they are combined with the virtual objects and sent to the monitors located in front of the user's eyes. AR applications can also be monitor-based (Fig. 2.). In this kind of configuration, the positions of the video cameras are tracked and used to calculate the virtual scene. The video of the real world and the graphic images are then combined and displayed on a monitor. Optionally, the images may be displayed in stereo on the monitor, which then requires the user to wear a pair of stereo glasses [2].

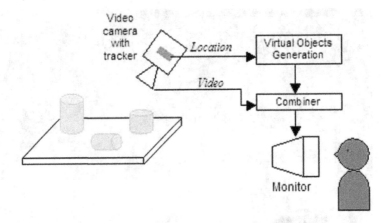

Fig. 2. Monitor based Augmented Reality System

The Augmented Reality Toolkit (ARToolkit) is a C publicly available library that enables the fast development of new AR applications [1]. ARToolKit uses computer vision techniques to calculate the real camera location by using predefined marked cards, and allows the programmer to overlay virtual objects onto these cards. We have used JARToolkit [8], a Java binding for the ARToolkit, to implement an Augmented Reality service for our telerobotics system ASSET.

3   Tools Overview

3.1 ARToolkit

The Augmented Reality Toolkit (ARToolkit) uses visual patterns (tracking markers) and their location in the real world to determine the camera viewpoint. The ARToolkit patterns are black squares with a black and white or color image in the middle. Markers' location is then used to overlay the pattern with its associated virtual object. This process is realized by the ARToolkit in several steps [9]:

1. The live video image is turned into a binary image based on a lighting threshold value.
2. The binary image is then searched for square regions. ARToolkit finds all the squares in the binary image, many of which are not the tracking markers.
3. For each square, the pattern inside the square is captured and matched against some pre-trained patter templates. If they match, then ARToolkit has found one of the AR tracking markers. ARToolkit then uses the known square size and pattern orientation to calculate the position of the real video camera relative to the physical marker.
4. The real video camera location is stored in a transformation matrix, which is used to set the position of the virtual camera coordinates.
5. Since the virtual and real camera coordinates are the same, the virtual objects rendered precisely overlay the real marker.

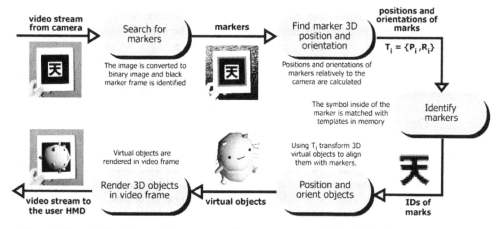

Fig. 3. The ARToolkit tracking process (Image courtesy of M. Billinghurst, HIT Lab, University of Washington [6])

3.2 JARToolkit

JARToolKit is a tool designed to offer the ARToolkit functionality to Java applications. JARToolkit uses Java Native Interface (JNI) in order to access ARToolkit services and allows the use of different rendering libraries (Java3D and GL4Java) as an alternative to the OpenGL API used in ARToolkit for drawing the virtual objects. By using Java, JARToolkit also provides ARToolkit with an object-oriented interface [5].

Two classes have been defined in JARToolkit in order to provide the ARToolKit functionality: JARToolKit and JARFrameGrabber. The JARToolKit class encapsulates all functions needed for tracking and some utility functions (e.g. to access the system time) and the class JARFrameGrabber provides all necessary functions to access video input from a camera. The two classes could be used separately in order to allow the development of different kind of applications.

3.3 ASSET

With ASSET we aim at providing a tool for helping development of telerobotics systems, following the philosophy of experimental platforms for virtual reality systems. We have also adopted distributed simulation techniques for minimizing the use of network bandwidth, and object-oriented development to offer a modular, flexible and easy to use system. Furthermore, because one of the major limitations of the actual systems is the number of platforms in which they are available (generally only one or a very few) we have chosen Java and Java3d to develop our system, so that it can run on any platform without further changes. Also, even though we can use high-end displays, we are using a conventional computer monitor to display the virtual world. Our system can thus be regarded as a low cost virtual reality solution that can be used for many applications in telerobotics research [21].

Fig. 4. depicts the ASSET architecture. There are two modules representing the local and the remote site and a third module that acts as a coordinator of the other two. In the local site, the operator generates commands for the robot by using the local site interface and the interaction devices. The commands are then executed by the simulation component and feedback is presented to the user. Only valid commands are sent to the remote site to be executed by the robot. The remote module transmits also commands to its simulation component and recovers real world state. If the difference between the real world state and the simulation state exceeds a user-defined threshold, the simulation state is updated in both, local and remote sites.

The communication between ASSET modules is managed by their Communications components. All the interaction between components of a module (simulation, virtual devices, visualization and communications) are defined by message passing and synchronized by means of the data space and event handling. Modules and components functionalities are described and accessed using specific interfaces so they can be modified without affecting each others. To allow the reuse of ASSET components, specific application information is processed only by the components – such as physical devices controllers or behavioral units- supplied for the application.

The particular application components and models are loaded from a configuration file, read at the initialization. This configuration file allows the customization of communication protocols, simulation objects (geometry and behavior), interaction devices, actuators and command validity rules. For analyzing different environment configurations and to allow fast prototyping, the user can change this file, rather than modify the source code and recompile.

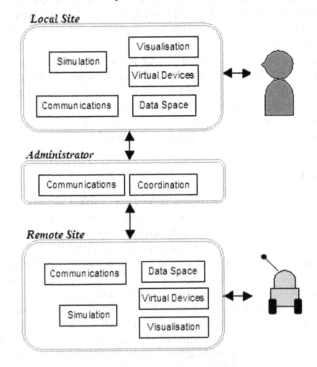

Fig. 4. Architecture of the ASSET System

4   Integration of the Augmented Reality Service

The Augmented Reality Service (ARService) that we have designed uses JARToolkit to allow operators and autonomous robots to collect information about the mission. Information points are represented in the real world by the tracking markers which,when recognized by the AR Service, trigger actions to be executed by the robot or activate virtual objects that provides information to the operator.

The AR Service has been integrated into the local and remote modules of the ASSET system. The remote AR Service captures the images and sends them to the local site. The local AR Service processes the image to detect patterns and superimpose the virtual objects. The final image, combining the image captured and the virtual scene, is then visualized by the user.

In order to implement this AR Service, some modifications has been made to ASSET and JARToolkit [19]:

- ASSET modifications: By default, ASSET modules communicate through TCP/IP sockets using text messages. Therefore, to support images transmission, the communication structure of ASSET needed some changes. In the new version, the sockets are read and written using the Java classes ObjectOutputStream and ObjectInputStream, which allows transmitting any Java object implementing the Serializable Java interface. Previously, the class Message was only able to store text messages. It has been modified to be able to store any Java object and to implement the Serializable[1] interface.

- JARToolkit modifications: JARToolkit has not been designed to work in a distributed configuration. To permit its integration in ASSET, a new class called ImageCam has been defined. This class, implementing also the Serializable interface, is used to store all the information about the image captured by the JARFrameGrabber. ImageCam also provides format conversion services to modify the image for network transmission and for processing in the local ARService.

A prototype of the AR Service was developed for Windows platforms. In this prototype configuration, we have a fixed camera viewing the environment and a mobile device being teleoperated. Our mobile device is a Khepera robot [10] with a tracking marker in its top face. This allows us to easily determine its location by using the ARToolkit tracking functions. Several tracking markers are disseminated in the environment, to be used as information points for the operator. The tracking markers are associated to virtual objects in the AR Service. When the robot walks over one tracking marker, the virtual object display is activated. In our current implementation, virtual objects are 3D text labels providing navigation clues (Fig. 5.). In the future, we will integrate more task related information. For instance, to assist in manipulation tasks, a virtual object (e.g. a virtual robot) could be superimposed in the location where the real robot will successfully pick or drop an object.

---

[1] Object Serialization supports the encoding of objects, and the objects reachable from them, into a stream of bytes; and it supports the complementary reconstruction of the object graph from the stream. Serialization is used for lightweight persistence and for communication via sockets or Remote Method Invocation (RMI).

Fig. 5. 3D Clues for Navigation

The AR Service can be activated and deactivated using the local site interface. When the user actives the AR Service, a new window is opened in order to display the images coming from the remote site. Therefore, there are two sources of information about the remote site: the 3D environment, which presents in real time actions results, and the AR display, which has an inherent delay due to communications latency. We are not interested in synchronizing the two sources because of the effect that this will have on the overall user response time. However, we allow the user to update the 3D environment with the information of the real world at anytime. We also planned to implement a function recovering the viewpoint of the captured image. This viewpoint can then be applied to the virtual camera. We think that this will ease the recognition of real (virtual) objects in the virtual (real) world based on their location.

ASSET is a work in progress and we can then improve our AR Service and the overall system by allowing the trackers markers to trigger actions to be executed by an autonomous robot. To do this, we have to add a vision module in the remote site in order to recognize patterns by processing the captured image. When a pattern is found (if the camera is on top of the robot) or when a condition is reached (e.g. distance between an environment pattern and the robot pattern in a fixed camera configuration), the vision process will send a message to the behavior controller of the robot in order to execute a predefined action.

We are also interested in studying time issues like latency reduction. To do so, we have to analyze the current network traffic generated by the Augmented Reality Service and investigate the use of protocols enabling video transmission such as RTP (Real-Time Transport Protocol).

5   Conclusions and Future Work

In this paper we have presented an Augmented Reality Service (AR Service) for teleoperation. It is based on the Java binding of the ARToolkit, a publicly available library allowing fast development of Augmented Reality applications. The AR

Service has been integrated in our telerobotics tool ASSET to provide additional data about the teleoperation mission being executed by an operator. In our current prototype, the operator can recover useful information by driving the mobile robot to the information points represented by visual patterns. When the AR Service recognizes a marker, a virtual object is superimposed into the real image at the marker location. The AR Service makes possible the combination of virtual objects and video images of the real world to indicate, for instance, particular features of the real objects.

Future work includes the improvement of our prototype in order to allow the AR Service to be used by autonomous robots. Additional developments to ease the correlation between the 3D synthetic world and the AR display are also planned. We are also interested in changing our fixed camera configuration with a camera fixed on the top of the robot to take full advantage of its mobile nature.

References

[1]   ARToolkit, http://www.hitl.washington.edu/artoolkit/
[2]   Azuma R.T.: A Survey of Augmented Reality. In Presence: Teleoperators and Virtual Environments, Vol. 6, No. 4 (1997)
[3]   Drascic D., Grodski J.J., Milgram P., Ruffo K., Wong P., Zhai S.: ARGOS: A Display System for Augmenting Reality. In Video Proceedings of INTERCHI '93: Human Factors in Computing Systems. Amsterdam, the Netherlands (1993)
[4]   Feiner S., MacIntyre B., Hollerer T., Webster A.: A Touring Machine: Prototyping 3D Mobile Augmented Reality for Exploring the Urban Environment. In: IEEE International Symposium on Wearable Computers (1997)
[5]   Geiger C., Reimann C., Stöcklein J., Paelke V.: JARToolKit – A Java Binding for ARToolKit. In: 1st IEEE International Workshop on the ARToolkit, Darmstadt, Germany (2002)
[6]   Human Interface Technology Lab, http://www.hitl.washington.edu
[7]   Ikeuchi K., Sato Y., Nishino K., Sato I.: Photometric Modeling for Mixed Reality. In: Proceedings of International Symposium on Mixed Reality, Yokohama, Japan, (1999)
[8]   JARToolkit, http://www.c-lab.de/jartoolkit
[9]   Kato H., Billinghurst M., Blanding R., May R.: ARToolKit Manual, PC version 2.11 (1999)
[10]   Khepera Robot, http://www.k-team.com/robots/khepera/index.html
[11]   Lawson S.W.,Pretlove J.R.G, Wheeler A.C.: Augmented Reality as a Tool to aid the Telerobotic Exploration and Characterization of Remote Environments, In: Presence: Teleoperators and Virtual Environments, Special issue on Virtual Environments and Mobile Robots, Vol. 11, No.4 (2002)
[12]   Lopes P., Calado Lopes A., Salles Dias J.M.: Augmented Reality for Non-Invasive Medical Imaging. In: 1st Ibero-American Symposium on Computer Graphics, Guimarães, Portugal (2002)
[13]   Lloyd J.E., Beis J.S., Pai D.K., Lowe D.G.: Programming Contact Tasks Using a Reality-based Virtual Environment Integrated with Vision. In: IEEE Transactions on Robotics and Automation, Vol. 15, No. 3 (1999)
[14]   Milgram P., Zhai S., Drascic D., Grodski J.J.: Applications of Augmented Reality for Human-Robot Communication. In: Proceedings of International Conference on Intelligent Robotics and Systems, Yokohama, Japan, (1993)

[15]   Nguyen L., Bualat M., Edwards L., Flueckiger L., Neveu C., Schwehr K., Wagner M.D., Zbinden E.: Virtual Reality Interfaces for Visualization and Control of Remote Vehicles, In: Vehicle Teleoperation Interfaces Workshop, IEEE International Conference on Robotics and Automation, USA (2000)

[16]   Piekarski W., Thomas B.: ARQuake: the Outdoor Augmented Reality Gaming System. In: Communications of the ACM, Vol. 45, No. 1 (2002)

[17]   Piekarski W., Thomas B.: Interactive Augmented Reality Techniques for Construction at a Distance of 3D Geometry. In: Immersive Projection Technology, Eurographics Virtual Environments, Zurich, Switzerland (2003)

[18]   Pook P., Ballard D.: Remote Teleassistance. In: IEEE International Conference on Robotics and Automation, Japan (1995)

[19]   Pulido L.J.: Augmented Reality Environments applied to Teleoperation. DEA dissertation (in French), Paul Sabatier University, Toulouse, France (2003)

[20]   Regenbrecht H.T., Wagner M.T., Baratoff G.: MagicMeeting: A Collaborative Tangible Augmented Reality System, Virtual Reality, Vol. 6, No. 3 (2002)

[21]   Rodriguez A.N.: ASSET: A General Architecture for Telerobotics, PhD thesis (in French), Paul Sabatier University, Toulouse, France (2003)

[22]   Sayers C.R., Paul R.P: An Operator Interface for Teleprogramming Employing Synthetic Fixtures. Technical report, Department of Computer and Information Science, University of Pennsylvania (1994)

[23]   Seitber F., Hildebrand A.: Stereo based Augmented Reality applied within a Medical Application. In Computer Graphik Topics, Vol. 11, No. 1 (1999)

[24]   Stork A.: Augmented Prototyping. In: Computer Graphik Topics Vol. 14, No. 1 (2002)

[25]   Wearable Computer Laboratory http://wearables.unisa.edu.au

VIBES: Bringing Autonomy to Virtual Characters

Stéphane Sanchez[1,2], Hervé Luga[1], Yves Duthen[1], and Olivier Balet[2]

[1] UT1/IRIT, Allées de Brienne, 31042 Toulouse cedex, France
{Sanchez,Luga,Duthen}@irit.fr
[2] Virtual Reality Department, C-S, Toulouse, France
{Stephane.Sanchez,Olivier.Balet}@c-s.fr

Abstract. This paper presents VIBES (Virtual Behaviours), a behavioural animation system for generic humanoid characters within dynamic virtual worlds. This system is based on stand-alone hierarchical behavioural modules. Each module performs a given task according to the perception of the virtual agent it belongs to. The main originality of VIBES is to combine Artificial Intelligence and Artificial Life techniques in order to obtain real-time reactions and adaptive behaviours. VIBES is a module of the V-Man character animation system developed in the frame of the V-Man project supported by the European Commission in the frame of the 5th framework program.

1 Introduction

Nowadays, virtual humans commonly inhabit the 3D virtual worlds of many educational, industrial or entertainment applications. Since the pioneering works of Brooks [1] and Reynolds [11], the quest for realism has not only aimed at improving rendering and animation of these characters but also at making them more autonomous and intelligent. In the last few years, several behavioural systems have been created. Among others, the Improv system [10] controls agents with behavioural scripts translated from a given script. The modular HTPS architecture (Hierarchical Parallel Transition System) [3] consists of a hierarchy of parallel automatons. Each automaton represents a behaviour, a sensor or an actuator. This system has been applied to several driving simulators. The ACE engine [9] provides a platform to connect behavioural modules to a scripted environment in order to convincingly simulate virtual humans evolving in a carefully chosen scenario. Finally, A. Iglesias [8] proposes a behavioural animation framework to simulate fully autonomous agents that act according to their perception and needs.

This paper presents a new system dedicated to the behavioural animation of virtual humans. This system aims at blending task resolution systems commonly used in both Artificial Intelligence (scripts, inference engines …) and Artificial Life (evolutionist algorithms, learning systems …) in a modular and efficient say to suit the needs of real time applications.

F. F. Ramos, H. Unger, V. Larios (Eds.): ISSADS 2004, LNCS 3061, pp. 19–30, 2004.
© Springer-Verlag Berlin Heidelberg 2004

This platform, named VIBES (Virtual Behaviours), is a module of the V-Man character animation system developed in the frame of the V-Man project[1].

2 Conception Premises

The main purpose of the V-Man project is to provide virtual worlds with generic and credible virtual humanoid actors (also known as virtual agents) and the intent of the VIBES sub-project is to make these agents autonomous and intelligent. "Intelligent" means that virtual agents can plan and execute tasks according to their intention and the perception of the world. Moreover, "Autonomous" means that they do not systematically require the conventional intervention of a real user to act.

Apart from the usual foundations of common behavioural engines (perception pipeline, cognition system and memory system), VIBES respects the following specifications.

First, the real user should control virtual actors but the latter must have the ability to act and take decision by themselves. Depending on the simulation planned by the user, this implies that the autonomy of an agent could be of three levels:

- *inexistent* to low in case of virtual actors directed by the user (player avatar in games or virtual actor in storytelling applications with highly detailed scenarios),
- *medium* in case of goal guided simulations (emergency evacuation simulation, fire squad intervention, team work in sport games, storytelling in case of highly abstract screenplays),
- *high* when the user does not specify a goal to the actors and these only act according to their inner stimuli and their contextual situation (habitat simulation, simulation of virtual societies …).

Besides, the behavioural system should allow mixing autonomous characters with user-controlled ones and so it must satisfy a complex twofold objective: on the one hand, the guided agents must react instantaneously to the user's request, and on the other hand the autonomous ones must act in an intelligent way according to their surrounding environment, and quickly enough for real time matters.

Then, the virtual agent must have a generic behaviour. This implies that if an actor knows how to go and grab a pen on a desk while following a scenario in any storytelling application, a fireman must also know how to go and grab the hosepipe to put out the fire while simulating a fire squad intervention. Obviously, this should be possible without any deep modification of the behavioural engine.

Moreover, the virtual agent must act in a natural way. This means that, on the one hand, in a specific situation with a specific intention, a virtual agent must act as a real human might have done.

On the other hand, two different virtual agents must not exactly act in the same way for the same context: two humans placed in the same environment and subjected

[1] The V-Man project [IST-2000-28094] is a project supported by the European Commission and gathering industrial and academic partners in a consortium striving toward the realisation of an intuitive authoring tool allowing non-computer specialists to create, animate, control and interact with autonomous virtual characters.

to the same conditions can act in many different ways. In fact, we could tell that the agents should have personality.

Finally, several agents together must be able to have social interactions in order to have crowd and group or team behaviours.

The first concept of VIBES is that each virtual agent within any application is a unique individual. So, the whole behavioural system is based on a bottom-up strategy [1]. Such a strategy implies that each agent has its own behavioural system and that any crowd or team behaviour emerges from their inner stimuli, their perception of the world (and of each other) and of their individual or common goals.

The three levels of autonomy imply that the virtual agent must perform simple, elementary tasks (input by the user or generated by the system) as *walk* and *grab* as well as more abstract ones as *evacuate the building* or *play football*. The fact is that each abstract task can consist of a set of less abstract sub-tasks. For example, the following figure shows a possible breakdown into sub-task (white) and elementary actions (grey) of the *evacuate* task.

This, linked to the intent of creating generic behaviours, forms the basis of the second concept of VIBES: hierarchical modularity. Each order given to a virtual agent represents a task that it must accomplish. The mechanism that allows this fulfilment will be stored in a stand-alone behavioural item called module. The role of each module is to generate new orders or actions according to the status of the agent and its surrounding environment in order to fulfil a unique associated order. Elementary modules are the ones that only trigger an action in the virtual world (as *push*, *close* or *walk*). They represent the simplest behaviour and the elementary actions a virtual actor can perform. Any combination of elementary or other existing modules potentially creates a more complex one.

It is important to note that each module is independent and adapted to its associated task: thus, it can be used indistinctly in any application that uses VIBES to animate virtual humanoid characters.

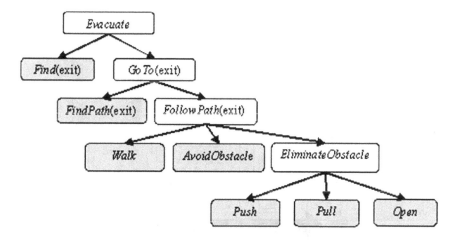

Fig. 1. Decomposition of *Evacuate* high level task

VIBES also requires a way to activate behavioural modules and to generate new tasks to fulfil. Most architectures usually use a set of deterministic rules and an inference engine to animate autonomous agents.

If such systems are sufficient to simulate an intelligent fulfilment of common tasks, they lack a little something to generate natural behaviours: no matter how complex they are, rule-based systems do not deal with uncertainties because they deterministically process situations and rules. In other words, similar conditions and knowledge always lead to the same output, if the system can compute one. Therefore, the third concept of VIBES deals with uncertainties. Due to the modular structure of the behavioural engine, the use of deterministic systems can be restricted to the case they apply the best and without uncertainty (as for example *open*(door) could be dealt with the simple script <*if in_range*(door) then *open*(door) else *goto*(door)>). More complex tasks can be satisfied using more adaptive systems as neural networks or classifiers systems.

Finally, in multi-agents simulations, even with the use of more stochastic mechanisms such as classifier systems, a simple copy of the behavioural modules from an agent to another could lead to unnatural behaviour. Indeed, they could all act exactly in the same way. The modular structure allows combining differently the behavioural modules to create personalities among the virtual actors. Besides, a learning system based on classifier systems and trials design may generate (more or less easily) a set of modules able to accomplish the same task but not exactly in the same way.

3   VIBES Framework

VIBES is linked to one agent consists of five main elements: the task manager, the perception system, the memory databank and the agent internal status data and, finally, the decision-making system.

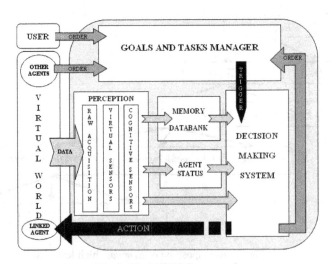

Fig. 2. The VIBES Framework

3.1 The Task Manager

The role of the task manager is to direct the virtual behaviour engine by collecting and handling orders from the possible sources and by triggering their process in a coherent and consistent way. There are three distinct kinds of sources for orders. The first one is the user of the application linked to the behavioural system, the second is one of the other agents in the virtual world and the last one is the virtual agent himself. Each time the manager collects an order or a list of orders, they are stored in a tree-like structure. Then, the manager triggers the activation of the decision-making process linked to the first eligible order. The first eligible order is the next order that is coherent and relevant with the current course of actions. It is important to note that the behavioural system tries to simulate autonomous agents and, so, a simple stored order could generate, during its processing, a complex dynamic subset of orders. The changes in the sets of orders is due to the probability that a planned action to solve a parent order fails and so cuts a branch of the tree of orders.

To ensure the coherence of the course of actions, the manager considers an order as active until the behavioural system has processed all its subtasks. The system considers an order as processed if all the actions it implies are successful or if it can never be fulfilled (i.e. it implies at least one suborder that can only fail).

Finally, the user or the linked application can choose to run behavioural simulations in planning mode (i.e. the system will process all the orders generated until succeeding in primary orders) or sequential mode (i.e. the application or the user chooses at which pace the next order will be processed). Besides, the user or application can request the task manager to stop, pause or reset the current process. Thus, the system can be easily adapted in matters of response time to function in any kind of applications included real time animated simulations or interactive ones.

3.2 The Perception System

The purpose of the perception system is classically to scan the virtual world in order to give relevant information to the components involved in the processing of orders. It consists of a pipe of three main kinds of components, the first ones being raw acquisition sensors, the second virtual sensors and we called the third ones cognitive sensors.

The raw acquisition sensors are used to convert all the data that the virtual world consists in into a formalism that the decision-making engine understands. The virtual sensors are principally meant to mimic common humanoid senses (essentially vision and hearing) but, in order to ease the decision-making and the use of the various components of the virtual world, we introduce another kind of sensor, the "focus sensor". Finally, the cognitive sensors transform the data issued from virtual sensors into refined relevant information for specific purpose.

The **vision sensor** allows the virtual agent to get visual information concerning its environment. It will provide essential data about the surrounding objects and other agents (position, size, type, name, velocity …).

As seeing is one of the main senses it will be used in finding and recognition tasks, in common movement behaviours such as path finding and obstacle avoidance, as well as in more complex ones like team work or crowd behaviour. To be accurate and realistic enough for simulation purposes, a horizontal field of view, a viewing distance and a viewing size threshold define the vision sensor. While the human field of vision is usually 200°, we chose to use one of 280° in order to simulate peripheral perception and head movements. The viewing distance is the maximum distance within which the agent is potentially able to view something. The viewing size threshold is the minimum size that an element of the environment requires to be perceived by the vision sensor. Therefore, any agent or object that is outside the field of vision, beyond the viewing distance, or of insufficient size will not be detected and so not provided to the behavioural engine. In order to push realism one step further, we use occlusion algorithms to eliminate entities that are totally hidden behind another.

The three main parameters of the vision sensor can be modified at initialization in order to mimic agents with non-accurate view as one-eyed or blind ones. Besides, the vision sensor acting as a filter applied to a global representation of the virtual world, we could easily implement altered vision sensors to mimic X-ray vision or anything particular the simulation needs. Finally, we plan to add lighting data in order to alter vision with notions of darkness and day or night vision.

The **hearing sensor**, which is still at the developing stage, works pretty much like the visual sensor. It consists of a "field of hearing" (usually 360°) and of a perception threshold that is the minimal intensity a sound requires to be heard. The intensity of a sound actually varies from 10 to 0 considering the distance of its source to the agent the sensor is linked to, 0 meaning silence and 10 maximum loudness. Actually, a perceived sound provides data on its emitter (essentially localisation and identification), its nature (conversation, music or distinctive sounds such as footsteps or breathing from another agent) and its intensity. Though simple, this conception of hearing is effective for our actual simulation purpose but we plan further improvements.

The **"focus sensor"** role is to mimic the fact that an entity of the world could become the centre of interest of the virtual agent. In such a case, the sensor is bound to the focused entity. It can constantly monitor its parameters and it can have access to more data about it. This sensor is useful because when an agent interacts with its environment it is usually with a specified object or agent ("open the door", "sit on the chair", "eat the food" ....).In theory, the "focus sensor" is unaffected by vision or hearing sensors for it is inconvenient to lose the object of attention during the processing of an order. Nevertheless, it is possible to link it to the virtual sensors in order to ignore the focused entity if they do not perceive it.

The output of the perception pipe, which is composed of focus, vision and hearing sensors, is a list of entities (agents and objects, and their various associated properties) that represent all the elements of the virtual world that the agent is able to perceive at the time the behavioural engine requests a scan of the environment.

If necessary, the cognitive sensors can process this set of perceived entities in order to extract more relevant and specific information. For example, a cognitive sensor can be a proximity sensor that selects among the perceived entities only the ones within a certain perimeter of the virtual agent. That kind of sensor is important to limit the data flow that the decision-making engine will have to process.

3.3 The Memory Databank and the Agent Status System

These two parts of the VIBES engine are used to bring realism into the decision-making process. For space limitation matters, they are not described in this paper but will be the subject of further work.

The memory databank stores various informations about the virtual world that might be useful to the decision-making engine (for example, cognitive maps of environment for path-planning tasks). The agent-status system monitors and stores the internal states of the virtual actor in order to simulate its knowledge of its actual situation, its needs and its emotions.

3.4 The Decision-Making System

The decision-making engine is the main core of the virtual behaviour. Its purpose is to determine a set of tasks or actions to accomplish in order to fulfil the orders collected by the task manager. It consists of a set of stand-alone behavioural modules dedicated to the fulfilment of a unique associated order. A module is a hierarchical structure that contains four elements: the task evaluator, the environment, the task solver and a subset of behavioural modules.

The **task evaluator** is the item that the task manager triggers. Its role is to initialize the task solver, to evaluate the completion of the solving process and, in case of use of any learning system, to handle the retribution engine.

The **environment** is the way to link the task evaluator and the task solver to the virtual world. Indeed, the environment receives a requested data flow from virtual and/or cognitive sensors and, if necessary, from the memory databank and the agent status system. Then, after processing the data flow to extract relevant information, it transmits it to the task evaluator (to evaluate completion of the task and, if necessary, retributions) and to the task solver in order to choose a way of action to complete the current task.

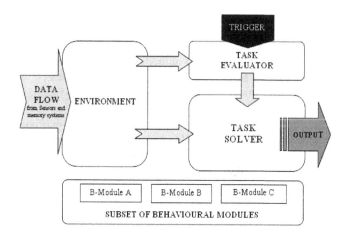

Fig. 3. Structure of a behavioural module (B-Module)

The **task solver** collects data from the task evaluator (in order to get the exact parameters of the aim to reach) and from its environment in order to make a decision about the next thing to do, and it reiterates this until it accomplishes the task or states a definite failure. The generated output can take three different forms: a new order (or a list of orders) to be processed, an action the agent must execute in the virtual world or an acknowledged signal that gives its actual state to the manager or to a possible parent order.

The **subset of modules** contains all the behavioural modules that the actual module might need for the completion of the new orders (output data) provided to the task manager. This inclusion is necessary to grant a behavioural module its stand-alone quality.

4 Learning System

One of the originalities of the VIBES engine is to include as behavioural module a learning system, specifically a Learning Classifier System (LCS), in order to teach virtual agents how to fulfil their task.

A LCS [6] [7] is an evolutionary computing system that uses a Genetic Algorithm (GA) [6] over a population of production rules in order to identify a sub-set of rules that can co-operate to solve a given task. A rule (a.k.a. classifier) consists of a condition, an action and a strength record. The condition acts as a matching receptor for a stimulus from the environment: each time the state of the environment matches the condition, its bound action is selected. The action is the decision that the agent makes (or, at least, a step toward the final decision). The strength record means the accuracy and the pertinence of the rule according to the task to solve and the environment. In case of competing selected actions, the LCS chooses the one that has the highest strength record. The modification of strength of rules applying the Q-Learning concept [15] ensures the learning process (however, while Q-Learning is restricted to a fixed sized space, in this case the learning method will apply to a changeable number of classifiers). The genetic algorithm role is to create potentially better new classifiers in order to improve the efficiency of the inference engine. Finally, a covering system (that creates new classifiers to match unexpected situations) allows the LCS to adapt to unpredictable dynamic environments.

Several factors (apart from the interest in LCS of our research team) motivate the choice of LCS as a learning system. First, as a rule-based system, the LCS stores its knowledge explicitly.

This allows the user to analyze the rules for simulation interpretation purposes or, in a more technical way, to manually add or modify the set of rules in order to compensate a failure in the improvement process (GA) or in the adaptation one (covering). Besides, a slight period of learning could contribute to improve a handmade a-priori set of rules that uses the LCS formalism.

Secondly, LCS are likely to be used as efficient memory systems. Indeed, in addition to the set of rules, LCS store the strength record of each classifier: this determines which rule is good or bad according to the current state of the environment, the task to solve and, eventually, the social rules of the agents' virtual world.

Afterwards, while conceiving a behavioural module for a complex task (*pushing an object in a crowded dynamic environment form A to B* for example) it could be more convenient to create a set of trial and let the virtual agent learn by itself than to implement an inference engine (or any other deterministic system) that could compute all the situations that the agent might encounter. Besides, when the user considers that the learning process is completed, the LCS can be used as a simple inference engine with its advantages (mainly the computing speed required for real time application) and disadvantages (particularly determinism).

Finally, the use of such a learning system is interesting as it enables to provide the virtual agent with some personality. Indeed, there could be many ways to fulfil a complex task and there is quite a chance that a classifier system randomly generated and evolving with a genetic algorithm only corresponds to a subset of them. Therefore, even if it uses the same wide variety of trials to solve a particular task, the learning engine can generate slightly different behavioural modules. Applying these modules to different agents in the world grants them a bit of personality as they do not exactly act as their neighbours in the same situation.

5   First Results: Motion Behaviours

Once the virtual behaviour framework was implemented, it had to be validated. This was done with the resolution of an essential complex task to accomplish: motion.

Moving is one of the basic behaviours of virtual agents. Indeed, most actions or decisions taken in order to interact in any environment usually imply moving towards a location (it could be near an object or another agent). As the agents should be autonomous, in order to go to a location they should be able to plan a path, follow this path, avoiding static or moving obstacles, and, if they cannot reach their planned destination, remove the obstacle or point out a failure.

Using VIBES, the **"GOTO"** module is a high-level module that is a script capable of triggering the following subset of modules: NAVIGATE, MOVETO, REMOVEOBSTACLE and COMECLOSEST.

The **NAVIGATE** module finds a path in the known topology of the virtual world. This knowledge is stored in the memory databank of the agent as a cognitive grid that indicates the latest space occupied by the known components of the environment (objects, walls, other agents …).

The path-finding algorithm is a standard A-star algorithm (optimized for real-time matters) that produces a smoothed path consisting of a minimal set of waypoints.

The **MOVETO** module ensures that the agent goes to a location B from its current location. In the case of GOTO, it makes an agent move from one waypoint to another and it is in charge of the collision avoidance behaviour. It triggers the action *walk* that signifies to the agent to take a step at a certain velocity and in a certain direction. This behaviour has two possible implementations. The main one is based on the works by C. Reynolds about steering behaviours [9]: the next move the agent will make (i.e. a new velocity vector meaning its speed and its heading) is calculated according to three computed vectors. The first one represents the direction towards the aimed destination; the second one is the needed deviation to avoid an anticipated collision with moving and static entities; finally, the third one represents needed correction to the deflected velocity to avoid any collision due to deviation. To avoid an unnatural determinism in the computation of avoidance deviation, stochastic values are integrated into the algorithms. Although this module prevents most of the possible collisions, in a highly crowded or encumbered environment, the support of a collision engine is highly recommended to prevent residual collisions. In order to add diversity to the moving behaviours of the agent, we can use a second MOVETO module. This one is related to the work of A. Champandard [2] about collision avoidance but instead of using neural networks, it is based on learning classifiers systems.

The **REMOVEOBSTACLE** is also a finite state machine that, if the agent is stuck and depending on the nature of the obstacle, triggers the correct way to handle it. If it is a door or a container, it activates the OPEN/CLOSE module (script). In case of another agent or several ones blocking the way, it triggers a classifier system that will handle communication between agents to solve the conflict. Finally, if it is an object, it can use a module based on a classifier system to *push* or *pull* the blocking entity out of the way.

The **COMECLOSEST** module role is to allow the agent to come as close as possible to an aimed entity. In case of an object put on another or contained into one, the recursive algorithm selects a position according to the closest accessible support or container. This module is used in case of a *goto*(object) kind of order (as in "go and grab the vase").

The GOTO module is the basis of most behaviours; nevertheless, in order to obtain a full range of moving usable abilities, we have also implemented the following modules:

- LEADTO: the agent leads a group of others to a destination.
- FOLLOW: the agent follows another one.
- BLOCK: the agent cuts the course of a quarry.
- INTERCEPT: the agent catches the quarry.
- EVADE: the agent flees a potential threat.

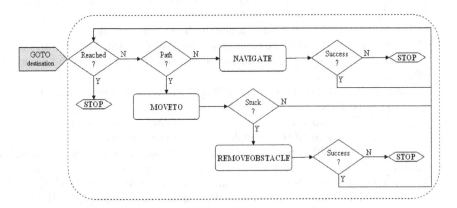

Fig. 4. GOTO module, functioning diagram in case of *goto*(destination) order

Fig. 5. Various applications of motion behaviours. Upper images: path planning and collision avoidance. Lower left: crowd behaviours. Lower right: building simulation and evacuation

6   Conclusion

In this paper we have presented VIBES, a new system for behavioural animation of generic virtual humanoid characters within real-time applications. A first implementation of this framework is already available and the first results are promising: virtual actors are able to move from one location to another, they avoid each other and possible obstacles and, they are also able to come within range of specified objects in order to interact with them. The use of an object oriented programming language (C++) to implement VIBES has preserved the modularity and the extensibility of the conceived framework, and the system is still being extended to more elementary actions and more low-level modules in order to simulate humans in storytelling applications and industrial simulations. Besides, VIBES will be used as a main part of our future research about cooperative and competitive behaviours.

However, implementing new behaviours, especially group or team ones, can be a complex and time consuming task. Improving the learning system in order to ease and accelerate their development seems necessary.

Acknowledgements

The authors would like to thank the European Commission for granting and supporting the V-Man RTD project in the frame of the Fifth Framework Program.

References

[1]   Brooks R.A. "A robust Layered Control System for a Mobile Robot" IEEE Journal of Robotics and Automation (1986), pp 14-23.
[2]   Champandard A. "Bot navigation tutorial", http://www.ai-depot.com.
[3]   S. Donikian, « HPTS: a Behaviour Modelling Language for Autonomous Agents », in Fifth International Conference on Autonomous Agents, Montreal, Canada, May 2001.
[4]   Funge J., Tu X., and Terzopoulos D. "Cognitive Modelling: Knowledge, Reasoning and Planning for Intelligent Characters", SIGGRAPH 99, Los Angeles, CA, August 11-13, 1999
[5]   Heguy O., Berro A., Duthen Y. "Learning System for Cooperation in a Virtual Environment". SCI'2001 The 5th World Multi-Conference on Systemic, Cybernetics and Informatics Orlando Florida, july 2001.
[6]   Holland J.H., "Adaptation in Natural and Artificial Systems", University of Michigan Press, Ann Arbor, 1975. Republished by the MIT Press, 1992.
[7]   Holland J. H., "Adaptive Algorithms for Discovering and Using General Patterns in Growing Knowledge Bases", International Journal for Policy Analysis and Informations Systems, vol 4, no 3, p 245-268, 1980.
[8]   Iglesias A., Luengo F. "Behavioral Animation of Virtual Agents". 3IA'2003 The 6th International Conference on Computer Graphics and Artificial Intelligence, Limoges(France), May 2003
[9]   Kallmann M., Thalmann, D. "A behavioural interface to simulate agent-object interactions in real-time", proceedings of Computer Animation'99, IEEE Computer society press, Menlo Park (1999) 138-146
[10]   Perlin K., Goldberg A. "Improv: a system for scripting interactive actors in virtual worlds", proceedings of SIGGRAPH'96, 1996, New Orleans, 205-216
[11]   Reynolds C.W. "Flock, Herds and Schools": a distributed behavioural model" in SIGGRAPH'87, vol 21(4) of Computer Graphics, pp 25-34. ACM Press, 1987. Anaheim(USA)
[12]   Reynolds C.W. "Steering Behaviors for autonomous Characters" in Game Developper Conference, 1999 San José(USA)
[13]   Sanza C., "Evolution d'entités virtuelles coopératives par systèmes de classifieurs', Thèse de Doctorat, Université Paul Sabatier (Toulouse), june 2001.
[14]   Thalmann D., Musse S.R. and Kallmann M "Virtual Humans' Behavior : Individuals, Group and Crowds " Proceedings of Digital Media Futures International Conference. 1999. Bradford (United Kingdom).
[15]   Watkins C., and Dayan   P. Technical Note: "Q-Learning", Machine Learning, 8, 279-292, 1992.

An Overview of the Virtuosi Toolkit

Alcides Calsavara, Agnaldo K. Noda, and Juarez da Costa Cesar Filho

Pontifícia Universidade Católica do Paraná
Programa de Pós-Graduação em Informática Aplicada
Rua Imaculada Conceição, 1155, Prado Velho, Curitiba, PR, Brazil
{alcides,anoda,juarez}@ppgia.pucpr.br
http://www.ppgia.pucpr.br/~alcides

Abstract. Currently, a number of distributed software systems development tools exist, but typically they are designed either to satisfy industrial standards – *industrial perspective* – or to experiment new concepts –
research perspective. There is a need for software development tools where
programmers can both learn about distributed computing – *pedagogical perspective* – and build quality distributed software systems through
prototyping – *experimental perspective*. This paper introduces the Virtuosi Project, which aims at building a toolkit to assist in developing
and executing distributed software systems from both pedagogical and
experimental perspectives. It combines virtual machine, object-oriented
programming and computational reflection concepts to give those perspectives. The Virtuosi runtime environment can be seen as a reflective
middleware, where objects can migrate and remote method invocation
is totally transparent by using a mechanism based on handle table.

1 Introduction

The importance of distributed computing has grown significantly in the last
years due to the incresing use of the Internet as a means of information systems
deployment. Many new applications have emerged and new ones are expected in
the near future, especially in the fields of embbeded systems and mobile devices
– the so-called ubiquitous computing This scenario promises a high demand for
distributed software system development in the next years.

However, distributed computing introduces great complexity in software systems development, deployment and maintenance. A number of requirements
which are not normally present in centralized systems may need to be fulfilled
in distributed systems, such as reliability of an interprocess message exchange
protocol. Also, requirements which are already present in centralized systems
may be more difficult to implement in distributed systems, such as security. As
a consequence, developing quality distributed software systems is hard and relies
fundamentally on programmers expertise and good tool assistance.

A programmer becomes an expert in developing distributed software systems firstly when she is properly taught distributed computing concepts and
secondly when she is properly trained to use specific technological artifacts,

F. F. Ramos, H. Unger, V. Larios (Eds.): ISSADS 2004, LNCS 3061, pp. 31–41, 2004.
© Springer-Verlag Berlin Heidelberg 2004

such as a distributed programming language or a middleware for distributed execution. Often, concepts are learned by experimenting with technological artifacts, where knowledge on theory and practice come together. The learning process is complex and the learning curve depends on many factors, but surely the technological artifacts employed are decisive.

A tool for developing distributed software systems can provide a series of features to programmers, from conceptual modeling to physical system installation. Naturally, the quality of a distributed software system is strongly influenced by the features provided by such a tool and how programmers use them. One such feature that is decisive for the success of a system is the capability to create prototypes easily, that is, create a preliminary version for the target system where its requirements – either established in the first place or introduced later – can be quickly implemented, debugged, tested and simulated.

Currently, a number of distributed software systems development tools exist, but they hardly favor learning about distributed computing and hardly favor prototyping because they are typically designed either to satisfy industrial standards – industrial perspective – or to experiment new concepts – research perspective. Industrial tools are concerned with productivity and software efficiency and robustness; they hardly permit a programmer to develop any task with simplicity and focused on a single problem, i.e., industrial tools invariably forces programmers to care about requirements that operational releases of real-world applications have and need to be considered despite the problem under study. That surely distracts programmers and may compromise both the developing and the learning curve. On the other hand, research tools normally have complex user interfaces and require the knowledge of particular concepts. Programmers often find it difficult to use research tools because they require a considerably large amount of work and time to build even small applications.

Therefore, there is a need for software development tools where programmers can both learn about distributed computing – pedagogical perspective – and build quality distributed software systems through prototyping – experimental perspective. A pedagogical tool should implement the main established principles of distributed computing in a clean way and should be open to be enhanced with trial concepts. An experimental tool should conform with the main established technologies, so that it would be possible to convert a prototype to a corresponding operational release.

The remaining of this paper is organized as follows. Section 2 presents the objectives of a new toolkit for building distributed applications named VIRTUOSI. Section 3 describes the main design principles of VIRTUOSI. Section 4 discusses how distributed objects are managed in VIRTUOSI, gives an overview on how they can migrate and how remote method invocation is implemented. Finally, Sect. 5 presents some conclusions and discusses future work.

2 Objectives

The VIRTUOSI Project aims at building a toolkit to assist in developing and executing distributed software systems from both pedagogical and experimental perspectives. From a pedagogical perspective, VIRTUOSI will permit programmers to be taught about distributed computing in a structured manner; distributed programming concepts and techniques would be introduced one by one and each studied separately from others. As a consequence, programmers should get a better understanding of distributed computing and the learning curve should get accelerated. From an experimental perspective, VIRTUOSI will permit programmers to create prototypes which are mature and robust; they will be mature because all typical system requirements will be implementable, and they will be robust because it should be easy to carry tests on separate units, followed by integration tests, where it would be possible to simulate all real-world operational configurations and circumstances, independtly of particular technological aspects. Because of their maturity and robustness, such prototypes will be the basis for easily developing the corresponding operational releases by using specific technologies. As a net effect, VIRTUOSI will assist in developing distributed software systems of great quality in a short period of time, since programmers will be better trained and will be able to implement and test critical system requirements in a controlled manner.

3 Key Design Decisions

The VIRTUOSI toolkit encompasses many aspects of distributed computing and of software engineering. It should comprise artifacts to build software systems and a full-fledged distributed runtime system. The pedagogical perspective requires an environment where a programmer can write a program by using a simple yet powerful set of abstractions, and then test that program in a way that all abstractions employed can be easily traced, i.e., translations from programming abstractions to runtime structures should be minimized. Another requirement from the pedagogical perspective is that the environment should be as neutral as possible with respect to the actual runtime platform in order to avoid unnecessary distractions. Finally, the pedagogical perspective requires an environment where the programmer can easily select which system aspects should be either transparent or translucent in a given moment. The experimental perspective, on the other hand, requires an environment where real-world applications can be quickly developed and carefully tested. The subsequent sections present the key design decisions made for the VIRTUOSI toolkit in order to satisfy the requirements discussed so far, namely virtual machine, object-oriented programming and computational reflection .

3.1 Virtual Machine

The VIRTUOSI runtime environment is composed of a collection of communicating virtual machines. In a simplified way, each virtual machine is a user-level process that emulates a real-world computer, including its hardware components and corresponding operating system. Thus, each virtual machine is able to host any typical software systems that store and process data and, as well, communicate with peripherals. Virtual machines are grouped in collections where each virtual machine can be unambiguously addressed and can exchange messages with any other in the collection. That allows a software system running on a certain machine to communicate with a software system running on a different machine, i.e., a collection of communicating virtual machines is a runtime environment for distributed software systems. In fact, this runtime environment can be seen as a middleware, similarly to systems based on the CORBA Standard [1], since a distributed software system can run on a heterogeneous computer network.

Such an approach to distributed computing – based on virtual machines – is in accordance with the objectives of the VIRTUOSI Project (Section 2) due to the following reasons:

Neutral Architecture A virtual machine is not tied to any particular computer architecture; it implements only core computer features which are common to standard computer technologies. From an experimental perspective, this ensures that prototype software systems which run on VIRTUOSI machines can be easily translated into operational releases that run on any typical real-world machines, while not precluding code optimization for better use of particular computer architeture features. On the other hand, from a pedagogical perspective, the simplicity of a VIRTUOSI machine architecture makes it appropriate for training computer programmers since the number of concepts to work with is small; consequently, programmers are forced to know how to combine such concepts to build complex applications.

Portability and Mobility A virtual machine sits between applications and the actual operating system; applications interact with the virtual machine which, in turn, interacts with the operating system. As a consequence, there must be a specific implementation of the VIRTUOSI machine for each operating system. Another consequence is that a software system that runs on a specific VIRTUOSI machine implementation will run on any other. In other words, VIRTUOSI applications are portable: they run on heterogeneous computers, as long as there is proper implementation of the virtual machine. From an experimental perspective, this portability helps building prototypes when a group of programmers who use distinct operating systems work cooperatively; they can share code without getting down to runtime environment specifics, thus improving productivity. From a pedagogical perspective, it helps programmers to write exercises in steps where several distinct computers can be employed without causing any distractions. Yet another consequence of the use of virtual machines is that VIRTUOSI applications are mobile: they can move through heterogeneous computers, at runtime, as long as proper implementations of the VIRTUOSI machine are provided. This mobility can be very useful since it is a requirement that often appears in modern applications, especially in ubiquitous computing.

Controlled Execution Because a virtual machine is a software system that controls the execution of other software systems, it can fully assist in debugging applications; a virtual machine can keep very precise data about execution context, thus providing programmers with more accurate information when some bug happens. From an experimental perspective, this is an essential feature to improve productivity. From a pedagogical perspective, it is also important because programmers can use debugging to understand better software systems behaviour.

Flexible Network Configuration Since a VIRTUOSI machine is a user-level process, there may exist any number of instances of the virtual machine running on a single computer. As a consequence, a collection of n virtual machines may run atop a network containing from 1 to n computers. In the extreme, there is no need to have a real computer newtork to run a VIRTUOSI distributed application. According to [2], this concept was first experimented by the IBM VM Operating System, where a set of virtual machines run on a single physical computer, giving the illusion that each user has its own computer; communication between the virtual machines happens through a virtual network. From an experimental perspective, such feature may easy the development of prototypes, since any network configuration can be simulated. From a pedagogical perspective, it may help programmers to experiment with distributed computing even when only a single machine is available.

3.2 Object-Oriented Programming

Probably, object-oriented programming is the most widely accepted paradigm for distributed computing, both in academia and industry. Object orientation was first introduced by Simula-67 [3] as a means to represent real-world entities for the purpose of simulation only, and got popularity after Smalltak-80 [4] and C++ [5]. Currently, there is a number of programming languages that support object-oriented programming concepts and they are largely employed in computer programmer training for more than a decade. More recently, with the incresing demand for Internet-based applications, new languages and tools have appeared and, practically, all of them are object oriented. Perhaps, the most significant example is Java [6], which, despite its industrial flavor, is very much used in introductory programming courses and also motivates much of the current research in distributed computing. Another important example is Eiffel [7], a languague that implements object-oriented concepts rigorously.

In fact, the object-oriented paradigm is present in almost every new architectural development in the distributed system community. For instance, both the Open Distributed Processing (ODP) and the Object Management Group (OMG), the main standardization initiatives for heterogeneous distributed computing, are based on object concepts. In the software industry, two important examples of the use of object-oriented concepts are the Sun Microsystems' Java-based J2EE and the Microsoft .NET platform.

The VIRTUOSI project adopts object orientation as the paradigm for both applications development and runtime system. Programmers should develop applications by employing solely object-oriented concepts, assisted by proper artifacts, such as a rigorously object-oriented programming language, and tools, such as a compiler built according to the pedadogical perspective, i.e., a compiler that helps in training rather than simply checking the source code. The runtime system – defined by a collection of virtual machines (Section 3.1) – should preserve all object-oriented abstractions in order to minimize translations that could make it difficult debugging applications; that helps in fast building prototypes – the experimental perspective – and helps programmers to understand better programming concepts – the pedagogical perspective.

3.3   Computational Reflection

Three different yet complementary approaches to the use of the object paradigm in concurrent and distributed contexts are discussed in [8]:

Library Approach Object-oriented concepts, such as encapsulation, genericity, class and inheritance, are applied to structure concurrent and distributed software systems through class libraries. It is oriented towards system builders and aims at identifying basic concurrent and distributed abstractions – it can be viewd as a bottom-up approach where flexibility is priority. Its main limitation is that programming is represented by unrelated sets of concepts and objects, thus requiring great expertise from programmers. Examples of the library approach are the ISIS System [9] and the Arjuna System [10].

Integrative Approach Object-oriented concepts are unified with concurrent and distributed system concepts, such as object with activity. It is oriented towards application builders and aims at defining a high-level programming languague with few unified concepts – it makes mechanisms more transparent. Its disadvantage is the cost of possibly reducing the flexibility and efficiency of the mechanisms. Examples of the integrative approach are the distributed operating systems Amoeba [11] and Mach [12].

Reflective Approach Integrates protocol libraries within an object-based programming language; the application program is separated from various aspects of its implementation and computation contexts – separation of concerns – by describing them in terms of metaprograms, according to the concept of computational reflection, firstly disseminated by [13]. It is oriented towards both application builders and system builders and, in fact, bridges the two previous approaches by providing a framework for integrating protocol libraries within a programming language or system – combination of flexibility and transparency.

The VIRTUOSI Project adopts the reflective approach, thus allowing programmers to change systems behaviour in two levels: application level and runtime system level. Such approach conforms to the established project objectives (Section 2) because, from a pedagogical perspective, programmers can selectively choose what system features should be transparent, so that it is possible to study each feature individually or combine just some of them. And, from an experimental perspective, programmers have a large degree of dynamism for developing software systems as components can be easily replaced and tested. In fact, the VIRTUOSI runtime environment can be seen as a reflective middleware, like the CORBA-based implementations DynamicTAO [14] and Open ORB [15]. The reflective middleware model is a principled and efficient way of dealing with highly dynamic environments yet supporting development of flexible and adaptative systems and applications [16]. Naturally, such flexibility may be difficult to achieve and should require a consistent model for composing meta-level system resources, such as the framework proposed in [17].

In VIRTUOSI, the combination of virtual machine and object orientation brings a particularly interesting feature for the implementation of computational reflection: objects and their corresponding code can be explicitly stored and manipulated at runtime, thus permiting reflection on practically any computation aspect, easing dynamic modification of system behaviour. The architecture of a VIRTUOSI machine is, therefore, oriented towards computational reflection, besides all aspects related to the pedagogical and experimental perspectives, discussed so far. In other words, a VIRTUOSI machine should have access to all the semantics of an application for providing good support for programmers for both pedagogical and experimental purposes and for permiting full reflection. This feature differs VIRTUOSI from other attempts such as the Guaraná Project [18], where the Java Virtual Machine was modified to support computational reflection, but entirely preserving its standard code format – the so-called bytecode – and programming language compatibility. It differs, as well, from the PJama Project [19], where the Java Virtual Machine is modified in order to support orthogonal persistence.

The solution found in VIRTUOSI for the purpose of having full application semantics at runtime is to represent and store program code in the form of a program tree: a graph of objects that represents all elements of a given source code, including their relationships. Program trees are successfully employed in the Juice Virtual Machine [20, 21] for transferring code through the network; when a program tree reaches its destination it is then translated to a specific machine code for execution. Since there is a direct mapping between a program tree and a source code, the rules for building a program tree are the same for writing an object-oriented program. Such rules are established by an object model formalized by means of a metamodel which are expressed in the Unified Modeling Language (UML) [22]; the objects of a program tree are instances of the classes present in the metamodel.

4   Distributed Objects

Objects reside within virtual machines and can reference each other locally and remotely. When an object has a reference to another, it can invoke methods; the invocation is local when the reference is local, otherwise it is remote. An object A obtains a reference to an object B by one of the following means:

- Object A creates object B.
- Object A receives a method invocation where a reference to an object B is passed as a parameter.
- Object A invokes a method of some object and receives a reference to an object B as return value.

Because in VIRTUOSI objects are always created locally, an object can only obtain a reference to a remote object either when it is passed as parameter or when it is returned. A third case may happen when an object migrates: a local reference may become a remote reference.

As discussed, the management of objects in VIRTUOSI can be very complex, thus requiring a proper implementation. The subsequent sections describes the handle table mechanism adopted and how migration and remote method invocation use it.

4.1   Handle Table

All objects are referenced through a structure called handle table, similarly to they way it is implemented in DOSA (Distributed Object System Architecture) [23]. Figure 1 illustrates how objects are referenced both within a virtual machine and between virtual machines. The VM named Alpha stores objects identified as 12 and 17, while the VM named Beta stores objects identified as 45 and 67. A handle table is an array of entries of two types: entry for local object and entry for remote object. Thus, for each object there is an entry in the handle table of the machine where the object resides. For instance, the object 12 is referenced by entry 0 of Alpha. An object cannot directly reference another; an object can only reference a handle table entry in the same machine. For example, object 12 references entry 1 of Alpha, which, in turn, references object 17; conceptually, object 12 references object 17. An object may also conceptually reference an object that resides remotely. For example, object 17 – that resides in Alpha – references object 45 – that resides in Beta. This is implemented through the entry 2 of Alpha, which references entry 0 of Beta. Therefore, an entry for local object must contain an object reference, while an entry for remote object must contain a virtual machine name and a handle table entry index.

4.2   Object Migration

An object can migrate from one virtual machine to another. Typically, object migrate for efficiency (load balance) and accessibility purposes. From a pedagogical perspective, it may be interesting to migrate objects to observe difference between local and remote communication. From an experimental perspective, it may be interesting to migrate objects to simulate applications where mobile devices carry some software.

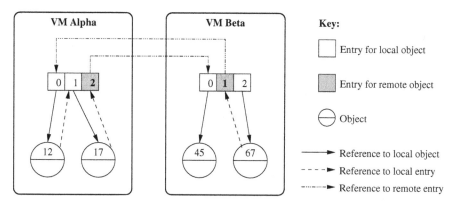

Fig. 1. Example of handle table

In VIRTUOSI, object migration can be programmed by using a set of operations defined according to [24], as follows.

move Moves a local object to another machine.
fix Fix an object on the machine where it resides, so it cannot migrate anymore.
unfix Undoes a previous fix operation, so that the object can migrate again.
refix Atomically, moves an object to another machine and fixes it there.
locate Returns the name of the virtual machine where a given object resides.

When an object migrates, the handle table of the originating machine and the handle table of the destination machine must be updated. In the destination machine, a new entry must be inserted: an entry for local object. In the originating machine's table, the existing entry for local object must be replaced for a entry for remote object that references the newly created entry in the destination machine.

The migration mechanism brings some constraints to object behaviour:

– An object cannot migrate while it performs any activity.
– An object cannot initiate a new activity while migrating.

Composed objects must migrate all together. As a consequence, the move operation has no effect for an object that belongs to another. Also, an object cannot migrate if it contains any object that is fixed.

4.3 Remote Method Invocation

The remote method invocation mechanism is totally transparent in VIRTUOSI. Like any Remote Procedure Call (RPC) mechanism [25], there must be parameter marshalling, message exchange and some level of fault tolerance. The handle table helps identifying whether a method invocation is either local or remote, thus providing access transparency [26]: a programmer does not need to concern about distinguishing local and remote calls. Also, the handle table helps finding an object when it happens to be remote, thus providing location transparency. The marshalling process is automatically done by using the information provided by program trees, which are available at runtime. In other words, there is no need to prepare stub code in advance. Some typical faults that may happen include: (i) remote machine disconnection from the network, (ii) message loss and (iii) target object is under migration. All these faults require proper treatment.

5   Conclusions and Future Work

We have introduced a new toolkit named VIRTUOSI for building distributed object systems with pedagogical and experimental perspectives. It combines virtual machine, object-oriented programming and computational reflection concepts to give those perspectives. A previous work [27] has shown that the main design principles of VIRTUOSI are feasible. Currently, a full-fledged version of the toolkit is under development.

References

[1] Soley, R.M., Kent, W.: The OMG object model. In Kim, W., ed.: Modern Database Systems. Addison-Wesley (1995) 18–41 34
[2] Silberchatz, A., Galvin, P.B.: Operating System Concepts. fifth edn. Addison-Wesley (1998) 35
[3] Dahl, O.J., Nygaard, K.: Simula-67 common base language. Technical Report S-22, Norwegian Computing Centre, Oslo (1970) 35
[4] Goldberg, A., Robson, D.: Smalltalk-80: The Language. Addison-Wesley, Reading, MA (1983) 35
[5] Stroustrup, B.: The C++ Programming Language. Addison Wesley, Reading, Massachusetts (1986) 35
[6] Arnold, K., Gosling, J.: The Java Programming Language. Addison Wesley (1996) 35
[7] Meyer, B.: Object-Oriented Software Construction. Second edn. Prentice Hall PTR (1997) 35
[8] Briot, J.P., Guerraoui, R., Lohr, K.P.: Concurrency and distribution in object-oriented programming. ACM Computing Surveys 30 (1998) 291–329 36
[9] Birman, K.P.: Replication and fault-tolerance in the ISIS System. ACM Operating System Review 19 (1985) Proceedings of the 10th ACM Symposium on Operating System Principles. 36
[10] Parrington, G.D., Shrivastava, S.K., Wheater, S.M., Little, M.C.: The design and implementation of Arjuna. USENIX Computing Systems Journal 8 (1995) 36
[11] Mullender, S.J., Rossum, G.v., Tanenbaum, A.S., Renesse, R.v., Staveren, H.v.: Amoeba: A distributed operating system for the 1990s. IEEE Computer 23 (1990) 44–53 36
[12] Boykin, J., Kirschen, D., Langerman, A., Loverso, S.: Programming under Mach. Addison-Wesley, Reading, MA (1993) 36
[13] Maes, P.: Concepts and experiments in computational reflection. ACM SIGPLAN Notices 22 (1987) 147–155 OOPSLA'87. 36

[14] Kon, F., Roman, M., Liu, P., Mao, J., T., Y., Magalhães, L., Campbell, R.: Monitoring, security, and dynamic configuration with the DynamicTAO reflective ORB. In: Proceedings of the IFIP/ACM International Conference on Distributed Systems Platforms and Open Distributed Processing (Middleware2000). (2000) 121–143 37

[15] Blair, G., Coulson, G., Andersen, A., Blair, L., Clarke, M., Costa, F., Duran-Limon, H., Fitspatrick, T., Johnston, L., Moreira, R., Parlavantzas, N., Saikoski, K.: The design and implementation of Open ORB. In: IEEE Distributed Systems Online. (2001) 37

[16] Kon, F., Costa, F., Blair, G., Campbell, R.H.: The case for reflective middleware. Communications of the ACM **45** (2002) 33–38 37

[17] Venkatasubramanian, N.: Safe composability of middleware services. Communications of the ACM **45** (2002) 49–52 37

[18] Oliva, A.: Guaraná: Uma arquitetura de software para reflexão computacional implementada em java. Master's thesis, Universidade Estadual de Campinas, Instituto de Ciência da Computação (1998) 37

[19] Atkinson, M.: Providing orthogonal persistence for java. Lecture Notes in Computer Science (1998) 383–395 ECOOP'98. 37

[20] Kistler, T., Franz, M.: A tree-based alternative to java byte-codes. In: Proceedings of the International Workshop on Security and Efficiency Aspects of Java '97. (1997) Also published as Technical Report No. 96-58, Department of Information and Computer Science, University of California, Irvine, December 1996. 37

[21] Franz, M., Kistler, T.: Does java have alternatives? In: Proceedings of the California Software Symposium CSS '97. (1997) 5–10 37

[22] Rumbaugh, J., Jacobson, I., Booch, G.: Unified Modeling Language Reference Manual. Addison-Wesley, Reading, MA (1997) 37

[23] Hu, Y.C., Yu, W., Cox, A., Wallach, D., Zwaenepoel, W.: Run-time support for distributed sharing in safe languages. ACM Transactions on Computer Systems (TOCS) **21** (2003) 1–35 38

[24] Jul, E., Levy, H., Hutchinson, N., Black, A.: Fine-grained mobility in the Emerald system. ACM Transactions on Computer Systems **6** (1988) 109–133 39

[25] Birrel, A.D., Nelson, B.J.: Implementing remote procedure calls. ACM Transactions and Computer Systems **2** (1984) 39–59 39

[26] Tanenbaum, Andrew S.: Distributed Operating Systems. Prentice Hall (1995) 39

[27] Calsavara, A., Nunes, L.: Estudos sobre a concepção de uma linguagem de programação reflexiva e correspondente ambiente de execução. In: V Simpósio Brasileiro de Linguagens de Programação. (2001) 193–204 In Portuguese. 40

Assessing the Impact of Rapid Serial Visual Presentation (RSVP): A Reading Technique

Barbara Beccue and Joaquin Vila

School of Information Technology, Illinois State University
Campus Box 5150, Normal, IL 61790-5150, USA
{bbeccue,javila}@ilstu.edu

Abstract. Currently there is a vast amount of information available on the World Wide Web (WWW). When trying to traverse this space, human reading speed and comprehension are limiting factors. These factors may be affected by poor website design and inconsistent presentation of text styles which can result in screen illegibility and disinterest on the part of the users. Most computer-based reading tools use book metaphors to display information. As designers continue to rely on mechanical-age paradigms, they are often blinded to the potential of the computer to do a task in a better, albeit different, way. The main objective of this research was to investigate the impact of a different reading technique (Rapid Serial Visual Presentation) on reading speed and comprehension.

1 Introduction

Currently there is a vast amount of information available on the World Wide Web (WWW). People are turning more frequently to this source of information rather than using traditional library resources. In fact, the abundance of readily available information via the Internet is often causing information overload. One of the bottlenecks experienced by humans when trying to traverse this information space is their reading speed and comprehension. More than ever, interface designers must be sensitive to users' needs and limitations; however, they continue to rely on mechanical-age paradigms as evidenced by the current use of book metaphors to display information. Designers' conventional mindset often prevents them from seeing the potential of the computer to better address the cognitive and physiological characteristics of users.

Reading psychology research about brain and eye functioning provides us with insights that could be used to address the problem of reading speed. Literature indicates that reading is a brain function that is effectuated by the eyes in a specific manner. One reads, not by sweeping one's eyes along a line of print, but by moving one's viewpoint in a series of little jumps, called saccades. In order to see, a reader focuses the image of an object on the retina. Various tests have revealed that the reader's visual acuity is sharpest in the center of the visual field, which is called the fovea. Vision is clearest in this region, and its clarity lessens with the decrease in density of the receptor cells as one moves away from the fovea.

F. F. Ramos, H. Unger, V. Larios (Eds.): ISSADS 2004, LNCS 3061, pp. 42-53, 2004.
© Springer-Verlag Berlin Heidelberg 2004

Insup Taylor from University of Toronto and M. Martin Taylor from Defense and Civil Institute of Environmental Medicine, Ontario, have conducted research in the field of reading psychology that suggests that if the eye movements are bypassed, people seem to read faster. Bypassing the eye movements does not impair comprehension since the fovea is the most receptive area of the eye. Thus, in their opinion, if words from a text are displayed in the center of a display area, one word at a time, the individual will save the time required for moving the eye from one word to another. Consequently, a reader will increase his or her reading speed and comprehension since the reader will only use the foveal region to read that single word at a given instant. This technique of reading text one word at a time has been referred to as Rapid Serial Visual Presentation (RSVP) [1]. This technique of reading text one word at a time is referred to as Rapid Serial Visual Presentation (RSVP) and was coined by Forster [2]. Forster's research used 16-mm film and variable speed projection to present text in a manner similar to Kolers and Katzman [3]. Later this technique was adapted for computer display by Aaronson and Scarborough [4]. The RSVP technique has been investigated in the areas of reading psychology and information technology [1, 5-14]. At this time, people who retrieve information from the web use conventional software applications such as Acrobat Reader or the ubiquitous web browser to display web content. Using these applications, the user can easily retrieve web resources; however, there are some inherent problems related to their use. The user has little control on how the information is displayed, and therefore, must often adjust to different text styles at each site. Various foreground and background colors, font sizes, and font types create a number of problems like illegibility (e.g., chromostereopsis), inaccuracy of reading, and disinterest on the part of readers [1]. These factors may have an impact on the reading speed and comprehension of the readers. If the style attributes of the text were under the user's dynamic control, each user would be able to adjust properties like font type, font color, background color, and font size, thus allowing for personalization of the reading experience.

The purpose of this study was to assess the impact of RSVP on the reading speed and comprehension of the subjects when reading computer-displayed text. In order to accomplish this assessment, a tool called Monolithic Reading Browser (MRB), which implements the RSVP reading technique, was developed and tested. Using MRB, the document is gradually displayed on the screen one word at a time. Essentially, saccades are avoided by bringing the words to the subject's eyes instead of his/her eyes going to the words.

The main objective of this research was to investigate the impact of computer-displayed RSVP on reading speed and comprehension. The following hypotheses were generated.

Ho. 1. There is no significant difference in the reading speed of subjects who used RSVP, as implemented for reading computer-displayed text, over those who did not.

Ho. 2. There is no significant difference in the reading comprehension of subjects who used RSVP over those who did not.

A secondary objective was to document how users personalized their reading environment by setting text style attributes such as font size, font color and background color.

1.1 Significance of Research Project

The research presented in this paper compares the effects of using computer-displayed RSVP versus traditional Western style text on users' reading speed and comprehension. A contribution of this research is the determination of whether or not RSVP can be used as an alternative reading technique to improve reading speed and comprehension and, thereby, enable users to be more productive in their acquisition of information from the web. This is of particular importance since most of the new wireless Internet appliances have small display units. One of the advantages of implementing RSVP in such devices is that there is a minimal requirement for screen real estate.

2   Literature Review

Reviewing the literature relevant to this research has revealed that physiological and psychological factors play an important role in the complex process of reading. Some research defines reading as a process and concentrates on the steps involved. Other studies describe reading in terms of who the reader is and adjust the definition for different groups or classes of readers.

Research in the physiology of reading shows that there are two types of eye movements: pursuit and saccadic [15]. Pursuit movements are smooth trajectories that the eye makes when following a constantly moving object. For instance, if one holds a pencil vertically and moves it in a smooth motion from left to right, at the same time fixing his vision on the eraser end of the pencil, the eye movement following the pencil is called a pursuit movement. The other type of movement, saccadic movement, happens when a person looks around his environment and his eyes hop from one object to another. For example, his eyes move from the chair to the computer, from the computer to the window, and from the window to something else. Thus, the eyes move in saccades. In other words, they jump from one object to another. Furthermore, research in reading psychology suggests that the eye movements involved in reading are saccadic [1].

Gibson and Levin [15] analyze saccadic movement into two basic components: the movement itself and the pause, or fixation that precedes and terminates the movement. According to them, "...the viewer voluntarily 'throws' his eyes to some area, at which point he may have to make minor adjustments to bring the desired display into maximum clarity."

In addition to studying the eye movements, it is essential to study the physiological and neurological aspects of reading to understand how the raw data acquired by the eyes is sent to the brain for processing and extracting information.

The retina is the light-sensitive inner surface of the eyeball. It consists of nerve cells that produce impulses in the optic nerve. As a whole, the retina covers a visual angle of 240 degrees. One section of the retina, the fovea, a tiny area that looks like a small depression in the retina, is of particular interest in the reading process. (See Figure 1.) The main difference between the fovea and other regions of the retina is that almost all the receptors at the fovea are slender cones. The density of the cones decreases as one moves away from the fovea and the density of the rods increases. Another difference is that the fovea contains equal numbers of ganglion cells and receptor cells which accounts for the fovea being the center of greatest visual acuity. According to 1970 research by Bouma [16], the visual acuity is approximately halved at a distance of 2.5 degrees from the point of eye fixation. Given a viewing distance of 19" from a display screen, the size of the screen area for optimum visual acuity is 1.67" [16].

According to Taylor and Taylor [1], reading eye movements are inefficient; therefore, when eye movements are bypassed, people seem to read faster without impairing their comprehension. RSVP entails presenting words of a sentence in rapid sequence at the point of fixation. Using this technique, they claim that one can read two or three times faster than the speed at which people normally read which is 250 words per minute (wpm). In fact, they found that subjects could read and recall individual sentences better when presented at a rate as high as 12 words/sec (720 wpm) using the RSVP technique. With traditional reading techniques, the reader has to move his/her eyes to the text because moving the text (book) to the eyes would be much more cumbersome [1].

3   Design & Implementation

The research design phase included the following steps: Experimental Design, Research Tool Implementation, and Instrument Selection.

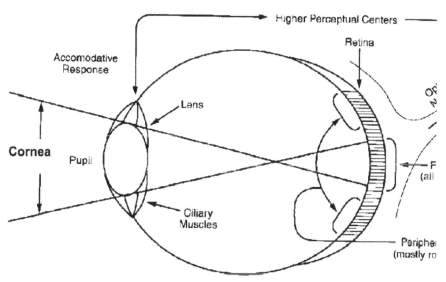

Fig. 1. The human eye. (Credit: National Eye Institute, National Institutes of Health)

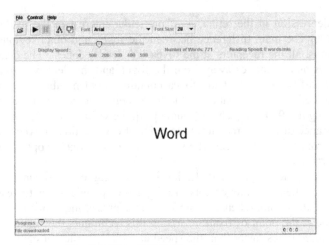

Fig. 2. MRB – RSVP Display Component

3.1 Experimental Design

An experiment was designed to determine the effects of using computer-displayed RSVP versus traditional Western style text on users' reading speed and comprehension. The randomized design experiment with a posttest only used a convenience sample drawn from students, faculty and staff at a mid-western university. The subjects were randomly assigned to treatment and control groups. The treatment group used computer-displayed RSVP to read selected text passages while the control group used computer-displayed traditional Western style text. For every subject, demographics, time required to read each text passage, number of questions correctly answered, and text styles selected were recorded.

The text style attributes that were used as independent variables in the experiments to investigate the effects of allowing personalization included font type, font size, font color, and background color. All text style attributes were assigned initial default values based on information obtained from the literature.

3.2 Research Tool Implementation

In order to assess the impact of the Rapid Serial Visual Presentation (RSVP) reading technique on reading speed and comprehension, a tool called Monolithic Reading Browser (MRB), which implements the RSVP reading technique, was developed [17] (See Figure 2.)

The subject has access to the tool functionality through a menu and a toolbar. The display speed slider specifies the reading speed. The reading speed can be fixed by the researcher or can be set by the subject (if allowed). The progress slider control depicts the progress of the reader through the passage. The subject can use this control to traverse the passage in either the forward or backward directions.

To engage the RSVP display component, the user can request a file (text passage). Once the requested file is available, the user may start reading it. The tool informs the reader when the end of the passage has been reached. The user can then proceed to the reading comprehension testing component. Once a user has started the examination, the reading passage can't be reentered.

The MRB includes the following four components: 1) survey, 2) display, 3) reading comprehension testing, and 4) tracking mechanisms.

Survey. The purpose of the Survey component is to collect demographic information from each subject who participated in this study. Variables collected included age, gender, computer literacy, university year and mother-tongue.

Display. The display component consists of two versions: 1) RSVP display and 2) traditional Western style display.

The RSVP display component converts a text document into a Rapid Serial Visual Presentation of text by displaying one word at time. The RSVP display allows the researcher to conduct controlled experiments by presetting the parameters which determine the visual display characteristics. Some of the parameters include word speed, font type, font size, foreground color and background color. Furthermore, the RSVP display enables researchers to track user preferences for the same parameters when conducting experiments that allow for personalization.

The traditional Western style display was similar to the ubiquitous web browser. Text was displayed left-to-right and top-to-bottom. The same personalization tools as in the RSVP display were available with the exception of the progress status and reading speed sliders. These sliders were irrelevant for this type of display method.

The default personalization settings that were used for both the RSVP display and the Western style display are shown in Table 1. The default color selection was based on an ISO [18] recommendation that suggests white background and black symbols as providing high contrast. Furthermore, most printed material and words processors still uses that color combination to present text; thus, it is familiar to users. In order to avoid saccade (eye) movements when reading the text in the RSVP mode a font size was selected to ensure that most words being displayed fell in the optimum acuity range of 1.67 inches (assuming a 19" distance between screen and user). For the screen resolution of the display units used during the experiment, the font size was set to 28.

Reading Comprehension Testing. The purpose of this component is to gather the answers to post-test questions so that reading comprehension could be determined or evaluated. These questions are presented in multiple-choice format.

Tracking Mechanism. The purpose of this component is to track total time spent by the subject to complete the reading assignment. When reading the text passage, MRB allows the subject to move forward, to pause, and to move backwards (regression).

Table 1. Personalization (Default Settings)

Attribute	Value
Font:	Times New Roman
Font Size:	28
Font Color:	Black (R:0, G:0, B:0)
Background Color:	White: (R:255, G:255, B:255)

3.3 Instrument Selection

A standardized test was the instrument selected for testing reading comprehension in the experiments. It has a basic format that is widely accepted. The authors of the standardized test developed the norms that are widely accepted. It is used for grade levels 9-16 and has been carefully designed to avoid racial and gender bias. The test contains several comprehension passages, which are drawn from commonly used high school and college texts, and questions are based on those passages.

4   Experiments

An experiment was designed and conducted to determine if using RSVP had an effect on an individual's reading speed or comprehension when reading computer-displayed text.

4.1 Pilot Test

A pilot test using participants that were representative of the intended user population was conducted prior to the experiment. The pilot test was used to refine the protocol and validate the MRB tracking mechanism.

4.2 Controlled Experiment

Before starting the tests, the subjects were given a brief verbal and visual introduction to the application and were apprised of the approved protocol. After the introduction, they were asked to answer a short questionnaire that collected demographic data. Both groups were asked to read the same passages from the selected standardized reading comprehension test (see section 3.3). The subjects read a total of seven passages from the standardized test and completed a posttest after reading each passage.

Treatment Group. After answering the demographic questionnaire, the participants belonging to the treatment group were asked to start using the MRB according to the instructions. For the first four passages, the values of the text style attributes (e.g. font type, font size, font color, background color) were fixed; therefore, subjects had no control over them. In order to study the subjects' personalization of the user interface, the values of the visual variables were under user control for the last three passages. For each passage, a tracking mechanism automatically recorded the time required to read it, participants' responses to the posttest, and changes made to the text style attributes.

Control Group. The control group used the traditional Western style display. The control group followed the same procedure for reading the passages as the treatment group. For each passage, a tracking mechanism automatically recorded the time required to read it, participants' responses to each posttest, and changes made to the text style attributes.

Table 2. Age Demographics

Experimental Group (N = 28)			Control Group (N=26)		
Age group	Number	Percent	Age group	Number	Percent
18-22	12	42.85	18-22	12	46.15
23-28	12	42.85	23-28	9	34.61
29-35	3	10.71	29-35	3	11.53
36-40	1	3.57	36-40	2	7.69
Over 40	0	0.00	Over 40	0	0.00

Table 3. Gender Demographics

Experimental Group (N = 28)			Control Group (N=26)		
Gender	Number	Percent (%)	Gender	Number	Percent (%)
Male	18	64.28	Male	18	69.23
Female	10	35.71	Female	8	30.76

Table 4. Computer Literacy Demographics

Experimental Group (N = 28)			Control Group (N=26)		
Computer Literacy	No.	Percent (%)	Computer Literacy	No.	Percent (%)
Low	0	0	Low	0	0
Medium	5	17.85	Medium	6	23.07
High	23	82.14	High	20	76.92

Table 5. University Year Demographics

Experimental Group (N = 28)			Control Group (N=26)		
University Year	Number	Percent (%)	University Year	Number	Percent (%)
Freshman	0	0	Freshman	0	0
Sophomore	1	3.57	Sophomore	0	0
Junior	1	3.57	Junior	2	7.69
Senior	12	42.85	Senior	14	53.84
Graduate	14	50	Graduate	10	38.46

5   Data Analysis

The major purpose of this research was to compare the effects of using computer-displayed RSVP versus traditional Western style text on users' reading speed and comprehension. This section presents the statistical analysis of the data collected during the course of the experiments.   Since the study utilized two groups, experimental and control, the Independent-Samples t-test and the 2 Proportion z-test were the tests of significance used.

Table 6. Mother Tongue Demographics

Experimental Group (N = 28)			Control Group (N=26)		
University Year	Number	Percent (%)	Mother Tongue	Number	Percent (%)
English	14	50	English	16	61.53
Marathi	1	3.57	Marathi	2	7.69
Hindi	1	3.57	Hindi	2	7.69
Spanish	0	0	Spanish	2	7.69
Gujarati	1	3.57	Gujarati	0	0
Malayalam	1	3.57	Malayalam	1	3.84
Polish	1	3.57	Polish	0	0
Telugu	3	10.71	Telugu	0	0
Ibo	1	3.57	Ibo	0	0
Konkani	1	3.57	Konkani	1	3.84
Vietnamese	1	3.57	Vietnamese	0	0
Bengali	1	3.57	Bengali	0	0
Chinese	0	0	Chinese	1	3.84
Not mentioned	2	7.14	Not mentioned	0	0

5.1 Demographics

Tables 2 through 6 show the demographical statistics of students belonging to each group. These tables show percentages and number among students of differing age, gender, computer literacy, university year, and mother tongue between control and experimental groups.

Over 80% of the subjects in both the control and experimental groups were in the age groups 18-22 and 23-28. There were no subjects over 40 years of age. In both, control and experimental groups, males represented about two-thirds and females one-third of the sample. Over 75% of the population rated themselves as being highly computer literate and none represented themselves as having low computer literacy. This self-ratings could be attributed to the fact that most subjects were either in computer related majors or minors. Over 90% of the subjects in each group were seniors or graduate students. English was the mother tongue of 50% of the subjects in the control group and of about 62% in the experimental group.

5.2 Reading Speed

The data collected during the experiment pertaining to the reading speed is presented and discussed in this section. Table 7 summarizes the mean (in min:sec), standard deviation (in min:sec), and p-value for the experimental and control groups for each of the 7 passages. The analysis shows that there is a significant difference ($p<0.05$) between the experimental and control groups for only passages 1 and 4. The first five passages were short text passages; whereas, passages 6 and 7 were longer text passages. The mean reading time of the first five passages is consistently less for the experimental group using the RSVP reading technique than for the control group. The mean reading time of passages 6 and 7 was greater for the experimental group than for the control group. These results are consistent with other study which also reports increased reading speed for RSVP when reading short text passages [14]. Öquist reported that for short text passages RSVP increased reading speed by 33%.

5.3 Reading Comprehension

The data collected during the experiment pertaining to the reading comprehension is presented and discussed in this section. As a result of the analysis carried out using the z-test, the resulting z-values were found to be not significant ($p<0.05$) for all passages (See Table 8). Thus, there is insufficient evidence to reject the null hypothesis (Ho. 2) that there is no significant difference in the reading comprehension of subjects who used RSVP over those who did not. Thus, the results of this research show that there is no difference in the reading comprehension performance of subjects who used RSVP and those who used the traditional Western style format.

Table 7. Reading Speed for Passages 1 – 7

Reading Passage	Experimental Group (N=28)		Control Group (N=26)		p - value
	Mean (in min:sec)	Std. Dev.	Mean (in min:sec)	Std. Dev.	
1	1:29	0:12	1:44	0:26	0.0109*
2	1:30	0:26	1:42	0:37	0.1778
3	1:17	0:11	1:28	0:35	0.1357
4	1:22	0:22	1:52	0:50	0.0080*
5	1:19	0:15	1:36	0:49	0.1003
6	4:22	1:11	3:55	2.35	0.4220
7	3:58	1:19	3:24	1:25	0.1340

(* $p<.05$)

Table 8. Reading Comprehension for Passages 1 – 7

Reading Passage	Experimental Group			Control Group			p - value
	N*	Mean+	%	N*	Mean+	%	
1	112	**50**	44.64	104	45	43.27	0.838
2	112	**61**	54.46	104	57	54.80	0.959
3	112	**99**	88.39	104	92	88.46	0.987
4	112	**62**	55.35	104	65	62.50	0.286
5	112	**64**	57.14	104	72	69.23	0.066
6	224	**140**	62.50	208	127	61.05	0.757
7	224	**143**	63.84	208	137	65.86	0.659

(* Total number of questions)
(+ Mean of correct answers)

5.4 Personalization

A secondary objective of this research was to document how users personalized their reading environment by setting text style attributes such as font color and background color. During the experiment, when subjects were asked to read passages 6 and 7, they were allowed to personalize the MRB display. Ninety percent of the subjects chose not to change the default settings of the MRB display.

6 Conclusion

The results of this experiment are consistent with other studies that suggest RSVP as a viable reading technique for short text passages. This is of particular importance since most of the new wireless Internet appliances have small display units. One of the advantages of implementing RSVP in such devices is that there is a minimal requirement for screen real estate. For example, RSVP could be used for Short Message Services (SMS) which allows the transmission of short text messages to and from IP addresses, mobile phones and other devices.

Acknowledgements

The authors wish to acknowledge the contribution of Ajit Dharmik to this research.

References

[1]   Taylor, I. and Taylor M. M. (1983). *The Psychology of Reading*. Academic Press Inc., 111 Fifth Avenue, New York, NY 10003.

[2]   Forster, K. I. (1970). Visual Perception of Rapidly Presented Word Sequences of Varying Complexity. Perception & Psychophysics, 8, 215-221.

[3]   Kolers, P.A. & Katzman, M.T. (1966). Naming Sequentially Presented Letters and Words. Language & Speech, 9, 84-95.

[4]   Aaronson, D. and Scarborough, H. S. (1977). Performance Theories for Sentence Coding: Some Quantitative Models. Journal of Verbal Learning and Verbal Behaviour, 16, 277-303.

[5]   Juola, J. F., Ward, N. J. and McNamara, T.(1982). Visual Search and Reading of Rapid Serial Presentations Of Letter Strings, Words, And Text. Journal of Experimental Psychology: General, 111, 208-227.

[6]   Masson, M. E. J. (1983). Conceptual Processing of Text During Skimming And Rapid Sequential Reading. Memory and Cognition, 11, 262-274.

[7]   Potter, M. C. (1984). Rapid Serial Visual Presentation (RSVP): A Method for Studying Language Processing. In Kieras D. E. and Just M. A. (eds), New Methods in Reading Comprehension Research, (Hillsdale, NJ: Erlbaum), 91-118.

[8]   Cocklin, T.G., Ward, N.J., Chen, H.C. and Juola, J.F. (1984). Factors Influencing Readability Of Rapid Presented Text Segments. Memory & Cognition, 12(5), 431- 442.

[9]   Muter, P., Kruk, R.S., Buttigieg, M.A. and Kang, T.J. (1988). Reader Controlled Computerized Presentation of Text. Human Factors, 30, 473-486.

[10]   Kang, T.J. and Muter, P. (1989). Reading Dynamically Displayed Text. Behaviour & Information Technology, 8(1), 33-42.

[11]   Fine, E.M. and Peli, E. (1995). Scrolled And Rapid Serial Visual Presentation Texts Are Read At Similar Rates By The Visually Impaired. Journal of Optical Society of America, 12(10), 2286-2292.

[12]   Rahman, T. and Muter, P. (1999). Designing an Interface to Optimize Reading with Small Display Widows. Human Factors, 1(1), 106-117. Human Factors and Ergonomics Society.

[13]   Castelhano, M.S. and Muter P. (2001). Optimizing the Reading Of Electronic Text Using Rapid Serial Visual Presentation. Behaviour & Information Technology, 20(4), 237- 247.

[14]   Öquist, G. (2001).   Adaptive Rapid Serial Visual Presentation.   Master's Thesis. Language Engineering Programme, Department of Linguistics, Uppsala University.

[15]   Gibson, E. J. & Levin, H. (1975).   The Psychology of Reading. The Massachusetts Institute of Technology Press, Cambridge, MA.

[16]   Galitz, W.O. (1997).   The Essential Guide to User Interface Design.   John Wiley & Sons, 605 Third Avenue, New York, N.Y. 10158-0012.

[17]   Vila, J., Beccue, B., & Dharmik, A. (2001). A Workbench for Investigating an Alternative Reading Technique. Proceedings of WebNet 2001 - World Conference on the WWW and Internet, Orlando, Florida. 1295-1299.

[18]   International Standards Organization (1989). Computer Display Color. Draft Standard Document 9241-8, ISO, Geneva.

An Open Multiagent Architecture
to Improve Reliability and Adaptability of Systems

Edson Scalabrin[1], Deborah Carvalho[2], Elaini Angelotti[2],
Hilton de Azevedo[3], and Milton Ramos[4]

[1] Pontifical Catholic University of Paraná
R. Imaculada Conceição, 1155, 80215-901 Curitiba (PR) Brazil
scalabrin@ccet.pucpr.br
[2] Tuiuti University of Paraná
Av. Comendador Franco, 1860, 80.215-090 Curitiba (PR) Brazil
{elaini.angelotti, deborah}@utp.br
[3] Federal Center for Technological Education of Paraná
Av. Sete de Setembro, 3165, 80230-901 Curitiba (PR) Brazil
hilton@ppgte.cefetpr.br
[4] Technology Institut of Paraná
R. professor Algacyr Munhoz Maedes, 3775, 81350-010 Curitiba (PR) Brazil
mpramos@tecpar.br

Abstract. We present an open multiagent architecture for intelligent collaborative information systems based on the concepts of cognitive agents and machine learning. We assume a double hypothesis: (i) agents collaborate to reach their goals; (ii) agents can find and interact with other agents in a network. This assumption implies specialized services that have as functions: (a) relate the needs of user agents with the services of supplier agents; (b) integrate several answers in order to produce better results; (c) send regular notification to user agents about changes in the world. The location of such services depends on the architecture one adopts. We focus on the definition of architecture able to dynamically integrate new agents into the system. Thus, agents shall have machine learning capabilities inherited from a generic agent. An open architecture brings some benefits to the system performance such as adaptability, availability of services, incremental development and improvement of lifetime. System proactive capabilities may extend the knowledge human users have about the process.

1 Introduction

Distributed artificial intelligence studies societies of agents working together to solve problems that are naturally distributed, too large or too complex to be solved by a single program. The efforts to design systems able to adapt themselves to either structural or environmental changes are leading to the conception of autonomous unities that can interact. Thus, we are interested in complex agents able to reason about their tasks, present proactive behavior and learn how to interact/communicate with other agents. Our framework is the open systems one – systems containing a variable number of agents which do not have to be halted when changes occur (i.e. when some agents join or leave the system). As a consequence of this approach, we

F. F. Ramos, H. Unger, V. Larios (Eds.): ISSADS 2004, LNCS 3061, pp. 54-66, 2004.

hope to simplify the way specific agents are built by offering an off-the-shelf generic agent containing some basic mechanisms (including machine-learning). The generic agent cloned serves as a starting point for the implementation of a specific agent.

Section 2 bears the reasons why studying open systems and presents an overview about multiagent systems and different kinds of architectures. Section 3 discusses the characteristics a generic agent should have. Section 4 presents how some machine-learning techniques can help agents learn about their environment. Section 5 presents an application scenario and some agents that would allow the system to learn about itself. Finally, section 6 presents some considerations regarding the interest in the development of multiagent systems.

2   Towards Open Systems

This terminology is used in several areas in computer science: (a) interconnection between architectures of different machines (OSI model); (b) dynamic *binding* between a client and a server (CORBA model); (c) dynamic reconfiguration and mutual selection (*Contract-Net* model); and (d) dynamic integration of an agent in a working context (agent model). The dynamic integration of an agent implies in its capability of learning about the current tasks going on.

The dynamic and complexity of systems are leading us to a new situation where to know how to design efficient, reliable and correct computational systems is no longer sufficient. Jacques Ferber [[11]] argues that the new software must easily adapt themselves to changes in the context of work: (a) change of operational system; (b) change of database management system; (c) change of graphic interfaces; and (d) addition of new software. The new computational systems must have capabilities to evolve in situations like: (a) inclusion of new functionalities; (b) changing in the way the software is used; and (c) integration of new software. In this sense we can talk about open systems that are strongly adaptable.

Multiagent systems are promising candidates to implementing open, distributed, heterogeneous and flexible architectures able to offer a great quantity of services in collective work environments without imposing a structure *a priori*. Multiagent systems can be classified according to their architecture (overall organization), the degree of autonomy of each agent, the type of protocol they use to communicate, or their complexity. A major distinction concerns reactive vs. autonomous agents. Reactive agents are very simple without any representation of their environment. They interact by stimulus-response type behavior [[12]]. Thus, intelligent behaviors can emerge from a population of numerous agents [[5]]. Autonomous agents are very complex ([[33]], [[2]], [[8]], [[6]], [[38]]).

Nowadays, several systems can be classified according to their architecture, communication capabilities and complexity of the basic agent they have.

Blackboard systems ([[20]], [[21]]) implement a particular architecture allowing several specialists (often called knowledge sources) to interact through shared data (posted on the blackboard). Normally, communication occurs only through the shared data, which leads to a form of strong coupling, and possibilities of bottlenecks. Furthermore, very often there is an overall control, done at a meta-level by a specialized control agent, or by a hierarchy of control agents. The architecture has been successfully deployed in many cases. It was extended to distributed blackboard systems in a multi-processor environment in MACE [[16]], and was also proposed for programming the internal structure of an agent [[37]].

In structured multi-agent systems [[18]] complex agents called facilitators, organize the work among simpler agents. The coordination process is carried out by a facilitator; service agents notify the facilitator of the tasks they are able to handle; and, when an agent sends a request to the facilitator, the latter finds a competent agent to execute the task; then, the facilitator is returned the result to be transmitted to the requesting agent. Some examples of such architectures are: the ABSI [[34]]; the SHADE matchmaker [[24]] used in the SHADE project, a framework for information sharing and decision coordination [[25]]; and the Knowledgeable Community, a framework for knowledge sharing and reuse characterized by ontology-oriented agent organization and multi-stage mediation mechanisms [[28]]. Facilitator architectures rationalize communication resources. However, because a facilitator operates as a bridge between agents, its failure may prevent communication between the agents.

"Democratic" multi-agent systems gather agents which all have the same status (i.e., all are first-class agents), like in the ARCHON project, a multi-agent platform used to implement industrial applications such as electricity distribution and supply or control of an application in robotics [[7]] or in our approach.

Since agents must perform collective actions ([[3]], [[8]], [[38]]) communication is an important issue. The communication process among complex agents is usually asynchronous, and is performed by means of various protocols. For example, the Knowledge Query and Manipulation Language (KQML) is a language letting agents express their beliefs, needs, and preferred modalities of communication [[13]]. KQML defines a set of message types describing the sender's attitude towards knowledge. The Cooperation Language (CooL) is another language where communication between agents is performed via a set of message types, called cooperation primitives [[23]]. The principle of cooperation in CooL is the Contract-Net Protocol [[35]].

The internal model of an agent is also an important feature [[33]].

Generally, modeling inside one agent the other agents brings some benefits that allows the agent: (a) to plan and to coordinate its actions; (b) to reason about the other agents beliefs and intentions (and doing so, choosing what to communicate to them) [[17]]; (c) to coordinate its actions without communicating [[19]]; (d) to make local decisions (decentralized control); (e) to reduce communication (only useful information is communicated, i.e. the subscriptions in KQML [[13]]); (f) to know who does what and to whom is useful to ask for information [[36]].

In this work, we focus in how one agent can represent the others. The objective is to define specialized channels to address the right information, to the right agent, at the right time and in the right measure. Basically it means identifying the profile of interest an agent has (artificial or human), processing information and send it in accordance with such profile.

Inside the OSACA system, to build an agent for an application one starts by cloning the Generic Agent.

3   The OSACA Generic Agent

A generic agent (GAg) is an entity possessing basic mechanisms, structures and skills, ensuring a minimal internal and external behavior, and allowing an agent to adapt itself to a new environment. Actual agents are produced by cloning the generic agent, and thus inherit the basic structure and mechanisms. Thus, an agent can communicate with other agents, learn what the others do, and organize itself in order to cooperate towards a common goal. Our objective is to include a set of minimal learning mechanisms in the GAg that make it easier to an agent to integrate an unknown environment and become specialized. Our aim is not to have a universal model, but to define an agent model that allows the development of multi-agent systems quickly and economically. GAg is also intended to favor the reuse of already defined structures and mechanisms.

3.1   Overall Project Organization

OSACA agents are complex. They must be able to function on several tasks at the same time. Indeed, it would not be economically reasonable to clone an agent each time it receives a new request, in the same way an actor is cloned in Hewitt's approach [[22]]. Thus, our agents are multi-threaded. In order to organize the work of an agent, one must provide a mechanism for distinguishing among the different tasks in which the agent is involved. The concept of project is adopted rather than the traditional concept of task [[32]].

3.2   Agent Architecture

A specificity of the proposed architecture is to let an agent manage projects with minimal previous knowledge. An agent has several functionalities as Fig.1 illustrates:

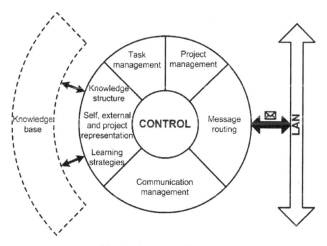

Fig. 1. Agent Architecture

The elements that embed knowledge inside an OSACA agent are:

- *Self-Representation*. It has information about: what the agent can do, the agent needs from other agents and the agent's identification and functions (name, language, ontology, address, communication protocols).
- *External-Representation*. It contains the information concerning the other agents: what the other agents can do, what the other agents could request, information on the requests that could not be satisfied, and concepts manipulated by different agents.
- *Project-Representation*. A project is represented in two levels: project model, and project instance. The model contains the skills (project-skills) required in the project and the associated useful information. The model can evolve with agent interactions. An instance represents a specific project based on the project-model. It can be active, suspended or finished.
- *Communication*. It has the communication protocols giving to the agent basic capabilities to exchange information and negotiate in a collaborative perspective. OSACA agents collaborate in order to reach their objectives. Examples of objectives are: reduction of the time to accomplish a task (stimulating parallelism); choice among local solutions proposed by other agents; improvement of the result quality by sharing and comparing results between agents; attribution of a problem to a limited number of agents in order to reduce the possibility of process duplication; reduction of the communication overload by exchanging only relevant information. These objectives where identified by [[10]]. All objectives suggest specific communication protocols (e.g. the choice of a performative set or the implementation of different forms of collaboration and control). This means that an agent must have a set of protocols and must know when to use them.

3.3 Messages Routing

In OSACA, all agents in the same LAN can see and retrieve all the messages passing through the network. In each agent messages are filtered and distributed by a dedicated process that places them in two waiting queues: W1 and W2. W1 contains the messages explicitly addressed to it and W2 contains the messages retrieved by the agent but which were not addressed to it. Two different processes treat the messages in W1 and W2. W2 allows an agent to learn about other agents and about projects in progress. We assume that W2 is an essential condition to have learning agents that can be proactive. Proactiveness is a characteristic that qualifies intelligent agents.

So, OSACA agents can learn from three basic sources of data:

- the interactions (W1) it can have with other artificial or human agents (e.g., producing the user profile and using it to be proactive and rational in the benefit of the user);
- the messages from W2 that can be used to identify new opportunities to act;
- the data obtained through its sensors.

The three elements above were defined in order to determine minimal conditions to testing and adapting machine learning algorithms in the OSACA agents.

4   Learning

The ability of learning by observation and experience seems to be crucial to any intelligent creature. "Learning is the ability of improving on some determined question".

One of the most used resources by the human brain to originate new knowledge is the induction. The inductive learning is accomplished from reasoning about examples provided by an external process to the learning system.

Machine learning algorithms use induction as a way of logical inference, which allows getting generic conclusions about a database. In a database, a case, register or data are vectors of attribute values. One case describes the object of interest: the collection of procedures adopted by a user, the report of clients from a determined company, etc. An attribute describes an example, characteristic or aspect: gender (male, female), salary (continuous values), etc. [[27]].

Some learning algorithms represent the discovered knowledge through a classifier, which must identify, for a new case, which class it belongs to, among a variety of previously definite classes. Each class corresponds to a unique standard of values of the attributes. This unique standard can be considered the description of the class. The collection of all classes is defined as C, and each C class correspondent to a D_i description of the selected properties. By using this description it is possible to build a classifier, which describes an e example from T collection of examples as being an example belonging to C_i class when that example fulfills D_i.

The main goal of a classifier construction is to discover some type of relation between the attributes and classes (Freitas, 1998). For example, on Fig. 2 the classifier has the objective of identifying the existent relation between the attributes A_1 and A_2 and the values of classes ("+" e "-"). The procedure of building that classifier is based on recursive share of data space. The space is divided into sub-areas and each one is evaluated if each sub-area must be divided into sub-areas in order to obtain a class separation.

According to Breiman et. al. [[4]], an extracted classifier from a collection of data is useful for two purposes: prediction of a value and understanding of the existent relation among attributes and class. To accomplish the second purpose it is required from the classifier not only to classify but also make explicit the knowledge taken from the database in a comprehensive manner.

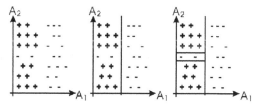

Fig. 2. Example of Classification [[14]].

In order to contribute to comprehensibility of discovered knowledge (relationship among attribute and classes), this knowledge is generally represented in form of rules "if" (conditions)… "so"…(class)…, whose interpretation is: "if" values of attributes fulfill the conditions of the rule "so" the example belongs to the class foreseen by the rule.

In the next section, machine-learning and its use on personalization search will be treated. For example, generated and disseminated information. To exemplify the system wanted to be built, an architecture will be presented involving four types of agents which will be detailed sequentially as well.

5   System Architecture

Below, we present a scenario to illustrate the system architecture.

Let's suppose that a company has three departments: finance, marketing, and management. The management department is responsible for the information distribution to the other two departments. It allows them to use such information to support their decision processes. Information can be obtained from the company own databases or from other internal sources.

Another task of the management department is to identify the information demand profile of the other departments. In this scenario, the constant interaction between the management and finance departments allows the management department to identify the finance agent profile. Another way for the management department to spot the profile of a department is by observing the communication and chat (information exchanging) between a specific department and the other ones inside the company. Computationally, a machine-learning algorithm can discover such profile from the data that documents the interaction between the agents. These interactions and messages exchanged between the system agents can be stored in *log* files over which, machine-learning techniques could be applied later.

In this context, the proposed architecture for the system consists of a set of cognitive agents oriented to the knowledge discovery and to the profiles identification in an open collaborative system. In a first moment, four kinds of agents were defined:

- Learning Agent: its objective is to extract the knowledge from databases (one or more) using the machine-learning techniques;
- Evaluation Agent: it is responsible for the evaluation of the discovered knowledge by using objective and subjective techniques. It also must distribute the discovered and evaluated knowledge to the respective assistant agents in accordance to their specific profiles;
- Personalization Agent: it has the objective of identifying the assistant agents profile in the system (that means, the different users profiles);
- Assistant Agent: this agent is the interface between the users and the system. It is responsible for specific information asking, and evaluation of the pertinence of the knowledge discovered by the learning agent (subjectively).

Such agents must cooperate in the dissemination of the decision taking useful information, in an intelligent way. This objective reveals an interest by the complex agents capable of reasoning over their tasks, exhibiting a pro-active behavior in the direction of the dynamic integration of an agent in a work context, aiming to increase the processing power, including new competencies (or agents), to provide assistance, etc.

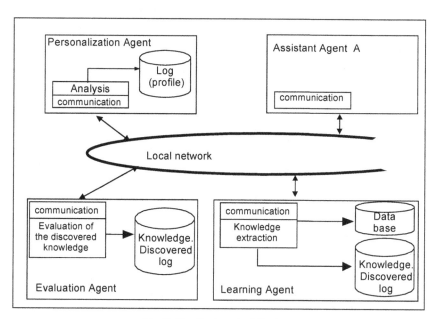

Fig. 3. The System Architecture.

Fig. 3 gives a simplified look on the system architecture, as well as on the internal agents one.   The learning capabilities can be identified in the Learning and Personalization Agents. The communication capabilities are present in all the agents and are implemented by the communication module, through of the communication language — for example the KQML language [[13]]. The communication module is responsible for the asynchronous message exchanging between agents, and implements some basic tasks, like performative recognition, message content extraction and the passing of such content to the specialized modules. The capability of evaluating the discovered knowledge is realized only by the Evaluation Agent.

It is important to note that in this architecture there can be more than one agent of each type, implementing different learning and evaluation algorithms. In such way, the architecture allows that a new agent be included in the system at any moment.

Initially, each particular agent is created as a clone of the GAg agent. The created agent inherits from the GAg agent a set of machine-learning methods, as well as the necessary capabilities to articulate the several internal processes oriented to the discovery and dissemination of knowledge. Besides, the agents can distribute the information following each agent profile. The Personalization Agent supplies such profiles.

The Evaluation Agent, after having executed an objective evaluation (section 5.2), asks the profiles from the personalization Agent and makes the discovered knowledge available according to each profile. As soon as the Assistant Agents receive the knowledge, they evaluate them or not, assigning one of the following qualities: too much abstract, too much specific, irrelevant, excellent, good, satisfactory, regular, etc. Such information is returned to the Evaluation Agent and it will be stored in a *log* file. This *log* file will be used by the Evaluation Agent (for measuring the interest on the supplied knowledge), and by the Personalization Agent (to find and update the profiles of system agents).

5.1 Learning (apprenticeship) Agent

The learning of an agent occurs by building a classifier from the algorithm, which induces trees of decision C4.5 [[31]], from a database. After the tree has been built this agent turns that same tree into a collection of rules. That collection contains the same number of rules and leaf-knots, which were on the generated tree. A rule is a way to be run between the root node and a specific leaf node. Intermediate nodes represent the rule antecedent - each node represents a condition - and the respective leaf node its respective consequent, the predictive class.

Once the collection of rules is generated, it is available to the others agents of the system.

5.2 Evaluation Agent

Most machine-learning algorithms produce, as a part of results, statistic nature information which allow the user to identify how correct and trustful the discovered patterns are. However, many times this is not enough for the user. Even though, the discovered pattern is highly correct from a statistic point of view, it may not be easy to understand. For example, the discovered knowledge (i.e., the collection of discovered rules) may be too big to be analyzed, or have redundancies. Besides, this knowledge may not be surprising, representing some previously known relationship. Few machine-learning algorithms produce, as part of the results, a measure of comprehensibility degree and of surprisingness of discovered knowledge. However, for algorithms, which do not supply those additional data, those can be computed in the phase of post-processing, as a form of additional evaluation of the quality of discovered knowledge, complementing (not substituting) statistic measures about the degree of correction of that knowledge. The goal of Evaluation Agent is exactly to accomplish the task of post-processing discovered patterns.

There is a large number of proposals in the literature to post-process the discovered knowledge. In general, proposals fit into two basic categories: subjective or objective methods. In subjective methods it is necessary that the user establishes previously the knowledge or beliefs, from which the system will mine the original collection of patterns discovered by the algorithm, searching for those patterns which are surprising for the user. Or, that evaluation can occur in process, meaning that, when it is available to the user, he/she provides it with a fulfillment degree.

On the other hand, the objective methods do not need this previous knowledge to be established. It is possible to say that the objective method is data-driven and the subjective one is user-driven [[15]].

The selected methods to be appropriated by the evaluation agent are distinguished by those two natures; the objective and the subjective. In the case of the subjective method it was adopted the evaluation in process, which is stored in a log file. The reason of this criterion is due to the fact of difficulties, which are inherent to the task of a previous establishment of expectation related to knowledge.

The evaluation agent also implements a metric of objective evaluation proposed by Freitas [[14]] who introduces a measure to evaluate the surprisingness of the rule, called AttSurp (Attribute Surprisingness). This paper proposes that AttSurp be defined parting from acquirement of information (measure of the theory of information) [[26]]. The rules, which are composed by attribute(s) with a low acquirement of information, tend to be more surprisingness. Those attributes can be considered irrelevant if taken individually. However, combined to other attributes it can become relevant.

The evaluation agent takes into account the obtained metrics, not only subjectively but also objectively to measure the interest degree of the discovered knowledge.

Mathematically, the calculation of AttSurp is expressed by:

$$AttSurp = 1/ \sum_{i=1}^{K} InformationGain(A_i)/K \tag{1}$$

where InfomationGain (A_i) is the acquirement from the i-th attribute which occurs in the antecedent of the rule and k is the number of attributes in this antecedent.

However, the original formula was later normalized to return values in the range 0..1 [[29]], as follows:

$$AttSurp = 1 - \left(\frac{\frac{\sum_{i=1}^{K} InfoGain(A_i)}{K}}{\log_2(Number\_of\_classes)} \right) \tag{2}$$

This measure has the advantage of being generic enough to allow its application in a pretty large number of data bases of distinct dominions; for example, it does not depend on the existence of small disjuncture or exception rules, etc. Another advantage that can be accentuated is the fact of being computationally "cheaper", for example.

5.3 Personalization Agent

As it has been said before, the personalization agent discovers the profile of an agent taking into account the interactions, the messages and any internal/external stimulus to the system.

Two metrics, which may be used to profile identification, are the objective and subjective measure obtained by means of the evaluation agent.

By analyzing a user, relating with the mean in which he/she interacts, it is possible to identify if there is any pattern on his/her behavior. For example, parting from a simple sequence of operations or even the type of achieved demands when interacting with a computational tool, it is possible to verify whether there is or not a pattern.

Once that identification is done, it is possible to foresee what kind of solicitation that same user could make in the future [[30]].

5.4 Assistant Agent

The assistant agents are the responsible for the interface and the interaction between the system agents and the users, using the services of the other agents. It is based on the model of an assistant that helps and supports an intellectual worker in his/her every day computer tasks [[1]]. Its main function is to manipulate the received knowledge and support the user on his/her subjective evaluation.

Each assistant agent, when receiving new information, should consider the degree of the user satisfaction over such information. This evaluation is made by the user by giving degrees of quality: too much abstract, too much specific, irrelevant, excellent, good, satisfactory, regular, etc. Such behavior allows the personalization agent to improve its actions, for example: avoiding overcharging a specific user with uninteresting information.

The justification to reduce the processing capabilities for the assistant agents is based on the distributed architecture. So it is possible for an assistant agent be operated on a computer without a heavy hardware configuration, even to run on other pieces of equipment like mobile phone and notepads.

6   Conclusions

It is a difficult task to assemble, in a unique intelligent system, all necessary knowledge (or expertise) to perform complex tasks (normally done by humans). Distributed or decentralized architectures seem to be more appropriate to handle with the intelligence existing in complex systems. In this sense, societies of agents are a promising approach because it may consider, in several cases, the natural characteristics of an application domain (e.g., physical and functional distribution of a problem or heterogeneity) and also some characteristics pushed by technological and social trends (e.g., network development pushes to distributed systems, the increase of complexity requires local vision, systems have to adapt themselves to structural and environmental changes, software engineering seems to go toward approaches that consider autonomous interacting unities).

Even if the distribution and decentralization of an application increase the complexity of both coordination and control mechanisms (and by doing so, the development environments used to create such application also increase in complexity); the use of distribution and decentralization can decrease the complexity of: (a) the information a human being or a machine can process in a period of time; (b) the necessary actions to accomplish one task; and (c) the necessary coordination to execute decomposed tasks. We argue that the distribution of processes must be done according to the physical location of knowledge in the system, as well as the system design/implementation team location and the level of knowledge about the relations between the system modules.

The text presented an open architecture to facilitate the development of open multiagent systems. The aim of the proposal is a generic agent (GAg) that has basic capabilities of: communication, coordination, reasoning about itself, reasoning about the others (acquaintances), reasoning about its tasks, and learning about its environment. One can create specific agents by cloning the generic agent and giving them domain competencies.

The system learning capabilities are implemented in specific agents that discover, personalize, and validate knowledge about the process through the use of different machine-learning mechanisms.

References

[1]   Barthès J-P. A., Ramos M. P.: Agents Assistants Personnels dans les Systèmes Multi-Agents Mixtes. Technique et Science Informatique. Vol. 21 (04) (2002) 473-498.

[2]   Beer R. D.: A Dynamical Systems Perspective on Autonomous Agents. In : Special Issue of the AI Journal on Computational Theories of Interaction and Agency (1992).

[3]   Bond H., Gasser L.: What is DAI ?. In Reading in Distributed Artificial Intelligence, Morgan Kaufman Publishers (1988).

[4]   Breiman, L., Friedman, J.H., Olshen, R.A., Stone, C.J.: Classification and Regression Trees. Wadsworth and Brooks, Monterey, Ca. (1984).

[5]   Brooks R. A.: Intelligence without representation. Vol. 47. Artificial Intelligence (1991) 139-159.

[6]   Castelfranchi C.: A Pont Missed in Multi-Agent, DAI and HCI. Decentralized AI, Y. Demazeau & J-P. Müller (Eds.), Elsevier Science Publisher B.V. (North-Holland) (1990) 49-62.

[7]   Cockburn D., Jennings N. R.: ARCHON: A Distributed Artificial Intelligence System for Industrial Applications. In O'Hara G.M.P., Jennings N.R., ed., Foundations of DAI, Wiley (1995).

[8]   Demazeau Y., Muller J-P.: Decentralized Artificial Intelligence. In Demazeau Y., MŸller J-P., Decentralized AI, Elsevier Science Publishers (1990).

[9]   Deschrevel J-P.: The ANSA Model for Trading and Federation. Rapport Technique, n° APM.1005.01 (ANSA Phase III), July (1993).

[10]   Durfee H. E., Lesser V. R., Corkill D. D., Cooperation through Communication in a Distributed Problem Solving Network. Vol 36 (11). IEEE Transactions on Computers (1987).

[11]   Ferber J.: Les Systèmes Multi-Agents. Interéditions, Paris (1995).

[12]   Ferber J., Drogoul A.: Using Reactive Multi-Agent Systems in Simulation and Problem Solving. In Avouris N.M., Gasser L., eds., Distributed Artificial Intelligence: Theory and Praxis, Kluwer Academic Publishers (1992) 53-80.

[13]   Finin T., Weber J., Wiederhold G., Genesereth M., Fritzson F., McKay D., McGuire J., Pelavin P., Shapiro S.: Specification of the KQML Agent-Communication Language, Technical Report EIT TR 92-04, Enterprise Integration Technologies, Palo Alto, CA, Updated in July (1993).

[14]   Freitas, A.A. Lavington, S.H.: Mining Very Large Databases with Parallel Processing, MA: Kluwer Academic Publishers. (1998).

[15]   Freitas, A: On Rule Interestingness Measures. Knowledge – Based Systems Journal 12 (5-6). (1999) 309-315.

[16]   Gasser L., Braganza C., Herman N.: MACE: a Flexible Testbed for Distributed AI Research. In Huhns M.N., eds., Distributed Artificial Intelligence. Vol. 1. Pitman Publishing, London (1987) 119-152.

[17]   Gasser L.: An Overview of DAI. In: Distributed Artificial Intelligence : Theory and Praxis, N.M. Avouris & L. Gasser, editors, Kluwer Academic Publishers (1992) 9-30.

[18]   Genesereth M. R., Ketchpel S. P.: Software Agents. Communications of the ACM. Vol. 37(7). July (1994) 48-53.

[19]   Genesereth M. R., Ginsberg M.L., Rosenschein J.S.: Cooperation without Communication. In: Readings in Distributed Artificial Intelligence, A.H. & L. Gasser, editors, Morgan Kaufmann Publishers, San Mateo, California (1988) 220-226.

[20]   Hayes-Roth B.: A Blackboard Architecture for Control. In Bond A., Gasser L., eds., Readings in Distributed Artificial Intelligence, Morgan Kaufman (1988).

[21]   Hayes-Roth B.: An Architecture for Adaptative Intelligent Systems. Vol. 72. Artificial Intelligence, (1995) 329-365.

[22]   Hewitt C.: Office are Open Systems. In Bond A., Gasser L., eds., Readings in Distributed Artificial Intelligence, Morgan Kaufman (1988).

[23]   Kolb M.: CooL Specification. Technical Report, SIEMENS AG (1995).

[24]   Kuokka D., Harada L.: Matchmaking for information agents. Proceedings of the Joint Conference on Artificial Intelligence (1995).

[25]   McGuire J., Kuokka D., Weber L., Tenenbaum J., Gruber T., Olsen G.: SHADE: Technology for knowledge-based Collaborative Engineering. Vol. 1(3). Concurrent Engineering Research and Application (1993).

[26]   Mitchell, T. M. Machine Learning, MacGraw-Hill, USA. (1997).

[27]   Monard, M. C., Baranauskas, J.A.: Indução de Regras e Árvores de Decisão. In Sistemas Inteligentes. Rezende, S. O. Editora Manole Ltda. (2003) 115-140.

[28]   Nishida T., Takeda H.: Towards the knowledgeable community. In Proceedings of the International Conference on Building and Sharing of Very Large-Scale Knowledge Bases, Japan Information Processing Development Center, Tokyo (1993).

[29]   Noda, E; Freitas, A.A., Lopes, H.S.: Discovering interesting prediction rules with a genetic algorithm. *Proc. Congress on Evolutionary Computation (CEC-99)*. Washington D.C., USA (1999) 1322-1329.

[30]   Podevin, J-F.: Learning to Personalize - recognizing patterns of behavior helps systems predict your next move. Communications of the ACM. Vol. 43 n. 8. August (2000) 102-106.

[31]   Quinlan, J. R.: C4.5 Programs for Machine Learning. Morgan Kaufmann Publishers. San Diego – California - USA. (1993).

[32]   Scalabrin E. E., Vandenberghe L., De Azevedo H., Barthès J-P. A., (1996), A Generic Model of Cognitive Agent to Develop Open Systems, In : 13th Brazilian Symposium on Artificial Intelligence, SBIA'96, Díbio L. Borges and Celso A.A. Kaestner (eds.), (Lecture Notres in Artificial Intelligence 1159, Springer), Curitiba, Brazil, October.

[33]   Scalabrin, E. E.: Conception et Réalisation d'environnement de développement de systèmes d'agents cognitifs. PhD Thesis. Université de Technologie de Compiègne, France (1996) 169.

[34]   Singh N.: A Common Lisp API and Facilitator for ABSI, Report Logic-93-4, Logic Group, Computer Science Departement, Stanford University, March (1994).

[35]   Smith R. G.: The Contract Net Protocol: High-Level Communication and Control in a Distributed Problem Solver. C29 (12). IEEE Trans. on Computers (1980) 1104-1113.

[36]   Smith R. G., Davis R.: Frameworks for Cooperation in Distributed Problem Solving. IEEE Transactions on Systems, Man and Cybernetics (1981).

[37]   Washington R., Boureau L., Hayes-Roth B.: Using Knowledge for Real-time Input Data Management, Report KSL-90-14, Knowledge Systems Laboratory, Stanford University, mars (1990).

[38]   Wooldridge M. J., Jennings N. R.: Agent Theories, Architectures, and Languages: A Survey, Workshop on Agent Theories, Architectures and Languages, ECAI'94, Amsterdam (1994).

Toward a Generic MAS Test Bed

Juan Salvador Gómez Álvarez, Gerardo Chavarín Rodríguez,
and Dr. Victor Hugo Zaldivar Carrillo

Instituto Tecnológico de Estudios Superiores de Occidente A. C.
Periférico Sur Manuel Gómez Morín 8585, Tlaquepaque, Jalisco, México.
{vithar,gchavarin,victorhugo}@iteso.mx

Abstract. One of the main obstacles of achieving a good performance when teaching or studying a MAS / DAI course in the undergraduate level is the lack of good development tools that allow the teacher and the students to focus on the main subject concepts rather than dealing with GUI and network problems. With this paper, we present such a development tool, which is intended to be as generic as possible, enabling the definition and use of several agent behaviors ,different agent communication and negotiation protocols. We begin by discussing the motivation of the project and its main goals to continue with some design and development issues and finally current results with future work that is presented.

1 Background

For several years, there has been a course in Multi-Agent Systems in the curricula for the Bachelor's degree in Computer System Engineering at ITESO University in Guadalajara; Mexico. Since the beginning, the teachers had to deal with several problems; that the students had to achieve the course objectives. These obstacles varied from conceptual gaps in logic and programming, the lack of adequate textbooks, to the lack of development tools or test beds for multi-agent systems.

Most of the problems could be solved, but the problem of obtaining an adequate platform to build experimental MAS remained unsolved. Indeed, there were many attempts at solving this problem by using the tools available on the internet ([ORBacus], [JAFMAS], [JADE]).

Those tools proved to be useless for our purpose mostly because they were built with a particular problem in mind and therefore they were useful in that problem context only or because they were such a general purpose tool that were difficult to understand and use. In the meantime, students continued to spend most of their project time dealing with GUI, network communication and synchronization problems, rather than focusing on MAS issues such as defining and monitoring agent behaviors, comparing and choosing between several agent communication and negotiation protocols.

Given those problems and the specific needs of the courses, we launched a project to build a fully customizable MAS Test bed, which would have at least the following features:

F. F. Ramos, H. Unger, V. Larios (Eds.): ISSADS 2004, LNCS 3061, pp. 67-77, 2004.
© Springer-Verlag Berlin Heidelberg 2004

1. A reliable Agent Communication Platform, based on TCP/IP and IPX protocols where messages could be sent and received.
2. A 3D Visualization Engine that would provide a graphic representation of agents and their behaviors (using OpenGL, for instance).
3. An Agent Communication GUI that provides a comprehensive real-time interface of communication, where it is easy to know which agent is the sender and who is the receiver of the message content. The protocol will be user specified. A final log will be saved for further analysis.
4. The Test Bed would be programmed in a language that ensures its future enhancement and portability (C++, for instance).

At the end of our project we will accomplish two main goals: 1) Provide a fully customizable Test Bed for Multi-Agent Systems (MAS). 2) Provide a complete implemented example of MAS project documentation using AUML modeling standard.

Using this MAS Test Bed, the MAS projects will start designing behavior algorithms, protocols ACLs(Agent Communication Languages), instead of wasting time with GUI, OS conflicts, and secondary problems, which are certainly important, but are not the focus of MAS projects. Therefore, we will provide a Test Bed capable of graphically representing agents, their environment, their communication, and it will be an easy-to-use tool for MAS designers.

2 Project Design Considerations

In this section, we will describe different Test Bed modules. The development status of each module varies. Therefore, some modules are almost finished while others are still on design stages, not yet implemented.

2.1 Test Bed Architecture – Overview

The Test Bed provides a 3D environment that could be adapted to different user needs, it could be a soccer field, a landscape terrain, a maze, etc. There are applications such as web searchers, travel agents, etc that only need web connection and a communication platform, but the Test Bed will also provide necessary tools to analyze and design agents.

2.2 Test Bed Control System

This is a core module. It contains all the blackboards, agent information (current connections, positions, etc). It controls the data flow between agents and the GUI. It is also responsible for controlling concurrency and avoiding agents to modify data at the same time.

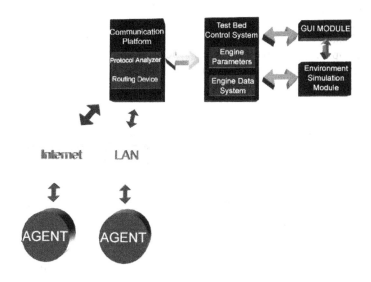

Fig. 1. Test bed architecture general diagram

2.2.1   Engine Parameters

Inside of the Control System, this module is used to define the kind of application we are coding, for instance this module is used to set up what kind of environment we are using, what protocols are allowed, it calls a GUI window if needed, etc. The GUI module uses this information to know what is going to be displayed on the screen.

2.2.2   Engine Data System

This module includes customizable global variables that are available to other modules. For instance, each agent position is stored in this module and can be used by the GUI module, while the Agent Communication Module stores in this module the whole conversation log that the Agent Communication GUI needs for displaying on screen.

Synchronization is required when many agents update common variables. This module uses semaphores and monitors in order to avoid data corruption.

2.3 Environment Simulation Module

The Engine Data System has the general information, which is shared between all the agents and modules, but more specific tasks for the simulation of the environment are done in this module. This module can provide the GUI module with the behavior of the environment, it could change the terrain parameters, provide rain, fog and so forth, changing environment conditions and agent perception.

The GUI module only reads and displays what it reads on the Control System and extra parameters provided in the Environment Simulation module.

Visual and communication noise could be added in this module to provide agents a more complex environment. We are considering adding controlled noise to the data reading by the agents. This could be useful when simulating sonar lectures which are noisy and mobile robots that could be more accurately simulated.

2.4 GUI Module

2.4.1   3D Engine

The engine is programmed using OpenGL and GLUT Libraries. These tools were chosen because of their portability and performance. In order to optimize the CPU time these libraries send the graphical rendering job to the video card.

Java was another option, but since Java is an interpreted language, it becomes slow when simulating complex graphic environments.

The 3D Engine allows the programmer to make different agents. In later versions, it will be possible to load 3d models, instead of simple colored sphere representations.

While the system is running, the user can choose the camera view point from a menu. This allows the designer to follow specific agents and analyze the agent's behavior.

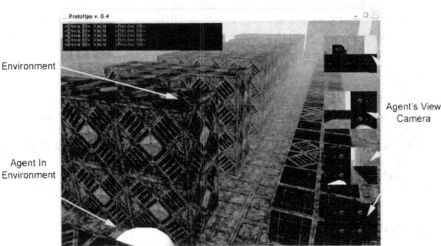

Fig. 2. Test bed prototype screenshot

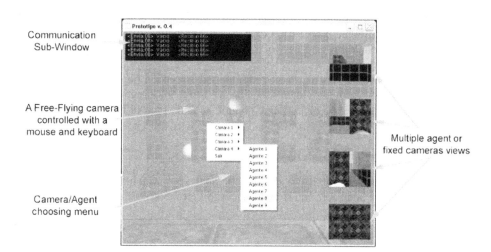

Fig. 3. Test bed screenshot

2.4.2   Agent Communication GUI

Once the 3D Engine has been briefly described, communication activities need to be displayed as well. The Communication Platform provides a full log of the communication of the system, where all sent messages, time and contents are saved. There are some different ways to access and watch this communication:

1. Access the log file generated by the communication module of the engine.
2. Sniff on the communication module, such as it works on Ethernet networks, this is useful when the communication module has been used as a Hub device (broadcasting messages).
3. Using programmed functions on the communication module to read all communication, or specific messages.

The Agent Communication GUI is another way to monitor the communication activities. This GUI sub-module adds a window inside the main GUI window. As shown in Fig. 3. Communication Sub-window. This sub-window display the messages that have been sent in real-time. The full message history will be logged for a deeper analysis.

2.5 Agent Communication Platform

Communication between agents is necessary for MAS. The system will allow communities of different kind of agents to share messages among themselves. We provide at this moment communication via TCP/IP sockets and IPX messages. The messages can be sent directly by Agent-Agent or by using a routing system, which could be conFig.d to work as a network hub, switch or router.

This switching/routing processes include protocol understanding, not just control on network sockets, the routing device is capable to redirect messages by understanding their contents in different protocols (such as KQML, FIPA's ACL or specifying a different protocol). Lexical and Syntactic analyzers will process the messages and could prevent network flood by eliminating (and Logging) erroneous messages.

There are some instructions programmed on the Engine that allows the programmer to provide agents with a fully bi-directional communication. Communication could be local (Same computer, same Lan) or remotely using TCP/IP protocol.

2.5.1   Protocol Analyzer

This module includes Lexical and Syntactic analyzers, which support different MAS protocols. These analyzers can stop broadcasting erroneous messages.

2.5.2   Routing Device

This device is capable of sending messages directly to the proper receiver. It is useful specially when the system starts or in contract-net services. After all agents know each other, they can establish direct connections. But they can still listen to broadcast messages. Broadcast messages are specially useful when the Test Bed Control System wants to send information or instructions to all agents (Agent Halt for instance).

The Routing Device also allows the creation of agent groups, each group could start a communication with one or more groups. Agent groups can be isolated as well.

At the time this document is written, the platform is fully operational, but the analyzers are still in development in order to provide a customizable protocol support.

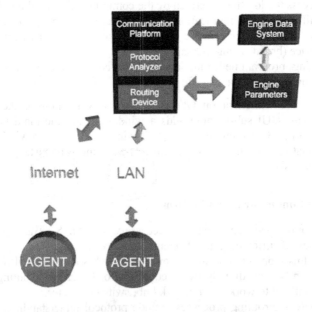

Fig. 4. Communication platform general diagram

2.6 Agents: Script Engine Module

Agents will be able to execute tasks specified in scripts. This will be useful to design complex behaviors. This means that a complex task will be separated in small simple tasks and the programmer will be able to write a script for each behavior and it will be much easier to update the behavior each time the agent fails.

There will be an agent "template", which by default, will perform the basic operations on the Test Bed, such as: GUI Updating (Position, state), Communication capability (establishing communication with other agents). Any particular needed behavior would be easily programmed in the agent's Script.

3   Current Status

While some modules are almost finished, some of them are not. We are still improving their performance and capabilities. Resuming for each component of the Test Bed have been obtained so far.

3.1 Test Bed Control System

The general aspect of this architecture is already discussed and defined, but there are still some details to define in order to provide the Control System with more robustness. Also, the documentation of the project is in process of being completely modeled under UML standards.

3.2 GUI MODULE

3.2.1   3D Engine

The 3D Engine is currently working. It can display agents in the environment. Camera views can be changed. Communication messages are shown as well, sent messages can be clearly identified (Agent Communication GUI). The environment at this time is defined to display mazes(2D Rectangular Grids), which are easily made and could be changed each time the engine is loaded. At this point, agents are just colored spheres. Each agent color indicates the type of agents.

3.2.2   Agent Communication GUI

The current prototype displays all the communication between agents. The messages are displayed in different colors according to their origin, destiny and type (Agent-agent, System, Agent-broadcast). For each message it is possible to read the basic information: Sender, Receiver, Protocol and Message content.

3.3 Communication Module

The Engine is capable of connecting agents and broadcasting messages. Agents also are capable of doing these two tasks(connecting to other agents and broadcasting). At this time, the agent communication module is embedded on the agent code. We are updating this module in order to provide more available protocols (BlueTooth for instance).

3.4 Script Engine Module

We are now in the design phase, specifying script requirements and defining everything the scripts need to cover. The agents will be updated to use this script module. This Engine is now being implemented.

4 Testing the Engine

We needed an application that was complex enough to test the engine's integrity and able to measure somehow the performance of the test bed, but also it was not intended to take much time of the project. We decided to design a game involving intelligent agents, using the 3D engine and using the communication platform, all together.

The game idea is a simple a 20 x 20 grid maze where different agents are interacting in two separated teams: Guards vs. prisoner. The goal of each group is simple as well, the Guards must capture the prisoner and the prisoner must find an exit before he is captured. The Test Bed simulates the environment (Maze/Jail) and provides the programmer with a 3D view of what is happening with the agents.

The following table shows more information about the behavior of the agents involved in this application:

Table 1. Test bed testing application: agents PAGE description

Agent Type	Perceptions	Actions	Goals	Environment
Guard Agent	Visual: other agents, maze walls. Communication: other agents messages. Other: prisoner generated noise.	Patrol, Pursuit, Chase prisoner, communicate with other agents. Hold prisoner.	Find and Hold prisoner.	One maze exit, other agents, prisoner.
Prisoner Agent	Visual: other agents, maze walls. Other: guards generated noise.	Walk inside maze, evasive / hiding maneuvers. Exit search.	Reach maze exit	One maze exit, other agents.
Dog Agent (Guard)	Environment: prisoner noise. Communication: messages to/from guard agents.	Search prison. Inform guards about perceptions.	Detect Prisoner position.	One maze exit, other agents. Maze noise, other agent's noise.

Agents are programmed to use the communication platform and to update the GUI in real-time. The programmer can also see the "agent view" of 4 different agents any time while he can also watch the flying camera on the screen. Also, communication is being shown on the screen, so the programmer can see how agents are reacting with their environment and how they are reacting to their communication.

We are currently working on this project; so, the agents are in development, while they are functional. They are sending and receiving correct messages, they change their current position updating the GUI. They also perform simple path planning at this point, which is useful for GUI testing purposes. We are now working on them to make more complex cooperation and distributed planning, which is easier to implement now since we have the GUI and Communication solved with the current Test Bed version.

5 Future Work

It is clear that there are many areas to improve. The most important task includes the development of more standardized communication tools to provide new functionality and use them in real applications. Also, it would be useful to provide more modules to agents in order to make them more like mobile robots, adding libraries for agents to simulate sensors, and the simulation of sensors errors, including odometry errors, radar noise, and so for.

We are capable of providing agent's view at this time, which is now for illustrative purposes, but the agent's view could be fixed to simulate real camera lenses parameters and be used for testing image recognition tasks, and it would be safer (and cheaper) to test agents on software environments than testing robots with the risk of collision and damage.

The current prototype has been made by using the MS Visual C++ v 6 Compiler provided by the university, but we are not using the MFC libraries that could make the engine dependent of the Compiler or Operative System. Therefore, the next stage is to make the Engine completely portable to Linux for instance, and the project will be an open source in order to make it portable to other OS such as Solaris, Mac OS, Irix, etc.

5.1 Architecture

At this moment, we are detailing the final diagram of the Engine, which will describe all the functions of each module, how they are connected, I/O's and all the documentation required to implement a MAS project. All this documentation includes: module functions, variables, and constants. Engine structure modeled on UML, which shows all modules and the relations among them.

5.2 GUI Module

The GUI module has two main tasks, which are now functional, but they are in the improvement process. Both parts are working correctly, but expanding possibilities is important too. The 3D Engine is becoming more detailed and the environment looks and works in a more realistic way each time.

5.2.1   3D Engine

Environments are becoming more complex than just simple boxes and mazes. Agents, eventually, will be 3D models instead of spheres. The environment design will be easier providing some design tools and libraries. Simulating information of GIS (Geographic Information Systems) systems is also considered in the future.

5.2.2 Agent Communication GUI Incorrect constructed messages will be marked up in order to locate the errors easily. Different protocols will display different useful information.

5.3 Agent Communication Platform

The Communication module will be used as a library, which the agent will use, instead of being part of agent's code. The library allows the use of IPX and TCP/IP protocols, but we are working on bringing up more communication technologies like BlueTooth that will allow testing many devices that will work like agents. The Communication module will be more than a broadcast/multicast tool, it will also perform routing and message analyzing functions. These analyzing operations need other modules such as the Scripting interpreter and protocol analyzers (KQML, FIPA ACL, etc).

5.4 Script Engine Module

This module defines the complete script specification. The implementation of the interpreter and debugger is our current work. After the script is completely defined we will design and implement the library, which allow agents to understand and execute the scripts. We are working to provide the Engine with the capability of executing different Script languages and the possibility of modifying the existing ones.

6   Conclusions

We have obtained very satisfactory results so far, the original goal is to be an aid in MAS courses. This project could be useful for different applications and simulations. We have analyzed common projects used in MAS courses and this test bed seems to reduce implementation time considerably, making possible to spend more time of the course designing MAS applications, completing course subjects, while spending less time coding GUI and the Communication platform.

A next version of the project will be a complete set of libraries, for GUI, Communication and analysis for MAS. Including the 3D Engine, and a set of supported ACL (initially KQML and FIPA's ACL).

It has been very useful to code modules separately and to be able to update each module independently, without having major problems of making it to work together. The most important thing about this modularity is its capability of expansion, the capability of adding more functionality, adding new protocols, and components that could make the Test Bed capable of being very customizable and implement new features.

References

[UML2003]   OMG Unified Modeling Language Specification V. 1.5, March 2003, formal/03-03-01.
[FIPAACL]   FIPA 97 Specification, Version 2.0, Part 2,Agent Communication Language, Publication date: 23 rd October, 1998.
[KQML01]   KQML as an agent communication language , Finin T., Labrou Y. & Mayfield J., 1995.
[MABS]   Multi Agent Based Simulation: Beyond Social Simulation, Paul Davidsson, Department of Software Engineering and Computer Science, University of Karlskrona/Ronneby.
[OGL]   OpenGL specification version 1.4, released on July 24, 2002.
[KQML02]   Tim Finin and Rich Fritszon, "KQML – A Language and Protocol for Knowledge and Information Exchange", Computer Science Department, University of Maryland, UMBC, Baltimore MD 21228.
[AIW2002]   AI Game Programming Widsom, Edited Steve Rabin, Charles River Media, INC. , 2002.
[AIW_Script01] Scripting: Overview and Code Generation, Lee Berger-Turbine, Entertainment Software.
[AIW_Script02] Scripting for undefined Circumstances, Jonty Barnes – Lionhead Studio, Jason Hutchens – Amristar.
[AIW_AStar01] Generic A* Pathfinding, Dan Higgins.
[AIW_Astar02] Basic A* Pathfinding Made Simple, James Matthews.
[MPMMRS]   Motion Planning for Multiple Mobile Robot Systems using Dynamic Networks, Christopher M. Clark & Stephen M. Rock, Aerospace Robotics Lab, Department of Aeronautics & Astronautics, Stanford University, Jean-Claude Latombe, Department of Computer Science, Stanford University.
[JAFMAS]   JAFMAS: http://www.ececs.uc.edu/~abaker/JAFMAS/   , Multi-Agent Technology at the University of Cincinnati.
[ORBacus]   ORBacus and Corba : http://www.iona.com.
[JADE]   JADE Framework: http://sharon.cselt.it/projects/jade/.

State Controlled Execution
for Agent-Object Hybrid Languages

Ivan Romero Hernandez and Jean-Luc Koning

Inpg-CoSy, 50 rue Laffemas, BP 54, 26902 Valence cedex 9, France
{Ivan.Romero,Jean-Luc.Koning}@esisar.inpg.fr,
http://www.esisar.inpg.fr/lcis/cosy

Abstract. This paper explores some ideas about the implementation of state controlled execution for a language centered on agent interaction protocols. Such an approach could be useful because there an increasingly strong interest on the notion of *role* in the multiagent system domain. The strong recurrence *role* and the almos spontaneous appearance of interactio protocols in most practical applications of MAS, and the strong similarities this situation has with the pre-existing notion of *class* on the object oriented sense, suggest the high relevance of roles and the need of having adequate notational and programming artifacts to represent them.

1 Introduction

Nowadays agent-oriented systems are attracting increasingly more attention from the industry of software development. Such growing interest stems from many reasons among which is the multiagent systems' capacity to almost naturally represent complex systems made of "intelligent" interacting entities. As growing complexity is more of a concern as time passes, this capacity to represent complex systems is a most welcome help.

Systems grow complex for many reasons: first the demand for extended features, or greater usability/intuitiveness increase the size of the source code and therefore, the work necessary to develop it. Next, there is the increasing demand for network aware systems and utilities.

This demand for network aware applications leads to a proliferation of application level protocols at development time, resulting in still another complexity layer added to those traditionally found in software engineering.

As protocols are usually a very complex piece of software, needing a careful analysis and design by themselves, it could be useful to have methodological frameworks proposing more straightforward processes for protocol engineering than those proposed nowadays, both via non formal development methodologies as UML and also by formal techniques (LOTOS [1], PROMELA/SPIN [2], etc.).

These development processes could be either notational improvements over preexisting notations, methodological or even reflected in the very syntax and semantics of programming languages.

F. F. Ramos, H. Unger, V. Larios (Eds.): ISSADS 2004, LNCS 3061, pp. 78–90, 2004.
© Springer-Verlag Berlin Heidelberg 2004

2   Application Protocols

As the network capacities of final user applications grow steadily but surely, there is also a growing need to use development tools fit for such tasks, i.e., we need tools capable to model, validate and develop communication protocols.

Communication protocols are not a new concept at all, for they exist from almost the very beginning of computer technology. But unfortunately they are largely absent from most current development approaches.

In a strict sense, protocols are algorithms that define a communication process between entities, and as most algorithms, they are specified, analyzed and developed using a set of specific purpose methodologies and notations, most of them grounded strongly on finite state automata theory.

Unfortunately, the methodological approaches for protocol engineering are out of the usual domain of software developers who are more concerned with the problem of system understanding/subdividing and implementation than with network related details. Most protocols are really complex and with very recurrent functionality (to take data packet X from A to B, by instance).

So, the usual approach is (1) to leave protocol development to protocol's specialists and once these protocols have been adequately specified and implemented, (2) to use them in a traditional approach of high level encapsulation of system services. Thus, most of the time, protocols become operating systems' low level services and are used correspondingly, through a high-level interface which hides the internal functionality and embarrassing details behind most protocol's complex behavior.

However, this approach reveals itself non satisfactory, as the number of application level protocols increases. The concept of application level protocols comes in a straightforward way from the once practical, now theoretical, OSI multi-layered model for networked systems [3].

It is out of the scope of this paper to discuss the OSI multi-layered approach for protocol development. It is enough to say that we call application level protocols those who make always use of other protocols to fulfill their task and that exist in a conventionally named high level (e.g. they are user applications, they are not OS services).

These application level protocols become increasingly common as developers face the migration from monolithic-centered systems to distributed network-aware ones.

It is a fact that current development techniques and methodologies are object oriented, and so they are strongly focused on a top-down problem subdivision, by creating a set of modules with specific capabilities and competencies; each object is intended to be specialized and solves only a subset of the final problem, delegating the solution as a whole to a concerted cooperation among objects via message calling.

When we take this approach to a networked scenario, software developers continue indeed to see the whole system as made of objects or modules. It is easy to see why. Problem subdivision comes more naturally in a distributed system than in a monolithic one, because there always are independent modules in a distributed system. This subdivision is inherent to the problem and gives a stronger hint to problem modularization than a somewhat artificial subdivision of competencies within a single monolithic system.

3   Distributed Objects

Object oriented systems are intended to be centered applications. This restriction comes from the fact that objects are basically abstract data types. Every class is created in order to establish an abstract link between data and the functions that modify it.

This modularization is helpful in more than one way, because we could relate better to events where personified entities (even abstract ones) interact than to mere sequences of instructions and control statements.

So, most object oriented languages and methodologies assume that every object is directly accessible via a simple function calling (method invocation is an instance of local function calling).

Continuous advancement have led to a increased awareness of the similarities between the object method invocation and communication protocols. ¿From the beginning of the object oriented approach it was clear that the pre-existing remote procedure call (RPC) infrastructures [4] could be perfectly well used to represent a method invocation. There are many examples of distributed object platforms with their own RPC schemes, some of them widely used so far [5, 6], where objects executed in different systems can execute methods on remote objects.

However, a remote procedure call infrastructure imposes severe restrictions to the system to be developed with it. Any remote procedure call scheme is a virtualization of a whole communication protocol enabling the invocation, parameter and result exchanges between the interacting network hosts.

This yields the problem of platform incompatibility, every RPC scheme defines its own protocol and functionality, and at the same time, isolates almost completely the objects from the actual communication mechanism they use to interact. It is true that the motivation of any RPC mechanism is actually to isolate the object from all those excruciatingly repetitive communication details, but the shielding is so efficient that any interaction among distributed objects via RPC mechanisms could hardly be named a protocol.

Obviously, any RPC scheme could be tricked using the appropriate message passing scheme with the right fine-grained protocol definition.

4   Agent Oriented Programming

The object oriented approach has shown to be satisfactory enough for most modern software development. However, there are some kinds of applications that even when using an object migration approach from centered to distributed infrastructures, have many properties that are either impossible to address using an object oriented approach, or very complex to do.

Industry shows a steadily but surely increase of interest on agent oriented systems which are commonly believed to be the next programming framework for computer science, right after the current object oriented approach. Whether they really are the heirs of objects is (still) debatable, it's certain that they have many interesting properties as a conceptual framework for programming, even in the case that they are mere object oriented and parallel programming extensions.

When we talk about an "agent" we are using the definition given by Odell et al [7]. An agent is a independent communicating entity (equivalent to a system process) with the capacity to answer "no" to a petition based on its own internal functionality or rules (non observable behavior) , and also able to say "go" using internal mechanisms in a way that would look "spontaneous" for an external observer of the entity.

This definition is wide enough to cover most multiagent systems, but restrictive enough to get rid of many object-oriented and structured systems. However, there is an abstract intersection between categories.

There are many examples of systems having the capacity of request denial and pro-activity, and these systems were not designed with any kind of agent-orientation in mind (e.g., network daemons like sendmail).

4.1   AUML

Agent-UML (AUML) [8] is an agent extension for UML designed to represent the specific requirements of an agent-oriented analysis and design process that UML as it is cannot adequately represent. It is not really surprising to find that AUML strongly focuses on interaction protocols.

The AUML proposal divides interaction protocol specifications on three closely related phases or layers (in fact, they call their proposition a layered approach to protocols) [9]:

Overall protocol representation Everything related to the creation of a general view of the protocol. The package notation is used and extended to represent the existence of interactions among related agents (roles) instead of simple class conglomerates semantically linked, as in UML. The UML template notation is quite useful here, as interactions are very often patterns of behavior repeated more than once in the final system behavior (e.g., session opening and closing), thus enabling an explicit representation of reusable protocol blocks.

Interaction among agents representation UML sequence diagrams are extended to be more expressive, thus allowing a richer notation for object lifeline branching and communication. In order to do this, a counterpart of execution operators found on some process algebra based languages are created, but they are separated into two kinds: those that affect the agent's lifelines and those that affect the communication acts. To a lesser extent, collaboration diagrams, activity diagrams and statecharts are also extended.

Agent's internal processing representation UML activity diagram and statecharts are used to enable a further understanding of the agents' internal behavior. However, such notation is not extended.

5   Roles and Scenarios

As mentioned before, we propose a programming approach linking object oriented programming with the agent oriented approach, focusing on interaction.

In order to enable this migration, we need to define a set of artifacts that could be useful for our purposes. First, let us define the concept of role. As far as we are concerned, a role R is a stereotypical behavior expressing the temporal ordering of the message exchange between an agent and others, in an analogous way to the concept of role in a theater piece where every actor has a well defined and ordered dialog. In fact, we consider the role to be an attribute assigned to a single agent.

There is another interesting analogy, if each agent has a role to perform, we could say that a set of interacting roles make a Scenario.

Let $S = (E, I, C)$ be a scenario where $E = \{A_1, A_2, ..., A_n\}$ is the set of agents participating within S. $I = \{i_1, i_2, ..., i_n\}$ is the scenario's set of interactions messages and $C = \{c_1, c_2, ..., c_n\}$ is the set of communication channels existing between entities within the scenario.

Each role $A \in E$ could be defined in different ways, but for comfort sake's, we are going to make use of the most common formal notation used to represent communicating systems: the extended finite state machine, or EFSM [10]. Let $A = \{Q, A_I, A_O, T, U\}$ be a role , where $Q = \{q_1, q_2, ..., q_n\}$ is the role's finite state set, $A_I \subseteq (I \times C)$ and $A_O \subseteq (I \times C)$ are two subsets of the Cartesian product of the input symbol set I and the scenario's communication channel set C, $T : A_I \longmapsto S$ is a function mapping from A_I to S and $U : S \longmapsto A_O$ is a function taking from S to A_O.

Each role R is defined from the participant agent's point of view, but is independent from the actor or agent finally taking the role (i.e., it could be assigned to any agent).

Let us exemplify our definitions on the FIPA definition of the Contract Net protocol as it is represented by means of the Agent-UML notation proposed by Odell et al [8]. Figure 1 shows the aforementioned Contract Net protocol.

This scenario holds two roles: the Initiator and the Participant. The interactions set is $I = \{$cfp, not_undestood, refuse, propose, reject_proposal, accept_proposal, failure, inform_done, inform_ref $\}$. The communication channel set C is not showed explicitly, but could be assumed from the moment an interaction takes place between two roles, so we could say that there is a communication channel c_1 linking the Initiator and the Participant, so $C = \{c_1\}$.

If we continue with the same Contract Net protocol, we could express the behavior of both Initiator and Participants roles as two distinct EFSM. Figure 2 shows a possible modeling for the Initiator's role. As this automata is an extended one, there are input and output symbols. The notation we use here to

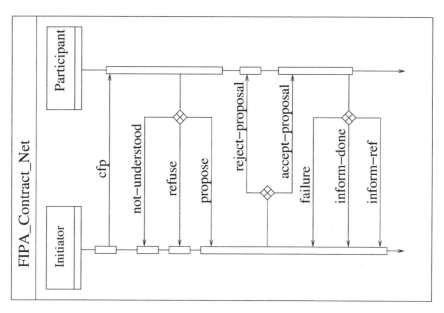

Fig. 1. AUML representation of the FIPA Contract Net protocol

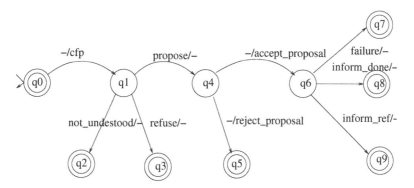

Fig. 2. The initiator's role automata

represent both kinds of symbols is `<input symbol>/<output symbol>`, if there is no output or input symbol in a transition, we use a score before (input) or after (output) the dividing slash.

Figure 3 is the corresponding automata model for the Participant role. As in figure 2 the input/output symbols are written separated by a slash and located side by side with their corresponding transitions. The translation from a graphic representation to a formal one, using our definition of Role as an extended FSM, is trivial and left out for space reasons.

6   Roles and Scenarios as Programming Artifacts

The reason for defining roles as extended finite state machines, and scenarios as tuples containing roles, interactions and communication channels, is to propose a way to include them within the context of a generic agent-oriented programming language, centered on the interaction aspect of agency.

Most formal specification techniques used for protocol specification, like LO-TOS [1] and PROMELA/SPIN [2], use algorithms provided by the theory of finite state machines to perform their tasks, even if there is not any explicit programming structure for that purpose.

However, there are previous examples of languages that explicitly enable a state controlled execution of autonomous entities, like for instance, the ISO standard FDT ESTELLE [11].

In ESTELLE, a specification is a text file describing the observable behavior of black-box entities linked by communication channels, ESTELLE's syntax is Pascal-like allowing a straightforward understanding of the function of every grammatical element.

```
body descrSwitch for Switch;
   state OFF, ON; {Records ON/OFF state}
   initialize to OFF
begin
end;
trans
{*** Activate/deactivate switch ***}
    when P.TurnOn
        from OFF to ON
            begin
            output P.TurnedOn
            end;
    when P.TurnOff
        from ON to OFF
            begin
            output P.TurnedOff
            end;
end; {SwitchBody}
```

This is the "body" specification (internal behavior) for a sample switch object in ESTELLE. The first statement declares the set of states of the entity (ON,OFF), the next one specifies which one is the initial state (OFF). The following part specifies the transitions and the input symbols that triggers them. There are only two transitions, from ON to OFF with a symbol P.TurnOn and from ON to OFF with an input symbol P.TurnOff. The begin-end pairs allow to insert code to be executed right after the preceding event expressed has been triggered.

ESTELLE is neither an object-oriented technique (there is no inheritance, polymorphism or method invocation) nor a pragmatic programming language

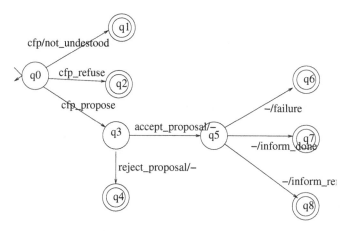

Fig. 3. The participant's role automata

(it lacks many usual programming facilities like I/O features, dynamic memory allocation and so on). However, it does have some interesting similarities to some well known and widely used OO languages, with a strong emphasis on data encapsulation and interface design, while at the same time it proposes a clear syntax for state-controlled execution. It was designed to be a formal specification language capable to verify a set of properties on the modeled system through the use of specialized software tools.

Having programming artifacts that enable to represent state-controlled execution paths, does not provide with any significant advantage. There are already some well known and used techniques to translate a finite state machine onto machine-compilable source code, most of them are used to implement compiler-compilers [12] or produce executable versions of formally specified systems, like for instance, ESTELLE to C translators [13].

However, if we could represent a communicating automata inside a class, nothing forbids to extend this same concept toward internal automata inheritance.

Now, state inheritance among agents is an interesting problem in itself, because if one accepts the notion of multiple parents for a single entity, it arises a number of internal state inconsistencies that are difficult to trace and eliminate. How does one "join" two automata in a purposeful way?

In order to answer this question, we could analyze the semantical meaning of state inheritance, and look for some formal equivalent in the finite state machine theory. For instance, one could take three basic operations and use them: union, concatenation and cross product of finite state machines.

The union of n languages is represented by $L(D_1) \cup L(D_2) \cup \cdots \cup L(D_n)$, and generates an automata that accepts any string s recognized by any of the automata $D_1, D_2, \ldots, D_n$. The union of languages could be used to represent any case where one wishes an entity to behave in different ways depending on the first input it receives. The automata resulting from a union should recognize all the strings in the original languages, but only one at a time. So, any entity inheriting the behavioral automata of a third one using the union operator, would choose to behave as its ancestor or as its eventual new definition, depending on the first symbol it receives (i.e., the first symbol of any string $s \in L(D_i)$ where $i = 1, 2, \ldots, n$).

The concatenation of n languages is represented by $L(D_1)L(D_2) \cdots L(D_n)$, and generates an automata that accepts any string resulting from the concatenation of any string $s_1 \in L(D_1)$, with any other string $s_2 \in L(D_2)$ and so on. This operator could be useful for creating sequenced scenarios, sub-protocols or something one could call sequenced roles. The behavioral automata of a role R_1 could be concatenated to that of a role R_2 to produce the combined behavior $L(R_1)L(R_2)$ that accepts the inputs and generates the outputs of both roles.

The cross product has the property of representing the parallel behavior of two or more FSM $D_1, D_2, \ldots, D_n$, thus allowing us to create an automata which recognizes the languages $L(D_1) \cup L(D_2) \cup \cdots \cup L(D_n)$ in a pseudo-parallel fashion, interleaving the symbols that form any string $s \in L(D_i)$ where $i = 1, 2, \ldots, n$. But the cross product could be inconvenient in many cases, first because two or more of the ancestors could react to one single stimulus, thus being unable to decide which behavior should the joint automata take. Second, even in the case that there is no non-determinism on the input, the semantics associated to a multi-parented agent could dictate that reacting to a stimulus is incorrect in certain states, likely rendering the behavior of the agent formally correct but semantically senseless. And last but not least, one faces the unavoidable exponential growth of the state space.

Our definition of a scenario as a set of roles, and of a role as an extended finite state machine is completely arbitrary. Its principal advantage is that it enables to propose a formal language, to express which kind of programming artifacts could be implemented, once the concept of scenario and role are viewed as programming artifacts, and overall, how they could be actually implemented.

A role, in general, represents a set of stereotypical behaviors that any given agent takes through time within a multiagent system containing it, it has been hinted by some experts that the notion of role could be used as a reutilization mechanism[14, 15], if there eventually are mechanisms enabling its use as formal declarative language constructions. However, it has been also pointed out that roles are not a perfect equivalent of a class. For instance, they are strongly interdependent one each other, and they could be time or context dependent.

7   Proposal for a Hybrid Agent-Object Language

Having defined the concept of role as an extended finite state machine, a scenario as a set of roles and the role inheritance operator as a product between the ancestor role's automata and the descendant's ones, we can see that these three

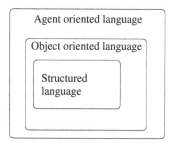

Fig. 4. General structure of an agent-oriented language

elements could create a programming artifact equivalent to the Interface (instanceless/virtual class) notion present in Sun Microsystem's Java language [16].

Figure 4 shows the structure of a hybrid agent-object oriented programming language, built adding new agent-specific elements to its syntax and semantics.

It is worth noting that our interests are centered on the interaction aspects of agency. We propose the notion of scenario, role, role Inheritance and implicitly, that of role instantiation, because those notions could be useful to represent sub-protocols and to solve a problem of particular interest for us: that of protocol reuse. However, there are many aspects of agency overridden by this partial view of the problem.

In [17] the concept of sub-protocol is proposed, sub-protocols are partial, reusable sequences of communication acts defining the temporal ordering of messages, within a specific communication process between roles. Roles, as said before, represent the behavior that any specific agent has through an interaction process.

While all the agents take on certain roles inside any given interaction process, the roles are not restricted to any entity, e.g., a function taking from roles to agents is not bijective. Entity A of type B could take on a role C, while entity D of type E could take on a same role C and still being two different agents.

Figure 5 shows a simple AUML package expressing the registering sub-protocol of an agent on a resource broker, this sub-protocol has two roles: **broker** and client, both represented with labeled boxes. Communication acts (individual messages) are represented using labeled arrows, where the label expresses the exchanged message and its parameters. The temporal ordering notation is conventional to UML and AUML sequence diagrams. The roles of client and broker in this sub-protocol are specific, but at the same time, applicable to many different entities (named A, B, C, D and E), represented in the figure as round boxes "containing" inside them the role. The dashed boxes around the roles and the arrow notation linking these roles to the agents the implement them is not AUML at all, but shows the presence of an abstract linking between the sub-protocol generated roles and the agents who take them on.

Odell's AUML notation [9] gives explicit support for template protocols and role specification, but not for specifying role-to-agent links and protocol reuse. It

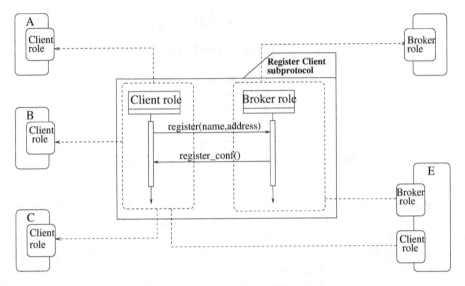

Fig. 5. Sample sub-protocol with two roles

could be useful to have such a notation, in order to extend the expressiveness of AUML. After all, the mapping of roles to agents is done in some way or another, but implicitly.

Figure 6 shows the same client registration sub-protocol, but using now our suggested notation based on the UML generalization graphical artifact. Other UML artifacts could be used, but we think they do not express adequately the intrinsic behavior modification an agent undergoes when implementing a role. It is likely a good idea to slightly change the notation in order to avoid confusion with the actual UML class generalization artifact, but context should get rid of this confusion.

Some authors note that well-designed template protocols and the roles they create could perfectly be used as a reuse mechanism. AUML is expressive enough to represent template protocols and roles, but lacks specific notation to link these roles to the agents that use them.

However, to hide the module's internal behavior as much as possible, and to base the system's functionality representation on weakly-coupled interfaces is not enough to fully model or implement a communicating modular system, either object- or agent-oriented. Even in object-oriented systems, internal variables have a very relevant part upon the system's behavior. Due to the usual presence of complex communication protocols between agents, the need for the agents to have an execution control mechanism increases.

There is always some internal processing involved in order for an agent to know how to react when faced with a specific stimulus and when to take the initiative and begin an interaction without any explicit input.

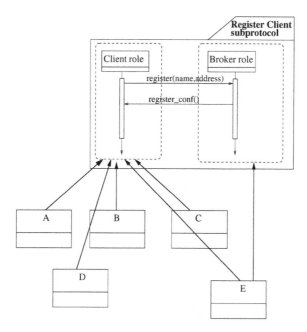

Fig. 6. Proposal for role generalization

As roles are indeed partial protocol specifications (they specify only one agent's perspective inside the communication process), we need some internal mechanism to control a role's state whenever we use that role inside an agent. For that purpose we could perfectly use the approach presented on section 5 to model and implement the final Agent, but how to do this is outside the scope of this paper.

References

[1] Courtiat, J.P., Saidouni, D.E.: A case study on protocol design. In: Lotosphere: Software Development with LOTOS. Kluwer Academic Publishers (1995) 201–217 78, 84
[2] Holzmann, G.J.: The model checker SPIN. IEEE Transactions on Software Engineering **23** (1997) 279–295 78, 84
[3] Tillman, M.A., Yen, D.C.C.: SNA and OSI: Three strategies for interconnection. Computing Reviews **31** (1990) 79
[4] Birrell, A.D., Nelson, B.J.: Implementing remote procedure calls. In: Proceedings of the ACM Symposium on Operating System Principles, Bretton Woods, NH, Association for Computing Machinery (1983) 3 80
[5] Sankar, S.: Introducing formal methods to software engineers through OMG's CORBA environment and interface definition language. Lecture Notes in Computer Science **1101** (1996) 52– 80
[6] Microsystems, S.: Jini Architecture Specification, 901 San Antonio Road, Palo Alto, CA 94303 USA. (2001) 80

[7] Odell, J., Van Dyke Parunak, H., Bauer, B.: Extending UML for agents. In Wagner, G., Lesperance, Y., Yu, E., eds.: Proceedings of the Agent-Oriented Information Systems Workshop at the 17th National conference on Artificial Intelligence, Austin, Texas, ICue Publishing (2000) 81

[8] Odell, J., Van Dyke Parunak, H., Bauer, B.: Representing agent interaction protocols in uml. In Ciancarini, P., Wooldridge, M., eds.: Proceedings of First International Workshop on Agent-Oriented Software Engineering, Limerick, Ireland, Springer-Verlag (2000) 81, 82

[9] Bauer, B., Muller, J., Odell, J.: Agent UML: A formalism for specifying multiagent interaction. In Ciancarini, Wooldridge, eds.: International journal of software engineering and knowledge engineering. Volume 11. Springer, Berlin (2001) 91–103 81, 87

[10] Byun, Y., Sanders, B.A., Keum, C.S.: Design patterns of communicating extended finite state machines in sdl. In: 8th Conference on Pattern Languages of Programs, Allerton House, University of Illinois, Monticello, Illinois, The Hillside Group, Inc. (2001) This paper gives a comfortable definition for extended finite state machine, it gives too some interesting ideas about the utilization of design paterns for protocol reutilization. 82

[11] International Organization for Standardization Geneva: Information processing systems — Open systems interconnection — Estelle — A formal description technique based on an extended state transition model. (1997) 9074. 84

[12] Waite, W.M., Goos, G.: Compiler Construction. Springer-Verlag, Berlin, Germany (1984) 85

[13] Thees, J.: Protocol implementation with estelle – from prototypes to efficient implementations. In Budkowski, S., Fischer, S., Gotzhein, R., eds.: Int'l. Workshop on the Formal Description Technique Estelle (Estelle'98), Evry, France (1998) 85

[14] Koning, J.L.: Automata for interaction protocols in multiagent systems. In Kawamura, K., ed.: IEEE International Conference on Systems, Man, and Cybernetics, Nashville, Tennessee (2000) 86

[15] Lind, J.: Specifying agent interaction protocols with standard uml (2001) 86

[16] Kendall, E.A., Malkoun., M.T.: Design patterns for the development of multi-agents systems. In Zhang, C., Lukose, D., eds.: Multiagents Systems: Methodologies and Applications, Proceedings of Second Australian Workshop on DAI. Volume LNAI 1286., Cairns, Australia, Springer-Verlag (1996) 17–32 87

[17] Koning, J.L., Huget, M.P., Wei, J., Wang, X.: Extended modeling languages for interaction protocol design. In Wooldridge, M., Ciancarini, P., Weiss, G., eds.: Second International Workshop on Agent-Oriented Software Engineering (AOSE-2001), Montreal, Canada (2001) 87

Cognitive Agents and Paraconsistent Logic

Elaini Simoni Angelotti[1] and Edson Emílio Scalabrin[2]

[1]Tuiuti University of Paraná,
Av. Comendador Franco, 1860,
80.215-090 Curitiba (PR) Brazil
elaini.angelotti@utp.br
[2]Pontifical Catholic University of Paraná,
R. Imaculada Conceição, 1155,
80215-901 - Curitiba (PR) Brazil
scalabrin@ccet.pucpr.br

Abstract. This work is part of the Multicheck[1] Project that defines architecture of cognitive and independent agents for the automatic treatment of Brazilian handwritten bank checks. The concept of autonomous agents allows us to organize the application knowledge and brings several benefits to the approach. A triple hypothesis supports this approach. First, the nature of the problem in question allows decomposition in well-defined tasks, and each of them can be encapsulated in an independent agent. Second, the natural capability of interaction of the agents makes the check treatment process more robust, solving situations apparently difficult. Third, the natural parallelism between the agents can contribute to implement an application with high performance.

Keywords: Artificial Intelligence, Autonomous Agent, Paraconsistent Logic, Task Distribution.

1 Introduction

In a bank environment, the manual verification of checks done by employees, in spite of being a trivial task, can cause some problems such as: technical incapability, person in charge's ability, delay in accomplishing tasks, etc. Automation allows a faster and more reliable processing of the task, offering reduction on costs as well as on check-compensation time. However, the automatic treatment of handwritten checks is a complex problem. As described by Scalabrin et al. [12] there is a great amount of diverse and complex knowledge involved, the need to dynamically reconfigure a treatment process, and the interaction between experts. The automation process requires the implementation of the operations as follows:

– image acquisition;

---

[1] The Multicheck Project is being developed by Pontifical Catholic University of Paraná, Brazil (PUCPR), with the financial support of the Brazilian Government (CNPq), in an international cooperation between *l'École de Technologie Supérieure* (ETS)/ Canada and PUCPR.

F. F. Ramos, H. Unger, V. Larios (Eds.): ISSADS 2004, LNCS 3061, pp. 91-104, 2004.

- suppression of irrelevant information given on the check;
- relevant information location and extraction;
- obtaining the logical structure of the document;
- discrimination between the pre-printed and the handwritten information;
- segmentation of each logical field;
- logical data interpretation (date, numerical and literal data and signature);
- check analysis for acceptance or rejection.

It is a problem where tasks are well defined. However, the implementation of each task requires large computer resources, and the sharing of some partial results can be decisive to obtain a correct interpretation of information on checks.

Therefore, we decided to automate the bank check-compensation process by using the concept of autonomous agent. This concept allows us to organize the application knowledge and brings several benefits to the approach. Such approach was chosen due to the following motivations:

- the nature of the problem in question allows a decomposition in well-defined tasks, and each of them can be encapsulated in an independent agent;
- the natural interaction capability of agents makes the check treatment process more robust, particularly as their exchanges leads to solving situations which are apparently difficult;
- the possibility of introducing learning and reasoning mechanisms in the agents, allows us to endow them with pro-active and adaptable behaviors;
- the modular aspect of the agents allows an effective fight against the complexity of the domain, as well as the development of a system in an incremental way, which means, an open system of agents [14].

Therefore, in a DAI (Distributed Artificial Intelligence) system, because of its distributed and non-synchronized nature, agents can easily obtain inconsistent information by working separately on the same problem. Thus, some of these agents must be complex enough to decide *how*, *when* and *with whom* to interact and behave correctly when facing contradictory information. The mechanism developed for this purpose uses some of the concepts and operators of paraconsistent logic, which integrates a natural inconsistent information treatment which cannot be treated through the classical logic [3], [5], and [15].

Empirically, the manual check treatment goes through the interpretation of the numerical and literal values in an interactive and approximated way, and then through the date and signature verifications. In this way and intuitively, the image treatment of the bank check requires specific knowledge to treat each relevant logical field of the document.

Section 2 presents the architecture of autonomous agents that takes into account this interaction in a very natural way. The next sections describe the system operation, enhancing the mechanisms of combination and interpretation (or validation) of the information given by the image segment classifiers of a check logical field. It is important to understand that the communication and validation processes work together, allowing the agents to exchange beliefs and to reason about them. To conclude, we present the conclusion of our work.

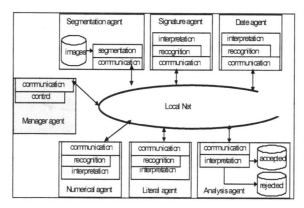

Fig. 1. Multicheck architecture

2   Architecture

The architecture of the Multicheck System consists of a group of relatively complex agents meant to perform the analysis and treatment of handwritten Brazilian bank checks images [13]. In this architecture, three types of agents are defined:

- The segmentation agent identifies, extracts and creates a logical model of a check (date, signature, numerical and literal values).
- The recognition agent recognizes the different logical fields extracted from a check.
- The analysis agent either accepts or rejects a check. The task consists of verifying whether all recognition agents have or have not given a positive interpretation of the same check. The information is kept in the accepted or rejected check database.
- The manager agent is responsible for monitoring the net and deciding whether an agent should be inserted or removed from the system.

Fig. 1. shows a simple view of the Multicheck System Architecture, as well as the architecture of each of its agents. The ability to recognize patterns – over image segments – is present only in the agents: date, signature, numerical and literal. The expertise to interpret and validate the patterns appears in all agents, except in the segmentation agent. The check acceptance or rejection is done by the analysis agent, which validates the information given by every recognition agent. The communication ability is present in all agents and is implemented by the communication module. This module is responsible for the exchange of non-synchronized messages between agents, and for the implementation of some basic tasks, such as: the recognition of a performance, the extraction of the message contents and its communication to specialized modules.

It is important to remember that in the implementation of this architecture, there can be several agents with the same competence. This redundancy allows us to aim for several parallel treatments and ensures the balance of the system load [14]. However, to interpret a check, the architecture has to have at least seven agents (one of each type).

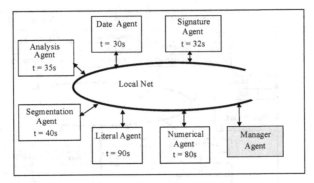

Fig. 2. Average time of calculus over a check

In order to manage the balance of the system load it was introduced a *manager agent* which monitors the agents of the net. The main tasks of this agent consist of inserting or removing agents from the system when necessary. This decision is made over the average time spent by one agent to end its calculus over a certain task. The ordered pair $< i, t >$ corresponds to information used by the manager for its making of decisions, where i is any agent and t is the average time spent by the agent to end its recognition task, as shown in Fig.2. E.g.:

$$< i, t > = \{< signature, 32s >, < date, 30s >, < numeric, 80s >, < literal, 90s >\}$$

The decision of whether inserting or removing a recognition agent is made by the manager agent considering the value βI, obtained as follows:

```
A = {32s, 30s, 80s, 90s}
for each element of A do:
```

$$\beta_i = \left| \left(\frac{\frac{A_i}{N_i}}{Min(A)} \right) - 1 \right|$$

```
apply rule 01
```

where N_i is the agents' number of the same type, A_i is the average time spent by the agent to end its task and *Min (A)* is the lower time spent by the agent to end its task.

The manager agent makes its decisions by evaluating the following rules:

```
Rule 01: insert a new recognition agent in the system
If (βi > 0)
then insert βi agents of the type Ai in the system

Rule 02:  insert a new analysis or segmentation agent in the
sytem
if (numbers of checks in the queue > 50)
then insert a new agent in the system
```

Rule 03: remove an agent in the system

$$\frac{A_i}{N_i} < Min(A)$$

If (   )
then remove the agent that spends more time to end its
recognition task

The main advantage of the Multicheck Architecture resides on the autonomous and cognitive agents. These entities are able to communicate and reason about beliefs, therefore making the interpretation process of a check more robust, besides allowing the repetition of treatment stages (if necessary). On the other hand, its biggest inconvenient lies in the complexity of the agents' implementation, especially the management and the treatment of its communication. E.g.: when and how an agent must communicate a piece of information? When and how an agent must ask for a piece of information? When and how the agents must organize themselves to accomplish the same goal? How must an agent treat a belief?

3   Scenario

The numerical and literal agents represent the most interesting aspect of this work, because the interpretation of the numerical and literal logical fields can be done in an interactive and approximate way, enabling these agents to exchange beliefs and reason about them. The Fig 3 shows summarily the working process of these agents.

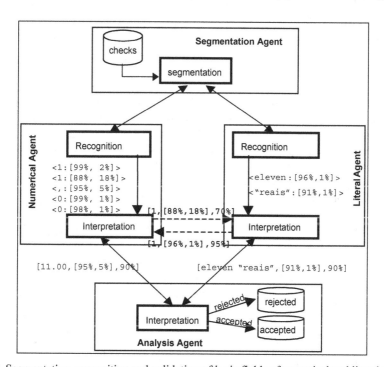

Fig. 3. Segmentation, recognition and validation of logic fields of numerical and literal values

Each recognition process corresponds to the range of classification algorithms applied on a certain logical field. The input of these processes are images and the output are pairs <n,[μv]>, where μ represents the favorable piece of evidence and v the opposite piece of evidence[2] on which n must be a digit in case of a numerical agent or a word in case of a literal agent. Each set of patterns obtained in a recognition process, is the input for an interpretation process.

The interpretation process of each pattern sets is accomplished in an interactive way, where, for example, the numerical and literal agents exchange information to solve certain internal conflicts and reach an agreement on the value of the check. These agents communicate their conclusions to the analysis agent, which accepts or rejects the conclusions or interpretations. The decision is based only on favorable and opposite evidential values about information given by recognition agents of the logical fields. The result is obtained through the application of some operators of paraconsistent logic on these values, as well as by using some domain heuristics.

It is important to remember that this work focuses on the validation or interpretation of patterns obtained in recognition processes; thereby it only concerns the implementation of the interpretation modules. The evidential values associated to the literal and numerical values were obtained by using an automatic data generator. The various modules of recognition are part of the following works: signature [6], date [10], numerical value [4], literal value [9], and segmentation [11].

3.1 Pattern Interpretation or Validation

The interpretation of information checking is an interactive, approximated and distributed task; therefore it is not limited to a mere local process. Each agent implements this task supported by a high-level communication protocol. This protocol activates responding to the state of each agent and its local knowledge. This knowledge is encapsulated in the decision process of each agent.

During the checking of a logical field process, concepts of evidential logic reasoning were used. In this type of reasoning, described by Subrahmanian [15], two values are associated to a proposition: one of them represents the favorable piece of evidence to the proposition and the other one the opposite piece of evidence [2], [12]. No restriction is set to these values, except that they belong to interval [0, 1]. In evidential logic favorable and opposite evidences; factors aren't directly related as in the Probability Theory [6].

In summary, the logical field process of a checking follows a determined flow: the recognition module of a certain agent receives an image segment σ_i – which corresponds to a certain logical field of a check, and decomposes σ_i in various parts σ_{ij}. These parts are classified through highly specialized classifiers. Its output format is $< \sigma_{ij} \in N_k : [\mu_j ; v_j] >$, where $\mu_j, v_j \in [0, 1]$, and represents coefficients of favorable and opposite evidence in relation to the class that contains a determined σ_{ij}. N_k are the possible classes.

---

[2] As Subrahmanian [15] says, the use of two evidences associated to a same p proposition, can reinforce its expressive capacity.

Given σ_1 the numerical value logical field, σ_{1j} the values of favorable and opposite evidence of each digit, and χ_{1j} the degrees of certainty, as shows Fig.4.

For example, σ_{11} can be read as follows: there is favorable evidence, up to 96%, that the first digit is "1", and opposite evidence, up to 1%, that this first digit is not "1".

The evidential values interpretation is done through operators and paraconsistent logic concepts, where the evidence is mapped in certainty degrees through the following function [2], [12]:

$$c([\mu j, vj]) = \mu j - vj = \chi ij \tag{1}$$

A certainty degree χ_{ij} associated to each classified σ_i segment. χ_{ij} shall be used in various situations, as to define when an agent must communicate with the others. The main valid rules for numeric, literal and analysis agents are:

```
Rule 04: If χij ∈ (50, 90]
then asks for information to the literal or numeric agent to
increase χij

Rule 05: If min (χij) ∈ (90, 100] then sends the result to the
analysis agent and other interested agents

Rule 06: If χij ∈ [0,50]then asks for segmentation σi+1

Rule 07: If the request for a new segmentation is rejected then
concludes that the numerical value cannot be recognized and sends
the result to every other agent

Rule 08: If one of the logical fields cannot be interpreted
correctly then rejects check else accepts check

Rule 09: If I/S ∈ [0,50] then accept check else reject check
[...]
```

The thresholds presented on the rules above are suppositions. In particular, an agent searches an interaction when he cannot recognize the logical field of its competence, it can decide to:

- ask a segmentation agent to take a new extraction of the logical field;
- ask a recognition agent to validate a belief;
- warn all system agents that the logical field of its competence could not be recognized.

The exchange of information between agents can result in new evidential coefficients, especially through successive combinations which occur at two different moments:

- during a local segmentation of a given logical field;
- during the interpretation of two or more logical fields that interact with each other.

σ		σ_{1j}	χ_{1j}
17,31	< 1 :	[0.96 ; 0.01]>	0.95
	< 7 :	[0.86 ; 0.01]>	0.85
	< , :	[0.70 ; 0.25]>	0.45
	< 3 :	[0.85 ; 0.36]>	0.49
	< 1 :	[0.70 ; 0.30]>	0.40

Fig. 4. Image segment, degrees of favorable and contrary evidence, and certainty degrees

$(\sigma_{1j}\ \sigma_{2j})$		(χ_{3j})
< 1 :	[0.99 ; 0.02]>	0.97
< 7 :	[0.86 ; 0.01]>	0.85
< , :	[0.90 ; 0.11]>	0.79
< 3 :	[0.80 ; 0.23]>	0.57
< 1 :	[0.99 ; 0.40]>	0.59

Fig. 5. Image segment, degrees of favorable and opposite evidences, and certainty degrees

Phase 1: Combination of Different Segmentations and Classifications on the same Logical Field

The segmentation agent identifies, extracts and creates the logical structure of a check (date, signature, literal and numerical value). In the first place the check global segmentation is accomplished and immediately followed by a local segmentation. This procedure allows any agent to ask the segmentation agent for a new extraction of a determined logical field. The recognition algorithms are applied to this new extraction, obtaining new evidential values and certainty degrees, which are consequently combined.

On Fig.4, the third, fourth and fifth components of σ_1 were recognized with certainty degrees lower than 50%. Applying Rule 06, a new segmentation is requested.

Given σ_2 a new segmentation for the numerical value of the logical field, σ_{2j} the values of favorable and opposite evidence for each digit, and χ_{2j} the certainty degrees, as shows Fig.5.

Each σ_{1j} value of the first segmentation (Fig.4) is compared to each σ_{2j} value of the second segmentation (Fig.5). If, for example, σ_{11} and σ_{21} belong to the same class, apply the supreme operator (**sup**) over χ_{11} e χ_{21}. The σ_{ij} that owns the highest certainty degree is selected. In this way, for σ_{11} and σ_{21} select <1: [0.99 0.02], 97%>. The supreme operator is used because it returns the highest degree of certainty in the selective process. However, if σ_{11} and σ_{21} do not belong to the same class, it is necessary to begin the process of information exchange between numerical and literal agents to discover which classification is correct. It is important to remember that even if the certainty degree of σ_{22} is higher than the certainty degree of σ_{12}, $\sigma_{12\ 1}$, it will be selected. This occurs because the literal value is more decisive than the numerical[3] value. In this case, the combination of the results to σ_1 and σ_2 will be shown in Fig.6.

---

[3] In the Brazilian legislation, for bank checks, the valid value is the written one.

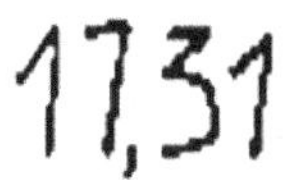

σ_2	σ_{2j}	χ_{2j}
	< 1 : [0.99 ; 0.02]>	0.97
	< 1 : [0.98 ; 0.01]>	0.97
17,31	< , : [0.90 ; 0.11]>	0.79
	< 3 : [0.80 ; 0.23]>	0.57
	< 1 : [0.99 ; 0.40]>	0.59

Fig. 6. Second segmentation of the numerical amount, degrees of favorable and contrary evidence, and certainty degrees

These data will be object of validation, rejection, or combination according to the results obtained, for example, by the literal agent.

Phase 2: Sharing of Partial Results from Different Logical Fields

The sharing of partial results is fundamental between *literal* and *numerical agents*, especially because they must obtain exactly the same information from different logical fields (codified in different formats). They can also obtain conflicting results and be led to interact with each other, obtain a consistent interpretation and increase its certainty degree.

Assuming that the literal and numerical agents have already concluded the Phase 1 independently and have recognized the same information, the consequent of Rule 04, of both agents, can be evaluated. The mechanisms used in this work to evaluate the quality of the information of an agent are: disjunction, conjunction, certainty degree and inconsistency/sub-determination degree [2], [5], [12] and [15].

– *the disjunction* allows values combinations to increase a certainty degree.
– *the conjunction* allows the evaluation of a set of values over a certain logical field as a whole.
– *the certainty degree* allows the individual study of each segmented part (χ_{ij}).
– *the inconsistency/sub-determination degree* allows the mapping of the inconsistency or sub-determination of the analyzed information in a unique value.

Disjunction

The disjunction operator ($\vee$) below, defined in [12], is applied when an agent needs to confirm a hypothesis or reinforces its beliefs about a certain component.

$$[\mu1, v1] \vee [\mu2, v2] = [\max(\mu1, \mu2), \min(v1, v2)] \tag{2}$$

Where the evidential factors are: $[\mu1, \mu2], [v1, v2] \in [0,1]$.

In the example of Fig.6, the certainty degrees of the numerical field three last Fig.s need to be increased, because they are smaller than the certainty degrees obtained by the corresponding literal field. Therefore, the numerical agent applies the disjunction operator on the information calculated locally and the information received from the literal agent, obtaining the following expressions:

Information obtained after the application of the disjunction operator over the local information of the numerical value and the information received from the literal agents.	$c([\mu, v])$	Information obtained by the literal agent by the segmentation: $\sigma_1, \sigma_2 \, e \, \sigma_3$	$c([\mu, v])$
	χ_{4i}	$(\sigma_{1i}, \sigma_{2i}, \sigma_{3i})$	χ_{4i}
< 1 : [0.99 ; 0.02]>	0.97	< eleven : [0.89 ; 0.02]>	0.87
< 1 : [0.86 ; 0.01]>	0.85	< " reais " : [0.88 ; 0.03]>	0.85
< , : [0.90 ; 0.02]>	0.88		
< 0 : [0.89 ; 0.02]>	0.87		
< 0 : [0.99 ; 0.02]>	0.97		

Fig. 7. Degrees of favorable and opposite evidence and certainty degrees after the application of disjunction operator

$$[0.90, 0.11] \vee [0.89, 0.04] \vee [0.90, 0.04] \vee [0.93, 0.06] \vee [0.91, 0.04] \vee [0.88, 0.06] = [0.93, 0.04]$$
$$[0.80, 0.23] \vee [0.89, 0.04] \vee [0.90, 0.04] \vee [0.93, 0.06] \vee [0.91, 0.04] \vee [0.88, 0.06] = [0.93, 0.04]$$
$$[0.99, 0.40] \vee [0.89, 0.04] \vee [0.90, 0.04] \vee [0.93, 0.06] \vee [0.91, 0.04] \vee [0.88, 0.06] = [0.99, 0.04]$$

The Fig.7 shows the information obtained after the application of the operator ($\vee$).

Conjunction

The conjunction operator ($\wedge$) below, defined in [12], is applied when an agent needs to obtain a closure value of each amount.

$$[\mu 1, v1] \wedge [\mu 2, v2] = [\min(\mu 1, \mu 2), \max(v1, v2)] \qquad (3)$$

Where the evidential factors are: $[\mu 1, \mu 2]$, $[v1, v2] \in [0,1]$.

The conjunction operator permits to generate a unique value for σ_i and χ_i from various values σ_{ij} and χ_{ij}. In other words, a unique favorable and opposite evidential value can be obtained, as well as a unique certainty degree for a given field.

For example, in the application of the operator ($\wedge$) on the numerical and literal agents' local information, it is obtained:

Numerical Agent:
$$[0.99 \; 0.02] \wedge [0.86 \; 0.01] \wedge [0.90 \; 0.03] \wedge [0.89 \; 0.03] \wedge [0.99 \; 0.03] = [0.86 \; 0.03]$$
Literal Agent:
$$[0.89 \; 0.02] \wedge [0.88 \; 0.03] = [0.88 \; 0.03]$$

This information will be sent to the analysis agent in order to interpret the evidential factors obtained for each value.

Inconsistency/Sub-determination (I/S) Degree

The calculation of the degree of I/S, defined in [3], [6], [15] allows to map in a single value the inconsistency or sub-determination of the analyzed information.

$$I/S = |\mu 1 + v1 - 1| * 100 \qquad (4)$$

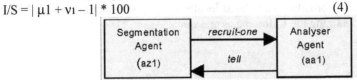

Fig. 8. Connection between segmentation and analysis agents

The calculation agent does this calculation in two stages:

- application of the conjunction operator on the information received by the recognition agents, obtaining in this case: $[0.86 \quad 0.03] \wedge [0.88 \quad 0.03] = [0.86 \quad 0.03]$
- the calculation for I/S is: $|0.86 + 0.03 - 1| * 100 = 11\%$

This means that the obtained information – from a given check – has 11% of I/S. The acceptation or not of the check is submitted to Rule 09 above, defining a 5% limit established according to statistic calculation on a test base of Brazilian check banks.

The calculations above are done locally, inside each agent. This implies that the agents should be endowed with communication mechanisms. In summary, these mechanisms include three distinctive phases:

- the settlement of a connection between agents;
- the solicitation and communication of determined information;
- the end of connection.

4   Communication

The communication in a multi-agent system is fundamental. It requires a common communication language, especially to codify the intentions during a dialog. For this purpose, the KQML language [7], [8], has been adopted: each message represents, intuitively, a part of the dialog between two or more agents.

In this implementation, the cooperation begins by the settlement of connections between task holder agents and the agents able to execute these tasks [1]. For example, the segmentation agent receives a check, segments it and sends it to the analysis agent (aa1), which owns the required competence (check analyzing).

Effectively, the *recruit-one performative* (Fig.8) makes the connection between these agents. The agent *aa1*, sender of *tell,* assumes the responsibility for analyzing the check. This analyzing task will be shared with the other agents of the system. For this, a process of competence recruitment – signature verification, date verification, literal and numerical value recognition – is done by the agent *aa1* (Fig.9). This process creates other connections between *aa1* and the other agents. Each sender of a *tell* assumes the responsibility for treating the logic field of its own competence. In this process, the agents start working in an individual way and as some partial results start to be obtained, they begin to share them.

The closure of these connections is done only after the ending of the calculations done by the recognition agents and their communication to an analysis agent. This agent decides (based on the received results) whether the check is going to be rejected or not. It is important to remember that the analysis agents are mono-task.

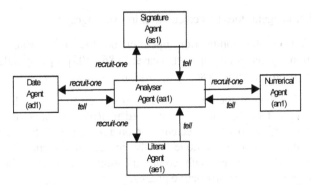

Fig. 9. Connections for logic field distribution to be treated

5   Results

The tests done to prove the robustness of the system were achieved on three different versions of the system:

- The v1 test corresponds to check analysis without any interaction between the agents;
- In the v2 test the recognition agents interact with a segmentation agent during the check analysis, for example, to request a new segmentation; and
- The v3 test represents the case where all agents are able to interact.

This graphic shows (Fig. 10) that the interaction between these agents results in a highly robust treatment process, as the exchanges among the agents can resolve situations which are apparently difficult or impossible to be resolved with a unique expert. Finally, it is important to notice, that in the case of this experiment, it did not have no false-positive classification.

6   Other Works

In this application domain, Montoliu [10] proposes a solution for the treatment of French bank checks, using the concept of reactive agent. In this proposal, three types of agent are defined:

- *base agents*, that are the classifiers (e.g. RN, PPV and HMM);
- *macro agents*, that are entities composed by base agents which are regrouped by specialties (e.g. words global treatment, number treatment);
- *meta agents*, are agents that combine the results produced by the base agents.

The main advantage of this method is the velocity in which a result can be produced, due to the use of classifiers in cascade. On the other hand, the main inconvenience is the lack of interaction between agents and the absence of intelligence at each agent level. Besides, there are no interactions between stages of treatment, which makes the check interpretation process sequential, direct and potentially little robust.

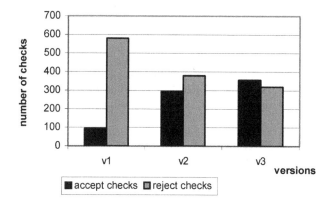

Fig. 1.0. Comparison of the results (v1, v2 and v3)

7   Conclusions

The treatment of handwritten Brazilian bank checks is a very complex problem and it requires large computing resources to automate them. However, it is a domain in which tasks are very well defined and the tasks encapsulation – signature verification, date verification, numerical and literal values recognition – in independent agents allows a progressive development of the system, as well as the reuse of these agents in other applications. The interaction between these agents makes the process of checks treatment robust, because the agents have abilities to learn, reason and resolve conflicts. The presence of inconsistent information is frequent in the interaction between *literal* and *numerical* agents, because they have to recognize the same information codified in different formats. Thus, to treat the inconsistency appropriately, some concepts and operators of paraconsistent logic were used.

References

[1]   Angelotti, E. S., Utilização da Lógica Paraconsistente na Implementação de um Sistema Multi-Agente, Dissertação de Mestrado, Pontifical Catholic University of Paraná, Curitiba, 2001, in Portuguese.

[2]   Ávila, B.C.; Abe, J.M.; Prado, J.P.A., Paralog_e: A Paraconsistent Evidential Logic Programming Language, XVII International Conference of the Chilean Computer Science Society, IEEE Computer Society Press, Valparaiso, Chile, November, pp.2-8, 1997.

[3]   Blair, H.A.; Subrahmanian V.S., Paraconsistent Logic Programming, Proc.7th Conf. on Foundations of Software Technology and Theoretical Computer Science, Lecture Notes in Computer Science, Springer-Verlag, Vol. 287, pp. 340-360, 1987.

[4]   Brito Jr. A.S.; Bortolozzi F.; Lethelier E.; Sabourin R., Numeral Slant Normalization Based on Contextual Informational, Accept on 7th International Workshop on Frontiers in Handwritten Recognition, Amsterdam, Netherlands, September, 2000.

[5]   da Costa, N.C.A., Calculs Propositionnels pour les Systèmes Formels Inconsistants, Compte Rendu Acad. des Sciences (Paris), 257, pp. 3790-3792, 1963, in French.

[6]   Enembreck, F.; Ávila B.C.; Sabourin, R., Decision Tree-Based Paraconsistent Learning, In: Proc. of XIX International Conference of the Chilean Computer Science Society, pp. 32-44, IEEE Computer Society Press, Talca, Chile, 1999.

[7]   Finin et al., Specification of the KQML Agent-Communication Language, DARPA Knowledge Sharing Initiative, External Interfaces Working Group, June 1993.

[8]   Finin T.; Labrou Y., A Proposal for a new KQML Specification, TR CS-97-03, 1997.

[9]   Freitas, C.; Bortolozzi, F.; Sabourin, R., Reconhecimento do Extenso Manuscrito em Cheques Bancários Brasileiros, ISDM98, Curitiba, Brasil, pp 149-167, Novembro, 1998, in Portuguese.

[10]   Morita M.E.; Bortolozzi F.; Facon J.; Sabourin R., Mathematic Morphology and Weighted Least Square to Correcting Handwritten, Proceedings of IEEE – ICDAR99 – The 50th International Conference on Document Analysis and Recognition, Vol.I, pp. 430-433, Bangalore, India, September,1999.

[11]   Oliveira, L.E.; Bortolozzi F.; Lethelier E.; Sabourin R., A New Segmentation Approach for Handwritten Digits, 15th International Conference on Pattern Recognition, Barcelona, Spain, September, 2000.

[12]   Prado J.P.A., Uma Arquitetura para Inteligência Artificial Distribuída Baseada em Lógica Paraconsistente Anotada, Universidade de São Paulo, São Paulo, 1996, in Portuguese.

[13]   Scalabrin E., Bortolozzi F., Kaestner C., Sabourin R., Multicheck : Une Architecture d'agents cognitifs indépendants pour le traitement automatique des chèques bancaires Brésiliens, In : CIFED'98, Canada, Maio, 1998, in French.

[14]   Scalabrin, E. E., Conception et Réalisation d'environnement de développement de systèmes d'agents cognitifs, Thèse de Doctorat, UTC, pp. 169, France, 1996.

[15]   Subrahmanian V., S.; Towards a Theory of Evidential Reasoning, Logic Colloquium'87, The European Summer Meeting of the Association for Symbolic Logic, Granada, Spain, July, 1987.

A Multiagent Infrastructure
for Self-organized Physical Embodied Systems:
An Application to Wireless Communication
Management

Jean-Paul Jamont[1] and Michel Occello[2]

[1] Laboratoire de Conception et d'Intégration de Systèmes
Institut National Polytechnique de Grenoble
F-26000 Valence, France
jean-paul.jamont@esisar.inpg.fr
[2] Université Pierre-Mendès France
Laboratoire de Conception et d'Intégration de Systèmes
Institut National Polytechnique de Grenoble
F-26000 Valence, France. michel.occello@iut-valence.fr

Abstract. The aim of this paper is to present an application of multi-agent systems (MAS) to communication management in wireless sensor networks (WSN). We propose an adaptive infrastructure of autonomous agents to route the information in the best way, in consideration to strong constraints on energy resources, dynamical topology, asymetric communication links etc. We design a multiagent system's architecture according to the AEIO method. We also introduce the ASTRO hybrid agent model. We apply our approach to the monitoring of an underground hydrographic network. Interesting simulation results are discussed.

1   Introduction

Recent developments in wireless technology and mobile computing foreshadow a promising future for wireless networking. The design of efficient routing techniques is a more complicated thing that it can appear. In such networks, the routing process is distributed to all the hosts and an efficient packets routing is difficult to obtain because links can be asymetric, topology is dynamic, bandwidth is limited. We can note that this type of network is called "ad-hoc network".

The cooperative, collaborative and negotiating capabilities allow the agents which evolve in an open system to increase the overall efficiency of this system. The multiagent systems are so well suited for analyzing and designing complex systems such as networks of distributed autonomous entities behaving in an open environment.

In this paper we intend to evaluate the contribution of a multiagent approach to communication management in a physical open system of interacting entities

F. F. Ramos, H. Unger, V. Larios (Eds.): ISSADS 2004, LNCS 3061, pp. 105–117, 2004.

i.e. a wireless network of intelligent sensors. In our case, we consider that the energy constraints are very strong.

We introduce in a first part multiagent systems and their use in the context of wireless sensor networks. We present the ad-hoc traditional approaches based on protocols. We then propose our multiagent approach based on self-organization in the context of communication management to wireless networks of autonomous sensors. Finaly, we present our application in the context of the instrumentation of an underground river system that involves an open network of intelligent sensors whose cooperation must be monitored in order to insure the best organization. Our simulation platform will be described and we conclude with some comments of the results obtained whith our approach.

2   Multiagent and Wireless Sensor Networks

2.1   AEIO Multiagent Method

A multiagent system is a set of agents situated in a common environment, which interact and attempt to reach a set of goals. Through these interactions a global behavior can emerge. The emergence process is a way to obtain, from cooperation, dynamic results that cannot be predicted in a deterministic way. It is important to note that the multiagent system intelligence is more than the sum of the agent local intelligence.

The power of an agent decomposition is the decentralization of the intelligence, i.e. the decision capabilities, and of entities' knowledge.

The multiagent methods aim at decreasing the complexity of system design by a decentralized analysis.

There are several multiagent system methods [11] among which most are centered on the analysis of agents'tasks as the methods Gaia [20] and MaSE [19], others on the roles or on the organization as the method AALAADIN [5]. We are thereafter going to be interested in the AEIO decomposition [4]. We will follow the method of multiagent design discussed in [16], associated to this MAS decomposition. It proposes a decomposition according to four axes collectively accepted today :

- The agent axis (A) gathers all elements for defining and constructing these entities.
- The environment axis (E). This part of the analysis deals with elements necessary for the multiagent system realization such as the perception of this environment and the actions one can do on it.
- The interaction axis (I) includes all elements which are in use for structuring the external interactions among the agents (agent communication language, interaction protocols)
- The organization axis (O) allows to order agent groups in organization determined according to their roles.

We chose to apply this multiagent method for our problem because it privileges an explicit description of the interactions and the environment. In our case, this method will be more adapted than the approaches previously mentioned.

2.2   Wireless Sensor Network Routing Protocol

Generalities. Networks of wireless autonomous sensors for monitoring physical environments are a recent but very active application and research area. These networks, where the routing process is distributed among all the hosts, are called ad-hoc networks. If the hosts are mobile they can be called MANET networks for Mobile Ad-hoc NETwork. The associated routing protocols are centered on the flooding techniques. Flooding techniques consists in sending messages all the members of the network to be sure the receiver gets the message. A node is both receiver and sender of broadcasted messages. The associated power cost is very high.

There are three differents ad-hoc routing protocols families :

- The reactive protocols using no routing table,
- The proactive protocols using routing tables, periodically updated, and for those it is necessary to exchange control packets,
- The hybrid protocols adopting the reactive protocol behavior and, if necessary, using routing tables for increasing efficiency.

In the case of reactive protocols, when a host wants to transmit data it never knows the way to reach the receiver. The main idea of this family is to reduce the flows by creating clusters for example. The Dynamic Source Routing protocol (DSR [13]), that we will see aftewards, is one of the simplest protocols.

The proactive protocols use adaptive routing tables for creating a "network model". Generally, the adaptive feature of these tables comes from periodical exchanges between the different nodes. The Destination Sequence Distance Vector protocol (DSDV [17]) for example is one of the first protocols of this family specified by the MANET work group and it takes the RIP functionning principe. The Clusterhead Gateway Switch Routing protocol (CGSR [2]) agregates the different hosts in clusters.

The clustering idea seems to bring a real benefit from an efficiency point of view, but we can create a better and more complex self-organization feature with a multiagent approach.

Difficulties of Communication Management for WSN. There are a lot of problems in the management of a wireless sensors network. An overview of these difficulties, collectively accepted today, is given in [21]. Some of them concern the sensors and other the whole system.

In such networks, the sensors are numerous. For cost reasons, the embedded chips have to be as cheap as possible : the CPU speeds are not very fast and memory capacities are low. Generally these devices have autonomous energy sources. These constraints must be taken into account in order to optimize the communication management (the energy devoted to communication constitutes an important part of the sensor energetic cost). The energetic parameter is important in the sense that it can create internal fault or that it can influence other parameters like the emission range. Furthermore the environment can be hostile (temperature, pressure, water flood environment...) and can cause internal fault.

The sensor collection system, the wireless sensor network, must be very adaptive, fault tolerant and self-stabilized : a sensor failure must not have an important impact on the system. This system must provide reliable communication (it is not always possible) and, sometimes, adapt to "real-time" constraints. Furthermore, in the case of mobile devices the infrastructure of sytems are not persistant.

2.3   Wireless Sensor Networks Management and MAS

This intelligence in communication networks usually comes from distributed artificial intelligence. We can use intelligent components in configuration management, security management, fault management, performance management and accounting management.

The distributed and open nature of sensor networks means that the multiagent system approach is an adapted answer. Another advantage of this approach is the external representation of the interactions and of the organization. External representations offer multiple possibilities such as the monitoring by an external observer.

A few works reaching the same objectives show that the approach is interesting. We can quote the ActComm [8] project which is a military project for which the routing of information is essential: it aims at studying the communication management between a soldier team and a military camp via a satellite. We can also mention the work of Petriu and al [18] on wireless networks of mobile autonomous intelligent sensors where agents are used to achieve flexible and open cell assembly.

Another example is the Unmanned Ground Vehicle Program ARPA's project [3] which approaches the information management resulting from a group of autonomous observation military vehicles. The problem described in [21] is very similar to our problem but the approach is very different since the used technique is based on distributed stochastic algorithms.

Multiagent systems are used in very active way for service descriptions and service discovery in ad-hoc networks [9, 1]. For this, FIPA [6] is the most commonly used standard. Some work on this standard have been proved to be efficient in environments where slow wireless networks are involved [10].

3   Our Multiagent Approach for Communication in Wireless Sensor Networks

We have selected the cluster idea to decrease the number of exchanges resulting of the flooding process.

3.1   AEIO Analysis of this Problem

As previously examined, this approach is articulated around four axes.

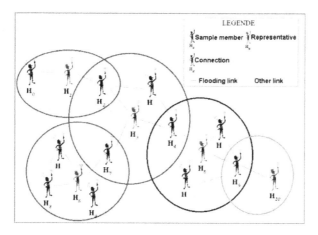

Fig. 1. Group organisation for communication management

The Environment Axis. The environment will be made of information the measurable by every agent. Agents are situated but don't know their position. This environment is deterministic, non episodic, dynamic and continuous.

The Organization Axis. The main property of this organization is that it will be dynamic. In this type of application no one can control the organization a priori. Relations between agents are going to emerge from the evolution of the agents'states and from their interactions. We are going to be content with fixing the organization parameters, i.e. agents'tasks, agents'roles.

The organizational basic structures (see fig 1) are composed of :

- one group representative agent managing the communication in his group,
- some connection agents: they know different representative agents and they can belong to several groups,
- some ordinary members : active in the communication process only for their own tasks (They don't ensure information relay).

The ideal representative agent is the one having the most important number of neighbors and the most important level of energy. The level of energy is an important parameter in the sense that the representative agent is the more sollicited agent in the group from a communication point of view. We use a role allocation based self-organization mechanism involving the election of a representative agent . Our election function integrates some data on neigbors and energy levels. This function estimates the adequation between it desire to be the representative agent and its capacity to be. The organization is modified only when a problem occurs. We don't try to maintain it if we have no communication.

The Interaction Axis. The agents will interact only with the agents in acquaintance (an agent is in acquaintance with another if it is aware of its existence). Agents interact by exchange of messages. We can distinguish two methods

for these communications: a synchronous and an asynchronous version. In the former, agents must be in rendez-vous. On the latter, the asynchronous version, messages are memorized. It is not necessary for the receiver and the sender to be synchronized. Our application having no particular constraint from a communication point of view, we opt for an asynchronous communication mode by messages sending, which is the most flexible method. Among the different protocols that we use, the choice of an introduction protocol is essential. Indeed, this protocol allows to the agents to be known, i.e. to bring their knowledge and their know-how to the agents' society.
We defined thirteen different types of small messages.

The Agent Axis. In our multiagent system, sensors are modeled by agents. These agents have hybrid architectures, i.e. a composition of some pure types of architectures. Indeed, the agents will be of a cognitive type in case of a configuration alteration, it will be necessary for them to communicate and to manipulate their knowledge in order to have an efficient collaboration. On the other hand, in normal use it will be necessary for them to be reactive (a reactive agent reacts to stimuli by a response) to be most efficient.
The agents have then to achieve several functions.

- A measuring function : It is the main work of a sensor, it consists in interacting with the environment to acquire information about one of the environment parameters.
- A communication task : giving (if necessary) the information to other devices or relaying neighbor's messages. All the agents have the same communication capabilities but the communicated data depend of their roles.

Using a hybrid architecture for the agents enables to combine the strong features of each of reactive and cognitive capabilities seen before. The ASTRO hybrid architecture [14, 15] have we chosen is especially adapted to a real time context. The integration of deliberative and reactive capabilities is possible through the use of parallelism in the structure of the agent.

4   Our Practical Case: The EnvSys Project

The purpose of the ENVironment SYStem project is to monitor an underground river network. Let us present the origin of this project and the problems occurring in such an application [12].

4.1   Origin of the Project

The ENVSYS project finds its origin in a statement: the measure of the various parameters in an underground river system is a complex task. In fact, the access to this type of underground galleries is difficult : it requires help from speleologists. Besides, the installation of wire communications networks is difficult, especially because the structure of an hydrographic system is very often chaotic. Finally, in the case of a radio communication network, the underground aspect complicates wave propagation and for the moment the techniques which are used are not totally mastered.

For some years, systems of radio communication have been introduced. They are generally used by the speleological rescue specialists. These systems are analogic, work with low frequencies and are used mostly for voice transmission. The general idea of the project is to study the feasibility of a sensor network from the existing physical layer. This will allow wireless instrumentation of a subterranean river system. Such a network would present an important interest in many domains: the study of underground flows, the monitoring of deep collecting, flooding risk management, river system detection of pollution risks, etc.

4.2   The Issue

In a subterranean river system, the interesting parameters to measure are numerous: temperature of air and water, air pressure and if possible water pressure for the flooded galleries, pollution rate by classical pollutants, water flow, draft speed, etc. All this information will be collected at the immediate hydrographic network exit by a work station like a PC. These data will be processed to activate alarms, study the progress of a certain pollution according to miscellaneous measuring parameters, determine a predictive model of the whole network by relating the subterranean parameters measures of our system with the overground parameters measures more classically on the catchment basin.

We do not wish to carry out this instrumentation with a wire network for obvious reasons of convenience. We shall use electromagnetic waves with low frequencies as a carrier. These waves have an interesting property: they are able to go through rock blocks.

Every sensor has a limited transmission range. This limitation results from three points: the technological solutions which are used to achieve the sensor transmission module (frequency, power, antenna), the implementation of these solutions and, finally, the environment. In this environment we can say that propagation is hardly anisotropic. Indeed, according to the obstacles it will have to go through, the electromagnetic waves will not be usable at the same distance for each direction. The transmission zone will not be modeled by a sphere. In fact, as we can se on the next figure (fig 2), the distance d1 which separates the sensors i1 and i2 is shorter than the distance d2 which separates the sensors i1 and i3. However, the rock separating the couple of sensors (i1 , i2) will degenerate the signal and will prevent sensor i2 from receiving the message correctly unlike i3. Links are so really assymetric.

Having defined the role of sensors, we can represent the structure of our communication network. It consists of a set of sensors and a listening station as illustrated on the following figure (see fig 3):

Here is a non-exhaustive list of problems which one needs to address:

- How to realize the physical layer?
- What level of protocol connection to choose above such physical layer?

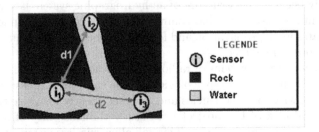

Fig. 2. Anisotropic signal propagation

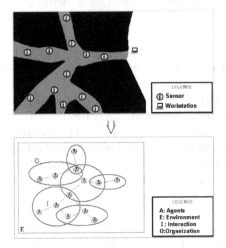

Fig. 3. Result MAS of our approach

- How to route the information in the best way? Each of the sensors cannot physically communicate with the workstation which collects the information. Which sensor should thus make the decision to repeat the information?
- How to monitor such a complex environment?
- What kind of intelligence giving to the network?

Our work deals with the analysis of the problem using a multiagent system approach. The main contribution of the work presented in this paper is situated at a logical level, concerning especially the last three points of the problems listed before.

4.3   Application of our Approach

The application of our approach on this case is very natural. We can see the resulting MAS on the figure 3.

5   The Experimentation

We can consider that we use agents as decisional structures for the intelligent sensors. In order to evaluate and improve such agents' software architectures and the cooperation techniques that they involve, we introduce a simulation stage in our development process. In this section, we describe this simulation step, the comparison against other ad-hoc routing protocols, and then give an insight to the operational embedded architecture.

5.1   The Simulation Step

The simulation first allowed us to experiment our approach and the software solutions that we provide for the various problems. We can also quantify the emergence inferred by the MAS approach in this case.

The simulation software structure is very basic. In fact, we have two types of components: SimSensor and SimNetwork (fig 4). A SimSensor component simulates the sensor behavior. It possesses its own model and architecture. All the sensors have the same communication capabilities. They transmit their requests to the SimNetwork component sends this information to all sensors which can receive them, in the environment. SimNetwork can appear as the inference mechanism for the simulation.

5.2   Simulation Results

We have compared our multiagent system to three other ad-hoc protocols. The DSDV protocol and the natural DSR protocol do not appear in this comparaison because its efficiency were lower than the ehanced version of DSR which use a route maintenance (memorization of main route).

We thereafter call efficiency the ratio between the theoretical useful volume (useful volume of the optimal path) and the real configuration volume added to the extra of the real useful volume. The extra of the real useful volume equals the real useful volume minus the theoric useful volume. Thus, a nonoptimal way will be suitably penalized. We can notice that DSR and DSR-ROUTAGE use optimal path to transmit messages contrary to our routing multiagent approach. Indeed, in our case the way is a succession of groups: it is this succession of groups which is optimal in our case.

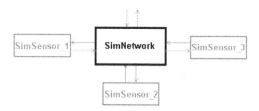

Fig. 4. Simulation plateform architecture

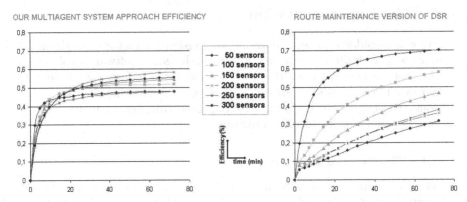

Fig. 5. DSR and self-organized MAS comparison for unidirectionnal use case

Use Case 1. At first, let us present some performances in the ENVSYS context. All sensors communicate only with the workstation situated at the end of the undergound river system : it is a unidirectionnal protocol. In this case, messages are small (five bytes : one for data type and four for the measure). For this example, three messages are send by five second. The same scenario is applied for the different protocols. In the real ENVSYS use case a sensor take one measure by hour.

We can see that the benefit (fig 5) of our approach is important. Quickly our routing method can deliver all messages with a good efficiency. Higher is the number of sensors better is the reactivity of our approach. We must note that if the system knows no pertubation or mobility variation, DSR will be better from an efficiency point of view. It is normal because in this case DSR learns all the routes (succession of sensors) allowing to communicate with the workstation. It is not really the case with our approach which reason from the group and not from the sensors. One consequence is that the route used by the messages with our approach are not optimal.

Use Case 2. In this case, we are in the ENVSYS context where the sensors communicate together for elaborating more complex measures. We choose to give to messages a size of thirty bytes.

In this case the behavior of our approach is much better than DSR because its route management is more complicated.

If we add some perturbations on these scenarios (one perturbation by three minutes) the efficiency is nearly the same (it is not the case for the DSDV protocol).

5.3   The Operational Embedded Architecture

Therefore, we will demonstrate the feasibility of our approach. For the sensors we have chosen a classical three-layers architecture of the following type:

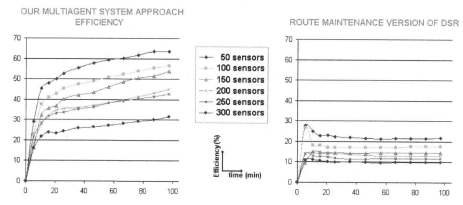

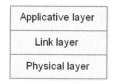

Fig. 6. DSR and self-organized MAS comparison for the multidirectionnal use case

We use the physical layer which is employed by NICOLA system, a voice transmission system used by the French speleological rescue teams [7]. This layer is implemented in a digital signal processor rather than a full analogic system. Thereby we can keep good flexibility and we are able to apply further a signal processing algorithm to improve the data transmission.

The link layer used is a CAN (Controller Area Network) protocol stemming from the motorcar industry and chosen for its good reliability. The applicative layer is constituted by the agents' system. The agents are embedded on autonomous processor cards. These cards are equipped with communication modules and with measuring modules to carry out agent tasks relative to the instrumentation. These cards supply a real time kernel. The KR-51(the kernel's name) allows multi-task software engineering for C515C microcontroller. We can produce one task for one capability. We can then quite easily implement the parallelism inherent to agents and satisfy the real-time constraints.

6   Conclusion

Our Multiagent System. This software agent architecture is embedded on autonomous processor cards. The multiagent system, which we are creating, has two important features. First of all it is an open system: adding a sensor does not require a manual reconfiguration. Most of sensors'dysfunctions should not threaten the functional integrity of the whole system which should be fault tolerant. Besides, our multiagent system is homogeneous. Indeed, all the sensors have a hybrid decisionnal architecture based on the ASTRO model. Through the simulation step , we can already notice what the MAS approach provides versus a classic approach. We summarize these contributions in three points:

- The emergent feature, which is inferred by the MAS approach, makes the system flexible and robust. Indeed, the system is fault tolerant to changes of the environment in which it evolves.
- Agents present interesting features of software engineering such as genericity allowing an easy evolution of the applications.
- Generic aspects of agents allows us to envisage differents applications for this network type such as diagnosis, risk management, data fusion, predictive model elaboration...

Future Work. In a near future, we want to analyse the effect of a recursive mechanism on this application. By this way, we hope to increase its efficiency in the case of a very pertubated context.

We project to apply our approach to other applications such as health monitoring and movement tracking. For these new applications, eavesdrop can introduce new problems on messages security.

References

[1] C. Campo. Service discovery in pervasive multiagent systems. In *Proceedings of Workshop on Ubiquitous Agents on embedded, wearable, and mobile devices*, Bolonia, Italy, 2002. 108

[2] C. Chiang, H.K. Wu, W. Liu, and M. Gerla. Routing in clustered multihop, mobile wireless networks. In *Proceedings of IEEE Singapore International Conference on Networks*, pages 197–211, Singapore, 1997. 107

[3] D.J. Cook, P. Gmytrasiewcz, and L.B. Holder. Decision-theoric cooperative sensor planning. *IEEE Transactions on Pattern Analysis And Machine Intelligence*, 18, October 1996. 108

[4] Y. Demazeau. From interactions to collective behavior in agent-based systems. In *European Conference on Cognitive Science*, Saint-Malo France, 1995. 106

[5] J. Ferber and O. Gutknecht. A meta-model for the analysis and design of organizations in multi-agent systems. In Y. Demazeau, editor, *Proceedings of ICMAS'98*, Paris France, July 1998. IEEE Computer Society. 106

[6] The Foundation for Intelligent Physical Agents. http://www.fipa.org. 108

[7] N. Graham. The Nicola Mark II – a New Rescue Radio for France. In *The CREG Journal*, volume 38, pages 3–6, December 1999. 115

[8] R.S. Gray. Soldiers, agents and wireless networks: A report on a military application. In *Proceedings of the 5th International Conference and Exhibition on the Practical Application of Intelligent Agents and Multi-Agents*, Manchester, England, April 2000. 108

[9] H. Chen, D. Chakraborty, L. Xu, A. Joshi, and T. Finin. Service discovery in the future electronic market. In *Proceeding Workshop on Knowledge Based Electronic Markets, AAAI*, Austin, july 2000. 108

[10] H. Helin and M. Laukkanen. Performance analysis of software agent communication in slow wireless networks. In *Proceedings of the 11th International Conference on Computer Communications and Networks*, pages 354–361, Austin, Oct 2002. 108

[11] C. Iglesias, M. Garrijo, and J. Gonzales. A survey of agent oriented methodologies. In *Proceedings of workshop on Agent Theories, Architectures, and Languages*, volume LNAI 1555, pages 163–176, Paris, France, July 1998. Springer-Verlag. 106

[12] J.-P. Jamont, M. Occello, and A. Lagrèze. A multiagent system for the instrumentation of an underground hydrographic system. In *Proceedings of IEEE International Symposium on Virtual and Intelligent Measurement Systems - VIMS'2002*, Mt Alyeska Resort, AK, USA, May 2002. 110

[13] D.B. Johnson and D.A. Maltz. Dynamic source routing in ad hoc wireless networks. In T. Imielinski and H. Korth, editors, *Mobile Computing*, pages 153–181. Kluwer Academic Publishers, 1996. 107

[14] M. Occello and Y. Demazeau. Modelling decision making systems using agents for cooperation in a real time constraints. In *3rd IFAC Symposium on Intelligent Autonomous Vehicles*, volume 1, pages 51–56, Madrid, Spain, March 1998. 110

[15] M. Occello, Y. Demazeau, and C. Baeijs. Designing organized agents for cooperation in a real time context. In A. Drogoul, M. Tambe, and J. Singh, editors, *Collective Robotics*, volume LNCS 1456, pages 25–73. Springer-Verlag, March 1998. 110

[16] M. Occello and J.L. Koning. Multi-agent based software engineering: an approach based on model and software reuse. In *From Agent Theory to Agent Implementation II - EMCSR 2000 Symposium*, pages 645–657, Vienna, April 2000. 106

[17] C.E. Perkins, E.M. Royer, and S. Das. Highly dynamic destination-sequenced distance-vector (dsdv) routing for mobile computers. In *Proceedings of ACM SIGCOMM'94*, August 1994. 107

[18] E.M. Petriu, G.G. Patry, T.E. Whalen, A. Al-Dhaher, and Z. Groza. Intelligent robotic sensor agents for enviroment monitoring. In *International Symposium on Virtual and Intelligent Measurement Systems - VIMS 2002*, pages 19–20, May 2002. 108

[19] M.F. Wood and S.A. DeLoach. An overview of the multiagent systems engineering methodology. In *The First International Workshop on Agent-Oriented Software Engineering*, 2000. 106

[20] M.J. Wooldridge, N.R. Jennings, and D. Kinny. The gaia methodology for agent-oriented analysis and design. In *Autonomous Agents and Multi-Agent Systems*, volume 3, pages 285–312. Kluwer Academic Publishers, 2000. 106

[21] W. Zhang, Z. Deng, G. Wang, L. Wittenburg, and Z. Xing. Distributed problem solving in sensor networks. In *AAMAS'02*, pages 15–19, July 2002. 107, 108

Tlachtli*: A Framework for Soccer Agents Based on GeDa-3D

Francisco Ocegueda, Roberto Sánchez, and Félix Ramos

CINVESTAV-IPN Unidad Guadalajara
Prol. López Mateos Sur 590, 45090 Guadalajara, Jal. Mexico
{focegued,rsanchez,famos}@gdl.cinvestav.mx

Abstract. Tlachtli is a framework for Soccer Agents based on the platform
GeDa-3D. It proposes a system for the simulation of the soccer game based on
cognitive intelligent agents. Tlachtli using GeDA-3D facilities offers a three-
dimensional graphic environment where the game is simulated. This work is
different from RoboCup platform because it includes a 3D interface and also
offers the facility to add personality to the players. Personality can affect or
modify the agents' responses to the environment. In a future work the emotions
of the players will be included in the agent architecture.

1 Introduction

Nowadays there exists much research developed for Soccer Agents simulators [1,2]
based on the RoboCup competition[2]. Our interest is the development of a platform
for the soccer game, where intelligent software agents are contemplated as key part
and to be able to develop some characteristics that have been few contemplated in the
platforms oriented to RoboCup. These characteristics include concepts such as:
Personality and Emotions. The present work outlines our platform: Tlachtli. This
platform was developed in a three-dimensional graphic environment GeDa-3D [3],
which allows carrying out simulations of the game in a three-dimensional
environment. Tlachtli also proposes an architecture of agents, which adds as
characteristic its personality and in near future it will include the emotions.

The remainder of this paper is organized as follows: Section 2 describes the
Tlachtli architecture. Section 3 describes the agent architecture used in this work.
Section 4 overviews the environment of Tlachtli. Section 5 presents an application
using Tlachtli

2 Tlachtli Architecture

This section presents the architectural design of Tlachtli, and describes how it is
customized to perform a simulation using soccer agents.

---

* Tlachtli was a game ball played by the Aztecs and some individuals have claimed that it is
over 3000 years old. The game involved passing the ball from side to side without it
touching the ground.

F. F. Ramos, H. Unger, V. Larios (Eds.): ISSADS 2004, LNCS 3061, pp. 118-124, 2004.
© Springer-Verlag Berlin Heidelberg 2004

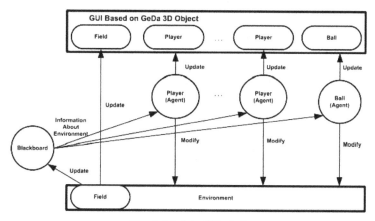

Fig. 1. Model of Tlachtli

The Figure 1 shows the model of Tlachtli. It is formed by the following components: The agents, the environment, the GUI and the blackboard. The environment includes the field, and represents the place where the agents interact. It has its representation in the GUI. The state of the environment is saved in the blackboard [4, 5], from where the agents obtain information about it. The agents perform actions and modify the state of the environment. The GUI is created using the GeDA 3D Editor [3]. Each element of the game has its own representation in the GUI, which is updated every time the element's state changes. The GUI's elements includes: the field, player and ball. The field is a 3D graphical representation of the field of indoor soccer game. Consequently it has four bounds which are like walls. The player is the name of the avatar representing the player agent; the ball is the graphical representation of the ball agent.

With respect to elements movements: The player has a set of possible movements (to walk, run, pass, kick, tackle) which was defined in the source object created in GeDA 3D; the ball moves in response to actions from player such as passing and shooting, also the ball obeys the physics laws that govern the parameters as velocity, angles, momentum, etc; and the field is static.

The architecture of Tlachtli is shown by means of an AUML class diagram (Figure 2) containing fundamental components in the Tlachtli. These components are the basic building blocks.

3   Agents

The kinds of agents implemented are usually known as cognitive agents [4, 5]. The actions performed by the agent as response to a signal from the environment are ruled by the behavior of each agent [4, 5]. Our approach includes, as novelty, the personality as characteristic of the agent. Personality is used to modify agent's behavior throughout the game. In order to implement the previous characteristic the agent contains two learning modules. The first one classifies the personalities of the others agents in the game. The second one allows the agent to select the action to perform taking into account the others agent personalities and his own.

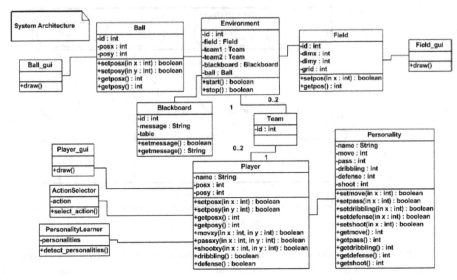

Fig. 2. The architecture of Tlachtli

3.1 Agent Personality

Every soccer player's personality is identified through his behavior in the field; personality determines the way he plays. It is possible to know player's personality observing his behaviors. For this reason, we include personality as a key part of the agent.

3.2 Soccer Agents Architecture

The Figure 3 shows the Architecture of soccer agents that Tlachtli drives.

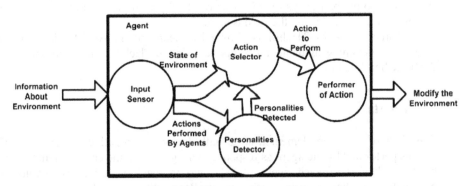

Fig. 3. Architecture of Soccer Agent

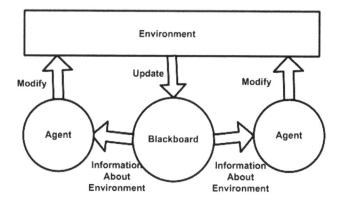

Fig. 4. Environment of Tlachtli

The agent contains an Input Sensor; this one receives signals from the environment such as: agent's position, ball's position, teammate's position, etc. Moreover the agent has two learning modules: Personalities Detector which detects the personalities of the others agents using the vector of the actions performed by them. And Action Selector that allows him to choose an action to be performed according to his personality, state of environment and the personalities detected by the Personalities Detector. Also the last one is the mechanism by means of which the agent learns how to play soccer. Finally the agent performs the action and it modifies the environment.

3.3 Personality Detection

The detection of the personality of a player is made by a learning module. It receives a vector where is stored the frequency of each action performed by the agent and then classifies the pattern and gives as answer the personality of the agent.

4 Environment

The environment is the place where the agents reside. We considered a centralized environment [1][4]. The Figure 4 shows the Tlachtli environment. The centralized environment has a representation which is saved in the blackboard. When the environment is modified by the actions of the agents, it is necessary to update the representation of the environment in the blackboard.

5 Example

This section shows an application developed using our framework. It is a soccer game where each team has two players. The objective is to score at the opponent's goal. This is a simulation of the game, the rules are next, but can be modified easily.

---

[1] The agents are not centralized, but they are distributed.

5.1 Rules of the Game

The rules of the game are the following:

- The match ends when someone scores: When one player scores, the match finish, and can be restarted.
- The game is based on indoor soccer: The field has walls surrounding it, so the ball can not leave the field.
- The game is played at the level of the floor. Currently, the ball has only movements in two dimensions.
- The kickoff is made by a team selected randomly in every match.

5.2 Personalities

We have defined four personalities, which are:

- Selfish: He hardly passes the ball, always wants to dribble and shoot.
- Aggressive: He plays in a rude way, hitting his opponents (accidentally or intentionally).
- Cooperative: He runs for the ball, passes it, dribbles. He plays for the team.
- Passive: He is not interested in running for the ball, neither in helping his teammates.

The user assigns to each player a personality (see Figure 5), which determines his behavior in the field.

5.3 Learning Modules

As previously described, each player has two learning modules: The first one is responsible of detecting the opponents' personality, and the second one for selection of action to be performed. In short: learning how to play. The learning modules are based on neural networks [6].

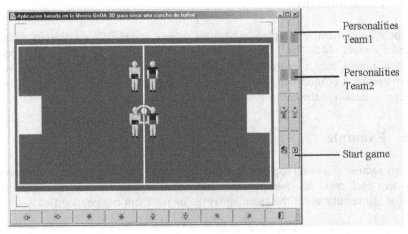

Fig. 5. Initial Screen

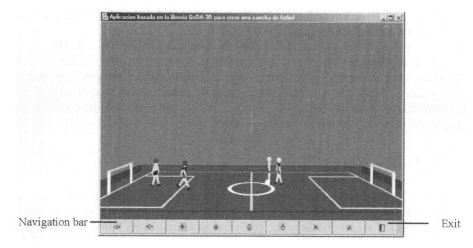

Navigation bar ———   Exit

Fig. 6. Complete view of the game

The networks used in this example are feed forward back propagation neural networks, with one hidden layer of neurons [6].

Supervised learning is used to train both neural networks. The first is trained using the patterns of a simple behavior from each personality. The second is trained considering as input the most important situations of the game. The second neural network receives information from the first, to decide the action to be taken on the game. To determine the personality of an opponent, we take into account the actions he has performed during the game (behavior).

The Figure 5 shows the initial screen, where the user assigns each player a personality, and places the players in the field.

The game in action is shown in Figure 6. A player of the dark team has the possession of the ball. This player has a selfish personality, so he tries to shoot when he has the opportunity although his teammate has a better position.

5.4 Simulation

This application was executed several times using at each episode a different combination of personalities, and then we observed the behavior of the players. We noted in general that different personalities in the agents cause they performed different actions over similar situations.

6   Conclusion

This paper proposes Tlachtli as a framework for soccer agents based on GeDA 3D. Tlachtli allows simulating the soccer game in a three-dimensional graphic environment. Players are modeled as intelligent software agents. They are a key part of this work and they include some characteristics that have been few contemplated in the platforms oriented to RoboCup. The proposed architecture for soccer agents allows assign personality to soccer agents. Personality is used to modify agent's behaviors throughout the game.

To prove our approach we also present an application using Tlachtli. The execution of this application showed results according to our expectations: The behavior of the agent was modified by his personality and the personalities of the others agents.

Finally, Tlachtli is an extendable framework, because it can take advantage of each new characteristic of GeDa 3D, which is in constant evolution. Moreover, it could incorporate new features, according to needs.

7 Future Work

Future work contemplate incorporate emotions over Tlachtli, in order the soccer players can modify their behaviors according to the emotions that they feel throughout the game because the behaviors of other players. Until now, the game is played at the level of floor. We are investigating how to implement the ball movements in three dimensions. This is useful to be close to real match.

Even if Tlachtli is open, we are thinking to add other personalities, and we are studying different learning algorithms.

Acknowledgements

We would like to thank to the students of the course: Distributed Systems II on 2003 from Cinvestav IPN – Guadalajara, México: Elvia Ruiz Beltran, Omar Zatarain Villanueva, Adriana Tovar Arriaga, Agustìn Zaragoza Gutiérrez and for their contributions in the development of the work originated this work.

References

[1]   Mao Chen, Klaus Dorer, Ehsan Foroughi, Fredrik Heintz, Zhan Xiang Huang, Spiros Kapetanakis, Kostas Kostiadis, Johan Kummeneje, Jan Murray, Itsuki Noda, Oliver Obst, Pat Riley, Timo Steffens, Yi Wang and Xiang Yin, "User Manual RoboCup Soccer Server for Soccer Server Version 7.07 and later", http://sserver.sourceforge.net/.

[2]   The Official Robocup HomePage: www.robocup.org.

[3]   Fabiel Zuñiga, Hugo I. Piza D., and F. Ramos, "A 3DSpace Platform for Distributed Applications Management." ISADS-2002, November 2002 Mexico, ISBN 9702703581.

[4]   Jacques Ferber, Multi-Agent Systems: An Introduction to Distributed Artificial Intelligence. Addison-Wesley Pub Co; 1st edition (February 25, 1999). ISBN: 0201360489.

[5]   Gerhard Weiss, Multiagent Systems: A modern approach to distributed artificial intelligence. The MIT Press,2nd edition (2000), London, England.

[6]   Simon Haykin, Neural Networks: A comprehensive foundation. Prentice Hall, 2nd edition (1999), USA.

Evaluating Location Dependent Queries Using ISLANDS

Marie Thilliez and Thierry Delot

LAMIH Laboratory - CNRS UMR 8530
University of Valenciennes, Le Mont Houy, 59313 Valenciennes Cedex 9 France
{marie.thilliez,thierry.delot}@univ-valenciennes.fr

Abstract. The recent emergence of handheld devices and wireless networks implies an exponential increase in the numbers of terminals users. Given this increase, today's service providers have to propose new applications adapted to mobile environments. In this article, we focus on distributed proximity M-services, in which several handheld devices, situated in close physical proximity to one another, can communicate and exchange data. Proximity M-services exploit a combination of mobile devices and heterogeneous mobile and/or fixed networks, and require a high degree of flexibility in order to permit easy and rapid application development. Because these applications are based on the Hybrid Peer-To-Peer (P2P) software architecture, such problems as scalability, deployment, security, reliability and information retrieval in M-services, can be more easily resolved than in other architectures. Within the framework of this software architecture, we focus on the localization problematic. Existing localization solutions are not well adapted to the mobility, dynamicity and heterogeneity of the Proximity M-service environment. Our solution to this lack of adaptation is ISLANDS, a service designed to aid the user in identifying and locating information and/or services within a communication area. ISLANDS is a decentralized service derived from the directory service model and adapted to the management of numerous distributed resources. In addition, ISLANDS provides querying facilities and a query evaluation model adapted to distributed directory management. Since most ISLANDS users are mobile, location dependent queries are also supported, thus enabling users to track down the closest theater or, more importantly in an emergency, the closest general practitioner's office. Doing so obviously requires pinpointing the location of the query issuer, and one of the original aspects of our approach is the adaptability of the localization process : given that few handheld devices today are equipped with geo-localization features, ISLANDS is able to return approximate solutions by estimating the position of the client terminal, although ISLANDS can also use GPS-like techniques if available.

Keywords : Localization Service, Location Dependent Queries, Evaluation

1 Introduction

The emergence of both handheld devices and wireless networks [19] implies an exponential increase in the numbers of terminals users. Given this increase, today's service providers have to offer new proximity services adapted to mobile

F. F. Ramos, H. Unger, V. Larios (Eds.): ISSADS 2004, LNCS 3061, pp. 125-136, 2004.
© Springer-Verlag Berlin Heidelberg 2004

environments [1, 3]. Among these services, proximity applications [16] deployed in highly distributed environments permit new possibilities for users of these handheld devices. These proximity applications exploit communication areas formed dynamically by juxtaposing several wireless and mobile networks. For example, a communication area can result from the association of a wireless LAN (Local Area Network) and a wireless PAN (Personal Area Network). Wireless communication areas are also highly dynamic since they evolve in relation to user mobility. These areas allow communications between different users who are physically close to one another. Indeed, depending on the location of these users, a certain set of services is proposed. For example, using a proximity service, users could buy goods, exchange data or communicate with other users. In addition, the set of services can evolve as the user moves from one area to another. A proximity service is created spontaneously when several users form a communication area and want to share information. This service then evolves dynamically in relation to the movements of the participants and terminates when there are no longer any participants.

Due to the dynamicity and the heterogeneity of both networks and devices, a high degree of flexibility is required to exploit proximity services. In an earlier article [16], we demonstrated the importance of the hybrid Peer-To-Peer (P2P) architecture model [24] in basic proximity applications. Clearly, the partial centralization and the flexibility of the P2P model make proximity applications developed using this model much more adaptable to changing environments.

In such environments, the information is distributed through different devices. Due to user mobility, the information available in the communication area evolves rapidly, and localization services are needed to provide correct and up-to-date information to users. Without such mechanisms, users cannot exploit the proximity services since they are unable to access the available information. For example, in a proximity electronic commerce application, the potential client has to be able to retrieve the different vendors and their propositions in order to benefit from the offers. Because existing localization solutions (naming services, trading services, discovery services, ...) do not deal well with the constraints imposed by proximity applications, in terms of distribution, dynamicity and heterogeneity of both terminals and networks, we propose ISLANDS[1] [18], a new distributed localization service, exploiting directory services technology and dedicated to mobile environments.

In a proximity applications, due to the users mobility, we have also to be able to evaluate queries in function of users locations. Thus, based on ISLANDS, we focus on the evaluation of location dependent queries such as "Where are the music stores closest to me ?". Location dependent queries are evaluated according to the user's physical location, and responses are designed to help the user localize the resources needed easily and precisely. The process for locating the user proposed in the paper and required for the evaluation of location dependent queries does not rely only on existing localization techniques, such as GPS, since they are only available on few handheld terminals today. Indeed, using ISLANDS, user location can also be estimated using the localization data usually stored in directory services for computing approximate query results.

---

[1] Information and Services LocalizAtioN and Discovery Service

The rest of this paper is organized as follows : Section 2 gives an overview of the localization service ISLANDS and present existing solutions in location queries evaluation and their limitations. Our proposition to evaluate location dependent queries is explained in section 3, with special attention given to the procedure for estimating the location of a mobile user. And finally, in section 4, in conclusion, we present our prototype and present the perspectives for future research.

2   ISLANDS

2.1 An Overview

A participant in a proximity service has to be able to locate the data available in his/her communication area, not only the information stored on the participant's device but also the information managed by the system's remote peers. Since existing localization solutions present severe drawbacks, we have proposed a dedicated solution: ISLANDS, an Information and Services LocalizAtioN and Discovery Service [18]. ISLANDS is based on the directory services technology because, compared to both naming and trading services, this technology provides very interesting features such as scalability, querying facilities, authentication and so on. However, the current directory services present also severe limitations in our environment. Thus, in ISLANDS, we have extended the directory services technology to be adapted to the constraints imposed by mobile, heterogeneous and dynamic environments. In order to support these constraints and to exploit the benefits of the underlying hybrid P2P architecture, our solution does not rely on a centralized server but rather on the deployment of ISLANDS for each peer able to interact in the communication area. As shown in Fig. 1, based on the hybrid P2P Model, two types of peers are distinguished : the light peers and the central peers. Peer type essentially depends on the underlying hardware configuration. Central peers generally correspond to robust servers, whereas light peers correspond to handheld devices. Central peers, as their name implies, centralize information to share it with the other peers. The most of time, every central peers are selected at the application deployment. Light peers correspond to thin clients exploited by users to submit their queries and consult the results. We choose to deploy ISLANDS on every peers (central or light) in order to stand up to the inherent mobility and dynamicity of the system. Naturally, ISLANDS can be customized in terms of the peer's resources (CPU power, memory space ...). For example, a powerful peer (as is generally the case for central peers) can easily store and share information about the other peers. On the other hand, the localization service as deployed for a light peer may only be able to store a small amount of information locally in addition to providing users with a means for retrieving the information stored on remote peers. Thus, the distribution between the instances of ISLANDS services is completely transparent for users. Indeed, in proximity applications, the data and services set is distributed over the different peers present in the communication area. ISLANDS queries are evaluated throughout the entire communication area and thus, if necessary, are forwarded automatically to remote directory services.

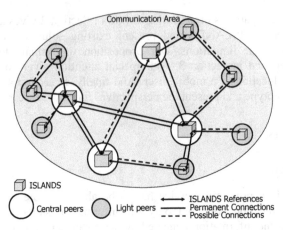

Fig. 1. ISLANDS Distribution

2.2 Location Queries

In the mobile context considered in this article, the different participants have to be able to query information in relation to their location. For example, a participant may want to identify and retrieve the location of the closest general practitioner. Traditionally, directory services propose very simple query languages. However, this is very restrictive. With ISLANDS, in order to select information in terms of location or proximity, several simple and user-friendly operators are used to verify proximity constraints : inside, closest and close [17]. First, the inside operator is used to retrieve elements within one area. For example, it can be used to retrieve every vendors at the ground floor of a shopping mall. Then, the closest operator is used to access a particular element located the shortest distance from the query issuer or from a specified location parameter. It can be used, for example, to retrieve the fast food closest to me or closest to Virgin. And finally, the close operator is an evolution of the closest operator. This operator is used to retrieve several elements close to the issuer or close to a specified location parameter. It may also be used with a distance parameter. This optional parameter is an integer representing the number of meters, which defines the maximal distance between the specified target and the issuer (or a specified location).

Since the presentation of the concept in 1992 [10], querying location dependent information in mobile environments has become an important field of research. A lot of studies concern questions of data management in mobile devices and the information about devices' location [4, 12]. Of those, several are worth mentioning. Sisla et al. [14, 15] have proposed the Moving Object Spatio-Temporal (MOST) data model to manage the locations of moving objects and to predict their future locations. The DOMINO project [20, 21, 22, 23], which complements our work quite nicely, proposes a model that represents moving objects in a database and tracks them efficiently. These same authors also propose Future Temporal Logic (FTL) as a query language for such a model. Several other interesting works deal with processing continuous location-dependent queries in mobile environments [5, 7, 8, 11]. These studies concentrate on query processing on mobile terminals. Such processing relies on a centralized environment and the use of handheld devices equipped with localization techniques, such as GPS. In this article, we have focused on evaluating issuer location in order to improve the quality of location-dependent query results. Similar studies have also been completed using URLs in a web context [2], but to the best of our knowledge, the problems of mobility and dynamicity have not yet been dealt with prior to the work described in this article.

3 Evaluating Location Dependent Queries

One of the main difficulties of the query engine concerns the evaluation of location-based queries. First, the evaluator has to define whether the query is location-aware or location-dependent [13]. A location-aware query, such as "retrieve the fast foods close to Virgin", does not depend on the issuer's location. On the other hand, a location-dependent query, such as "retrieve the TV set vendor closest to me", requires that the user's position be known. In this section, we firstly focus on the evaluation of the client location. Then, we present the evaluation of the location queries.

3.1 Evaluation of the Location

One of the original aspects of our approach is the adaptability of its localization process, which can be adapted to the resources of the underlying peer. The process can be based on geographic localization technologies like GPS; however, given that today's handheld devices often do not have GPS-like features, localization will generally be based on the location data stored in the Directory Information Tree (DIT), particularly the referenced directory services. Using stored data means that localization can be approximated. Some studies [9, 25] have proposed broadcasting geographic information to wireless device users so that they can evaluate their position. However, such solutions make it difficult for a particular user to estimate the correctness and the precision of the broadcast information. To increase the precision of the location information broadcast to users, one solution is to increase the number of servers used to broadcast location information. Unfortunately, seeing as the information may come in from several different servers, this solution complicates matters by making it very difficult for the handheld devices to choose which location information should be used. Our solution, which exploits the P2P environment, relies on information-sharing between neighboring peers, as explained below.

If the query issuer is using a stationary computer, its location is well known, and the location evaluation is negligible. Indeed, stationary computers always have the same location, which is specified only once. On the other hand, defining the location of mobile peers is a major difficulty because issuer location can change at any moment and potentially must be re-evaluated for each evaluated query. For those cases when location cannot be provided by geo-localization techniques like GPS, we propose to compute approximate and relative locations that are nonetheless sufficient for evaluating location dependent queries. Specifically, the approximate location of one peer is determined using location information from the peers connected to it.

```
<locationDescription>
  <symbolicLocation>
    <building name = « Building 1 »>
      <floor name = « first »>
        <section name = « North »>
          <room name = « Virgin »>
          </room>
        </section>
      </floor>
    </building>
  </symbolicLocation>
  <physicalPosition>
      <lat> 27.7 </lat>
      <long> -15.1 </long>
      <alt> 197.4 </alt>
  </physicalPosition>
</locationDescription>
```

Fig. 2. Example of a locationDescription attribute file

Indeed, the location evaluation is based on remote peers data. This information can be stored locally on the peer. Indeed, for each remote neighbored peer, several attributes are retrieved and can be stored on the local peer. To estimate the issuer location, we use four of these attributes for each remote peer :

- The *locationDescription* attribute describes the geographic location of the referenced directory service. As shown in Fig. 2, the symbolic location (building, room ...) and/or the physical location (using GPS for example) [6] can be represented in XML because it allows a trace of the location data semantic to be preserved and also facilitates location data management.
- The *locationLastUpdate* attribute represents the date of the last update of the *locationDescription* attribute file.
- The *connectionRange* attribute provides a range which allows to estimate the distance between the peer and the remote peer.
- The *connectionState* attribute allows to know if the peer is connected to the remote peer.

The algorithm (the evaluation function) described in Fig. 3, used to evaluate the location of a light peer employs an approximation degree, calculated from the *locationLastUpdate* and the *connectionRange* attributes, to estimate the quality of the computed location. The smaller the degree, the better location. This algorithm provides a list of couples (location, approximation degree), sorted by approximation degree. In this algorithm, the Nb variable is defined in terms of environmental constraints and indicates the maximal number of locations to be computed. The smaller the Nb variable is, the shorter the execution time of the evaluation will be.

First, if the light peer is connected to other peers, the d_i and r_i variables for each connected referenced peers are defined. The d variable corresponds to the difference between the current date and the *LocationLastUpdate* attribute. Thus, the larger d is, the more out-of-date the location data is. The r variable defines a proximity index corresponding to the *connectionRange* attribute (which defines an approximate value of the distance separating the light peer from their connected peers in function of the network rate quality) in order to select the closest peers. The d_i and r_i variables are stored in two tables : respectively tables d and r. In the case of central peers, the d_i variable is null because their location is always updated. Then, for each connected peer, we calculate their approximation degree. This degree is $a*r_i$ for a central peer or $b*d_i + c*r_i$ for a light peer. The a, b and c coefficients allow the priorities used to compute the "best" locations to be balanced. Then, a location list of Nb couples is sorted in function of this approximation degree. Nb corresponds either to the Nb variable defined in the evaluation function or to the number of connected peers (*nbConnectedPeers*) if $Nb > nbConnectedPeers$.

Example

In this example, a peer p has express a location dependent query, thus, to evaluate this query, his/her location has to be evaluated. The following illustration of the location evaluation is based on a configuration in which the peer p has 6 neighbored peers : 3 central peers and 3 light peers. The different attributes of the neighbored peers are stored on the peer p, these attributes are described in the table 1.

```
Function Evaluation return LocationList
{
Nb := LocationListNb() ; //returns the number of desired
elements in the LocationList
RefPeerList := RefPeerList() ; //retrieves the set of
referenced peers
ConnectedPeerList := Connected(RefPeerList); //the attribute
connectionState > 0
nbConnectedPeers := nbPeer(connectedPeerList) ;
LocationList := null ;
If ConnectedPeerList is not null then
    {
    Int d[nbConnectedPeers] ;
    Int r[nbConnectedPeers] ;
    For i=1 to nbConnectedPeers loop
  {
    d[i] := coeff_d(connectedPeerList, i) ; //defines the d
coefficient : the difference between the current date and the
locationLastUpdate attribute
    r[i] := coeff_r(connectedPeerList, i) ; //defines the r
coefficient in function of the connectionRange attribute
    approxDegree := approxDegree(d[i], r[i]) ; //returns a*r[i]
if the peer i is a central peer or b*d[i] + c*r[i] if the peer
i is a light peer
    locationList := concat(locationList, (location(i),
approxDegree(i))) ;
    }
If Nb > nbConnectedPeers then Nb := nbConnectedPeers ;
LocationList := Sort(LocationList, Nb); //returns a list of Nb
couples sorted in function of the approximation degree
Return LocationList ;
}
```

Fig. 3. Evaluation Function

Table 1. Example of referenced directory services entries

Referenced Light Peers	*Referenced Central Peers*

`LP = LP1`
`locationDescription  = «LP1.xml »`
`locationLastUpdate = Oct-14th-2003 1:00 pm`
`connectionRange = 2`
`connectionState = 0`
`...`
	`CP = CP1`
	`locationDescription  = «CP1.xml »`
	`locationLastUpdate = sysdate`
	`connectionRange = 60`
	`connectionState = 30`
	`...`

`LP = LP2`
`locationDescription  = «LP2.xml »`
`locationLastUpdate = Oct-14th-2003 2:33 pm`
`connectionRange = 3`
`connectionState = 30`
`...`
	`CP = CP2`
	`locationDescription  = «CP2.xml »`
	`locationLastUpdate = sysdate`
	`connectionRange = 90`
	`connectionState = 0`
	`...`

`LP = LP3`
`locationDescription  = «LP3.xml »`
`locationLastUpdate = Oct-14th-2003 2:16 pm`
`connectionRange = 30`
`connectionState = 40`
`...`
	`CP = CP3`
	`locationDescription  = «CP3.xml »`
	`locationLastUpdate = sysdate`
	`connectionRange = 30`
	`connectionState = 60`
	`...`

The current date in the example is Oct-14th-2003 at 2:43 pm. a, b and c are respectively set to 1, 10 and 1. *Nb* is set to 3. Then, the Evaluation function (Fig. 3) is executed.

```
Function Evaluation :

Nb := 3
The RefPeerList is {LP1, LP2, LP3, CP1, CP2, CP3}.
The ConnectedPeerList is {LP2, LP3, CP1, CP3}.
nbConnectedPeers := 4

The set of variables is defined : d = [10,27,0,0], r = [3,30,60,30]
For each connected peer, an approximation degree is calculated (a*r[i]
for a central peer or b*d[i] + c*r[i] for a light peer)
Thus, the locationList is :
 {(LP2.xml, 103), (LP3.xml, 300), (CP1.xml, 60),(CP3.xml, 30)}

Then, the list is sorted in function of approximation degrees.
Thus the final result is the LocationList = {(CP1.xml, 30), (CP3.xml,
60), (LP2.xml, 103)}
```

This location evaluation returns a list of locations sorted in terms of their approximation coefficients. The approximation coefficient is very important and will facilitate the location query evaluation described in the next section. In rare cases, the light peer location cannot be evaluated because the evaluation function returns a null/empty list. In this case, an interactive system can be proposed which will allow the user of the light peer to describe his/her location.

3.2 Evaluation of Location Queries

The previous section explained how the issuer location is determined when the query is location-dependent. Then, let us call QL the location resulting from the query and PL, the parameter location, which can be explicitly specified in the location operator or computed. For example, to retrieve the fast food closest to me, the QLs will be every fast food locations and the PL is my location (one XML file if my location is exact or several XML files if my location is computed using the location evaluation solution described in the precedent section). For each location operator, the evaluator must compare each PL of the locationList with each QL. If the query is location aware or if the peer location is fixed and known, there is only one element in the locationList and the approximation degree is null. For example, for the location-aware query : "Retrieve the fast foods close to Virgin ?", each QL corresponds to each location of one fast food in the shopping mall and PL corresponds to the list containing the unique couple {(VirginLocation.xml, 0)}.

We choose to base the location description on the same fixed DTD to facilitate the comparison between XML files. Therefore, for each proximity application, a DTD could be defined. Based on fixed DTD, the comparison of the different location files is more easily computed. In a XML location file, the location can be represented in different ways : for example, such as the location described in Fig. 9, the location is described in symbolic data and in physical data. Indeed, some central peers can be provided with a GPS module.

Firstly, we consider the inside operator, which has a LocationType parameter. The comparison of two locations is possible only if the two location XML files contain a symbolic description. The LocationType parameter represents a XML element, for example the "stage" element to retrieve the fast foods of my stage. Then, each PL is compared with each QL : when there is a match to the LocationType element, the QL is selected. And finally, for each selected location, a correctness degree is computed : Correctness_Degree = 1/(Approximation_Degree + 1).

Table 2. Comparisons in function of XML files contents

		QL's XML file content		
		Symbolic representation	Physical representation	Symbolic & physical representation
PL's XML file content	Symbolic representation	Symbolic Comparison	-	Symbolic Comparison
	Physical representation	-	Physical Comparison	Physical Comparison
	Symbolic & physical representation	Symbolic Comparison	Physical Comparison	Physical Comparison

Table 3. An example of correspondence table for the similarity coefficient between two locations

Physical comparison (distance in meters)	Symbolic comparison (similarities in %)	Similarity Coefficient
<100 m	>0%	10%
<80 m	>20%	30%
<60 m	>40%	50%
<40 m	>60%	70%
<20 m	>80%	90%

Secondly, let us consider the close and closest operators. As shown in table 2, the comparison between two locations is computed in different ways according to the XML files contents. For example, if the PL corresponds to symbolic data, the comparison is possible if the QL is represented in symbolic data or in both symbolic and physical data.

When there is a match between two locations, a similarity coefficient is computed. This coefficient is based on the percentage of values similarities in the case of symbolic representation comparison. In the case of physical representation, this similarity coefficient is based on the distance between the two physical locations : the larger the distance, the smaller the similarity coefficient. This distance is $\sqrt{[(lat1-lat2)^2+(long1-long2)^2+M*(alt1-alt2)^2]}$. The M constant is used to penalize the altitude. Then, a correspondence table is established in function of the application environment, this table allows to obtain a same similarity coefficient for the different representations. An example of this table is shown in the Table 3.

Thus, for each comparison between a PL and a QL, we obtain a similarity coefficient.

If the location operator is close, when the distance parameter is specified, the query manager selects the QL solutions for which the similarity coefficient corresponds to a distance lower than the distance parameter. When the distance parameter is not specified, the query manager computes a correctness degree for each couple (PL,QL). The correctness degree is based on both the similarity coefficient and the approximation degree : Correctness_Degree = Similarity_Coefficient / (Approximation_Degree +1). Then, QL is sorted in function of a correctness degree. And the query manager selects a set of QLs, which have a correctness degree superior with a degree specified by the user. If the location operator is closest, the query manager selects the best QL solution in terms of the correctness degree.

4   Conclusion & Perspectives

In this paper, we have presented the evaluation of location dependent queries in ISLANDS. Indeed, ISLANDS is a localization service, designed to support mobility and thus, it offers a query evaluator that provides distribution transparency and supports location dependent queries. Indeed, to evaluate location-dependent queries, the originality of our approach resides in the possibility of using not only localization techniques like GPS but also the data description localization that is usually stored in directory services. A prototype of ISLANDS, as presented in this paper, has been implemented. The Proximity Electronic Commerce application is selected to validate the prototype. In this prototype, the different peers are connected with Bluetooth or Wifi technologies. Pocket PCs Compaq Ipaq H5450 are used as light peers and represent the potential clients. Their data are stored in XML files. The central peers represent the vendors and their data are stored in the OpenLDAP directory server. The content of these directories is exported in DSML files in order to evaluate location dependent queries. To optimize the performances at the time of the updates, the different attributes of the neighbored peers are stored in indexes files.

In the near future, we will have to consider query distribution optimization. Indeed, for the moment, the query is forwarded to every connected peers; however, this may prove to penalize light peers (query execution time, resource consumption). Consequently, distribution strategies are needed for optimizing the query evaluation.

References

[1]   M. Bechler, H. Ritter, J. H. Schiller, Quality of Service in Mobile and Wireless Networks: The Need for Proactive and Adaptive Applications, Int. Conference on System Sciences (HICSS), 2000.

[2]   O. Buyukkokten, J. Cho, H. Garca-Molina, L. Gravano, N. Shivakumar, Exploiting geographical location information of web pages. Int. ACM SIGMOD Workshop on the Web and Databases (WebDB), 1999.

[3]   Y.-F. R. Chen, C. Petrie, Ubiquitous Mobile Computing, IEEE Internet Computing, Vol. 7, N° 2, 2003.

[4]   M. H. Dunham, V. Kumar, Location dependent data and its management in mobile databases, Int. Workshop on Mobility in Databases and Distributed Systems (MDDS), 1998.

[5]   G. Gok, O. Ulusoy, Transmission of Continuous Query Results in Mobile Computing Systems, Information Sciences, vol.125, no.1-4, 2000.

[6]   J. Hightower, G. Borriello, Location Systems for Ubiquitous Computing, IEEE Computer, 2001.

[7]   S. Ilarri, E. Mena, A. Illarramendi, Monitoring Continuous Location Queries using Mobile Agents, East-European Conf. on Advances in Databases and Information Systems (ADBIS), 2002.

[8]   S. Ilarri, E. Mena, A. Illarramendi, Dealing with Continuous Location-Dependent Queries: Just-in-Time Data Refreshment, IEEE Int. Conf. on Pervasive Computing and Communications (PerCom), 2003.

[9]   J. Il-dong, Y. Young-ho, L. Jong-hwan, K. Kyungsok, Broadcasting and Caching Policies for Location-Dependent Queries in Urban Area, ACM Int. workshop on Wireless sensor networks and applications (WMC), 2002.

[10]   T. Imielinski, B.R. Badrinath, Querying in Highly Mobile and Distributed Environments, Int. Conf. on Very Large DataBases (VLDB), 1992.

[11]   K. Lam, O. Ulusoy, T.S.H. Lee, E. Chan, G. Li, An Efficient Method for Generating Location Updates for Processing of Location-Dependent Continuous Queries, Int. Conf. on Database Systems for Advanced Applications (DASFAA'01), 2001.

[12]   D. L. Lee, J. Xu, B. Zheng, W-C. Lee, Data Management in Location-Dependent Information Services, IEEE Pervasive Computing, 2002.

[13]   Y. Seydim, M. H. Dunham, V. Kumar, Location Dependent Query Processing, Proceeding of MobiDE, 2001.

[14]   P. Sistla, O. Wolfson, S. Chamberlain, S. Dao, Modelling and Querying Moving Objects, Int. Conf. on Data Engineering (ICDE), 1997.

[15]   P. Sistla, O. Wolfson, S. Chamberlain, S. Dao, Querying the Uncertain Position of Moving Objects, Temporal Database: Research and Practice, LNCS, 1997.

[16]   M. Thilliez, T. Delot, S. Lecomte, N. Bennani, Hybrid Peer-to-Peer Model in Proximity Applications, Int. Conf. on Advanced Information Networking and Applications (AINA), 2003.

[17]   M. Thilliez, T. Delot, A Localization Service for Proximity Applications, Workshop on Mobile and Ubiquitous Information Access in conjunction with the 5th Int. Symposium on Human Computer Interaction with Mobile Devices and Services, 2003.

[18]   M. Thilliez, Y. Colmant, T. Delot, Query Evaluation in ISLANDS, Les 19èmes journées de Bases de données Avancées (BDA), 2003.

[19]   U. Varshney, R. Vetter, Emerging Mobile and Wireless Networks, Communications of the ACM, Vol. 43, Issue 6, 2000.

[20]   O. Wolfson, B. Xu, S. Chamberlain, and L. Jiang, Moving objects databases: Issues and solutions, Int. Conf. on Scientific and Statistical Database Management (SSDBM), 1998.

[21]   O. Wolfson, A. P. Sistla , B. Xu, J. Zhou, S. Chamberlain, DOMINO: Databases fOr MovINg Objects tracking, Int. SIGMOD Conference, 1999.

[22]   O. Wolfson, A. P. Sistla, S. Chamberlain, Y. Yesha, Updating and Querying Databases that Track Mobile Units, Distributed and Parallel Databases Journal on Mobile Data Management and Applications, 1999.

[23]   O. Wolfson, S. Chamberlain, K. Kalpakis, Y. Yesha, Modeling Moving Objects for Location Based Services, NSF Workshop on Infrastructure for Mobile and Wireless Systems, 2001.

[24]   Yang, H. Garcia-Molina, Comparing Hybrid Peer-To-Peer System, Int. Conf. on Very Large DataBases (VLDB), 2001.

[25]   J. Zhang, L. Gruenwald, Prioritized Sequencing for efficient Query on Broadcast Geographical Information on Mobile-Computing, ACM Int. Symp. on Advances in geographic information systems, (GIS), 2002.

Conceptual Information Retrieval

Emerson L. dos Santos, Fabiano M. Hasegawa,
Bráulio C. Ávila, and Fabrício Enembreck

Pontifical Catholic University of Paraná
Curitiba PR, Brazil
{emerson,fmitsuo,avila,fabricio}@ppgia.pucpr.br

Abstract. A regular and demanding task in legal offices is the search for documents upon an arbitrary subject. The point lies in the fact that each new process is analysed according to similar ocurrent ones which have already — occurred the past analyses support the current one. Nevertheless, this search is time-consuming since the number of documents is generally large. Classical IR tools usually retrieve a significative amount of irrelevant documents — where the terms of the query do not express the meaning intended — and may miss relevant ones —- where the meaning intended is represented by different terms. In this paper, a search engine based on Conceptual Analysis is presented. The search engine enables the retrieval of documents based on the meaning expressed by the terms of a query rather than on their lexical representation. Therefore, it attains a more effective analysis of past processes in legal offices.

1   Introduction

In legal offices, the analysis of processes upon past ones is a task performed on a regular basis.. Past cases provide knowledge and support for the analysis itself. However, that task is usually demanding, once there is often an abundant number of documents available for search.

The legal domain requires accuracy and the retrieval of irrelevant documents can make a search engine uninteresting for it. As classical IR tools are based on term-oriented approaches, they usually retrieve a significant number of irrelevant documents — because the terms of the query might not express the intended meaning in the documents — and, moreover, miss some relevant ones where the meaning desired might be conveyed by different terms.

In this paper, we present a knowledge-based IR tool. It uses Conceptual Dependecy (CD) to represent knowledge of the domain and a Conceptual Analyser (CA) to translate a sentence in natural language into a sentence in CD. The engine searches documents where terms express the meaning intended with the terms of the query, rather than documents containing those terms. The result set is more accurate and may contain even documents where none of the terms provided in the query appear.

In Section 2, the formalism for knowledge representation is presented. Next, Section 3 presents some sentences from the Legal Domain and their respective

F. F. Ramos, H. Unger, V. Larios (Eds.): ISSADS 2004, LNCS 3061, pp. 137–144, 2004.
© Springer-Verlag Berlin Heidelberg 2004

representations. The search engine and its architecture are described in Section 4. Last, Section 5 shows a compilation of the ideas discussed in the paper.

2   Knowledge Representation

As in this work knowledge was associated with natural language, the formalism should be able to take into account natural language. Conceptual Dependency (CD) [5, 7] allows the handling of natural language through the use of a memory manually developed. Some of its advantages are:

- Two different sentences in natural language which share the same meaning have both a unique representation in CD;
- The availability of Conceptual Analysers (CAs) in the literature [2] which can be expeditiously developed[1].

The structure of a unit of memory is exposed in (1):

$$predicate([role_1(filler_1), \ldots, role_n(filler_n)]) \tag{1}$$

where:

- $predicate$ identifies a type of structure, which packages a list of Slots;
- A $slot$ has the form $role(filler)$ and expresses a perceptible item in a structure along with its value;
- $role_i$ identifies the perceptible item i in a structure;
- $filler_i$ is the value of the perceptible item i — which can itself be another structure — in a structure.

Since the value of a perceptible item i in a structure s_1 can be another structure s_2, some structures will obviously be aggregating others; therefore, structures can link to each other. Thus, basic structures can be packaged by top-level ones. Moreover, fillers can contain patterns, what allows the use of matching constraints: if a filler contains a pattern, only instances which match that pattern can fill the respective slot; if a filler is unbound, no constraint is applied.

The hierarchy for generalization/specialization is not explicit in the formalism presented. They were expressed as pairs $(s, [a_1, \ldots, a_n), n > 1$, where s is either a specialization or an abstraction and a_i is an abstraction. The use of abstractions can be better understood in Subsection 4.1, where some slots are filled only with objects which respect constraints.

---

[1] CAs are programs which translate sentences expressed in natural language into sentences expressed in CDs.

3   From Documents to Memory

Case-based Reasoning is the default strategy used by the staff of a legal offices in the analysis of documents. This work concentraded on the development of an IR tool based on Conceptual Analysis and Conceptual Dependence [4, 6, 3, 7]. In addition, a memory was created with terms of the domain as a knowledge source. The following examples demonstrate how a memory can be modeled — only a significant part of the legal document was chosen to represent the whole document:

1. Sentence: "Hypothesis in which the faltering accord does not suffer from the referred omission." — Figure 1 for graphical modeling. The concept hypothesis aggregates the content "the faltering accord does not suffer from the referred omission". The concept hypothesis has an object accord in the state faltering. In this case, the state is just a form under which the object presents itself. The concept suffer was represented by a state upon which the operator does not acts. Whereas, this state is acting upon a concept representing an act of omission. In this example, the following concepts were used:
   - hypothesis: a concept which has an object as the content of the hypothesis;
   - not: an operator which produces the negation of a concept;
   - state: an observation of an object or another state in a certain moment in time, providing the notion of a static behaviour;
   - omission: a concept which represents the notion of an act of omission;
   - accord: a concept which represents a type of legal document;
   - faltering: this concept represents and describes the state faltering.
2. Sentence: "Embargos of declaration against decision which does not contain obscurity, contradiction or omission are inconsistent." — Figure 2.
   - implication: this concept represents a relation between two other concepts where one is the cause for the ocurrence of the other;
   - embargo of declaration: a concept which represents a special type of embargo;
   - critic: represents the notion of criticism, where an argument criticises a theory;
   - or: operator of disjunction;
   - obscurity, omission, contradiction: represent their respective notions;
   - inconsistent: a concept which describes the state of the concept declaration embargo.

The graphical models facilitate the creation of the respective entries in the memory. The models also help define what kind of request[2] will be necessary, what the request will do when the term is read and how the term will eventually be represented. The following example demonstrates a piece of the memory coded in Prolog:

---

[2] A request is a sort of trigger in Conceptual Analysis [2].

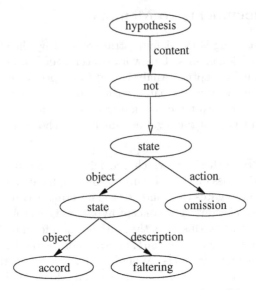

Fig. 1. First sentence's conceptual model

```
word(declaration,
     [request(1,
      [before(mental_object, O)],
      [set_slot(O, typo(declaration([]))),
       set_mode(normal)])]).
word(hypothesis,
     [request(1,
      [],
      [add_cd(hypothesis([]), CD),
       set_mode(noun_group)]),
      request(1,
      [after(lexical_item, which)],
      [activate([request(1,
      [after_destructive(mental_object, C)],
      [set_slot(CD, object(C))])])])])]).
```

4   The IR System

The search engine of the system is based on CD similarity, rather than mathematical approaches adopted in most of the current search engines. Next, the system itself and its architecture are described.

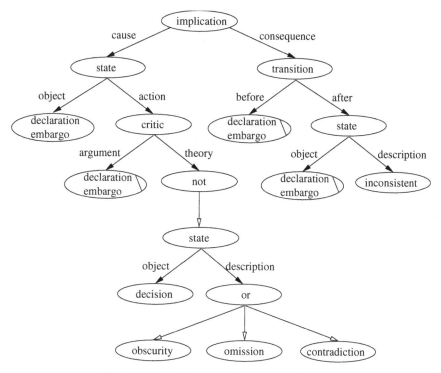

Fig. 2. Second sentence's conceptual model

4.1   Parsing Sentences

The Conceptual Analyzer (CA) is the parser that maps sentences in natural
language into conceptual representations [2] — each term is read from left to
right. Expectations perform an important role in CA: they are used to fill in the
slots in the CD representing the meaning of the input sentence. Expectations
or requests are triggers which may be activated whenever a term is read. Using
the concepts available in the short-term memory, the triggers perform actions
on CD structures. Each concept, after recognized, is stored in the short-term
memory. If a request is not satisfied, it is placed in a queue to be satisfied later.
The following example ilustrates the use of requests in Conceptual Analysis:

- Input sentence: "Jack read a book".
- Term "Jack": indicates a reference to a male human being named Jack. This
  reference is stored in the short-term memory under the token jack;
- Term "read": instance of the concept reading, which, in CD, is represented
  by the concept $mtrans([\,actor(\_),\, object(\_)])$ and supplies some expectations
  which will help to fill in the empty slots in the CD frame;
  - requests for the slot actor: if there is some animated being before this
    concept in short-term memory, fill in the slot actor with it — this expec-

tation (request) is satisfied and the resultant CD is $mtrans([actor(jack), object(\_)])$;
- requests for the slot object: if there is some physical object after this concept, fill in the slot object with it — this request is not satisfied at this moment.
- Term "a": indicates that an instance of a concept should come next;
  - requests of the term "a": if a concept is found after this position in short-term memory, it is marked with ref(indef) (indefinite reference) — this request is not satisfied at this moment either.
- Term "book": indicates an instance of a concept which is known to be a physical object and a source of information. Now the request belonging to the term "a" is satisfied and the current concept is marked as book([ref(indef)]). Furthermore, the request of the concept "read" that was waiting to be satisfied too is indeed satisfied and the slot object is filled with book([ref(indef)]);
- Output: the CD structure mtrans([actor(jack), book([ref(indef)])]).

In the legal domain, the output of the parser upon an input would be similar to the following examples:

- Sentence: "Hypothesis in which the faltering accord does not suffer from the referred omission."

```
hypothesis([object(not([object(state([object(state([object(accord([])),
                                                     description(faltering)]))),
                                description(omission([]))]))]))])
```

- Sentence: "Declaration embargos against decision which does not contain obscurity, contradiction or omission are inconsistent."

```
implication([cause(state([object(embargo([type(declaration([]))]))),
               action(critic([argument(embargo([type(declaration([]))])),
                  theory(not([object(state([object(decision([actor(_),
                                                             object(_)])),
                     description(or([object1(or([object1(omission([])),
                                                 object2(obscurity([]))])),
                           object2(contradiction([]))]))]))]))]))]))))]))))]))))))))),
               consequence(transition([before(embargo([type(declaration([]))]))),
                  after(state([object(embargo([type(declaration([]))])),
                     description(inconsistent)]))]))])])])
```

4.2   Case-Based Information Retrieval

Classical IR techniques use, as theoretical basis, statistical and mathematical methods [1]. Some problems may arise in classical IR tools, such as retrieval of documents which contain the terms of the query in different meanings. Also, some documents which do present the intended meaning are not retrieved because the terms of the query are different from the terms used in the documents. These problems can be reduced if semantic is properly handled.

The search engine of the proposed system uses CD similarity to determine how similar the user query is to the sentences in documents. This similarity is recursive — a CD slot could be filled with another CD structure. The similarity function takes two elements of a CD for comparison:

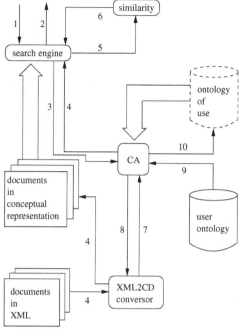

1. User Query
2. Most similar Documents
3. Natural language sentence
4. Sentence in CD
5. Sentences in CD for comparison
6. Documents similarity
7. Representative part of document
8. Sentence representing the document
9. Terms
10. Expanded terms

Fig. 3. System Architecture

- predicate: has higher weight in the similarity; if two CD's have both the same predicate, then their similarity is already relevant;
- slots: has lower weight in the similarity; both roles and fillers are compared.

4.3 System Architecture

The system modules are depicted in Figure 3. An "ontology of use" is created by expanding the terms in the "user ontology" into a suitable representation for the Conceptual Analyzer (CA)[3]. Next, the module XML2CD is responsible for

---

[3] The "user ontology" utilizes a simple notation to facilitate its creation, however that is not the format used by the CA.

the conversion of the relevant part of a XML document into a CD representation[4]. A CD document base is then obtained[5]. These two processes are executed separately as well as the searching process — although the creation of the "ontology of use" is fast, the generation of CD documents may require a substantial amount of processing time depending on the size of XML base.

When the user enters a query in natural language, that sentence is mapped into a CD structure — as seen in Section 4. Next, the search engine retrieves each CD document and compares each of them to the CD format of the query. In the module similarity, the similarity between the document and the user query is returned[6]. Finally, the resultant documents are returned ranked by similarity.

5   Conclusions

The construction of a memory model which properly represents a domain facilitates and clarifies the development of memory-based systems.

The effectiveness of the CA is determined by the ontology — or memory. If the ontology is well defined, the results will be satisfactory. The use of knowledge instead of statistical or mathematical methods in the search engine attains more precise results.

Thus, memory-based IR systems could improve the current accuracy of information retrieval. As meaning is manually defined, a search engine can rely upon a much more accurate method when deciding whether a document is relevant or not according to an ordinary query.

References

[1] R. Baeza-Yates and B. Ribeiro-Neto. *Modern Information Retrieval*. ACM Press, New York, 1999. 142
[2] L. Birnbaum and M. Selfridge. Conceptual Analysis of Natural Language. In Schank and Riesbeck [7], chapter 13, pages 318–353. 138, 139, 141
[3] S. W. Russel. Semantic categories of nominals for conceptual dependency analysis of natural language. Technical Report STAN-CS-72-299, Computer Science Department, Stanford University, Stanford, Jul 1972. 139
[4] R. C. Schank. Intention, memory and computer understanding. Technical Report STAN-CS-71-193, Computer Science Department, Stanford University, Stanford, Jan 1971. 139
[5] R. C. Schank. Conceptual Dependency: A Theory of Natural Language Understanding. *Cognitive Psychology*, 3:552–631, 1972. 138
[6] R. C. Schank. The fourteen primitive actions and their inferences. Technical Report STAN-CS-73-344, Computer Science Department, Stanford University, Stanford, Mar 1973. 139
[7] R. C. Schank and C. K. Riesbeck, editors. *Inside Computer Understanding*. Lawrence Erlbaum Associates, Hillsdale, NJ, 1981. 138, 139, 144

---

[4] The legal documents were originally in XML format.

[5] A document may generate many CD representations: the one with higher similarity is chosen to represent the whole document.

[6] The similarity is normalized from 0 to 1.

Semantic Search Engines

Alcides Calsavara and Glauco Schmidt

Pontifícia Universidade Católica do Paraná
Programa de Pós-Graduação em Informática Aplicada
Rua Imaculada Conceição, 1155, Prado Velho, Curitiba, PR, Brazil
{alcides,glauco}@ppgia.pucpr.br
http://www.ppgia.pucpr.br/~alcides

Abstract. Typical electronic business applications need to make queries about products and services made available by sellers and service providers through the Web. Unfortunately, it can be a very time consuming task to discover information as simple as those, since every site has its own metaphore. The so-called search engines can facilitate such task because a client provides some keywords and obtain a list of Uniform Resource Locators (URL) that point to the target sites, but it does not prevent from interacting with each site. We propose and define a novel kind of service for the Web: the semantic search engine. Differently from traditional search engines, a semantic search engine stores semantic information about Web resources and is able to solve complex queries, considering as well the context where the Web resource is targeted. We show, through examples, how a semantic search engine may be employed in order to permit clients obtain information about commercial products and services, as well as about sellers and service providers which can be hierarchically organized. Semantic search engines may seriously contribute to the development of electronic business applications since it is based on strong theory and widely accepted standards.

1 Introduction

A common requirement in electronic business applications is the ability to make queries about products and services made available by sellers and service providers through the World-Wide Web (WWW), or just Web, for short. For example, clients may wish to discover the lowest price of a certain product or may wish to know all shops in town that sell that product. Since normally each seller or service provider maintains its Web site organized in a particular way, clients need to interact with each target site, one by one, by using specific metaphores. As a consequence, it can be a very time consuming task to discover information as simple as those. Such a task is facilitated by the so-called search engines, where a client provides some keywords and obtain a list of Uniform Resource Locators (URL) that point to the target sites, but it does not prevent from interacting with each site.

Obviously, a client would benefit from a service that could understand its queries and give the proper answers. Such a service should know the precise

F. F. Ramos, H. Unger, V. Larios (Eds.): ISSADS 2004, LNCS 3061, pp. 145–157, 2004.
© Springer-Verlag Berlin Heidelberg 2004

semantics of products and services, besides keeping information about organizations that sell their products and services. For that reason, we call this type of service a semantic search engine.

Typically, in a electronic business environment, information objects – which represent commercial products or services – are categorized according to a certain taxonomy. Therefore, a straightforward means of representing semantic information about products and services is to devise a standard taxonomy and a standard language to make queries by using terms of the taxonomy. Also the organizations that sell products and services can be hierarchicaly organized, thus permitting a query to be issued not only considering the products taxonomy but also the hierarchy of organizations.

The remaining of this article is organized as follows. Section 2 presents other works that also attempt to provide some kind of semantic information. Section 3 presents a conceptual model for semantic search engines based on the General Theory of Signs. Section 4 presents a framework to express metadata, the data stored and managed by semantic search engines. Section 5 presents a protocol for clients to query semantic search engines. Section 6 discusses some implementation issues for a semantic search engine. Finally, Sect. 7 presents some conclusions and proposes some future work.

2   Related Work

The literature reports several efforts to the development of platforms to support metadata representation and corresponding applications. In this section, we discuss some documented research projects that influenced our model and design of a semantic search engine.

2.1   Metadata for Scientific Bibliography

– Content Standards for Digital Geospatial Metadata (CSDGM) This standard, also known as FGDC (US Federal Geographic Data Committee) [1], aims at providing a set of terminologies and definitions which are common for describing digital spatial data. Its main purpose is to help getting availability, precision and access means to geographical data. The groups of metadata elements are the following: identification information, data quality information, spatial data organization information, spatial reference information, entity and attribute information, distribution information and metadata reference information.
– Umwelt-DatenKatalog (UDK) This standard, also known as Environmental Data Catalog [2], is a meta-information system and a tool for navigating documents and retrieves collections of data related to environment which are produced by government agencies and other institutions. Developed with the support from the German and Austrian governments, it is the official tool in Austria for manipulating environmental data. Its data model contains three kinds of objects: environmental objects, environmental data objects

and UDK objects, which correspond to the metadata itself. There are seven classes that represent collections of environmental data objects: project data, empirical data, installation data, map and geographical information, studies and reports, product data and model data.

2.2 Metadata for Interoperability

- Open Information Model (OIM): This standard emerged from a partnership between several companies with the purpose of providing support to interoperability between development tools [3]. It permits to verify all phases of a software development process. The OIM standard is a specialization of the UML submodels and concepts. The following data are managed within this standard: analysis and design model, object and component model, business engineering model, knowledge management model, database and data warehousing model.
- Common Warehouse Metamodel (CWM): This standard permits integration of data warehouse systems, e-business systems and intelligent business systems, in heterogeneous and distributed systems [4]. Metadata is organized according to the following subjects: Warehouse Deployment, Relational, Record-Oriented, Multidimentisonal Database, XML, Transformation, OLAP, Warehouse Process and Warehouse Operation.
- XML Metadata Interchange (XMI) : This standard provides interoperability between CASE tools in the context of object-oriented software development, through XML documents [5].
- Rigi Standard Format (RSF): This is a reverse engineering tool to extract graphs that represent the architecture of a system [6].
- eXtensible Interchange Format (XIF) : This standard permits the exchange of models developed by Microsoft [7].

2.3 Generic Metadata Architectures

- Meta Content Framework (MCF): This open architecture can be used for describing Web sites structures [8]. Its main elements are: Node Set, Label Set, Arc Set.
- Platform for Internet Content Selection (PICS): This platform is promoted by the W3C Consortium and, initially, aimed at helping parents to control what their children would access on the Internet[9]. Its main metadata components are rating service and contents label.
- Resource Description Framework (RDF): The RDF standard, amongst other related technologies, is developed by the W3C Consortium, especifically by its Semantic Web group [10]. It defines a set of concepts which can be employed to model the semantics of Web resources.

3 Conceptual Model

The conceptual model of semantic search engines presented in this work is based on the General Theory of Signs. Firstly, in this section, we summarize the main concepts of that theory for the sake of completeness; a rich discussion on this subject can be found in [11]. Secondly, we show how the General Theory of Signs is used for defining the conceptual model of semantic search engines.

3.1   General Theory of Signs

Semiotics is the name used mainly by North American authors – fellows of Charles Sanders Pierce (1839-1914) – to refer to the science that studies the Theory of Signs; others, fellows of Ferdinand de Saussure (1857-1913), prefer the term Semiology. According to Peirce, the act of meaning involves three inseparable terms: sign, object and interpretant. A sign is something that takes the place of something else, it exists as a stimulus in the act of meaning because it can be perceived for interpretation by a sense – a visual stimulus, a sound stimulus, etc. The term used to refer to the act of meaning is semiosis. In a formal language, each sign is mapped unambiguously and univocally to a single object, while this is not necessarily true in natural languages. An object, on the other hand, is something physical or abstract that may be evoked. An object may have several signs. An interpretant is a representation – another representation for the object –, that is, it has a cognitive state of the object internally. An interpretant has such a state because it is placed in a specific environment – called ground – where it can find references to realize semiosis.

3.2   The Core Model

Our model is based on the relationship of tree elements: URL, semantics and context. A URL is a sign that refers to an information object, which can represent a commercial product or a service. A semantics is the meaning of that information object, according to a taxonomy that categorizes products and services. A context is the domain where such information object has the corresponding semantics, such as an organization or a country. Domains are normally organized hierachicaly, and so are contexts in our model. For example, the context that represent all supermarkets, say Supermarket, may contain specific sub-contexts, such as Carrefour and WalMart. By observing how Web resources are stored and referred to, we can come to the following conclusions:

1. Every Web resource has a semantics.
2. The semantics of a Web resource depends on the context where it is inserted.
3. The semantics of a Web resource is unique within a given context.
4. A Web resource may have the same semantics in distinct contexts.
5. Distinct Web resources may have the same semantics, independently of context.

To summarize, in our model, there is a set of URL (references to information objects that represent products and services), a tree of contexts (Web domains) and a tree of semantics (the taxonomy of products and services). By applying the General Theory of Signs, we can say that a URL is a sign that refers to an

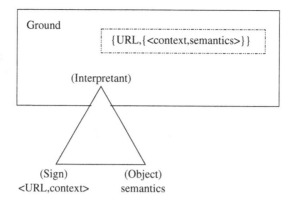

Fig. 1. Semiotic model for semantic search engines

information object. The ground, where an interpretant should be able to say the semantics of a given URL, must store a set of tuples $< context, semantics >$ for each known URL, that is, the interpretant needs to know the context where a URL is used in order to say its semantics. Fig. 1 illustrates a semiosis done by an interpretant where the resulting object for a sign defined by a tuple $< URL, context >$ is the semantics of that URL within that context, according to the information stored by the ground where the interpretant is inserted. In the next sections, we will refer to the information stored by the ground as metadata, the data managed by a semantic search engine, while the interpretant is the algorithm implemented by a semantic search engine in order to solve queries.

4   Metadata Representation

In this work, metadata is the information maintained by a semantic search engine about Web resources. Such a metadata includes a set of context trees, a set of semantics trees, a set of URL and their corresponding relationships, that is, all tuples $< URL, context, semantics >$ that exist. A semantic search engine must store its metadata in a proper data structure in order to solve queries efficiently. Thus, there must exist a means to load metadata into a semantic search engine. Moreover, the metadata maintained by a certain semantic search engine must be serializable in order to store it in a persistent form and to transfer it through the network to another semantic search engine. The persistent form of a metadata is useful to ensure the reliability of a semantic search engine; if a semantic search engine stops intentionally or crashes due to some failure, its metadata will be reloaded when it is restarted. Transfer of metadata from a semantic search engine to another permits them to cooperate as a group in order to answer queries; it makes it possible to replicate the metadata (fully or partially) and distribute those replicas strategically to improve system performance and response time.

Several techniques for metadata serialization can be envisaged, varying from a highly compressed binary format to a well structured and documented textual format and, orthogonally to that, varying from a private format to a open standard format. Traditionally in Web environments, the preference is for open standards and textual representation, since they easy information exchange between people, applications and distinct platforms. Currently, the eXtensible Markup Language (XML) is the standard most widely used for that purpose. However, XML alone does not solve the whole problem of metadata serialization; roughly speaking, XML is just a language that permits to express typed records composed of fields (attributes and tags) and associated values. Metadata has a complex structure, thus requiring a means to model it properly before expressing it. Again, several modelling techniques can be envisaged to model metadata maintained by a semantic search engine. However, such metadata is basically information about Web resources and, fortunately, there is a standard modelling technique specific for such type of information objects: the Resource Description Framework (RDF) standard. Another advantage of RDF is that the instantiation of a RDF model is well realized through XML documents: one document expresses the model itself, while other documents express instances of the model, which correspond to metadata in this work. Therefore, a good technique for metadata serialization is one that employes RDF and XML.

We have created a RDF model and corresponding XML definition named Web Resource Semantics (WRS) for expressing metadata. So, a WRS document expresses a set of context trees, a set of semantics trees, a set of URL and their relationships. The RDF model for WRS is shown in Fig. 2. For each URL there is an Extension, which is a set of occurrences in different contexts with different semantics; each occurrence is denoted as an Instance and they are organized as a Bag. So, for each instance there is a Context and a Semantics, each one implemented by a tree of nodes which are occurrences of TreeNode. Both trees – the context tree and the semantics tree – are composed by a root node, intermediate nodes and leaf nodes: any TreeNode must have another as its Father, except the root node; any TreeNode may have another as its Child, except the leaf nodes. The Value associated with each TreeNode as its Subject is a simple name within a certain taxonomy.

Let us consider, for example, the metadata represented in Fig. 3, where the tree with root node labeled Supermarket corresponds to a context tree, while the tree with root node labeled Goods corresponds to a semantics tree. The metadata is completed by a set of URL corresponding to products which are associated with at least one context tree node such that, for each association between a given product and a given context tree node, there is a corresponding semantics represented by a semantics tree node. For the sake of clarity, Fig. 3 shows only one such URL: the ficticious URL http://a.b.c , which belongs to two distinct tuples $< URL, context, semantics >$ – one denoted by a dashed line polygon and another by a dotted line polygon – that is, the same product has distinct semantics within each context (for the context Supermarket.Carrefour, its semantics is Goods.Electronics.Computers, and, for the context Supermarket.WalMart, its semantics is Goods.Toys.Games).

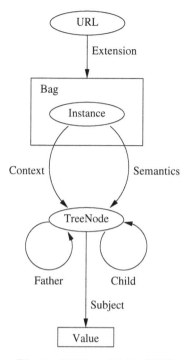

Fig. 2. RDF model for WRS

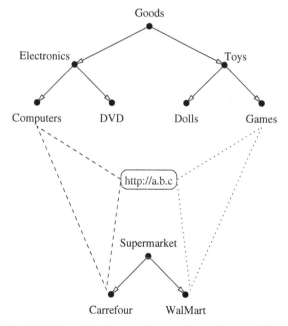

Fig. 3. Example of semantic search engine metadata

According to WRS model, the metadata represented in Fig. 3 contains seven occurrences of TreeNode that define a semantics tree root at the one whose Subject is Goods, tree occurrences of TreeNode that define a context tree root at the one whose Subject is Supermarket, one occurrnce of URL named http://a.b.c whose Extension is the Bag containing two occurrnces of Instance (one for each tuple $< URL, context, semantics >$ described above). For that URL and pair of instances, the corresponding XML code compliant with WRS (without heading information) can be expressed as follows.

```
<WRS

  xmlns:rdf=''http://www.w3.org/rdf-syntax-ns#''
  xmlns:wrs=''http://www.pucpr.br/wrs-rdf-schema#''>

<rdf:Description about=''http://a.b.c''>
  <wrs:Extension>
    <rdf:Bag>
      <wrs:Instance>
        <wrs:Context>
          Supermarket.Carrefour
        </wrs:Context>
        <wrs:Semantics>
          Goods.Electronics.Computers
        </wrs:Semantics>
      </wrs:Instance>
      <wrs:Instance>
        <wrs:Context>
          Supermarket.WalMart
        </wrs:Context>
        <wrs:Semantics>
          Goods.Toys.Games
        </wrs:Semantics>
      </wrs:Instance>
    </rdf:Bag>
  </wrs:Extension>
</rdf:Description>

</WRS>
```

As shown, a semantic search engine metadata can be easily expressed in XML by following the WRS definition, so that a XML/WRS document contains the serialized form of metadata.

5   Query Protocol

Once a semantic search engine is loaded with its metadata, it is ready to answer queries triggered by clients. A query, however, must be structured according to specific rules, transferred through the network from a client to the engine,

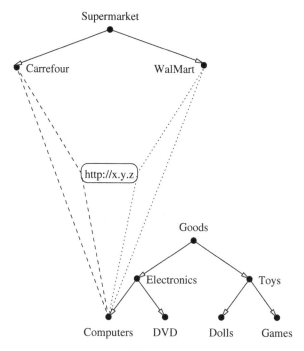

Fig. 4. Semantic search engine metadata additional to the metadata shown in Fig. 3

and the corresponding answer must be sent back to the client. Thus, a proper conversation between a client and a semantic search engine requires a formal protocol.

We have created a protocol named Context&Semantics Transfer Protocol (CSTP) that permits clients to query a semantic search engine and also permits two semantic search engines exchange metadata as well as solve a certain query in a cooperative way. CSTP permits a client to obtain information about context, semantics and URL, in a combined way. The forms of query are explained as follows and exemplified by using the metadata shown in Fig. 3 with the additional metadata shown in Fig. 4.

1. Return a collection of context trees: A client application may whish to learn what context trees are stored by a certain semantic search engine in order to formulate future queries. A semantic search engine, on the other hand, may whish to capture part of or the whole collection of context trees stored by another semantic search engine in order to enlarge its domain of knowledge and, therefore, be able to answer to a broader range of queries. In our example of metadata, such query returns the only context tree that exists: the tree rooted at the node Supermarket.

2. Return a collection of semantics trees: Analogously to the previous case, a client application may whish to learn what semantics trees are stored

by a certain semantics search engine in order to formulate future queries. A semantic search engine, on the other hand, may whish to capture part of or the whole collection of semantics trees stored by another semantic search engine in order to enlarge its domain of knowledge and, therefore, be able to answer to a broader range of queries. In our example of metadata, such query returns the only semantics tree that exists: the tree rooted at the node Goods.

3. Return the set of URL that matches a given tuple$< context, semantics >$: A client application or a semantic search engine may whish to learn what information objects (represented by their URL) have a certain semantics within a certain context. Example:

   query:$<$
   Supermarket.Carrefour, Goods.Electronics.Computers
   $>$
   return: {http://a.b.c, http://x.y.z }

4. Return the set of contexts that matches a given tuple$< URL, semantics >$: A client appplication or a semantic search engine may whish to learn the contexts where a certain information object has a certain semantics. Example:

   query: $<$http://x.y.z, Goods.Electronics.Computers$>$
   return: {
   Supermarket.Carrefour, Supermarket.WalMart
   }

5. Return a semantics given a tuple $< URL, context >$: A client application or a semantic search engine may whish to learn the semantics a certain information object has within a certain context. Examples:

   query:$<$http://a.b.c, Supermarket.Carrefour $>$
   return: Goods.Electronics.Computers

   query: $<$http://a.b.c, Supermarket.WalMart$>$
   return: Goods.Toys.Games

6. Return the set of tuples$< context, semantics >$ given a URL: A client application or a semantic search engine may whish to learn all contexts and corresponding semantics where a certain information object is present. Example:

   query: http://a.b.c
   return: {
   $<$Supermarket.Carrefour,
   Goods.Electronics.Computers$>$,
   $<$Supermarket.WalMart, Goods.Toys.Games$>$
   }

7. Return the set of tuples $< URL, semantics >$ given a context: A client application or a semantic search engine may whish to learn the information objects and corresponding semantics within a certain context. Example:

query: Supermarket.WalMart
return: {
<http://a.b.c, Goods.Toys.Games >,
<http://x.y.z, Goods.Electronics.Computers >
}

8. Return the set of tuples $< URL, context >$ given a semantics: A client application or a semantic search engine may whish to learn what information objects have a certain semantics and in which context that happens. Example:

query: Goods.Electronics.Computers
return: {
<http://a.b.c, Supermarket.WalMart >,
<http://x.y.z, Supermarket.Carrefour >,
<http://x.y.z, Supermarket.WalMart>
}

Additionally, it is possible to replace the name of a context or a semantics in a query for a wildcard, meaning that the target context or semantics must include all direct child nodes. Thus, the two queries given as example in the case return a semantics given a tuple $< URL, context >$ above, can be redone as follows.

query:<http://a.b.c, Supermarket.* >
return: {
<Supermarket.Carrefour, Goods.Electronics.Computers>
<Supermarket.WalMart, Goods.Toys.Games>
}

Now, by using wildcards, the return may be more complex, as the example above shows. Since the context is Supermarket.*, all child nodes of Supermarket must be included as target contexts, that is, the target contexts are Supermarket, Supermarket.Carrefour and Supermarket.WalMart. As a consequence, it is possible to exist a specific semantics for each context in the list of targets. Thus, the answer to the query has to be a set of tuples $< context, semantics >$, one tuple for each context in the list and corresponding semantics. The same discussion applies to all other forms of queries listed above where a semantics and/or a context is expected as part of the query.

6   Implementation Issues

We have implemented a semantic search engine and a client application for the purpose of experimenting the ideas described in this work.

The semantic search engine was implemented using the Java programming language and works as a servlet on a Internet server. Its main responsibilities are to store metadata in a properly structured manner and answer to queries efficiently. When started, the semantic search engine loads its hash tables with semantic information available from WRS documents. Then it opens a TPC/IP socket at the port number 8181 and awaits incomming requests (queries), according to the CSTP protocol. (CSTP works directly on top of TCP/IP.) Everytime a new request arrives, a new thread of execution is created specifically to process the corresponding query. Three hash tables are managed by the semantic search engines: the first one stores the set of semantics trees, the second one stores the set of context trees and the third one stores relationships between URL and entries of the other tables, thus reconstructing the tuples $< URL, context, semantics >$.

The client application is a graphical browser that allows a user to issue queries of the kind return the set of tuples $< context, semantics >$ given a URL. The user can navigate through a returned set of contexts and check their corresponding semantics with respect to the given URL. This client application does not intend to be an electronic business application; it simply shows the possibility of creating applications that interact with a semantic search engine.

7 Conclusions

We have proposed and defined a new kind of service for the Web: the semantic search engine. Differently from traditional search engines that solve queries based solely on keywords, a semantic search engine stores semantic information about Web resources and is able to solve complex queries, considering as well the context where the Web resource is inserted. We have shown through examples how a semantic search engine may be employed in electronic business applications in order to permit clients obtain information about commercial products and services which are categorized according to a certain taxonomy, as well as about sellers and service providers which can be hierarchically organized. The conceptual model of semantic search engines was formalized by using the General Theory of Signs, and its design was based on standard languages and frameworks such as XML and RDF. A prototype implementation was developed for the purposes of verification of ideas and, although still very limited, it has shown to be satisfactory.

Our main contributions can be summarized as follows:

1. A conceptual model that relates Web resource, context and semantics, based on a widely accepted theory – The General Theory of Signs – and that works very well in cases where a taxonomy for resources can be established.
2. Formal specification of the conceptual model by using a standard framework – the RDF framework.
3. Definition of a framework named WRS to express metadata based on a standard languague – the XML language.

4. Definition of a protocol name CSTP for clients to query a semantic search engine and for semantic search engines cooperate.

Many system design issues still need to be tackled, including efficiency, security, reliability. One possible path of future research is to implement the model here presented atop an open directory platform, such as LDAP. Another design issue to study is the way CTSP works. Instead of working directly on top of TCP/IP, as implemented so far, CSTP can work on top of HTTP, like the SOAP protocol. That would require to define a set of XML tags to enable representing CTSP messages (queries and answers).

We belive that our work may seriously contribute to the development of electronic business applications since the model we created is based on strong theory and widely accepted standards, besides the fact that it worked very well in the experiments carried so far. Since semantic search engines, as we defined, is a novel approach for obtaining information about Web resources, many new research projects can be started, especially in the field of electronic business.

References

[1] Simon, E., Tomasic, A., Galhardas, H.: A Framework for Classifying Scientific Metadata. American Association for Artifitial Intelligence (1998)   146
[2] Gunther, O., Voisard, A.: Metadata in Geographic and Environmental Data Management. McGraw Hill (1997)   146
[3] Open Information Model Version 1.1 (proposal) (1999)   147
[4] OMG Common Warehouse Metamodel Specification (1999)   147
[5] XML Metadata Interchange Specification Version 1.1 (1999)   147
[6] University of Victoria Victoria, Canada: Rigi User's Manual - Version 5.4.4. (1998)   147
[7] XIF eXtensible Interchange Format (2002)   147
[8] Guha, R., Bray, T.: Meta Content Framework using XML (1997)   147
[9] Krauskopf, T., et al.: PICS Label Distribution Label Syntax and Communication Protocols Version 1.1 (1996) W3C Recommendation   147
[10] Resource Description Framework (2002)   147
[11] Santaella, L.: A Teoria Geral dos Signos. Editora Pioneira, Sao Paulo (2000)   148

The Internal-Local-Remote Dependency Model for Generic Coordination in Distributed Collaboration Sessions

José Martin Molina Espinosa[1], Jean Fanchon[2], and Khalil Drira[2]

[1] ITESM-CCM
Calle del Punte 222 Col. Ejidos de Huipulco Tlalpan, 14380, México D.F.
jose.molina@itesm.mx
[2] Laboratoire d'Analyse et d'Architecture des Systèmes (LAAS-CNRS)
7, Av. du Colonel Roche - 31077 Toulouse, Cedex 04 - France
{fanchon,drira}@laas.fr
http://www.laas.fr

Abstract. This paper considers Distributed Collaboration Sessions (DCS) where distributed users interact through multi-component communicating applications. The paper develops a formal framework that identifies the dependency relationships and the associated coordination rules that should be considered in controlling and managing the interactions between the actors of DCS including software components and human users. Components of the same application are associated with the same category. The users constitute a unique category of actors. We identify three classes of dependency relationships: (1) internal dependency relationship dealing with constraints related to the intra-actor level. (2) local dependency relationship dealing with constrains related to the intra-site level. (3) remote dependency relationship dealing with constraints related to the intra-category level. These three relationship classes are then applied to define dependency management laws for session management including controlling state change, communication scope, role distribution and group membership. Building the multi-actors interdependencies management rules is achieved by composing elementary dependencies relationships that we express as first order logic formula.

1 Introduction

Different research works aim now at providing a software support of distributed collaborative activities. These works aim to develop new architectures and new software to be used for a new organization of the work process around geographically distributed groups which cooperate. The members of these groups meet periodically or according to specific needs to coordinate their contributions during work sessions according to a preset or impromptu planning.

Two categories of collaboration sessions are distinguished: asynchronous sessions and synchronous sessions. In the first category, the users act according to sequential or parallel procedures on local data. The research tasks within the

F. F. Ramos, H. Unger, V. Larios (Eds.): ISSADS 2004, LNCS 3061, pp. 158–169, 2004.
© Springer-Verlag Berlin Heidelberg 2004

framework of this category generally concern the field of business process automation according to organizational and sociological theories. These are Workflow approaches.

The second category concerns the synchronous sessions during which the participants act simultaneously from distributed access points on shared objects according to implicit or explicit collaboration rules and using a set of collaboration applications which enable them to progress in a coordinated way. Our contributions are in this second category and deal with online consistency management in multi-application collaboration sessions which includes in particular defining and managing the constraints of coordination related to the collaborative applications and the collaborating participants. Such constraints state that starting (or stoping or any other action) of a given component (or application) must be preceded or followed by such other action related to the component itself on a given site or within a given group, or related to the communication and collaboration medium (communication channels, notification services, etc...).

Dependency management also includes group membership related rules. Such rules state that the entry (or the leave) of a given participant must be (preceded or followed) by the entry (or the leave) of such other participant, or is prohibited (or necessary) during such phase of the activity or as long as this participant plays such role or has such privilege.

We propose, in this paper, a formal framework allowing dependencies to be classified and specified by extending and refining our initial work based on three elementary relationships expressing "enabling", "inhibiting" and "preceding" formulas. In the proposed paper, we refine this decomposition and introduce new elementary relationships. As in our previous work, our model framework defines distributed collaborative sessions as labelled partial orders and dependency constraints as First Order Logic (FOL) formulae which apply to the labelled partial order model. Contrarily to our past work [10], we do model the distributed architecture of the collaboration support system and consider formulae that express dependencies explicitly within the distributed architecture. Three classes of dependencies are distinguished. The intra-actor dependencies represent the ordering constraints for internal actions of a given software component or actions of its user. The intra-site dependencies represent the ordering constraints for actions involving different components having concurrent but local interactions. The intra-category dependencies represent the ordering constraints for actions involving software component hosted by distant sites or involving their respective users.

The rest of the paper is divided as follows: Section 2 presents our model of dependencies coordination in collaborative sessions. First we present the formalization of collaborative sessions by labelled partial orders, next we present the syntax and semantics of first order logic and presents the elementary sentences which form the base of the model. Before Conclusion, Section 3 presents the generic coordination rules.

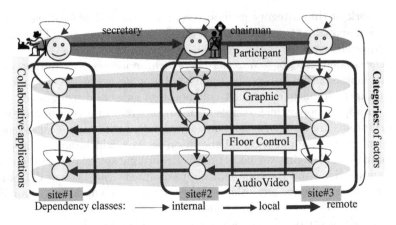

Fig. 1. Dependency classes for multi-users, multi-applications collaboration session

2   Related Work

Session and group management are coordination functions that are common to various types of collaborative activities. Many problems are considered, and various approaches can be planned to solve them. Various teams of research in the world were interested recently in these problems. Various work was carried out in this field. The addressed problems vary from the coordination of interactions [13, 5, 6] to the management of the structures of group to configure and control communications [14, 4]. One can classify the approaches in two main families: - those that consider that the collaboration sessions are always implicit and involve all the participants who access the same space such as [1, 2, 13] who consider spontaneous unstructured collaboration. - those who consider that the sessions are explicit and must be prepared before starting the collaboration activity such as [7] and [11] who are interested respectively in management of the communications and the interactions of the collaborating group, and [3] for the management of the authorizations for collaborative learning.

In each one of these families one can distinguish the approaches which treat only one application at the same time and those which treat various applications simultaneously. Contrarely to most of the works cited previously, we consider here multi-application collaboration sessions similarly to the approaches of session management in the Habanero project and ISAAC [2, 8] and Tango [12]. Contrarily to our work, these approaches are limites to the management of communication connexions and floor control. Moreove, only intra-application dependencies are considered.

A collaboration session (Fig.1) is viewed as a group of participants each of them having one or more roles (chairman, secretary, simple participant) and a set of collaborative applications symmetrically distributed on different sites. Each application is composed of 'n' cooperating components distributed on 'n' sites. Each application has a 'representative component' on each site. Each component

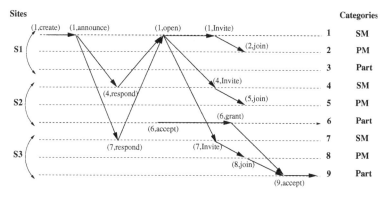

Fig. 2. Part of the partial ordering of session events involving 3 collaboration sites during session opening

belongs to a unique application characterized by its category. Such application categories are AudioVideo Conferencing, Graphic editing, text processing, floor control, instant messaging, session Management, Group Management.

Formally, we denote P the finite set of **actors** (human participant or software component) which are instances of the different categories. The set of **categories** is denoted C. The association between actors and categories is defined by the mapping: $Cat : P \rightarrow C$. We also use S to denote the set of **sites** where actors are located. The association of actors with sites is defined by the mapping: $Site : P \rightarrow S$.

Fig.1 illustrates an example of such a system where we distinguish four categories of actors: the "Participant" category, the "graphical application" category, the "audio-video conferencing" category and the "floor control" category.

2.1   Collaborative Sessions

In the following, we will consider that a collaborative session involves distributed actors (elements of a finite set P) executing **coordination actions** from a finite set A and generate events. Each event is the occurrence of a given action executed by a given actor. The pair (actor, action) is called the event name, and the set of event names is $\Sigma = P \times A$. Several events may be occurrences of the same event name during a session.

Definition 1 (Collaborative session). A **collaborative session** p over the set of event names Σ is a triple $p = (E, \leq, l)$ where

E is a finite set (called events) ,

$\leq$ a binary reflexive, antisymmetric and transitive relation on E, and

$l : E \rightarrow \Sigma$ a labelling function on events . An event $e \in E$ is an occurrence of the action name $l(e)$.

We recall, in the following definition, the semantics of first order logic as a background of the formal description.

2.2 Session Property Specification

Definition 2 (First order logic). We denote by $FO(\leq, \Sigma)$ the set of first order formulas built on the relation $\leq$ and the alphabet Σ. These formulas are defined by the grammar:

$$\varphi := P_\alpha(x) \mid x \leq y \mid \varphi \wedge \varphi \mid \neg\varphi \mid \exists x.\varphi$$

We write $\varphi(x_1, \ldots, x_n)$ when $(x_1, \ldots, x_n)$ are free variables that may occur in a formula $\varphi \in FO(\leq, \Sigma)$. These free variables must be instantiated by session event when the formula is applied to a session. Let $p = (E, \leq, l)$ be a collaborative session and $e_1, \ldots, e_n \in E$, we note $(p, e_1, \ldots, e_n) \models \varphi(x_1, à, x_n)$, to mean that φ is satisfied by p when x_i is given the value e_i for $i = 1, \ldots, n$. The satisfaction relation is defined inductively as follows:

$(p, e) \models P_\alpha(x)$ iff $l(e) = \alpha$

$(p, e_1, e_2) \models x \leq y$ iff $e_1 \leq e_2$

$(p, e_1, \ldots, e_n, e_{n+1}, \ldots, e_{n+p})) \models \varphi(x_1, \ldots, x_n) \bigwedge \psi(y_1, \ldots, y_p)$ iff

$(p, e_1, \ldots, e_n) \models \varphi(x_1, \ldots, x_n)$ and $(p, e_{n+1}, \ldots, e_{n+p}) \models \psi(y_1, \ldots, y_n)$

$(p, e_1, \ldots, e_n) \models \neg\varphi(x_1, \ldots, x_n)$ iff not $(p, e_1, \ldots, e_n) \models \varphi(x_1, \ldots, x_n)$

$(p, e_1, \ldots, e_n) \models \exists x.\varphi(x, x_1, \ldots, x_n)$ iff for some $e \in E$,

$(p, e, e_1, \ldots, e_n) \models \varphi(x, x_1, \ldots, x_n)$

The connectors ($\vee$ and $\forall x$)) and the different implications ($\Longrightarrow$, etc...) are derived in a standard way.

The immediate precedence predicate (" $\rightarrow$ ") is a derived operator defined by:

$$x \rightarrow y \stackrel{def}{\equiv} (x < y \wedge \forall z.(x < z \leq y \Longrightarrow z = y))$$

Particularly, if ψ is a sentence (i.e. ψ does not contain free variables) then it describes a property of p and we note $p \models \psi$.

2.3 Characterizing the Internal, Local and Remote Dependency Classes

The alphabet $Alph(\varphi)$ denoting the set of event names associated with the formula φ is defined inductively by:

$$Alph(P_\alpha(x)) = \{\alpha\}$$
$$Alph(x \leq y) = \emptyset$$
$$Alph(\varphi \wedge \varphi) = Alph(\varphi) \cup Alph(\varphi)$$
$$Alph(\neg\varphi) = Alph(\exists x.\varphi) = Alph(\varphi$$

The three classes of dependencies are associated with three classes of predicates that are characterized in the following.

- **Internal dependency predicates** are predicates defining intra-actor dependencies, also called **internal** properties. These are predicates having always the same actor in their set of event names, and they describe the internal consistency of the actor's behavior. Most of the time they are defined for all the actors of the same category. Formally, a formula φ is said to be internal iff:

$$\forall(n, a), (m, b) \in Alph(\varphi) : n = m$$

These formulas allow to describe properties of the kind : the actors of the category "Session Manager" cannot execute the action "delete a session" before having executed the action "open a session".

– **Local dependency predicates** are predicates defining intra-site dependencies, also called **local** properties. These are predicates having their associated actors located on the same site and they describe the mutual consistency of the behaviors of the actors acting on that site. They are generally common to all the sites of a collaborative session. Formally, a formula φ is said to be local iff:

$$\forall(n, a), (m, b) \in Alph(\varphi) : Site(n) = Site(m)$$

These class of predicate allows to describe properties of the kind: the actors of the category "Floor Control" cannot execute the action "start FC" before the actor of the category "AudioVideo Conferencing" has executed the "start AV" action.

– **Remote dependency predicates** are predicates defining intra-category dependencies, also called **remote** properties. These are predicates having their associated actors belonging to the same category and located on different sites. They describe the mutual consistency of the behaviors of the distributed actors of that category. Formally, a formula is said to be remote iff:

$$\forall(n, a), (m, b) \in Alph(\varphi) : Cat(n) = Cat(m)$$

These class of predicate allows describing properties of the kind: an actor of the category "Users" cannot execute the action "accept" before a remote actor of the same category has executed the action "grant".

2.4   Specifying the Basic Dependencies

We introduce the different basic relations expressing internal, local and remote dependencies relating intra-actor, intra-site and intra-application dependencies. These relations are formalized by logic formula over the action alphabet and are presented below.

Definition 3 (Precedence). For any pair of actions $\alpha, \beta \in \Sigma$, the precedence sentence, noted by $Pred(\alpha, \beta)$, is defined as :

$$Pred(\alpha, \beta) \overset{def}{\equiv} \forall x.\, P_\beta(x) \implies (\exists y.\, y < x \wedge P_\alpha(y))$$

This sentence is interpreted as: whenever action β is executed, the action a must have occurred previously at least once.

Definition 4 (Late enabling). For any pair of actions $\alpha, \beta \in \Sigma$, the precedence sentence, noted by $LEnable(\alpha, \beta)$, is defined as :

$$LEnable(\alpha, \beta) \overset{def}{\equiv} \forall x. \, P_\alpha(x) \implies (\exists y. \, x < y \wedge P_\beta(y))$$

This sentence is interpreted as: any occurrence of action α is must be followed by an occurrence of the action β.

Definition 5 (Inhibiting). For any pair of actions $\alpha, \beta \in \Sigma$, the inhibiting sentence, noted by $Inhib(\alpha, \beta)$, is defined as :

$$Inhib(\alpha, \beta) \overset{def}{\equiv} \forall x. \, P_\alpha(x) \implies (\forall y. \, x < y \Rightarrow \neg P_\beta(y))$$

This sentence is interpreted as: once action a is executed, then action β cannot be executed

Definition 6 (Immediate Precedence). For any pair of actions $\alpha, \beta \in \Sigma$, the enabling sentence, noted by $ImPred(\alpha, \beta)$, is defined as:

$$ImPred(\alpha, \beta) \overset{def}{\equiv} \forall x. \, P_\beta(x) \implies (\exists y. \, y \to x \wedge P_\alpha(y))$$

This sentence is interpreted as: any occurrence of the action β is immediately preceded (covers) an occurrence of the action α.

Definition 7 (Immediate Enabling). For any pair of actions $\alpha, \beta \in \Sigma$, the enabling sentence, noted by $ImEnable(\alpha, \beta)$, is defined as:

$$ImEnable(\alpha, \beta) \overset{def}{\equiv} \forall x. \, P_\alpha(x) \implies (\exists y. \, x \to y \wedge P_\beta(y))$$

This sentence is interpreted as: any occurrence of the action α is immediately followed (covered) by an occurrence of the action β .

Definition 8 (Non concurrency sentence). For any pair of actions $\alpha, \beta \in \Sigma$, the enabling sentence, noted by $InSequence(\alpha, \beta)$, is defined as:

$$InSequence(\alpha, \beta) \overset{def}{\equiv} \forall x. \forall y. \, P_\alpha(x) \wedge P_\beta(y) \implies (x < y \vee y < x)$$

This sentence is interpreted as: the actions α and β cannot be executed concurrently.

The absence of internal concurrency in the actors behavior is expressed by the formula:

$$\bigwedge_{n \in P, \, a,b \in A} InSequence((n, a), (n, b))$$

In practice, this property holds for the sessions we consider.

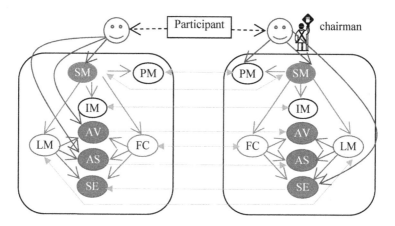

Fig. 3. Description of a given configuration and role distribution for a collaboration session

3   The Generic Coordination Rules
for Collaborative Session Management

In this section, we identify the generic coordination dependencies necessary for the coherence management in a multi-applications and multi-users distributed collaboration session according to the set of categories defined above. By using the different classes presented above we have modeled the coordination rules for the session management within the frame of the Distributed System Engineering European project (DSE) [9]. The set of commonly used collaboration applications is composed of 8 collaborative applications represented by the 8 categories: SM: Session Manager, PM: presence Manage, FC: Floor Controller, IM: Instant messaging, LF: Life cycle Manager, AV: Audio Video conferencing, AS: Application Sharing, SE: Shared editing. Formally: $C = \{Participant, SM, PM, FC, IM, LF, AV, AS, SE\}$. The chairman is a special participant who is allowed to execute more management actions than other (general) participants. The chairman can be played by different participants owning the chair attribute. But there exists in the participants set a unique participant who is the current chairman of the session.

Description of a given configuration and role distribution for a collaboration session.

3.1   Internal Dependency Management Rules

These rules express correct Ordering of events executed by single actors in the different categories including the Participant category. They allow ensuring internal state consistency.

Specifying the "Session Manager" Properties. The rule of coordination represented in Equation 1 shows the state transitions laws for a co-operation session. A session begins its life cycle after the execution of the event initialize which sets the state of the session to initialized. After its creation, a session can go to the states "announce" or "delete", according to the occurring event. The state "announce" means that the participants were invited to the session. While the state "delete" is the state of termination of the session. In addition, an announced session either is opened, in this case it goes to the state "open", or it is cancelled, in this case the session goes to the state "delete". The state "open" marks the beginning of collaborative activity which ends when reaching the state "close". Collaborative activity can be canceled while passing from the state "open" to the state "delete". The closed session is finished by passing from "close" to the state "delete".

$$\delta_1 = \bigwedge_{Cat(t)=SM} \begin{pmatrix} Pred((t, create), (t, announce)) \wedge \\ Pred((t, announce), (t, open)) \quad \wedge \\ Pred((t, open), (t, close)) \quad\quad \wedge \\ Pred((t, close), (t, delete)) \end{pmatrix} \tag{1}$$

Specifying the "Participant" Properties. Equation 2 defines the coordination rule which specifies that a participant can disconnect himself only if and only if he was connected before.

$$\delta_2 = \bigwedge_{Cat(p) = Part} Pred(p, join), (p, leave)) \tag{2}$$

Specifying the Collaboration Components Properties. Equation 3 defines a property of safety, which consists in ensuring that a collaboration component (actors belonging to one of the 3 categories: AV, AS or SE)can be stopped only if it were started beforehand. Consequently, the session manager must handle the list of the started components.

$$\delta_3 = \bigwedge_{Cat(t) \in \{AV, AS, SE\}} Pred((t, start), (t, stop)) \tag{3}$$

3.2   Local Dependency Management Rules

These rules express the correct ordering of the events executed by the actors behaving on a given site. They allow ensuring state consistency on a single site.

The rule of Equation 4 defines that the components must be stopped automatically after the termination of the session.

$$\delta_4 = \bigwedge_{Cat(t_1) = SM, Cat(t_2) = LF} ImEnable((t_1, delete), (t_2, stop)) \tag{4}$$

The rule shown by Equation 5 specifies the chairman role transfer scope. It indicates that the participant who can accept the role of chairman of the session must belong to the group and be connected to the session.

$$\delta_5 = \bigwedge_{Cat(t) = SM, Cat(p) = Part} Pred((t, join), (p, accept)) \qquad (5)$$

Group Membership Rules

This set of rules specifies the actions that the participant must undertake according to the session's state.

Admission Only by Invitation. We considered that the connection of the participant in a session is possible if and only if they were invited to this session. This rule is illustrated by equation 6

$$\delta_6 = \bigwedge_{Cat(t_1) = SM, Cat(t_2) = PM} Pred((t_1, invite), (t_2, join)) \qquad (6)$$

Admission Only before Termination. The rule illustrated by Equation 7 indicates that the participants cannot connect to a session which was finished. This rule ensures the prohibition of connection to a session which does not exist any more.

$$\delta_7 = \bigwedge_{Cat(t_1) = SM, Cat(t_2) = PM} Inhib((t_1, delete), (t_2, join)) \qquad (7)$$

Managing Group dissolution, Managing Leave of Participants. The rule of Equation 8 defines that the participants are automatically disconnected after the termination from the session.

$$\delta_8 = \bigwedge_{Cat(t_1) = SM, Cat(t_2) = PM} ImEnable((t_1, delete), (t_2, leave)) \qquad (8)$$

Communication Scope Inside and Outside a Collaboration Group

Only Group Members are allowed to Communicate. The rule represented by Equation 9 indicates that the participants must join before sending and receiving information. This is a local interdependency rule.

$$\delta_9 = \bigwedge_{Cat(t_1)=PM, Cat(t_2)=IM} \left(\begin{array}{c} Pred((t_1, join), (t_2, send)) \quad \wedge \\ Pred((t_1, join), (t_2, receive)) \end{array} \right) \qquad (9)$$

Only Connected Group Members are allowed to Communicate. The rule of Equation 10 shows that the participants can neither receive any more nor send information after their disconnection.

$$\delta_{10} = \bigwedge_{Cat(t_1)=PM, Cat(t_2)=IM} \left(\begin{array}{l} Inhib((t_1, leave), (t_2, send)) \quad \wedge \\ Inhib((t_1, leave), (t_2, receive)) \end{array} \right) \tag{10}$$

3.3 Remote Dependency Management Rules

Only One Chairman at the Same Time. Equations 11 and 12 represent the rules which define the transfer of the chairman role between participants. Equation 11 uses the previously defined predicate InSequence, and ensures that all the grants and the accepts are sequentially ordered (i.e. we cannot have concurrent accepts or grants).

$$\delta_{11} = \bigwedge_{Cat(p)=Cat(q)=Part} \left(\bigwedge_{a,b \in \{grant, accept\}} InSequence((p, a), (q, b)) \right) \tag{11}$$

Equation 12 indicates that a participant can accept the role of the chairman if, and only if, the chairman of the session granted him this role. This property is ensured by two predicates, Accept and Grant, that ensure that two consecutive grant (resp accept) actions must separated by an accept (resp. grant).

$$\delta_{12} = \bigwedge_{Cat(p)=Cat(q)=Part} (Accept(p,q) \wedge Grant(p,q)) \tag{12}$$

With:

$$Grant(p,q) = \forall x, y.(P_{(p,grant)}(x) \wedge P_{(q,grant)}(x) \wedge x \leq y)$$
$$\implies (\exists z.(P_{(q,accept)}(z) \wedge x \leq z \leq y)$$
$$Accept(p,q) = \forall x, y.(P_{(p,accept)}(x) \wedge P_{(q,accept)}(x) \wedge x \leq y)$$
$$\implies (\exists z.(P_{(p,grant)}(z) \wedge x \leq z \leq y)$$

4 Conclusion

We have presented a formal framework for multi-users multi-applications collaboration model which defines the coordination rules for dependency management during a cooperative session. We have identified and formalized three classes of coordination rules: internal, local, and remote dependency rules related respectively to intra-component, intra-site and intra-application dependencies. A session management system is in conformance with the coordination rules if the (internal, local and remote) events that modify the session's state are correctly ordered. We have applied the model to define the basic coordination rules of the Distributed Systems Engineering project. We have implemented a session management package, which is compliant to the coordination rules we have presented in this paper.

References

[1] L. Beca, G. Cheng, G. C. Fox, T. Jurga, K. Olszewski, M. Podgorny, P. Sokolowski, T. Stachowiak and K. Walczak. Tango - a Collaborative Environment for the World-Wide Web. Northeast Parallel Architectures Center, Syracuse University, New York, http://trurl.npac.syr.edu/tango/papers/tangowp.html , 1997. 160

[2] A. Chanbert, E. Grossman, L. Jackson and S. Pietrovicz. NCSA Habanero- Synchronous collaborative framework and environment, Software Development Division at the National Center for Supercomputing Applications, white paper, 1998. http://habanero.ncsa.uiuc.edu/habanero/. 160

[3] F. Costantini , C. Toinard, Collaborative Learning with the Distributed Building Site Metaphor. IEEE Multimedia juil-Sept 01.pp. 21-29. 160

[4] H.-P. Dommel et J. J. Garcia-Luna-Aceves, Network Support for Group Coordination, 4th World Multiconference on Systemics, Cybernetics and Informatics (SCI'2000), Orlando, FL. 160

[5] Dommel HP. et Garcia Luna Aceves J. J. 1997. Floor Control for multimedia conferencing and collaboration. Multimedia Systems (1997) 5:23-38. 160

[6] H. P. Dommel and J. J. Garcia Luna Aceves. Group Coordination Support for synchronous Internet collaboration, University of California, Santa Cruz, IEEE Internet Computing, pp. 74-80, Mars-Avril 1999. 160

[7] R. Hall, A. Mathur, F. Jahanian, A. Parkash, C. Rassmussen. CORONA: A Communication Service for Scalable, Reliable Group Collaboration Systems. International Conference on Computer Supported Cooperative Work, Cambridge , MA, USA, pp.140-149, 1996. 160

[8] ISAAC : Framework for Integrated Synchronous And Asynchronous Collaboration http://www.isrl.uiuc.edu/isaac/. 160

[9] Martelli A., "Distributed System Engineering". Data Systems in Aerospace - DASIA - 2001 Symposium, 28 May - 1 June 2001, Nice France. 165

[10] J. M. Molina-Espinosa , J. Fanchon , K. Drira. A logical model for coordination rule classes in collaborative sessions. IEEE Wetice International Workshop on Distributed and Mobile Collaboration (DMC'2003), Linz (Autriche), 9-11 Juin 2003, 5p. 159

[11] C. Schukmann, L. Kirchner, J. Schümmer, J. Haake, Designing Object-oriented synchronous groupware with COAST. International Conference on Computer Supported Cooperative Work, Cambridge , MA, USA, pp.30-38, 1996. 160

[12] TANGO Interactive (TM) http://www.webwisdom.com/Technologies/collaboration.html, http://trurl.npac.syr.edu/handout/tango.html. 160

[13] G. Texier, N. Plouzeau, Automatic Management of Sessions in Shared Spaces. International Conference on Parallel and Distributed Processing Techniques and Applications (PDPTA'99), Las Vegas (USA), 28 Juin - 1er Juillet 1999, Vol.IV, pp.2115-2121. 160

[14] E. Wilde, Group and Session Management. Thèse de doctorat ETH No. 12075, ETH Zürich, et Livre publié par Shaker Verlag en 1997 ISBN 3-8265-2411-X. 160

About the Value of Virtual Communities in P2P Networks

German Sakaryan[1], Herwig Unger[1], and Ulrike Lechner[2]

[1] Computer Science Dept.
University of Rostock, 18051, Rostock, Germany
{gs137, hunger}@informatik.uni-rostock.de
[2] Dept. for Mathematics and Computer Science
University of Bremen, 28359 Bremen, Germany
lechner@tzi.de

Abstract. The recently introduced peer-to-peer (P2P) systems are currently the most popular Internet applications. This contribution is intended to show that such decentralized architecture could be served as a suitable structure to support virtual communities.

This contribution is focused on the social and economic importance of topological aspects of P2P network communities. It shows that, besides the content offered, the structures of the connections and interactions of the users play an important role for the value of the whole network.

Different from social networks, the topology of P2P systems can be influenced by different working automatically in the background algorithms. The paper introduced distributed content-oriented and traffic-oriented methods for doing so. The simulation shows the results for the structure- and topology-evolution in the community.

1 Introduction

Significant research efforts have recently been invested in the development of peer-to-peer (P2P) computing systems. The interaction protocols distinguish P2P systems from client-server systems as all nodes that can contribute as peers, i.e., with the same rights and obligations in the interaction. P2P systems typically have a dynamic topology, unintermediated interaction and autonomy of all nodes. Peer-to-peer networks are organized as logical networks at the application level. Peers directly communicate with each other without using any central entity. Peer-to-peer networks have this basic principle in common with the basic interaction architecture of virtual communities, where the members contribute information, establish an atmosphere of trust and increase the stickiness or loyalty to a business model. In peer-to-peer networks, the contribution goes one step further. The members of the network act as content, service and network managers.

Communities are constituted by a set of agents and a medium. The medium assigns the agents a place in terms of rights and obligations [1, 2]. We employ the term virtual community to refer to communities that utilize mostly electronic

F. F. Ramos, H. Unger, V. Larios (Eds.): ISSADS 2004, LNCS 3061, pp. 170–185, 2004.

media for interaction. Virtual communities may emerge when people get involved in repeated, emotional on-line interaction [3]. Virtual communities can utilize centralized servers and only recently- distributed peer-to-peer platforms as their media for interaction. The interest in P2P has at least two reasons. First, the communities which share files with their enormous popularity utilize p2p systems as their platform. Second, p2p systems have a lot of advantages also for other kinds of communities, e.g., communities with interest of sharing information or transaction communities.

In this paper, we are particularly interested in the question that how far decentralized structures can support virtual communities (Sect. 2). We discuss P2P networks and their benefits and challenges (Sect. 3). We analyze content management in virtual communities and propose an integrated approach to manage contents and community on a peer-to-peer network in order to increase its value (Sect. 4). The empirical results are presented in Section 5. The paper is concluded with a discussion (Sect. 6).

2 Benefits and Challenges of P2P

Most communities rely on their interaction in a shared space. The community platform is typically implemented as a platform on the server. Some communities, such as the USENET used to rely on replicated structure). This shared space is typically a centralized structure. It can be attacked; it need to be implemented and maintained; and the cost must be covered. The one who provides the platform has a position to manage and even to exploit a community. For example, all the consumer communities are managed by the various on-line shops. Communities are so important that they realize on-line transactions: they positively influence the transaction-ere by establishing a trustworthy environment for transaction and help to establish a long-term relationship that can complete single transaction on a market. Moreover, they provide information for products and recommendations as well as reviewing knowledge that is invaluable for on-line transactions. Think of the value of the information consumers contribute, e.g., at Motleyfool.com, Ebay.com or Amazon.com [4].

The distributed nature attracts a lot of the potential users. According to different estimations, the size of the Gnutella network is in the range of 80-100,000 nodes (www.limewire.com) [5]. The number of the downloads of the SERVENT (SERver-cliENT) Kazaa Media Desktop is more than 200 million (March'2003) [6] with a growth of 100 million within 7 months. Such peer-to-peer communities share huge amount of data, which can hardly be shared by centralized systems. Napster is one example for this. The users contribute many of the resources for the sharing of files. The centralized server that is only responsible for directory services is fairly easy to implement and "cheap" to run. A centralized server that provides both content and directory services is prohibitively expensive to run.

The distributed and decentralized structure of peer-to-peer and in particular the design of current peer-to-peer systems bring a great number of challenges at the application level.

- **Services.** It is still unclear which service can be implemented in a decentralized way. Information search is still a central problem since existing approaches employ flooding-based mechanism that is not suitable for large systems. The scaling problem is crucial for scalability of peer-to-peer platforms.
- **Resources.** Even though Peer-to-Peer systems were introduced only a few years ago, peer-to-peer communities are now one of the most popular Internet applications and have become the major source of Internet traffic. According to [7], the estimated traffic in the Gnutella network (excluding file transfers) is about 330 TB/month (March'2001). The volume of generated traffic is an important obstacle for further growth. Moreover, the traffic is not an abstract size for the members of the Peer-to-Peer network. They experience the load of routing messages of frequent queries on the computers. Modern P2P system realizes traffic management of the single user, i.e., the user who decides on how much bandwidth and other resources could be contributed.
- **Relation content - social structure.** Currently most peer-to-peer systems are anonymous - this is partly due to the legal problems of file sharing and the lack of digital right management systems suitable for P2P systems. Quality management therefore is an issue. In communities it works over the relation content -social position of the one who contributes it (rating of contributions, rating of the reliability of transaction partners . . .). There is a danger that the quality of the content deteriorates since content is not related to people and their social structure that it enable quality management by "social pressure".
- **Positive feedback and network effects.** There is no relation between the contribution of the individual member of a p2p network and a reward for contributing to the network. There is no social status, or benefit in terms of resources. On the contrary - the individual contribution even demands more contribution of resources. For example, when one contributes thought after a piece of content, many users will access this file and this consumes resources from the contributor. There is no incentive to contribute. This leads to a deterioration of quality and quantity of available content. This is not a factor that contributes to the growth of communities [8].

The main challenge in the peer-to-peer systems is therefore the design of the interaction in an holistic sense: The P2P network, the interaction and the social network need to be designed so that content management becomes possible.

This however means that, to some extent, the social structure of the community must be mapped onto the platform and there needs to be implementation of services, that fits the decentralized structure of the networks. This structure must be adapted to the needs of the community. Therefore, this topology evolution includes the design of the network. We argue that this should be done in peer-to-peer style, i.e., in a decentralized way.

3   Contents in P2P Systems

Content and content management are the key to the success of any network. Content management on digital media and therefore in virtual communities and peer-to-peer networks differs from the content management approaches of conventional media. Subsequently we analyze the properties of content and the challenges of content management.

3.1   Characterization of Contents

Virtual communities utilize (mostly) electronic media for interaction. This electronic medium is often referred to as the community platform. The community platform plays an important role for the management of digital content. It structures and organizes the communication and makes the interaction persistent [9].

As the notion of content is closely related to medium that transfers it, content management on digital media cannot be separated from the management of the community that builds around the content. Moreover, the architecture of the community platform and its services influence content and community management.

In traditional one-way mass media, content is typically a product of the media industry. Newspaper articles, television spots and etc. are produced, packed, duplicated, and distributed by the media industry. A piece of content, such as a television show or a newspaper article is a self-contained unit. The traditional communication channels assemble pieces of content according to their format, and then copy and distribute the (packaged) content. This is changing through the Internet and its technology. Due to the characteristics of the Internet and its digital technology, content has a much broader meaning in the sense of information goods. Content on digital media can be characterized in terms of four aspects [10].

1. Content is digital. Most content is digital or have a digital counterpart. Foe example, mp3 format is a digital counterpart to analogue as well as other digital data formats in this case like compact disks and cassettes. Digital content can be distributed, processed and stored in high volumes by means of information technology. As the digital technology becomes commodity goods, anyone can easily create, pack, or modify content. Moreover, digital content is accessible to machines for all kinds of processing and distribution, which increases the availability of content and content management becomes a commodity, too. For example, all the peers distribute content and support through search and routing primitive functions in content management. Digital technology facilitates a new design of the whole value chain of content management [10]. Content cannot be separated from the media technology.

2. Content is linked. As the Internet can be seen as an electronic network, the content is embedded in and part of this network. This is mostly easily seen when one compares an isolated web page to the page as a part of a Web site or an information system or an on-line application. An isolated site

or a single web page is of little utility or value - it will hardly be visited. However, when a page is linked, it will be accessed through customers and become valuable. In many cases, the value of the content results from a direct link from information to transaction. Hyperlinks between pure information on products to transaction services to buy those products [11]. Still, this content and its links need to be structured and organized [9]. Network and content management cannot be separated.

3. Content is interactive. As every participant is both a recipient and sender, the Internet allows interactivity in a much broader way than traditional media does. There is traditional passive content consumption as is usual with books, television, or broadcasting. However, unique to new media, there is also interactive content with interaction between user and application or among users. Interactive contents may solve problems presented to them and adapt themselves to users' needs. Therefore, the producer of content is not only the media industry, but potentially every participant on the Internet. As a consequence, content changes over time as the media and community interacting with it. Content management and interaction management cannot be separated.

4. Content is embedded in a social, economic and organizational environment. Individual content is sometimes very valuable for other participants. The Internet not only has the cultural function of information as found in traditional media, but also the economic function of commerce and the social function of community. This content spills over to these functions. In the Internet, everybody can provide information about products. The experience shared by consumers is considered more trustworthy and valuable than information provided by producers [4, 12]. Reviews and recommendations in on-line shops or at file-sharing communities are good examples of it (cf. the participatory product catalog of [12, 13, 4]). Content management and community management cannot be separated.

The above characteristics of content have several consequences on the entire value chain of the management of content. The participants play new roles in the creation of economic value [14, 10]. Particularly for electronic media, everybody can contribute contents due to the interactive nature of the channels. The sources of content are much broader, as every participant is a potential creator and sender of content. However, the Internet does not only allow one-to-many communication as in traditional media, but also many-to-one or many-to-many kinds of communication. Moreover, the means for processing facilitate management of the interaction by digital media. Herein, network, content and social environment of the community become inseparable.

3.2   Value of Virtual Communities for Content Management

Peer-to-Peer networks offer new possibilities for the communities and content management. As the content and social structure of a community are interwoven, content and community management in virtual communities need to be

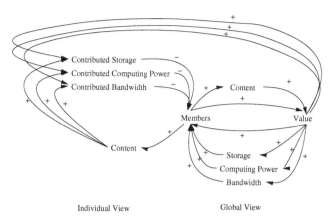

Fig. 1. Network and feedback effects in P2P networks

managed as an entity. In this respect, peer-to-peer networks differ from traditional centralized client server platforms. A key issue is hereby the benefit one obtained from contribution to a network. The relations are depicted in Fig. 1. In P2P systems there seems to be an inherent problem in the feedback that the individual gets. In every network, the value of the networks increases with the number of members. More members means more contents and more resources (bandwidth, storage and computing power). More content and more resources increase the value which again brings new members. This is the global perspective on the whole network. The individual perspective is to analyze the individual view on the feedback for the individual contributor. A high value allows a contribution of content. A higher value means that the individual can contribute more and still get value from the system. Contribution of content also means contribution of resources so that the content becomes available in the network. This contribution of resources positively correlates with the amount and attractiveness of the contributed content. This contribution, however, decreases the value of the network. The greater the number of members is, the more contribution of resources will be necessary to ensure content management and content accessibility to all members. This relation between number of members and contribution of resources makes it possibly unattractive for users to contribute to networks with a high number of members.

In communities on peer-to-peer networks, it is content, community and communication infrastructure that need to be managed in an integrated way.

The social network of the community – which exists outside the computer system – is the structure to which services, content relations and infrastructure need to adapt for an optimal quality parameters of the network and content management. Moreover, it is the correct reflection on the relations of the social network that builds the value of the network and makes it work. The community rewards the ones that contribute content and other resources through a positive feedback and an attractive social position in the network. In virtual communities, this is often the reason why many contribute – and adequate awareness of the social status provided. Communities in peer-to-peer networks need some sort of management so that the above mentioned challenges are overcome and only an integrated approach that includes community, content and network aspects seems to be adequate.

We propose an approach to community management which includes content-oriented network topology self-organization and content- oriented search. The reason behind is, that the most relations in a P2P network are formed by a number of point-to-point connections between peers. As a result, each peer is connected with a set of other peers typically called neighbors. We argue that these relations (topology) influence on the operations of P2P systems and on built above communities both from global and individual views. Since no peer is able to oversee this topology or to know all available information, our approach is decentralized to adapt this structure to the social dependencies of the considered community.

4   Influence of the Topology on the Community Operations

4.1   Basic Aspects

The above cited benefits can not be reality without technical entities. The topology of the community significantly influences the benefits brought by community to its members and includes the following aspects.

- **Communication Channels**. In order to participate in the community, every peer should be able to communicate with other community members. From the topology point of view, it means that out-degree (the number of available on-line neighbors) of any peer should be bigger than zero.
- **Reachability**. To insure high coverage of the community in the ideal case, each peer should be able to get content from any other peer. As well as there are no central entities providing directory service, message sent by a peer makes jumps (hops) from one peer to another until a required peer (or peer with required content) is found. Therefore, ideally, the topology directed graph should be strongly connected, which means that there is at least one direct path between any two peers.

  For real communities, it is almost impossible to achieve due to unpredictable arrival and departure of the peers. For practical purpose, any topology self-organizing algorithms should be able to increase peer's in-degree, and to increase number of the **connected pairs** (the pair of the node is considered connected if there is at least one direct path between them).
- **Reasonable Traffic**. Traffic in the communities is very important. It brings limitation for further growth of the system due to limited bandwidth capacity. Message which represents a user query is discarded if a peer can not handle it accordingly (overload situation). A network peer can be overloaded due to many reasons, where a "bad" topological structure plays an important role.

– **Time of the Search**. In spite of the advantages brought by decentralized systems, the data search is still a central problem. The search time depends on how effectively message routing algorithms use underlying topological structure. The famous approaches which use random forward or broadcast can cause high search time or high traffic. To improve this situation the content oriented search and respective content-oriented message forwarding algorithm (CF) [15] was proposed. The basic idea behind CF is that the peer forwards (routes) a message to the neighbor which stores the most similar content to the search query represented by the message.

4.2   Topology Self-Organization

The topology of a community is changed with time. The change is mostly caused by two main reasons. First, because of the uncoordinated and unpredictable addition and removal of nodes, these processes can be modeled by Poisson distribution and an exponential distribution accordingly [16, 17]. Second, algorithms may run and self-organize a community so that topology can be changed (cluster building, content oriented structure creation, traffic adaptation etc.). As far as search time and generated traffic are almost the main open problems of current P2P systems, two topology distributed algorithms were proposed: content-oriented restructuring and message flow control (MFC) [15, 18].

– **Content oriented restructuring**. Intuitively, in the human society, people who are interested in information will generally get faster, if they know other people with the same interests.
  As far as topology in human society reflects social connections between people, it makes sense to organize the topology of the P2P community in a way that connections reflect interests of the users represented by consumed and/or offered content. For example, to extract users of the same interests and connect them organizing closer-connected groups. For doing so, the following strategies to organize a neighborhood of peers are considered.
  - **Social strategy**. A peer keeps neighbors who share the most similar content to the one shared locally. A respective restructuring algorithm is called social restructuring (SR).
  - **Egoistic strategy**. A peer keeps neighbors who share the most similar content to the one user is interested in. User interests are represented by user's request history (consumed content). Accordingly -ER.
  - **Intergroup strategy**. A peer keeps neighbors who share the least similar content to the one shared locally. Accordingly -IR.
  The different strategies could be mixed (e.g. SER, SIR). In this case, neighborhood of a peer is divided between different strategies (in the given contribution equally). It should be noted, that the discovery of other peers in a network is done by traveling messages which are used for search [15]. In addition, search messages store data about visited peers. This data is used later for restructuring purposes.

– **Message flow control**. This kind of restructuring is caused by local traffic problems and leads to the creation of alternative paths around the overloaded nodes while controlling message flow to overloaded peers. Each peer constantly monitor its incoming message flow. If incoming traffic is bigger than some fixed level a peer sends warning messages (WMC) to predecessors. The data carried by a WMC includes a list of randomly selected outgoing neighbors of the overloaded peer, so the receiver may update its neighborhood by new peers creating bypaths. In addition, the receiver temporarily stops sending messages to overloaded peer.

Both approaches change the topology of the community dynamically, thus the changeable part of the P2P communities is ideally organized. Content restructuring uses knowledge about other peers which are visited by traveling messages used for search (IMC). In this way, extra traffic only for restructuring purpose is avoided. The content-restructuring ideally corresponds to the concept of the content oriented message forwarding. The creation of the content oriented topology may lead to a traffic concentration around nodes with the most requested information. In this case, the traffic restructuring is required. And vice versa, only traffic restructuring partially breaks content-oriented topology and may lead to increasing search time. That is why the combination of the two approaches is mostly indicated.

5   Empirical Results

In the given section, the influence of the proposed content-oriented topology self-organization, message flow control and content-oriented search algorithms on P2P community operations is evaluated. Especially two aspects are investigated:

– **Quality of Service (QoS)**. In the given contribution the quality of service is considered from user- perceived perspectives and represented through:
  - **Ratio of successful search queries to all search queries.** The query is successful if the respective message has found requested data and has reached starting peer-search initiator.
  - **Average number of hops per successful query.** This parameter depends on the topology of P2P as well as on how effectively routing mechanism uses it. The less hops are required in average to find requested info, the less traffic is generated and the less time is required for search.
  - **Ratio of discarded search queries to all search queries.** The queries discarded in congestion are considered.
  - **Average query rate.** This parameter indicates how many queries in average are sent by each network peer during statistic collection intervals.
– **Global Organization**. The influence of locally executed algorithms on global topological organization in P2P networks is studied. For doing so, the following sets of parameters are used:
  - **In-degree.** The in-degree influences on the traffic concentration and reflects number of incoming links.

- **Level of connectivity.** This parameter reflects "connectivity" aspects of a network. It represents a number of connected pairs of peers. This parameter is calculated as a number of connected peers divided by the maximal possible number of connected pairs calculated as n*n, where n -network size (number of peers).
- **Graph diameter.** The diameter of the graph indicates how close are peers to each other from number of overlay hops.
- **Number of changes caused by restructuring algorithm.** The target of a topology organization algorithm is to be able to create a reliable and stable topological structure. That is why the number of topological changes caused by restructuring algorithm is important parameter, which should be observable during the all simulation time.

In the given contribution the dynamic P2P network with static membership is considered. Such networks have constant peer population and dynamic is represented through changing topology. The similar behavior of algorithms was also observed in networks with dynamic membership.

To get reliable results, the size of a network must be large enough. On the other hand, simulating large communities becomes a problem since simulation time will rapidly increase. Considering both arguments, a community size of 2048 peer was chosen with neighborhood size - 10. The experiments were also conducted for 1024, 4096 and 8192 peers with different sizes of neighborhood (10 and 20 accordingly). The similar behavior was observed.

The simulation consists of the certain number of simulation steps typically 100. It will be shown later that majority of topological changes are done within the first 20 simulation steps. Each simulation step consists of the certain number of simulation cycles. By the end of one step, statistical data about community operations is collected and all messages which are still traveling are discarded to avoid "phantom messages" from the previous simulation step, which may influence the statistics. The next simulation step starts with the topology achieved during the last step. A simulation cycle is a big control loop, each peer sequentially receives a control. Number of such cycles within one simulation step is chosen equally to the number of peers in a network (2048). Thus a message has at least the theoretical possibility to visit all peers in a network.

To test the worst conditions each query is represented by only one message; no replication used; content is equally distributed and unique; and user requests are skewed to requesting popular content more often [15].

The initial topology of the community was created as a random graph, which may not be strongly connected with average in-degree less than 2. It is also assumed that peers are homogeneous from power, bandwidth and executed algorithms point of views.

All tested combinations of algorithms are presented in Table 1.

Each combination of the strategies is tested for the same initial network structure to compare system performance and investigate influence.

Table 1. Dynamic Networks with Static Membership: Tested Algorithms

Abbreviation	Comments
CF	content routing and no restructuring used
MFC+CF	study influence of MFC
SER+CF	study influence of content restructuring
SER+MFC+CF	study influence and used to compare strategies
SIR+MFC+CF	used to compare strategies
SR+MFC+CF	used to compare strategies
ER+MFC+CF	used to compare strategies

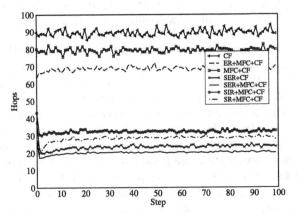

Fig. 2. Average Number of Hops per Successful Query

5.1 Quality of Service

The conducted experiments clearly demonstrate positive influence and effectiveness of proposed dynamic distributed message flow control algorithm. It improves situations in systems which use content-oriented topology organization as well as in systems which do not. The ratio of discarded messages (in congestions) in systems which use MFC is significantly lower vs. combinations without MFC (9% -CF vs. 4%-CF+MFC, 2.5% SER+CF vs. 1% SER+MFC+CF).

An application of content oriented organization algorithm (SER, SIR, SR, ER) significantly influences the quality of service in P2P networks. It significantly improves the ratio of successful search queries about 97% (SER+MFC+CF) - 90% (ER+MFC+CF) compared with average 83% (CF) or 87% (CF+MFC).

Due to the formation of content-oriented topology, the average number of hops needed for successful query to locate target pieces of data is about 20-30 hops (SER+MFC+CF, SER+CF, SR+MFC+CF, SIR+MFC+CF) compared with 80-90 hops (CF, MFC+CF) (Fig. 2). Since less hops are required to find data, traffic in the system is decreasing. Thus, the ratio of discarded messages is decreasing accordingly (e.g. 2.5% for CF+SER vs. 9% for CF).

At the same time, decreased number of hops causes the increase of query rate, which indicates how many queries each peer in a network can generate. The highest query rate is achieved for SER+MFC+CF - 32 in average. The increased query rate value indicates ability of the system to proceed more messages during the same time, while not decreasing ratio of successful queries. Thus, an user may request data more often.

Another interesting observation comes from analyzing different content oriented strategies to form a neighborhood. The combinations of algorithms which use social strategy to form content of a peer's neighborhood (e.g. SER+MFC +CF, SER+CF, SR+MFC+CF and SIR+MFC+CF) introduce lower number of hops required to locate a piece of data than pure egoistic strategy (ER+MFC +CF). The reason behind lies in the fact that mostly messages are routed using social part of peer neighborhood (or so-called social topology) in both combinations SER+MFC+CF and SIR+MFC+CF.

The pure egoistic strategy introduces high average number of hops. Even though all neighborhood is devoted to keep peers, which store the most similar content to user's interests. It may happen, that required piece of data cannot be located on direct neighbors. In this case, the further routing is required. During the simulation only peers which have direct neighbors keeping data which is asked by users of that peers may enjoy this egoistic strategy. Even if it happens during the simulation, it is not a case in real P2P systems, since users are not likely to find and download the same piece of data (file) from a network according to fetch-at-most once behavior [19]. Even during the simulation, the big part of the requests can not be satisfied by direct neighbors, so additional routing is required.

Accordingly, systems which utilize social strategy have bigger query rates, improved ratio of successful queries and decreased ratio of discarded queries. The pure social strategy (SR+MFC+CF) is better than pure egoistic. In the same time it presents a decreased quality of service compared with to SIR+MFC+CF or SER+MFC+CF combinations. These results are caused by the fact that users may be interested in the content which is different from the one which is locally stored and shared. This difference is included in principals of our simulation. If a generated query is targeting data which have nothing in common with locally stored content, the probability of having direct neighbors (for pure social strategy) which may have similar content to what query is looking for is very low. That is the reason that, in average, it is necessary to make more hops to find at least a group of peers storing content similar to target data. And then, the social topology is effectively used to route a message within a group.

The comparison demonstrates that the best combination of different strategies uses social and egoistic content-oriented strategies (in addition to MFC) to dynamically form a neighborhood. This combination (SER+MFC+CF) demonstrates the best quality of service in all investigated terms: successful ratio, discarded ratio, query rate, and the number of hops. The egoistic part of the neighborhood serves mainly to route a generated query as close as possible to the target group of peers storing interesting content. The social part of a neigh-

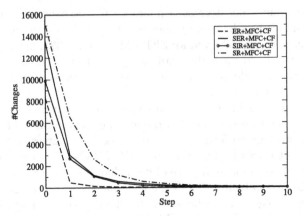

Fig. 3. Topological Changes Caused by Content Restructuring

borhood is in charge of routing within a group, which actually accounts the majority of routing.

5.2   Global Influence of Distributed Algorithms

One of the reasons behind delivered quality of service achieved by content-oriented topology self-organization lies in the improved network graph properties in addition to content oriented search.

The conducted experiments demonstrate that the topological changes caused by content oriented topology self-organization activity are decreasing with time. During the first 10 simulations steps a number of changes decreased down to zero for all of the tested content-oriented strategies (Fig. 3). Thus, the stable topological structure is achieved.

The number of isolated peers (those who have no predecessors) is decreasing with time for all content -oriented strategies except pure social one SR+MFC +CF (Fig. 4). In the initial network, 273 peers had no predecessors, which means that none of the peers kept them as outgoing neighbors. By the end of the simulation number of isolated peers as following: SER+MFC+CF -64, ER+MFC+CF -54, SIR+MFC+CF-130, SR+MFC+CF -313. For the best combination, the number of isolated peers was decreased more than 5 times.

These improvements are caused by virtual warehouse concept used by the developed routing algorithm [15]. Briefly speaking, messages met on the particular peer could use each data about visited peers. In this a way, there is a probability, that, if an isolated peer is active (generating many queries), it could be noticed by other peers in a network. The usage of that virtual warehouse is at the level of 20% of all routings.

The negative impact of pure social strategy SR+MFC+CF is caused by chosen simulation conditions. In these simulations, social interests of the peers (represented through stored and shared content) are very limited. Thus, only limited number of peers can be of interest to any other peer if they use only social

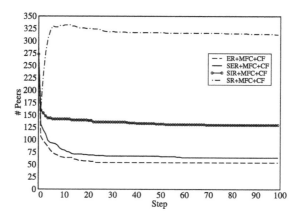

Fig. 4. Isolated Peer Dynamics

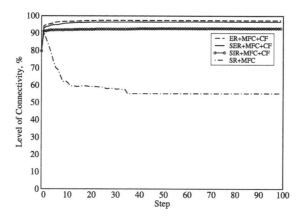

Fig. 5. Level of Connectivity

strategy. In more realistic environments, it could be assumed that this negative impact will disappear.

The wider interests (shared content) or more strategies peers have, the higher probability of integrating isolated peers discovered during a search. The more queries an isolated peer generates, the higher the probability of meeting those queries with queries coming from the other peers and the higher the probability of isolated peer discovery and integration will be. The integration helps to utilize peer resources for content sharing and routing.

During the simulation, the level of connectivity is increasing from about 80% to 92-97%, striving to maximum 100% value (Fig. 5). This is a direct outcome of decreased number of isolated peers as well as of increased number of directed paths in a network. As the same, pure social strategy has a negative impact.

The conducted experiments have demonstrated positive impact of the proposed topology organization algorithms on network graph diameter. The initial value of 23 was decreased to 7, which reflects the distances from overlay hop perspective in modeled network.

For all content-oriented strategy, dynamic of the average in-degree of a peer is almost the same. During the first two simulation steps, the average in-degree grew from 1.99 -for initial network up to 10 (maximum size of a neighborhood).

Experiments proved our expectation that topology of the community influences on the QoS and users can get benefits from membership. We have also proved that local behavior of the individual peers has global impacts Running locally algorithms are able to form a predictable content- oriented network structure with improved topological properties. It was also confirmed, that using community and content aspects (both from social and egoistic perspective) on a network level to organize operations of a P2P system brings benefit to its members.

6 Conclusion

The contribution discussed about the social and economic importance of topological aspects of P2P network communities. It shows that, besides the content offered, the structures of the connections and the interaction of the users play an important role for the value of the whole network.

Different from social networks, the topology of P2P systems can be influenced by different working automatically in the background algorithms. The paper introduced content-oriented and traffic-oriented methods for doing so. With a simulation, the results for the structure- and topology-evolution in the community are shown.

In future work, this algorithms should be included in real systems like Gnutella or KaZaa to prove their efficiency finally.

References

[1] Beat F. Schmid. A new model of media. In *Proc. Research Symposium on Emerging Electronic Markets, Maastricht*, 1997. 170
[2] Ulrike Lechner and Beat F. Schmid. Logic for media — the computational media metaphor. In Ralph Sprague, editor, *Hawaiian Int. Conf. on System Sciences (HICSS 1999)*. IEEE Press, 1999. 170
[3] H. Rheingold. *The virtual community: homesteading on the electronic frontier.* Addison-Wesley, 1993. 171
[4] J. Hagel III and A. Armstrong. *Net Gain: Expanding markets through virtual communities.* Harvard Business Press, 1997. 171, 174
[5] LimeWire LLC. http://www.limewire.com, March 2003. 171
[6] Kazaa. http://www.kazaa.com, June 2003. 171
[7] Matei Ripeanu and Ian Foster. Mapping the Gnutella network: Macroscopic properties of large-scale peer-to-peer systems. In *Peer-to-Peer Systems, First International Workshop, IPTPS 2002, Revised Papers*, volume 2429 of *Lecture Notes in Computer Science*, pages 85–93, Cambridge, MA, USA, March 2002. Springer-Verlag, Berlin. 172

[8] Ulrike Lechner, Johannes Hummel, and Claus Eikemeier. Business model peer-to-peer. is there a future beyond filesharing. In Peter Kropf, Herwig Unger, and Dietmar Tutsch, editors, *Proc. of the First Conference on Design, Automatization and Simulation of Distributed Systems*. SCS, 2003. 9 pages on CD-Rom. 172

[9] Katarina Stanoevska-Slabeva and Beat F. Schmid. Community supporting platforms. *EM - Electronic Markets. The International Journal of Electronic Markets and Business Media*, 10(4), 2000. 173, 174

[10] Johannes Hummel und Ulrike Lechner. The community model of content management. a case study of the music industry. *JMM – The International Journal on Media Management*, 3(1):4–15, 2001. www.mediajournal.org. 173, 174

[11] Cal Shapiro and Hal Varian. *Information Rules: A Strategic Guide to the Network Economy*. Harvard Business School, 1999. 174

[12] Petra Schubert. *Virtuelle Transaktionsgemeinschaften im Electronic Commerce: Management, Marketing und Soziale Umwelt*. Josef Eul Verlag, 1999. 174

[13] Petra Schubert and Mark Ginsburg. Virtual communities of transaction: The role of personalization in electronic commerce. *EM - Electronic Markets. The International Journal of Electronic Markets and Business Media*, 10(2), 2000. 174

[14] Ulrike Lechner and Beat F. Schmid. Business model community. the blueprint of MP3.com, Napster and Gnutella revisited. In Ralph Sprague, editor, *Proc. of the 34th Int. Hawaii Conference on System Sciences (HICSS 2001)*. IEEE Press, 2001. 174

[15] German Sakaryan and Herwig Unger. Topology evolution in P2P distributed networks. In *IASTED: Applied Informatics (AI 2003)*, pages 791–796, Innsbruck, Austria, 2003. 177, 179, 182

[16] Gopal Pandurangan, Prabhakar Raghavan, and Eli Upfal. Building low-diameter P2P networks. In *42th IEEE Symp. on Foundations of Computer Science*, pages 56–64, Las Vegas, USA, 2001. 177

[17] Jacky Chu, Kevin Labonte, and Brian Levine. Availability and locality measurements of peer-to-peer file systems. In *SPIE ITCom: Scalability and Traffic Control in IP Networks*, volume 4868, July 2002. 177

[18] German Sakaryan and Herwig Unger. Influence of the decentralized algorithms on topology evolution in P2P distributed networks. In *Design, Analysis, and Simulation of Distributed Systems (DASD 2003)*, pages 12–18, Orlando, USA, 2003. 177

[19] Krishna P. Gummadi, Richard J. Dunn, Stefan Saroiu, Steven D. Gribble, Henry M. Levy, and John Zahorjan. Measurement, modeling, and analysis of a peer-to-peer file-sharing workload. In *19th ACM Symposium on Operating Systems Principles (SOSP-19)*, Bolton Landing, NY, USA, Oct 2003. 181

Search in Communities:
An Approach Derived from the Physic Analogue
of Thermal Fields

Herwig Unger and Markus Wulff

Fachbereich Informatik
Universität Rostock, Rostock, Germany
{hunger,mwulff}@informatik.uni-rostock.de

Abstract. Peer-to peer communities are used to share information between users with common interests. This article describes an approach to locate nodes which are frequently accessed and therefore keep very new and/or important information for the community. Using an approach derived from the physic analogue of thermal field, the search for this attractive nodes becomes faster and creates a self organizing system for a more efficient information management.

1 Introduction

Nowadays, the Internet appears to be an important medium for the exchange of information in different languages. In this environment, the client-server architecture dominates the landscape as the most commonly used system. The major part of available services in the Internet are offered by a central service provider. On the other hand, peer-to-peer (P2P) systems becoming to play a more and more important role. These are networks consisting of machines which are more or less equal. Each member node can act as a server as well as a client.

P2P systems have a completely decentralized architecture which introduces some disadvantage caused by the lack of central instances. Different strategies for locating resources are required. On a central server or catalog, the client can directly ask for a certain service. In peer-to-peer systems, all resources are scattered over the whole network. Therefore, a search for the required resources becomes necessary. The situation becomes even more difficult, as no member of the network necessarily knows all other members. It means that special algorithms are needful [3, 4].

In a so called P2P-community, all members are considered to have common interests and offer or request resources which are probably interesting to all members of this community. Nevertheless, a keyword search for services or information would probably not be satisfactory due to the lack of a common vocabulary. It can be an entry point to find related information. Every user may give the same thing a different name or affiliation.

In the following sections, the community concept is analyzed more deeply and the thermal filed idea is explained in detail.

F. F. Ramos, H. Unger, V. Larios (Eds.): ISSADS 2004, LNCS 3061, pp. 186–196, 2004.

2   Main Ideas

The introduction and [2] describe how users can build up communities and use these structures. Furthermore, it was figured out how cross-connections between different communities can be made and used by the members.

For example, built of billions of Web pages as nodes connected by hyper-links the World Wide Web can be regarded as a P2P network community. If any Web pages are considered, it seems that a cycle of life of any page can be defined in the following manner.

1. A new site is developed according to the need that new information must be presented.
2. The Web page will be updated, in case the user is interested in such a change.
3. The support of the Web page was interrupted through rough changes, but the page still exists.
4. The page has removed from the Web (but search engines may still index it for a longer period).

The existence of these life cycles is supported by the considerations made in [1]. From the above content it is clear that every phase in the given life cycle is defined by the respective activity. Altogether, the following activities could be identified, which may give hints about the actuality, timeliness and importance of a document in the Web.

− the number of changes/updates of a document in a given period,
− the number of successful search operations having a document as result,
− the number of access operations to a given document,
− the number of links contained in a document or
− the number of links pointing to the document.

Nevertheless, the problem of an effective search still leaves room for improvement. Normally, a user searching the Web seeks documents which have similar (but not an equal) content to his own. Therefore it is necessary to follow the links from the respective user and reach, after some hops, the required information. However, the problem is that the more nodes were visited, the more (exponentially more) suitable links are known to the user. It is reasonable to assume that many users browsing the Web or community content are looking for "what's new". Search engines commonly used in the Web, like Google, are of limited use here. The user can only search by known keywords for new content.

The search for new content is usually not taken into account by search engines currently available. If a user of a community is a member for a longer time, he might want to know which resource was recently updated or which node has the newest information.

In this article, an approach is introduced to locate special nodes inside a P2P community. These nodes can be new, very frequently accessed, recently updated or may have a long uptime. The main idea is to enable the user to locate such attractive nodes efficiently. This is realized by adding a "temperature" value to every node. This temperature value is increased with the number of accesses, number of new information on this node or other criteria. A small part of the temperature of one node vests in its neighbors and therefore propagates over the community and a temperature field like shape is build. This temperature gradient leads the search requests directly to the temperature peak. Thus, the most attractive nodes of a community can be found efficiently.

3   The Search Algorithm

Using the above method, it is now helpful to the idea using an effect known from the physics. There, any dynamics of small particles (e.g. in a gas) are represented in the temperature of the medium, which is defined to be the average speed of the particles. Using this analogue, it might make a sense to speak about the temperature of a node/page in the Web. Hereby, the "temperature" may be defined through the intensity of the activities/changes connected through a node in the community.

Further developing this idea it becomes clear that through thermal conduction a high temperature of any part of a whole body affects a spatial dispersion of heat in the body around the part and is not a dot-like phenomenon. Convection and radiation results in the heated part which has the highest temperature in the environment, while the temperature of the remaining parts is sinking depending on the distance between the hot part and the measurement point. Heat generated from several hot parts will overlay their impact. Last but not least, any part of a body will become colder if no more heat will be fed.

Finding the hottest part in a body means to follow the maximal temperature gradient in the body (resp. to the scalar field of temperature).

This model of heat distribution can be easily applied to a Web environment, when assuming that communities exist and every node will cooperate with others to contribute to the success of the whole community.

Remember, every node is considered to be a part of the whole body called the Web community. It stores its actual temperature related to one of the above criteria in a common accessible data structure. Whenever an access to a given node is made, the access operation acts like a temporary connection to this node and allows the transport of a special amount of heat to the accessing node. This causes a heating of the accessing neighbor node. It is clear that the neighbor node can never reach the temperature of the origin of heat.

Different from the physic process, the accessing node is able to remember the temperature a neighbor has had during the last access. In such a manner, any request arriving at this node can be transferred to the 'hottest' neighbor kept in the memory of the considered node. Finally, a continued decrease of the actual and kept node temperatures models the effect of the described loss of temperature.

The intended method can be well used in the community environment, since the used message chain communication mechanism (see also [2] and [5]) ensure a frequent contact of different machines. Such a message chain is an extended communication mechanism, which transfers information from the source node by sending the information successively from one node to one of its (direct) neighbors until a suitable target node is reached.

Generally, a message chain contains the address of the original node and a hop counter beside the data or the requested operation itself. The hop counter is decreased every time the message is forwarded to the next node to ensure that this operation is finite. In accordance to its contents, a message can cause any kind of action at every way point as well as at the destination node and will be forwarded to a chosen neighbor in each case, unless the hop counter has reached zero. Thus, every node of the network is able to find information at previously unknown nodes and learn about any other node in the community. Since the forwarding procedure of the message chain is normally a random procedure, every node of the community can be reached with a certain probability. Therefore, a probabilistic search over the whole community can be realized.

If a temperature field approach is used, the random forward of a message chain must be replaced with a temperature depending method. The hop counter of the message must be high enough to reach any maximum and the temperature of each neighbor y of the node x is kept in the neighborhood warehouse. The message here also contains an array to keep the already found maximums. Thus, it can be assured that the already known maximums are recognized. To enable the message to locate every (or almost every) maximum, a randomness must be introduced again. Otherwise, the temperature gradient will always lead the message to the same (local) maximum. Therefore, the message is randomly forwarded with the probability of p_r.

The following algorithm is periodically executed on each node x of the community:

1. Initialize all values of the node (all node temperatures are set equal 0).
2. Update the kept temperature of the current node x $\theta(x)$ depending on the respective access and update activities made since the last update or compute $\theta(y) = \theta(y) \cdot e^{-\lambda t}$, if no update or access operations were made.
3. Decrease the kept node temperatures $\theta(y)$ from all neighborhood nodes y of x, $(y \in N(x))$ by $\theta(y) = \theta(y) \cdot e^{-\lambda t}$.
4. Repeat, until a message chain is arriving or the next node update time is reached.
5. If a message chain was received
   (a) With the probability of p_r select a node $Next\_node$ randomly from the warehouse $N(x)$ and goto 5c.
   (b) If there is a node $y \in N(x)$ in the set of neighbors of x, $N(x)$, with $\theta(y) > \theta(Next\_node)$ set $Next\_node = y$ otherwise determine $Next\_node$ randomly from the set of neighbors.
   (c) If $\theta(x) \leq \theta(Next\_node)$ or this node is already known as a maximum then forward the message chain to $Next\_node$ otherwise terminate the message chain, x is a new maximum. Send the answer to the origin and goto 6.

(d) Receive the temperature of $Next\_node$ with the acknowledgment of the forward operation and update the kept temperature $\theta(Next\_node)$ on x.[1]

(e) In case the temperature slope $\theta(Next\_node) - \theta(x)$ is big enough (i. e. $\geq const \cdot \theta(x)$), increase $\theta(x)$ by a given, fixed value corresponding to the amount of transported heat[2].

6. If the next node update time is reached then goto 2, otherwise goto 4.

The above described method makes sure that the temperature field is built up and will be maintained by the nodes as well as the fast forwarding of a message chain containing a search request to the "hottest" areas of the community. Some experimental results are given in section 4.

4   Experimentation

4.1   Simulation Setup

A simulation was set up in order to explore the above discussed methods. It is clear that the efficiency of the described method depends on the development of the temperature field in the community. Therefore, a community with 1024 resp. 4096 nodes was used in the simulation. The respective structure was built by using the edge-reassignment-method described in [1].

In every run of the simulation loop, the temperature of all nodes was calculated according to the algorithm. Some of the measurements were made to get the impression how the temperature field is developing over time. For the measurement of the search times in the thermal field, the field was kept in a stable state to achieve comparable results. It can be assumed that the changes in the thermal field are going slower than a search for a maximum.

Figure 1 shows the tool used for the thermal field simulation. It has some widgets on the right panel to adjust the simulation parameters and on the left side the graphical representation of the P2P network community. To get a reasonable picture, the number of nodes was set very low. The structure of the network can be seen in the graphic as well. The nodes are placed on the outer ring.

4.2   Results and Discussion

At the beginning, one or more machines have a high initial temperature (100), all other machines were initialized with a value (0) representing that no changes were made on these nodes. Now every machine of the community starts its search for changes in the community, i. e. it searches the hottest node in the community. Through the activities of the message chain the temperature field develops.

---

[1] Note, that this vary from the behavior of the continuously dispersing temperature field.

[2] This is another, strong simplification to the physic model, but it shortens the necessary computation and acts in a similar, suitable manner.

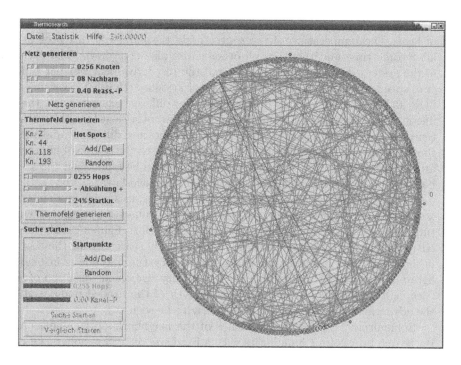

Fig. 1. Screenshot of the used temperature field simulation tool

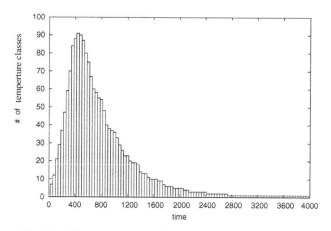

Fig. 2. Characterization of the built temperature field

Figure 2 shows, how the number of distinct and different temperature classes on all machines of the system is changing depending on the (simulation) time. At the beginning, this number is very low, but more and more nodes get higher temperatures through the system activities. Because of the required slope, different temperatures can be distinguished according to the distance from the source of heat. The temperature of the source node is sinking, so this process stops after some time and therefore all other nodes also cool down. The parameter of the system (the heat conductance and the respective heat loss per time unit (i. e. speed of cooling down) and number of system activities) determines, how high and broad the curve will be. The more different classes exist, the more fine-grained decisions can be made later. The lower the heat loss, the further the temperature field will cause a measurable temperature difference and therefore the more machines can directly detect a short way to the source of high temperature. Hereby, it is clear that high temperatures can be found near the source of heat and that the impact of different heat sources overlaps.

Besides the observations in accordance to physics, it is much more interesting how the search procedure in this system can be influenced using the temperature field. Figure 3 shows the respective results. Both figures clearly show the advantage, if the message chains are not randomly searching for the "hot spot" in the community but using the additional temperature parameter instead. Subfigure 3(a) shows the influence of the community size on the duration of search. Although both curves show significant growth of the needed number of steps, the advantage of the new method is clearly to be seen.

Subfigure 3(b) shows the influence of the neighborhood warehouse size on the search process in communities with a fixed size of 1024 members. Of course, problems exist for very small warehouse sizes due to the low connectivity of the graph. Therefore, the necessary search time becomes very high in this case. With a growing warehouse size, there are more alternatives on each node to reach another one, so the probability is also higher to find the "hot spot" in the network. Because of the good dispersion of the temperature field and good possibilities to distinguish temperatures on the way to the search target, this fact does not influence our new method very much. In such a manner, the use of our new method is indicated especially, if the warehouse size is small compared with the size of the whole community. This result seems to be very important to Web communities, since more and more nodes will be added while the memory of the machines keeps relatively unchanged.

In a community with many active members exist most probably more than one temperature maximum. Therefore, the search message is not in every case forwarded following the temperature gradient. If a new maximum is found, the message is returned to the node which has sent the request. To find all maximums, this path must be left from time to time. The figure 4 shows approximate search time to find 5, 10, ..., 50 maximums depending on the probability p_r that the message not following the link with the highest temperature.

If p_r is low or high, it takes long to discover all maximums in the community. In the first case, because the search message is always heading for the one maximum, the temperature gradient leads it to and in the second case, the community is searched almost randomly. Thus, the advantage of following the temperature gradient to find a maximum can not take effect. The best results were achieved with a probability around 0.5.

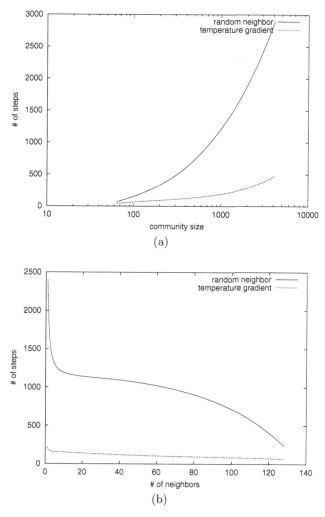

Fig. 3. Simulation of the search procedure using randomly forwarded message chains and message chains following the temperature gradient; 3(a) depending on the community size, 3(b) depending on the number of warehouse entries and a fixed community size of 1024 machines

The next example (Fig. 5) shows, how long it takes to find 32 maximums by using different values for p_r. Again, a probability around 0.5 shows the best results. And another characteristic is to be seen in this figure. The first maximums are found after a short time. It takes quite a long time, to find the last one. The search message starts always from the same node and some maximums can only be reached if the message is randomly forwarded.

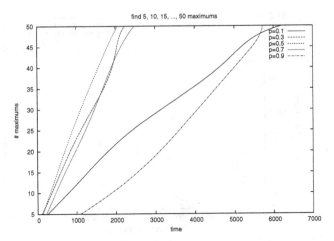

Fig. 4. The time needed to find all of 5, 10, ..., 50 maximums depending on the probability p_r that the search message does not follow the temperature gradient

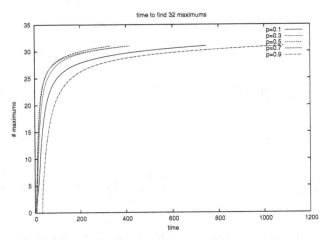

Fig. 5. Progression while searching 32 existing maximums depending on the probability p_r that the search message is forwarded randomly

The last figure (6) clearly shows that the search time for a different number of maximums is shortest with a value of p_r around 0.5.

The simulation results show that the approach works and can be used to find maximums in a community. In some cases, not all maximums were found. This depends on the structure of the underlying peer-to-peer network which is also a proximity of a real world network. However, it is mostly not necessary to find all maximums for the mentioned applications.

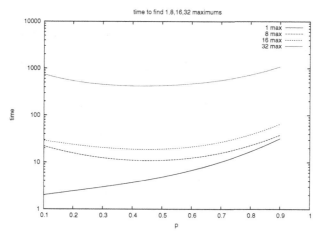

Fig. 6. The search time versus probability p_r for locating 1, 8, 16 and 32 maximums

Finally, a few words about trust and honesty. One weak point of the approach introduced in this article is, that there is no way to prevent the nodes from faking their temperature and thus becoming very attractive. This can be inhibited by a rating mechanism. For instance, only if a node has successfully downloaded information the source nodes temperature will be increased instead of just counting the accesses to that node. The basic idea of the thermal field approach is not affected by this problem, though.

5 Summary and Outlook

With simulation, it could be demonstrated that the information given from a dynamic scalar field may be used to improve the information management and organization in a community in a large distributed system. Hereby, the dispersion of the field depends on the communication activities between the nodes. It is normally fairly high in a collaborative environment given by communities (and the used message chain communication mechanism within).

The presented results are the first ones in an ongoing research. Probably there are much more applications in distributed systems, which might use the merit of the described approach, e. g. load balancing algorithms based on a fast distribution of load information of all participating nodes. Suitable applications and start point must be figured out and considered more detailed.

In addition, it was assumed in this paper that the community is a homogeneous one, i. e. that all members have the same set of parameters influencing especially the dispersion of the field. Future simulation and application should take into account that personalized parameter set may result in a more detailed adaptation of the search results to the belongings of the community structure.

References

[1] N. Deo and P. Gupta. World Wide Web: A Graph Theoretic Approach. CS TR-01-001, University of Central Florida, 2001. 187, 190

[2] H. Unger and T. Böhme. Distribution of information in decentralized computer communitites. In A. Tentner, editor, *ASTC High Performance Computing*, Seattle, Washington, 2001. 187, 188

[3] H. Unger, P. Kropf, G. Babin, and T. Böhme. Simulation of search and distribution methods for jobs in a Operating System (WOS). In SCS A. Tentner, editor, *ASTC High Performance Computing*, pages 253–259, Boston, 1998. 186

[4] H. Unger and M. Wulff. Concepts for a decentralized search engine for p2p-networks. In *11th Euromicro Conference on Parallel, Distributed and Network based Processing*, pages 492–499, Genua, Italia, 2003. 186

[5] M. Wulff and H. Unger. Message Chains as a New Form of Active Communication in the WOSNet. In A. Tentner, editor, *ASTC High Performance Computing*, Washington, 2000. 188

A Component-Based Design Approach
for Collaborative Distributed Systems

Francisco Moo-Mena* and Khalil Drira

Laboratoire d'Analyse et d'Architecture des Systèmes (LAAS-CNRS)
7, Av. du Colonel Roche - 31077 Toulouse, Cedex 04 - France
{fjmoomen,drira}@laas.fr
http://www.laas.fr

Abstract. In this paper we propose the Cooperative Component Approach (CCA), for the design of Collaborative Distributed Software (CDS). In this approach, we propose initially an analysis based on functional requirements necessary to the design of CDS. The functionalities are structured according to three functional levels: cooperation, coordination, and communication. We introduce the concept of "cooperative component" for the implementation of functional requirements into the suggested levels. The inherent aspects in the design of cooperative components are managed in a formal way by introducing a notation based on the Architecture Description Language Darwin. In order to prove its feasibility, we applied our CCA approach to the design of an application that supports the activity of collaborative document editing.

1 Introduction

During last years component-based development has taken a significant rise in the field of the software in general and particularly for distributed software systems. Thus, many projects and prototypes were developed to consolidate this new technology. So that, this new paradigm promises a revolution in the way of designing and developing distributed applications, comparable to the evolution of the procedural approach towards the object-based approach.

In agreement with [1], we view a component as "a unit of composition with contractually specified interfaces and explicit context dependencies, which can be deployed independently and is subject to composition by third parties". In this manner, starting from the composition of multiple components, it is possible to build applications much easier to maintain and to evolve.

In a particular way, main efforts are given to take benefit from inherent advantages of the component approach in the design of CDS. In this direction, it is now assumed that this new paradigm is important to answer the most significant requirements to this type of systems. However, being a relatively recent paradigm, nowadays there exist no development standard of CDS according to component-based approach.

---

* First author thanks PROMEP and UADY financial support, under grant UADY-117 for the accomplishment of this work.

F. F. Ramos, H. Unger, V. Larios (Eds.): ISSADS 2004, LNCS 3061, pp. 197–206, 2004.

Thus, often the development of CDS is based simply on the intuitions or the experiences of teams in charge of this development. This is at the origin in the majority of the cases of applications strongly attached to vendor technologies. This fact involves obviously the generation of applications that are not flexible, that are difficult to maintain and to evolve [2].

In this paper, we propose a new approach, called the Cooperative Component Approach (CCA), for the design of CDS. This approach is based on an analysis of the functional requirements necessary to the design of this kind of systems.

We propose to structure these requirements according to three functional levels widely accepted in the literature [3],[4],[5],[6] related to the design of CDS, namely, cooperation, coordination and communication. Then, we define the cooperative component design concept to facilitate the implementation of the collaborative application requirements in the suggested levels.

The inherent aspects in the design of cooperative components, in particular the definition, and the composition of their interfaces are managed in a formal way by defining a notation based on the Architecture Description Language (ADL) Darwin [7] which constitutes a reference in this field.

And, finally, so as to prove its feasibility in the development of CDS, we apply our approach to the design of a distributed application in the collaborative work domain, which supports the activity of collaborative document editing.

The remainder of the paper is structured in the following way: section 2 corresponds to the analysis of the state of the art, and presents the results of the study of the recent research works with regard to the software development using the component-based approach. Section 3 describes the CCA approach. Section 4 applies CCA approach to the design of a collaborative document editing system. Finally, we present the conclusion and future work.

2   Software Development According to Existing Component-Based Approaches

The DSC (Distributed Component Software) [8] is a framework and an environment of development, which supports the implementation of distributed component-based communication architectures. In DSC, the components are self-contained packages of code that can be linked dynamically into a program. The components offer their functionality through operational interfaces. Moreover, the components can be grouped to form composite components.

In [9], the authors describe a framework for the development of component-based applications, which separates in three views the concepts of architecture, component, and infrastructure of distributed objects and defines the existing relations between them. The view of architecture defines the components in the system, their functionalities, and their way of interacting. The view of components refers to the composition and implementation of components. And, the view of infrastructure of objects refers to the communication between components with specific parameters of quality of service, such as performance, reliability, and safety.

Jarzabek et al. [2] propose an environment of development of applications based on an approach of generative programming, with an aim of contributing with the customization and the evolution of the components which require much flexibility. In agreement with their work, the generative programming refers to various analyses making it possible to handle programs in a meta-level, such as the generators of applications, the transformation of systems, the treatment of macros and the automatic assembly of systems.

The CORBA Component Model (CCM) [10] is the answer of the OMG (Object Management Group) in regard with the component technology. In the CCM context, attributes and ports define a component. The attributes represent the configurable properties of the components. The ports represent the interfaces provided or required by the components.

The CoCoWare .NET Architecture [11] is defined within the framework of the GigaCSCW project of the Telematica Instituut in the Netherlands. The principal goal of this architecture is to help designers and developers to create the cooperative software, which matches the needs for a specific cooperative group. To achieve these goals, they define the following four services: enabling services, conference management services, communication and collaboration services, and coordination services.

2.1   Discussion

Nowadays, in the literature there is a lack of complete results for component-based collaborative software design methodologies. Moreover, the majority of the proposals define the components starting from the composition of class libraries by applying various strategies, which contribute to the necessary adaptation for the system [8],[2].

The framework proposed by [9] offers an appropriate high-level structure for the analysis of definition and interaction between components. On the other hand, in this proposal there are no formal aspects for description of components.

It is not efficient for us to use the CORBA abstract model of component, which is flat (only one description level is possible). In this model, it is not possible to design composite components (aggregation of components), which are themselves components and thus handled in a similar way.

The proposal of CoCoWare architecture does not define an original approach of description and of assembly of components and, on the contrary, the basic components proposed limit its level of flexibility.

3   The Cooperative Component Approach

In this section we present the CCA approach for the design of CDS.

3.1   Three Functional Level Structure

The first part of our proposal requires the development of an application functional analysis. This analysis must be structured in agreement with the three functional categories identified in CDS, i.e., the cooperation, coordination, and communication levels.

This type of exercise enables us to structure the functionality required by the system and constitutes a good basis for the mapping of each functional level to the appropriate cooperative components in a rather simple way.

Moreover, with this structure, we can have a first vision in advance with regard to the support necessary for the functional and non-functional requirements, which provides us the CDS design.

3.2   Cooperative Component Design

In the second part of our approach, starting from the functional structuring we define the necessary components which provide the required functional support. For this, the first step aims to the design of elementary components, which offer support for the specific requirements of CDS. Then, by interconnecting the points of interaction of elementary components (interfaces and events) we define the components of higher-level called cooperative components.

ADL Extensions. To provide the description of the components and their interconnections, we introduce a notation based on the ADL Darwin. In general, ADLs provide a concrete syntax for the description of software or hardware architectures, in a declaratory way, in terms of assembly of components.

There is no consensus on specific ADL offering the best description of a component-based architecture, and on the contrary, the studies show the limits of existing languages [12],[13],[14].

Darwin provides a simple notation for the expression of software compositions. From a description of interconnected software components, connections can be carried out in order to form an achievable specific architecture.

To overcome the lacks of Darwin we propose elements of extension for its notation so that its semantics enables us to represent in a unified way CDS requirements. Thus, the extensions proposed are the following:

- The notions of interfaces and events do not belong to the initial Darwin language notation; here we introduce them simply to facilitate identification of these two component elements.
- The specialization (specialization of) is used to avoid rewriting (inside another component of higher level) a component specified beforehand. Thus, we make it possible to extend Darwin functionality.
- Since in the graphical notation of Darwin there is not the description of the events; we use a black triangle to represent a service of produced events and a white triangle to represent a service of consumed events.

Cooperative Component. We define a cooperative component as: "A composite component made of a set of well defined interfaces which make it possible to have sufficient flexibility for well-adapting to functionality support required by a CDS".

Description of component dependencies is as significant as definition of component interfaces. Component dependencies include not only the interfaces required by components, but also the events that can be produced or to be consumed between them.

Elementary Component. We define an elementary component as: "An indivisible component designed to deal with a particular functional level, having a set of well defined interfaces; which enable it to offer and to use functions which contribute to component realization of a higher level".

4   Collaborative Document Editing System Design

In this section we will use the presented notations in order to prove its feasibility for CDS construction. For this, we study the design of a collaborative document editing system. This kind of system makes it possible for a group of users to participate in a distributed way to simultaneous creation of documents. This type of system is particularly useful for several group activities such as collaborative Web pages creation and collaborative software development.

4.1   Functional Classification

We cover the principal functionalities required by a collaborative document editing system according to the work of recent literature [15],[16],[17],[18]. Then, we can relate each one of these requirements with the implied functional levels, as depicted in Table 1. Taking into account this structuring, we made the design, in a first time of elementary components and in a second time of cooperative components, which we will compose in order to build the required application. That is shown in the following section.

Table 1. Structuring between requirements and functional levels

Requirements	Functional levels		
	Cooperation	Coordination	Communication
1. Text processing	x		
2. Interoperability of formats	x		
3. Awareness handling	x	x	
4. Conflict handling		x	
5. Session handling		x	
6. Version management		x	
7. Event ordering and diffusion	x	x	x

Table 2. Interfaces and events used by UserComponent

Interface Name	Role	Function	Type
A	Provided		
B	Required	Text update operations	
C	Provided		User-
D	Required	Awareness update operations	Component-
E	Provided		Data
F	Required	Messaging session update operations	
W1	Provided		
W2	Required	User's data processing operations	
G	Provided		
H	Required	Audio stream operations	UserMediaAudio
I	Provided		
J	Required	Video stream operations	UserMediaVideo
Y	Provided	Collaborative session	
Z	Required	processing data operations	UserCoordConf
Event Name	**Role**	**Function**	**Type**
a	Provided		
b	Required	Text update notifications	
c	Provided	Awareness	
d	Required	update notifications	UserNotify
e	Provided	Messaging session	
f	Required	update notifications	
w1	Provided		
w2	Required	User's data notifications	
g	Provided		
h	Required	Audio stream notifications	AudioNotify
i	Provided		
j	Required	Video stream notifications	VideoNotify
y	Provided	Collaborative session	
z	Required	data notifications	SitesNotify

4.2   Cooperative Component Design

While taking into account requirements of the cooperation level, we propose defining a first cooperative component in order to reach the whole set of system functionalities. In this direction we define a cooperative component called UserComponent, which of course, should be in connection with the cooperative components on the other levels in order to achieve its objectives.

Table 2 presents interface and event descriptions, whereas Fig. 1 shows graphical design of this first component. As presented, it is formed of the interconnection of six elementary components:

- Edition. This component is in charge of text processing functionalities.
- AwarennesMgr. This component is in charge of collaborative awareness functionalities.
- ConfShow. This component is in charge of instant messaging visualization.

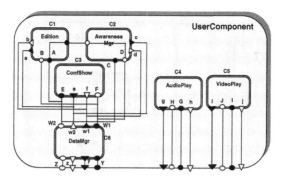

Fig. 1. Cooperative component UserComponent (graphical description)

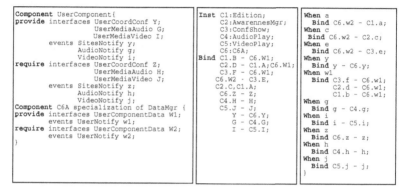

Fig. 2. Cooperative component UserComponent (language description)

- AudioPlay. This component is in charge of audio playing.
- VideoPlay. This component is in charge of video playing.
- DataMgr. In its producer-consumer function, this last component compiles information and sends it to the corresponding recipient; the reverse process is also supported.

In order to complete UserComponent description, in Fig. 2 we show this component using our extended notation of Darwin.

With regard to the coordination level, we define a component called Coordinator, which is formed of the interconnection of four elementary components:

- ConcurrenceMgr. This component is in charge of conflict handling.
- VersionMgr. This component is in charge of version management.
- SessionMgr. This component is in charge of session management.
- DataMgr. This component is another instance of the same one presented above.

For the communication level, we distribute the necessary functionalities on two cooperative components:

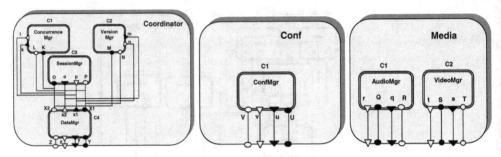

Fig. 3. Cooperative components Coordinator, Conf, and Media

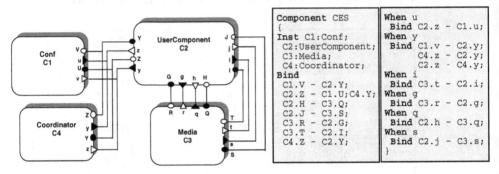

Fig. 4. Interconnection of cooperative components by defining the collaborative editing system

- The first one called Conf aims to provide the instant messaging management support. This component is formed of only one elementary component; of course, interconnecting other elementary components could satisfy an extension of its functionality.
- The second one called Media aims to provide the audio/video management support. This component is formed of the elementary components AudioMgr (charged of audio management functionalities) and VideoMgr (charged of video management functionalities) interconnection.

Coordinator, Conf, and Media graphical description are depicted in Fig. 3, whereas interface and event description are presented in Table 3.

By supplementing the integration of designed components in order to form the collaborative document editing system, we present in Fig. 4 interconnection of cooperative components. This interconnection shows an one-to-one relation between the various cooperative components. However, in an analysis closer with regard to system implementation we would see whether this relation is adequate, or to make necessary interconnection adjustments otherwise.

Table 3. Interfaces and events used by components Coordinator, Conf and Media

Interface Name	Role	Function	Type
K	Provided		
L	Required	Conflict handling operations	
M	Provided	Document version	
N	Required	control operations	CoordinatorData
O	Provided	Collaborative session	
P	Required	control operations	
X1	Provided	Coordination data	
X2	Required	processing operations	
Q	Provided		
R	Required	Audio control operations	UserMediaAudio
S	Provided		
T	Required	Video control operations	UserMediaVideo
U	Provided		
V	Required	Messaging session control operations	UserCoordConf

Event Name	Role	Function	Type
k	Provided		
l	Required	Conflict handling notifications	
m	Provided		
n	Required	Document version notifications	CoordinatorNotify
o	Provided		
p	Required	Collaborative session notifications	
x1	Provided		
x2	Required	Data coordination notifications	
q	Provided		
r	Required	Audio control notifications	AudioNotify
s	Provided		
t	Required	Video control notifications	VideoNotify
u	Provided		
v	Required	Messaging session notifications	SitesNotify

5   Conclusion and Future Work

In this paper we presented CCA, a design approach we introduced to design cooperative components as units of collaborative software architectures. Considering the absence of significant methods for the design of this kind of software, the results presented in this paper contribute towards a solution to these problems.

Using the developed notations, we presented the design of a collaborative document editing system. The expressiveness of our approach has been then evaluated according to this example and seems to be satisfactory. We plan to apply it to additional collaborative software examples in order to complete its evaluation.

References

[1] C. Szypersky: Component Software. Beyond Object-Oriented Programming. Addison-Wesley (1999) 197

[2] S. Jarzabek and R. Seviora: Engineering components for ease of customization and evolution. In IEE Proceedings Software **147** (2000) 129–138 198, 199

[3] K. Drira and M. Diaz: Graph-Grammar Based Coordination in Inter-Corporate Computer Supported Collaborative Activities. In: Annual Review of Scalable Computing. Chung kwong yuen edn. Volume 2 of Scalable Computing. Singapore University Press (2000) 1–27 198

[4] C.A. Ellis, S.J. Gibbs, and G.L Rein: Groupware: Some issues and experiences. Communications of the ACM **34** (1991) 38–58 198

[5] K. L. Kraemer and J.L King: Computer-based systems for cooperative work and group decision making. ACM Computing Surveys **20** (1988) 115–146 198

[6] H. Krasner, J. McInroy, and D. B. Walz: Groupware research and technology issues with applications to software process management. IEEE Transactions on Systems Man and Cibernetics **21** (1991) 704–712 198

[7] J. Magee, N. Dulay, S. Eisenbach, and J. Kramer: Specifying distributed software architectures. In: Proceeding of the 5th European Software Engineering Conference, ESEC '95. (1995) 198

[8] JL Bakker and H. Batteram: Design and Evaluation of the Distributed Software Component Framework for Distributed Communication Architectures. Technical report, Lucent Technologies, Bell Labs Innovations (1999) http://www.lucent.com/businessunit/pdf/commarch.pdf 198, 199

[9] G. Wang, L. Ungar, and D. Klawitter: Component assembly for oo distributed systems. IEEE Computer **32** (1999) 71–78 198, 199

[10] OMG: Corba component approach specification. Technical Report 3, Object Management Group (2002) 199

[11] R. Slagter, H. T. Hofte, and H. Kruse: CoCoWare .NET Architecture. Technical report, Telematica Instituut (2001) 199

[12] N. Medvidovic and R. Taylor: A classification and comparison framework for software architecture description languages. IEEE Transactions on Software Engineering **28** (2000) 200

[13] F. Plasil and S. Visnovsky: Behavior protocol for software components. IEEE Transactions on Software Engineering **28** (2002) 1056–1076 200

[14] M. Riveill et A. Senart: Aspects dynamics des langages de description d'architecture logicielle. Revue L'Objet: Coopération et systèmes à objets **8** (2002) 109–128 200

[15] M. Koch: Multi-user editor. In CSCW **5** (1996) 201

[16] D. McKechan and C. Allison: Design considerations for creditor: A collaborative report writing editor. In: Proceeding of Third Annual Collaborative Editing Workshop. (2001) 201

[17] E. Roblet, K. Drira, and M. Diaz: Formal design and development of a corba-based application for cooperative html group editing support. The Journal of System and Software **60** (2002) 113–127 201

[18] A. Zafer, C. Shaffer, R. Ehrich, and M. Perez: Net edit: A collaborative editor. Master's thesis, Department of Computer Science, Virginia Tech (2001) 201

Architecture for Locating Mobile CORBA Objects in Wireless Mobile Environment

Mayank Mishra

Information and Communication Technology
Dhirubhai Ambani Institute of Information and Communication Technology
Gandhinagar, Gujarat, India
+91-79-30510506
mayankmishra@msn.com

Abstract. In a wired environment, object oriented middleware facilitates the development of distributed objects. Common Object request Broker Architecture is a prominent example of the Object Oriented Middleware. CORBA is a solution provided for distributed computing taking into consideration Wired Environments. A number of issues are present in the design of CORBA architecture, when wireless environments are considered. The issues to address and the complexity of design increase as the entities hosted in CORBA in wireless mobile environment also become mobile. This paper identifies the issues and presents the design and implementation of architecture when CORBA objects are mobile and the environment of systems is also dynamic i.e. wireless mobile in nature.

1 Introduction

The global architecture of CORBA consists of Object Request Broker Architecture. The Object Request Broker (ORB) forms the core of CORBA, as it is responsible for enabling communication between objects hosted in various ORB's while at the same time hiding distribution, location and other related from the CORBA Clients. General Inter-ORB Protocol (GIOP) defines a standard protocol for inter-ORB communication to take place. Internet Inter-ORB Protocol (IIOP) is the mapping of the GIOP over the TCP\IP stack. The IIOP protocol is not designed taking consideration wireless mobile environment in mind. The issues to be considered in this paper are not only considering wireless host for CORBA objects, but also considering CORBA objects to be hosted in wireless environment to be mobile. In designing such a distributed system, fundamentals of distributed systems need to be considered. One of the main fundamental issues of a distributed system is Location Transparency. Location Transparency requires that the components can be identified in the service request without knowing the location of the component. Migration Transparency means that the component can be migrated from one location to another without users or clients to be notified about the relocation of the server object. Access Transparency is also a dimension of Transparency requirement of the Distributed Systems.

F. F. Ramos, H. Unger, V. Larios (Eds.): ISSADS 2004, LNCS 3061, pp. 207–218, 2004.

In a Wireless Environment, Physical Host mobility causes the mobile host connection end-points changes as the physical host gets connected and disconnected from the access point. The Inter Operable Reference (IOR) created by the Object Adapter in the ORB consists of host name and port along Object Key, which in turn includes the Object Id of the Server Object. For a fixed environment, the host name and port number is static as the host resides at the same end-point, which is not the case in the mobile environment. This paper discusses the design issues related to the proposed architectural framework, which enables the CORBA server client applications running on the Mobile Host can relocate and can communicate with each other and also with standard CORBA applications using IIOP. The solution provided in this paper is on Ipv4, that is CORBA servers and clients residing on the mobile hosts are on network that supports the basic Ipv4, which is mostly used and are able to connect to the access point on the network which is also on the Ipv4. Ipv6 addresses some of issues but adaptability of IPv6 is very rare at present. Also, in case of IPv4, no lower networking layer changes are required. The naming service in CORBA is a solution like centralized repository, in which communication overhead is very much and becomes a very critical factor as the updating entities become too far from the Naming Service repository.

The issues in locating mobiles entities are that transparency is needed to be consider while accessing the mobile entities, locating the mobile entities and in migrating the mobile entities. The design consideration also needs this in the way that client objects should access the CORBA servant objects irrespective of the current location of the servant objects. This paper is factorized as the following as it discusses the architectural framework. First, Section 2 discusses related partial work in the same area. Section 3 discusses the problem definition; Section 4 discusses the design aspects of the framework. Section 5 discusses the implementation aspects and finally section 6 discusses the future work.

2   Related Work

MobileIP, is also a modification to the wire-line IP. In MobileIP, two addresses are associated with each mobile host, one is Home Address and the other is care-of-address. MobileIP is transparent to the network and to the other fixed hosts. MobileIP suffers from ingress filtering, triangle routing. As specified, traffic to the mobile node is tunneled, but traffic from the mobile node is not tunneled. This results in packets from the mobile node(s), which have source addresses that do not match with the network where the station is attached. As such, the mobile IP solution could solve the mobility issues, as it transparently routes all IP traffic to the mobile terminal. However, there are some issues, which make mobile IP less useful. In mobile IP, all IP traffic is routed through the home location agent, which might be located in a remote network, as shown in figure 3. As a result, the network route can become very long, even though the mobile terminal is within the same network. For a distributed application based on CORBA, this can result in unacceptable delays. Furthermore, the mobile IP specification states that it solves the macro mobility (that is, the mobility between home and office) and is not well suited for micro mobility with quick handovers between devices with short ranges, like BlueTooth.

ALICE, Architecture for Location Independent CORBA environment, is an architecture, which defines the initial work done in this area. ALICE environment defines the concept of Mobile Host, Mobility Gateway and Fixed Host. ALICE Architecture solves the problem of server or client residing on mobile host at the session and application layer. ALICE Architecture does not approach the problem of mobile objects in mobile host. ALICE architecture also suffers from the chaining problem of the references of the server. ALICE Architecture requires heavy amount of change in the internal architecture of CORBA, the solution provided in this paper however eliminates the chaining problem of ALICE architecture and also requires Lightweight changes in CORBA.

3   The Problem

The problem is the reliable location tracking of the mobile objects, which are hosted in the mobile host, which suffers from the intermittent connectivity nature of the mobile wireless devices. During paper mobility of server CORBA objects are taken into the consideration, since the mobility of client CORBA objects can be addressed using a subset of the solution provided by paper.

The Disconnection of the object residing on the mobile host in intermittent connectivity conditions may be caused by one of the below reasons, voluntary disconnection by the mobile user, involuntary disconnection due to physical wireless communication and migration disconnection in which the service object it-self moves from the specific end-point to another host. Thus, the issues in such scenarios are mobility of server objects due to physical mobility of Mobile Devices and logical mobility, location tracking of server object and message exchange between communicating entities, adhering to the transparency paradigm of distributed systems.

4   Solution - Architectural Design Issues

For attending the issues in this intermittent connectivity environment, the modular approach has be used for attending the mobility concerns of both host and objects and to integrate the solutions. The solution architecture - RUDRAKSHA would facilitate the residence of service object on mobile host also adhering the transparency requirements posted by distributed system clients.

4.1   Architecture Elements

Mobile Host Mobile Host is the mobile entity that is connected to the fixed environments with the wireless LAN USB cards. Mobile host's mobility is dependent on the user and his specific requirements. The Mobile-nature of the

Mobile Host also varies from user to user and from conditions to conditions, as user walking in the environment as in the case of customers walking in shopping malls or stationary as in the case of sitting in a Airplane. Mobile applications run on resource-scare devices, with generally limited battery power, hence the disconnections could occur voluntarily from the Mobile Host user, or may occur due to physical movements of mobile entities.

Mobile Gateway Mobile Gateway is the access point stationary system, acts as connection point of the Mobile Host to the fixed wired LAN network in a region. Mobility Gateway in the sense lies in between the Fixed Host and the Mobile Hosts. Mobility Gateway can have wireless access points attached to them or they can be in network where access point are working.

Fixed Clients Fixed Client is a non-mobile system in nature and is stationary in nature. There can be many Fixed Clients residing in a region serviced by a Mobility Gateway of that region. As the solution to this problem has to be provided at the layers above transport layer, the solution concentrates on the session and Application layer as [1].

4.2   Addressing Physical Mobility of Mobile Host

Considering issues related to mobility of Host, two requirements have to be addressed, namely, Connectivity management and Location Tracking of mobile host where network connection endpoints are not fixed. For Connectivity management, a Mobility Layer is introduced as in [1] which makes connection attempts at the network level to the Mobile Gateway and inform layers above the network layer about the current connection end-points of the Mobility Gateway. On Mobile Host, this layer continuously monitors the state of the connection to the peer layer on the Mobile Gateway for current state of connection and accordingly informs the same to the layer above it, so as to logically handoff the Mobile Host. For Location Tracking, specially in the Mobile Host situation a layer is included in between the IIOP Layer and the Mobility Layer. This layer would make the IIOP Layer independent of the mobility endpoint aspects, which are related to the Interoperable Object References. A Layer named as Swapping Layer is introduced for the same purpose.

Mobility Layer This layer has been introduced so as to facilitate as the connection establishment of the Mobile Host with Mobile Gateway at Transport layer. This layer resides on Mobile Host and Mobility Gateway both. Transport layer module is written which connects with the peer entity using lower network layer. Mobility layer is hence independent of CORBA and IIOP. Mobility layer maintains the current connection endpoints details with the Mobility Gateway and makes transparent reconnection attempts to the Mobility Layer on the Mobility Gateway. This layer provides the connection information to the Swapping layer

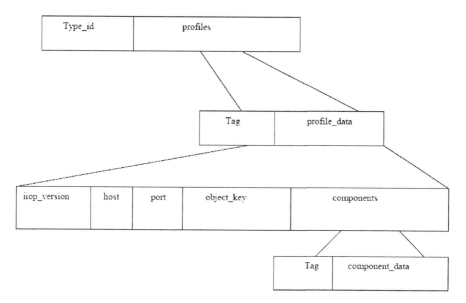

Fig. 1. This shows the components of Interoperable Object Reference

described below. Mobility layer is also responsible for providing initial connection and communicating IOR specific required details between Mobility Gateway and Mobile Host. The IIOP endpoints on which Mobility Gateway listens would be dynamically allocated by Mobility Gateway and communicated using Mobility Layer to Mobile Host, Mobile Host process this information while processing IOR.

Swapping Layer Swapping Layer resides on the Mobile Host and on the Mobile Gateway both. Swapping Layer lies in between the IIOP Layer and the Mobility Layer. The work of Swapping Layer at the MH is to introduce Swapping of the MH's Host and Port end-Points in the IOR(Interoperable Object Reference) with the MG's Host and Port end-points. This allows Fixed Client request to be processed by the Mobility Gateway instead of Mobile Host. The Swapping Layer at the MG reads the IOR information of the client's request and seek in the register maintained by it's mobility layer for referencing the recent connection state of the mobile host requested in the client request, and forwards the client request to the appropriate entities as determined by seeking in the MG's Register. This process can be called as Re-Swapping or Request Forwarding. Before Swapping or Re-Swapping, the Swapping Layer on both entities conforms from the Mobility Layer, which is concerned about the transport level connections, about the recent connection status of the MH. The Swapping layer is used by the above IIOP layer in publishing, reading and swapping IOR.

Interoperable Object Reference (IOR) Structure All object references consist of three essential terms: Repository ID: IDL related information is stored in it. Protocol-Specific Information: This part carried one or more addresses that identify a communication endpoint. For IIOP, each address IIOP (General Inter-ORB Protocol and Internet Inter-ORB Protocol), each address is an Internet domain name or IP address, and a TCP port number. The address (or addresses) can either identify the server, or identify a location broker that can return the address of the server. Object Key: The object key contains the ObjectId and ORB-specific information. ORB-Specific Information, consist of POA id, POA time of start and other vendor specific information.

Regions Since the issues to address range from the mobility issues of host to the mobility issues related to the Server Objects. The overall architecture of the network can be divided into various regions, this can be done according to the network topologies and physical environments: each region would be hosted by one Mobility Gateway and various Fixed Clients. Mobility Gateway can have wireless access points attached to them or they can be in network where access point are working. Mobile Host connects to access point of a region in the nomadic environment. Each Mobility Gateway would facilitate the Mobile Host connection with the fixed clients in its region. Mobility Gateway would be referred as MG, Mobile Host as MH and Fixed Clients as FH in the rest of the paper. Any further references would be as and when in the remaining paper.

Dividing of regions is irrelevant to the concept of paper and can be chosen as per physical environmental conditions.

Object Request Broker residing on the Mobility Gateway is free to decide the connection end-points of IIOP request coming from clients and informs the MH to publish the swapped IOR using Swapping Layer that results in the acceptance of FH client request on the mobility gateway on the specified connection endpoints. Based on this MH prepares the IOR using the host, port number and object key of the MH swapped with the same of the MG and MH introduces a Uniquekey, at the end of ObjectId of the ObjectKey. The swapping of object key in the swapped IOR is needed since the Object key as explained above contains contains the ObjectId and ORB-specific information. ORB-Specific Information, consist of POA id, POA time of start and other vendor specific information. Hence, in case only ObjectId is swapping rather then ObjectKey absence of other ORB specific information about POA id, POA start up time and other vendor specific information in the swapped IOR would cause an exception thrown by ORB at MG side when the client request contains ORB specific information about MH in the swapped IOR. This swapped IOR is given to the Clients for their connection attempts to the server. The distribution of IOR can be any mode and is not considered as a concept of paper is concerned.

As the FH Client gets the IOR from the server, client attempts to logically get connected to the server on MH. As the client calls a method through it's Stub, Client request is in turn directed to the MG since the protocol specific information in the swapped IOR specifies the MG IIOP endpoints, as the IOR

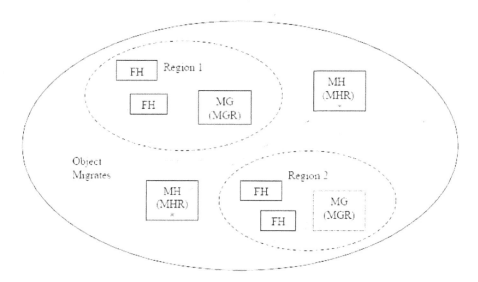

Fig. 2. This shows a figure consisting of Nomadic Environment Entities

client has received from the server is the swapped IOR, which handles authority of the region and currently hosting a MH. As the request arrives at the MG, it looks into the register for corresponding entry for the MH and Redirects the same request to the appropriate MH.

Mobile Host Register This is a register that resides on the Mobile Host. Only one Mobile Host Register (MHR) resides on each MH. This register contains information related to inform the request of client about the current location of the server object. There are three categories of entries in MHR. Server Object is residing on the MH. Server Object is on the other MH, which lies in the same region as the MH. That is both the MH are connected to the same MG. Server object resides on the MH, which is in the other MG's territory.

MHR contains entry like (Uniquekey, x) Where Uniquekey is the Uniquekey generated by MH while incarnating servant object(at the time of it's birth). Note that further incarnation of server objects on other MH would not create the Uniquekey, since Uniquekey is needed for unique identification of the servant object and same Uniquekey is associated with the servant object through out it's various lifetimes of different MH. By time of Birth we mean when the MH incarnated the servant first time, a unique identifier has been associated with the server object, this is in the state of information that is transferred as the server object is moved to another MH, so that the server object can be traced with the same.

Where x is,

1. μ, the same host is hosting the server object hence request is delivered to the MH servant and response is sent back to the client.

Table 1. This shows an entry of MHR

Uniquekey	Location
10011	μ
10012	MGR1@da-iict.org

2. MGR pointers, refers that another host in the same MG region or in different MG is hosting the Server object. This entry is included in the MHR so that if the MG has directed the client request to the MH, but the server object has moved to another MH, hence to avoid MH as terminal node of the Finite State Machine of the request hops, the request of the client would be redirected to the hosting MG for recent residing state of server object. Note that, pointer could also be set to the other MGR or MHR from this MHR, this has been knowingly chosen as due to behavior of network connectivity with MH and network bandwidth on the MH. Otherwise, each MHR has to be updated regularly of each event that occurs in the network.

As clear in example entry in Table 1, server object 10011 resides at the current MH, hence request would be delivered to the servant incarnated on the current host and server object 10012 may be in host MH region or in different MG region, that would be clear at the request would be handled by the MG and would be given to the MGR for further lookups.

Mobile Gateway Register This is the register, which resides on the Mobility Gateway. One Mobile Gateway Register (MGR) is used in each MG to store information related to swapping of the client request, so that it can be directed to the MH. Clearly, the information about the recent servant state information is maintained by the Mobility Layer of the MG. Design of MGR is also crucial in design since otherwise chain-referencing problem that lies in [1] would affect the system.

MGR contains a entry like (Uniquekey, x) Where, Uniquekey is defined above, and the x is

1. MHR pointer of the MH hosting the server object. This is the case when the MH hosting the server object is in MG's own region.
2. MGR pointer of the other MG. This is the case when the MH hosting the server object resides in the other MG.

As clear from example entries in Table 2, entry 1 and 4 lies in the MH host in the same territory of the MGR i.e. MGR1@da-iict.org and entry 2 and 3 are pointing in the other MGR.

Table 2. This shows an entry of MGR (MGR1@da-iict.org)

Uniquekey	Location
10011	MHR1@da-iict.org
10012	MGR4@ril.com
10025	MGR3@da-iict.org
20031	MHR2@da-iict.org

4.3   Analyzing Client Request Scenarios

Fixed host clients depends on regions MG to process their request for the service from the server object. As the client request is swapped, this would be delivered to the birth region MG, by birth region MG we mean that the MG that is/was associated with the MH when the MH has incarnated the servant and made the swapped IOR.

In a case, the MG to which FH client is associated may be the MG where the MH may have incarnated the server object, hence in that case MG would seek in the MGR and forwards the request using the locationforward interface in CORBA to the indigenous MH (if object resides in the indigenous MH is currently associated with the MG), or to other MH (if the object has moved from the birth MH to some other MH in the same MG territory.

In another scenario, where MG to which client is associated is different to the MG where MH has incarnated server object then request would be arrive at the Birth MG, MG seeks in its MGR to retrieve the information about the current location of the server object and the request would be forwarded to MG which is hosting the server object in one of its MH. A typical scenario may be that the MG forwarded by the Birth MG has handed-off the server object to another MG, in this case that MG forwards the request to the latest MG. Note that this case would arrive if the time of arrival of request from the Birth MG to the current MG is more than the time of migration of the server object from one MG to next MG. Since, forwarding of the server object requires code and state information to be forwarded, hence probability of this scenario is very low. In any of the above two cases request would be delivered to the MH and MH would in turn look into its MHR to get the very latest location of the server object.

4.4   Handoff of the MH

Handoff of the MH is between the MG's; this is initiated by the user and as according to the conditions or requirements of the user. Mobility Layer on MH hosting a server object would initiate the callback function to the Mobility Layer on new MG, New MG in turn communicates with the old MG at the Mobility Layer and takes buffered client request and other relevant information. Note that Handoff of the MH implies that as the MH connects the new MG, MH would be allocated a new end-point pair by the DHCP Server on the region of the new MG. Old MG would update its MGR information respective to the Uniquekey of the server object, handled by the new MG, to point to the new MG, old MG also call callback function to the Birth MG to forward the request to the new MG. This alleviates the chain-referencing problems associated in Architectures like ALICE or which follows path-proxies methodologies.

4.5   Handoff of the Server Object

Handoff of the server object means that the server object has been migrated to the new MH either in the same MG territory or in different MG territory.This can be classified into two scenarios

1. Across different MH in same MG: the MHR of the new MH to value $'\mu'$, MHR of the old MH to the MG, and the MGR of the MG of the same region is updated to MHR of the new MH.
2. Across MH in different MG: this would be handoff involving from MH in one region to the MH in the another region, as we are assuming that one MG would there in a particular region hence this handoff can be said to be inter-region or inter-MG handoff.

Now, MHR of the new MH has entry value as $'\mu'$, the MGR of the new MG points to the new MH hosting the server object, MGR of the previous MG would be updated to new MG reference for the new handoff of the MH. Old MG's Mobility Layer would also in turn call the callback method on the Birth MG's Mobility Layer to update its MGR to point to the MGR of the new MG. Server Object mobility can be classified into three categories,

1. Servant Classes as dynamically transferred to the MH, MH incarnates the servant object into it's POA and publishes a new IOR having same unique key but swapping Protocol specific and ORB specific information with the information of the MG connected with.
2. Servant state information also transferred from the old MH to the new MH. CORBA Externalization and Life-Cycle services can be used for this specific purpose.

This signifies the use of Uniquekey while publishing the IOR, this facilitate the transparency of the handoff of servant object from one MH to another MH without affecting any request related protocol specific information on the client side. Client can use the same IOR published by the servant object which was published previously by old MH while incarnating servant object. Hence, the Old IOR contained with the client does not get Invalidated while the servant object incarnates in the new MH's POA and publishes its recent IOR. Note that Publishing of the new IOR facilitates that the clients using new IOR does not get overhead of contacting previous Birth-Region 's MG while request the service from the servant object.

5 Implementation Aspects

This has been implemented in CORBA 2.5 compliant ORB ORBacus 4.1.0 with JAVA as the programming language. Network communications were achieved using sockets available in Java environment. Since currently Externalization service and Life-Cycle service is not supported with the ORBacus, hence the state information of the servant object can not be transferred using CORBA services, for experimentation purposes Servant implementation has been implemented with Externalizable interface, for transferring the state information of the servant objects. Codebase server has also been implemented, so as to facilitate the on-fly download of the classes required in the incarnation of the servant objects on the MH which do not have the required servant classes.

This section describes the experimental setup regarding the architecture. The mobile host was 2 Laptop PC enabled with wireless LAN card running Windows2000 working as MH, 2 MG's and 4 FH each MG are on the fixed network taken into the experimental setup. The experiment was run with constant request/reply size but varying method invocation times from the clients, the server object was moved using a simple algorithm and the invocation time were measured. The emphasis was given to reliable locate the mobile objects in mobile conditions.

6 Future Work

Work is currently being going on in studying various behavioral aspects of mobile Middleware. Reflective behavior of middleware can also be utilized to achieve better adaptability to the unpredictable mobile environment. Future work would deal with other optimized co-ordination related issues like group communication, impromptu service discovery and also with some real time performance issues of CORBA and of mobile environment.

7 Acknowledgements

The author is very grateful to the generous support, motivation and valuable guidance given by Prof. Sanjay Chaudhary, DA-IICT, Gandhinagar, India. I am also thankful to Mads Haahr, Trinity College, Dublin, Ireland for his valuable help.

References

[1] Object Management Group. 2001. The Common Object Request Broker: Architecture and Specification. Revision 2.5. ftp://www.omg.org/pub/docs/formal/99-10-07.pdf. Framingham, MA: Object Management Group.

[2] IONA Technologies, Inc. 2003 ORBacus for C++ and Java 4.1.0 http://www.orbacus.com MA: IONA Technologies, Inc.

[3] Object Management Group. March 2003.Wireless Access and Terminal Mobility in CORBA Specification. Version 1.0 formal/03-03-64 MA: Object Management Group.

[4] Mads Haahr, Raymond Cunningham, and. Vinny Cahill. Supporting corba applications in mobile environment. In Proceedings of the 5th International Conference on Mobile Computing and Networking, (Mobi-Com' 99) pages 36.47, ACM, August 1999.

[5] Object Management Group. The Common Object Request Broker: Architecture and Specification, V2.5. Object Management Group

[6] Ad Astra Engineering. Jumping Beans White Paper.

[7] IEEE TRANSACTIONS ON PARALLEL AND DISTRIBUTED SYSTEMS, VOL. 13, NO. 8, AUGUST 2002 Locating Mobile Agents in a Wide Distributed Environment, Antonella Di Stefano, Member, IEEE, and Corrado Santoro, Member, IEEE 2002.

[8] Denis Conan, Sophie Chabridon and Guy Bernard: Disconnected Operations in Mobile Environments

[9] Kimmo Raatikainen, Nokia Research Center/Software Technology Lab, University of Helsinki. CORBA in Mobile Computing.

[10] Irfan P. and Douglas C. Schmidt, Washington University, Missouri, An Overview of the CORBA Portable Object Adapter

[11] Armin Stranjak, Igor Cavrak, Damir Kovacic, Mario Äagar: "Autonomous Mobile Objects in CORBA-Based Distributed Systems"

[12] Object Management Group. April 2000. Externalization Service Specification. Version 1.0 MA: Object Management Group.

[13] Fahd Albinali, Prasad Boddupali, Nigel Davies, University of Arizona, USA, Lancaster University, UK: The Sabino System, An Inter-Access Point Handoff Mechanism for Wireless Network Management

[14] Giacomo Cabri, Letizia Leonardi, Franco Zambonelli: Weak and Strong Mobility in Mobile Agent Applications

[15] S. Choy, M. Breugst, T. Magedanz, IKV++ GmbH, Berlin, Germany, "A CORBA Environment Supporting Mobile Objects"

Integration of Load Balancing into a Parallel Evolutionary Algorithm

Miguel Castro[1,2,*], Graciela Román[1,**], Jorge Buenabad[2],
Alma Martínez[1], and John Goddard[1]

[1] Departamento de Ing. Eléctrica, Universidad Autónoma Metropolitana, Izt.
Ap. Postal 55-534, D.F. 09340, México
{mcas,grac,aaml,jgc}@xanum.uam.mx
[2] Sección de Computación, Centro de Investigación y de Estudios Avanzados del IPN
Ap. Postal 14-740, D.F. 07360, México
{jbuenabad}@cs.cinvestav.mx

Abstract. Generally evolutionary algorithms designed for parallel environments improve their execution time. However, if the algorithm has different individual evaluation costs, or if it is executed under multiprogramming or in heterogeneous platforms, performance can be adversely affected. This paper presents the integration of a load balancing scheme designed in order to improve the execution time of a parallel evolutionary algorithm. This scheme dynamically balances the load by transferring data from overloaded nodes to underloaded nodes. Data migration is relatively simple, both because the application data is represented as a list of individuals, and because each individual is evaluated independently. The balance mechanism is integrated by means of a single call, contrary to other works where the application code and the balance service are mixed. This proposal can be extended and integrated into any application with similar data representation and management. It is shown how under certain system conditions, the approach offers good performance.

1 Introduction

Today, clusters are a convenient way to run parallel applications, in order to obtain good performance [3, 5]. However, the best performance in clusters requires the appropriate distribution of the workload which, unfortunately, is not easy to determine. The distributed organization of processing nodes, their heterogeneity or multiprogramming, are factors that must be considered when the workload of a parallel application is divided among the processing nodes of the system. These factors are taken into account by load balancing tools in order to improve performance. However, when the workload of an application changes during the execution it must also be considered. In this paper, load balancing is designed

---

* Thanks to CONACyT for the institutional support.
** This work is supported by the CONACyT Project 34230-A: Infraestructura para la construcción de aplicaciones fuertemente distribuidas.

F. F. Ramos, H. Unger, V. Larios (Eds.): ISSADS 2004, LNCS 3061, pp. 219–230, 2004.

for an evolutionary algorithm that produces a variable workload by generating different size neural networks.

Evolutionary algorithms are stochastic optimization methods that subject a population of individuals to genetic operators inspired by Darwin's theory of evolution (selection, crossover, mutation, etc.). This population evolves from one generation to another, applying elitism so that the best adapted individuals survive. As each individual represents a solution to the given problem, at the end of the evolution the last generation contains the best adapted individual, providing the best solution to the problem [10].

Evolutionary algorithms have been executed in parallel systems in order to reduce their execution time [8, 1]. When evolutionary algorithms are required to process large populations, or when the evaluation of each individual's aptitude (evaluation cost) is too expensive, a parallel solution can be obtained by dividing the population among the total number of processors.

However this approach may not be appropriate if the evaluation cost of each individual varies, and in fact the execution time may increase. The execution time also increases in multiprogramming environments, where one or more processors are shared with other users, and in a heterogeneous environment, the evaluation costs will be different due to the differences in the processors speed.

In each of the previous cases, the execution time can be improved if individuals belonging to a subpopulation are balanced among the system processors. With this approach it is possible to dynamically balance the load of the nodes by removing data (individuals) from overloaded nodes and migrating them to less loaded nodes.

Currently there are load balancers at the operating system level [2] and others at the application level [6, 4]. The first make a general system-wide balance, and the latter usually requires application programmers to modify the code and data structures of the applications.

In this paper the integration of a load balancing service is proposed that migrates individuals in order to improve the execution time of a parallel evolutionary algorithm. This service requires that application data be organized as a list, and each element in the list be processed independently. The service is then invoked with a single call, receiving a pointer to the list to be balanced. To evaluate this approach the execution time of the parallel evolutionary algorithm was compared to that which did not use it. The results obtained show that this approach offers a better execution time under certain system conditions.

The structure of this paper is as follows. In Section 2 the evolutionary algorithm is described. The parallel version of this algorithm is presented in Section 3. Sections 4 and 5 present the proposal for integrating a load balancing mechanism into the evolutionary algorithm. Section 6 presents the results, and in Section 7 some conclusions and suggestions for future work are given.

2   The Evolutionary Algorithm

The purpose of the evolutionary algorithm is to find a multilayer perceptron neural network to perform a specific classification task. Classification consists in grouping objects according to their characteristics [15]; a group of objects with common characteristics forms a class. This task is very common in diverse areas such as health diagnosis, automatic speech recognition, wine classification, etc., and it is very complex to carry out manually, usually due to the large volumes of data and characteristic similarity amongst the classes.

Artificial neural networks, particularly the multilayer perceptron, have been used as a solution for the classification problem [14]. One of the difficulties involved in using an artificial neural network for this task is deciding on the topology of the network. This is not obvious and is often defined by trial and error. For this reason evolutionary algorithms are used to find the topology of the neural network.

The neural network used here has a single hidden layer, the number of nodes of the input layer is determined by the number of attributes of the classification problem and the number of nodes in the output layer is determined by the number of classes. The weights are initialized with numbers chosen randomly.

The task of the evolutionary algorithm therefore consists in determining a suitable number of nodes for the hidden layer for the solution of a specific classification problem; in addition, it determines the best weights for the whole network. A detailed description of a general neural network is given in Patterson [14] and Martínez [12].

2.1   Individual's Code

In the evolutionary algorithm each individual represents a multilayer perceptron network. An individual determines the number of nodes that the hidden layer will have and the weights of the connections that link entry nodes to hidden layer nodes and the weights of the connections that link hidden layer nodes to exit nodes. Each individual is implemented as a list, where each list element represents a hidden node of the multilayer perceptron together with the numeric weights of its connections [12]. A typical individual is shown in Fig. 1, together with the multilayer perceptron that it represents (with two hidden nodes).

2.2   Genetic Operators

The genetic operators used in the evolutionary algorithm are: structural mutation, weight mutation, replacement and elitism. These operators are used in order to increase or diminish the number of nodes in the hidden layer of a neural network, as well as to change the weight values causing an evolution that improves the fitness of individuals [12, 13].

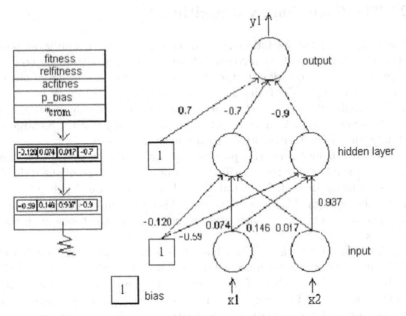

Fig. 1. Multilayer perceptron representation by means of an individual in the evolutionary algorithm

2.3 Evaluation of an Individual

To determine which individual has the best fitness inside a population, each one has to be evaluated with an aptitude function. This function is the half quadratic error, which evaluates the difference between expected and obtained results. In other words, the individual fitness is measured by the percentage of successfully classified examples. In our case each individual is evaluated when it classifies a database that contains cases of heart disease diagnoses, deciding if a person is ill or not.

The cost in time of the evaluation of an individual depends on the number of hidden nodes and the size of the database to classify.

3   The Parallel Evolutionary Algorithm

The parallel version of the evolutionary algorithm is obtained by dividing the total population into several subpopulations with the same size, that is, the total number of individuals is divided among the total number of processors (nodes) Fig. 2. With this division a time gain is obtained when smaller size subpopulations are evaluated in parallel [8, 1].

During each iteration of the algorithm, after the genetic operators are applied to the subpopulations, each node identifies the best local individual and this is sent to the other nodes (Fig. 3). Each node then determines the best global

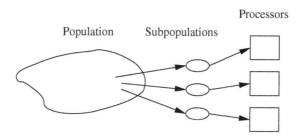

Fig. 2.   Population division of an evolutionary algorithm

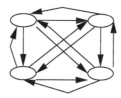

Fig. 3.   Broadcast of the best local individuals to identify the best global individual

individual, i.e., the best of the best. The worst individual in each subpopulation
is then substituted by the best global individual.

Because the best global individual substitutes the worst local individual in
each node, the global population size always remains constant.

The parallel evolutionary algorithm is as follows:

```
Begin
      Iteration=0
      Do-While (Iteration < TOTAL_ITERATIONS)
        Begin
          Apply genetic operators to the subpopulation
          Evaluate the subpopulation
          Send the best individual to all nodes
          Receive the best individuals from the other nodes
          Find the best global individual
          Substitute the worst local individual for the best global one
          Iteration=Iteration+1
        End {Do-While}
      Solution=Best global individual
End
```

Each processor executes the previous code (the total population is already
divided among the processors before each processor executes this code).

It should be noticed that, in each iteration this parallel evolutionary algorithm requires that all calls to send and receive be completed before proceeding
to the next iteration. This behavior is similar to other parallel evolutionary algorithms, and can adversely affect execution time under multiprogramming, on

a heterogeneous cluster or in situations where the subpopulation evaluation cost changes during the execution.

Under multiprogramming if several applications are executed at the same time on the parallel system, some of the processors will be overloaded. In this case it will take longer both to send and receive the best individuals from the overloaded processors increasing the execution time of the evolutionary algorithm.

Similarly, if a heterogeneous cluster is used, that is the nodes have different capacities (processor, memory, etc), the execution time is affected because nodes with less capacity will delay the algorithm.

When the evaluation cost of subpopulations changes during the execution, as in the evolutionary algorithm that is used here, processors can spend different amounts of time evaluating the same size subpopulation due to the different structure of each individual.

4   Load Balancing

For any of the three previous conditions, load balancing can improve performance. To balance the load in the parallel evolutionary algorithm, the migration of individuals between nodes is proposed. This load balancing, based on balancing data, is possible because there are no data dependencies, that is, the individuals can be evaluated as part of one subpopulation or another. In the evolutionary algorithm each subpopulation is implemented as a data list, where each list element represents an individual. In this section the proposed approach to data balancing is explained.

4.1   Structure of a Load Balancing Algorithm

The structure of a load balancing algorithm is basically composed of 2 complementary elements, information and control [11]. The information element collects information about the workload of the processors. This information is used by the control element to identify nodes with less workload and, if possible, to send them the workload of other nodes.

There are several ways to quantify the workload in a processor or node. Some researchers consider the total number of processes, others measure the processor use percentage [7]. The latter is the one chosen here as different processes make different use of their processors.

An important parameter is the quantification frequency, which determines how recent the information is. It may seem that information should be as recent as possible. However if information is collected too frequently there can be a high overhead which adversely affects the execution time. This parameter should usually be adjusted for a particular application. In the experiments reported here the quantification frequency was fixed at ten seconds (the application finishes in 150 seconds on average with/without load balancing).

The information that is collected can be global or partial, from all the processors or only from some.

The control element determines when to transfer or balance the load, and where to transfer the load. The control element can be of two types, centralized or distributed. In a centralized control, a single processor is responsible for balancing the workload; it is the only processor that knows the system workload state. In a distributed control all the processors have an estimate of the workload, and each one is able to balance it.

In the present paper the load balancing algorithm collects global information and has a distributed control.

4.2   Proposed Data Balancing

The data balancing that is proposed is achieved by a group of processes, that run simultaneously in each node of the system. This group is integrated by 3 processes: the Count, the Administrator and the Distributor processes. The interaction amongst them is illustrated in Fig. 4

Their functions are:

- Count process. This process is in charge of measuring the workload state of the node where it runs (local load). The measure can be UNDERLOADED or OVERLOADED. When a change occurs in the local workload state, the Count process sends a message to the Administrator and Distributor local processes, indicating to them the new state.
- Administrator process. The main tasks of this process are:
  a) Maintain a global view of the system workload (information element). Sends to the Administrator process of each node the workload upgrade detected by the Count process. With the same objective of maintaining a global vision, this process receives the remote workload state information sent by the other Administrators. Based on this information, the Administrator process can determine which are the less loaded nodes.

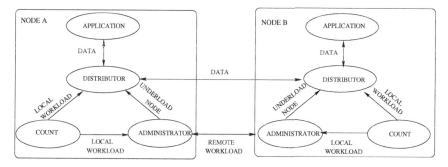

Fig. 4.   Interaction among the balance processes executed in the nodes A and B

b) Send to the Distributor process the id of the less loaded node in the system. If all the nodes have equal workload state then the local node is chosen as the less loaded.

- Distributor process. This process has three functions:

a) Transfer data towards the less loaded node based on the information provided by the Administrator and Count processes. The Distributor process works as follows:

```
If(less loaded node != the local node) then
    If (local workload state = OVERLOADED) then
        {Sends data toward the Distributor process
         in the less loaded node}
    Else
        No datum is sent
```

b) Receive the data that was possibly sent by other remote Distributor processes.

c) Interact with the Application process to balance their data list.

4.3 Interaction between the Load Balancer and the Application

The application interacts with the load balancing mechanism through the Distributor process of each node. At some point in its execution, the application sends its data list to the local Distributor. The Distributor process receives the list and combines it with the data list received previously from other remote Distributors (if the remote data list is not empty). Next, it carries out the transfer of data which was explained in the previous section. Finally the balanced list is returned to the Application process.

5 Integrating Load Balancing into the Parallel Evolutionary Algorithm

The integration of the load balancing mechanism can occur at different places in an application. The application programmer must take responsibility for choosing exactly where to apply the load balancing.

In the parallel evolutionary algorithm presented in Section 3, load balancing should happen before applying the genetic operators to the population. In this algorithm the initial partition, made before the Do-while cycle, represents a first load balance; the subsequent load balances therefore should go at the end of this cycle, as illustrated in the code below:

```
Begin
    Iteration=0
    Do-While (Iteration < TOTAL_ITERATIONS)
      Begin
        Apply genetic operators to the subpopulation
        Evaluate the subpopulation
```

```
         Send the best individual to all nodes
         Receive the best individuals from the other nodes
         Find the best global individual
         Substitute the worst local individual for the best global one
         BALANCE SUBPOPULATION
         Iteration=Iteration+1
      End {Do-While}
   Solution=Best global individual
End
```

This pseudocode is very similar to the previous parallel evolutionary algorithm, the only difference is the call to the procedure "BALANCE SUBPOPULATION", which receives the structure that contains the list of individuals together with its size as a parameter.

Organizing the load balancing as a procedure, facilitates its integration into different applications through a simple call. Also, when organized as a procedure, the load balancing can receive parameters which change its behavior. For example, the evolutionary algorithm doesn't vary its evaluation costs significantly from one iteration to another. For this reason it is convenient that load balancing is not executed during each generation, thus diminishing its cost.

Other utility parameters are: the threshold workload level at which load balancing must be carried out [9], the frequency of collecting information, and the maximum and minimum numbers of individuals to migrate in a load balancing action.

The threshold workload level specified by the user is compared with the real workload from the system when load balancing is requested. Only if the real workload is greater than or equal to the threshold level is the balancing conducted.

The information collection frequency indicates the period of time to upgrade the local workload state.

The last parameters, maximum and minimum number of individuals that migrate, determines the granularity of each load balancing action. If the difference among the workload of the nodes is relatively small, the individuals that migrate tend to the minimum number and vice-versa.

POOGAL is a parallel library used to execute genetic algorithms [4]. This object-oriented library has a load balance class. Contrary to our proposal, this class uses a centralized control. One other disadvantage is that this class doesn't allow an adjustment of parameters as in our approach.

6   Results

The results show the execution time of the parallel evolutionary algorithm under MPI [16] with and without load balancing, both in a dedicated environment and non-dedicated environment. In the dedicated environment the six processors were used exclusively for the evolution algorithm, whereas, in the non-dedicated environment 3 processors were also assigned to execute an application that calculates several trigonometric functions during the whole execution of the parallel evolutionary algorithm.

The number of iterations (received as a parameter) for applying load balancing is 90 and 100 for the dedicated and the non-dedicated environments, respectively.

For the above four experimental settings, the time of ten runs executed in a cluster of 6 processors, each processor with an initial population of 8 individuals was measured.

6.1   Results Obtained in a Dedicated Environment

Fig. 5 shows the execution times with and without load balancing in a dedicated environment. Load balancing improves execution time in nine of the ten cases and the remaining case is a tie. Load balancing improves the execution times because it makes an adjustment to the individuals when the evolutionary algorithm has different evaluation costs.

6.2   Results Obtained in a Non-dedicated Environment

When the parallel evolutionary algorithm is executed in a non-dedicated environment, Fig. 6, the execution time of the evolutionary algorithm with load balancing was better in all cases than that without load balancing. In multiuser non-dedicated environments, a high disparity of the evaluation costs occurs because some nodes are more overloaded than others; consequently load balancing significantly improves the execution of the evolutionary algorithm.

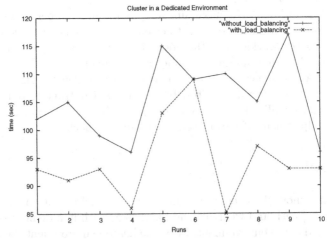

Fig. 5.   Execution times in a dedicated environment with six processors, with and without balancing of individuals

To obtain smaller execution times using load balancing, the threshold workload level of processor use was adjusted in the dedicated environment to 98% and in the non-dedicated environment to 75%. When a processor reaches the threshold load balancing level, it executes the load balancing. A higher value for the threshold diminishes the balance frequency and vice-versa. It was observed that, in dedicated environments, nodes used their processor on average 95% of the time. In this case it is not convenient to balance since all the processors are loaded, and there are no processors available to migrate loads. Hence balancing would adversely affect execution time. However, in non-dedicated environments the extra load at some nodes, makes the nodes without extra load use the processor 65% on average, because of the waiting for the messages from the nodes with extra load. Hence making load balancing is convenient.

7   Conclusions and Future Work

In this paper, an approach to integrating data load balancing into a parallel evolutionary algorithm has been proposed, and applied to the individuals of the algorithm. This load balancing service was designed using parallel computing together with message passing and implemented in a cluster with 6 processors.

The evolutionary algorithm was tested in both dedicated and non-dedicated environments, and with and without the load balancing service. In a dedicated environment, the execution time of the evolutionary algorithm was reduced by 10%, and in a non-dedicated environment by 22%. As to the integration of the service, the programmer has to specify the list to be balanced, and pass certain arguments. It is also required that independent processing be possible for the individuals.

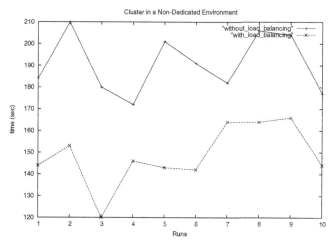

Fig. 6. Execution times in a non-dedicated environment, with and without balancing of individuals

The proposal considers several calibration parameters. In particular the threshold level is useful when the balance algorithm is used with and without extra workload, improving the execution time.

In future work we plan to integrate and evaluate a similar load balancing mechanism in other parallel applications. Our approach is to redesign the application so that its data can be described as a list which is suitable to balance by techniques outlined in the present paper. We believe that a general purpose load balancing service can be devised for applications whose workload is managed as a list.

References

[1] Panagiotis Adamidis. Parallel evolutionary algorithms: A review. http://citeseer.nj.nec.com/17679.html, Web Page. 220, 222

[2] Amnon Barak. Official mosix web. http://www.mosix.cs.huji.ac.il/. 220

[3] Michael Allen Barry Wilkinson. *Parallel Programming, Techniques and Applications Using Networked Worstations and Parallel Computers*. Prentice Hall, 1999. 219

[4] Marian Bubak and Krzystof Sowa. Parallel object-oriented library of genetic algorithms. page 12, 1996. 220, 227

[5] Rajkumar Buyya. *High Performance Cluster Computing: Architectures and Systems*, volume 1. Prentice-Hall, 1999. 219

[6] Rajkumar Buyya. *High Performance Cluster Computing: Programming and Applications*, volume 2. Prentice-Hall, 1999. 220

[7] Román Alonso G. *Contribution a l'etude des algorithmes d'allocation dynamique sur des machines MIMD a memoire distribuee*. PhD thesis, Universite de Technologie de Compiegne France, 1997. 224

[8] J. Williams G.A Riessen and X. Yao. Pepnet: Parallel evolutionary programming for constructing artificial neural networks, 1997. 220, 222

[9] Ming-Chang Huang and S. Hossein. Load balancing in computer networks. In *International Society for Computers and Their Applications ISCA*, 2002. 227

[10] Merelo Guervós J. *Algoritmos Evolutivos en Perl*, September 2002. 220

[11] Castro García M. A. Balance de carga en un sistema paralelo con memoria distribuida. Master's thesis, CINVESTAV IPN. Computer Section, May 2001. 224

[12] Goddard Close J. Martínez Licona A. E. Definición de una red neuronal para clasificación por medio de un programa evolutivo. *Revista Mexicana de Ingeniería Biomédica*, XXII(1):4–11, March 2001. 221

[13] Goddard Close J. y Fernandez Trejo O. Martínez Licona A. E., Román Alonso G. Alternativa para la solución del problema de clasificación por medio de un programa evolutivo. In *XXV Congreso Nacional de Ingeniería Biomédica*, 2001. Monterrey N. L. México. 221

[14] Dan W. Patterson. *Artificial Neural Networks: Theory and Appliations*. Prentice-Hall, 1 edition, 1998. 221

[15] Peter E. Hart Richard O. Duda. *Pattern Classification*. Wiley, John and Sons, Incorporated, 2 edition, 1999. 221

[16] MPI The Message Passing Interface Standard. http://www.netlib.org/mpi. Web Page. 227

Random Distributed
Self-stabilizing Structures Maintenance

Thibault Bernard, Alain Bui*, and Olivier Flauzac

Département de Mathématiques et Informatique
Université de Reims Champagne-Ardenne
BP 1039 F-51687 Reims Cedex 2, France
{thibault.bernard,alain.bui,olivier.flauzac}@univ-reims.fr

Abstract. Self-stabilization is a solution for many fault-tolerance problems. In this paper, we present a self-stabilizing solution to compute random local spanning trees rooted in each site. The computation is achieved thanks to random walks. We present an algorithm that works in a fully distributed environment: asynchronous message passing model is used.

Keywords: distributed systems, self-stabilization, random walks.

1 Introduction

The construction of structures such as spanning tree in networks is a fundamental one and is essential for managing a distributed system. Such constructions has received great deal of attention. Many tasks in networks, election, broadcast etc., can be efficiently carried out by maintenance of adapted structures.

In this paper, we address the problem of constructing and maintaining structures with a protocol that tolerates faults and adapts itself to topological changes. Indeed, fault tolerance is very important in distributed systems where numerous kind of failures may occur: processors may crash or get corrupted, communication links may fail or erroneous messages may be delivered. In particular, the concept of self-stabilization introduced by [7], is the most general technique to design a system to tolerate arbitrary temporary faults. A self-stabilizing algorithm can be started in any global state which may occur due to failures. From any arbitrary starting point it must be ensure that the task of the algorithm is accomplished. If, during a sufficiently long period no further failures occur, then eventually the algorithm converge to the intended behavior in finite time.

We present a spanning structures construction algorithm based on random walks. Random walks are often used in the design of distributed algorithms providing an efficient solution to cover the network without any knowledge of its topology. For example, a spanning tree can be easily computed by a random walk: each site, when receiving the token for the first time, sets its parent variable to the sender, and sends the token to one of its neighbours chosen uniformly

---

* corresponding author

F. F. Ramos, H. Unger, V. Larios (Eds.): ISSADS 2004, LNCS 3061, pp. 231–240, 2004.
© Springer-Verlag Berlin Heidelberg 2004

at random [4]. The successive positions of the token constitute a random walk. In distributed computing, the power of random walks has been successfully exploited to provide uniform and efficient solutions for many important problems. In [12] authors present a self-stabilizing mutual exclusion algorithm through random walk token circulation. In [6] solutions using random walks have been designed for mobile agents in wireless network. In [2] random walks are used as a network traversal scheme for spanning tree construction in wireless networks.

In [11], the author proposes an algorithm, using a random circulating word, to insure topological information gathering and dissemination over a network. In this paper, we present a self-stabilizing version of this algorithm. Fault-tolerance requirements are motivated by two aspects. Selection of random structures implies that probability that a bad communication link in the network will disconnect some node from the random structure is small. Self-stabilization properties completes the case of transient failures.

2   Preliminaries

Distributed systems A distributed system can be viewed as an undirected connected graph $G = (V, E)$, where V is a set of processors with $|V| = n$ and E is the set of bidirectional communication links with $|E| = m$. (We use the terms "node", "vertex", "site" and "processor" interchangeably). A communication link (i, j) exists if and only if i and j are neighbors. Every processor i can distinguish all its links and i maintains its set of neighbors denoted as N_i. The degree of i is the number of neighbors of i, i.e. $|N_i|$, denoted as $deg(i)$. We consider an asynchronous distributed system where all site's identities are distinguished.

Process Every process of the distributed systems executes the same code. The program consists of a set of variables and a finite set of rules. A process proceeds to internal actions (for exemple, write to its own variable, compute something, send a message, consult his message queue, or get message from its message queue) upon reception of a message.

Self-stabilization A self-stabilizing algorithm, regardless of the initial state, eventually reaches the intended behavior (see [7, 8]).

$\mathcal{C}$ being the set of all configurations in the system. A algorithm is self-stabilizing if there exists a set of legal configurations LC such that:

 - The system eventually reaches a legal configuration (convergence)
 - Starting from any legitimate configuration, the system remains in LC (closure)
 - Starting from any legitimate configuration, the execution of the algorithm verify the specification of the problem.

Random walks A random walk is a sequence of vertices visited by a token that starts at i and visites other vertices according to the following transition rules: if the token is at i at time t then at time $t+1$ it will be at one of the neighbors of i.

This neighbor is chosen uniformly at random among all of them. Various papers deal with random walks e.g. [1, 14]. More formally, a random walk is a finite homogeneous Markov Chain with states set V and with probability transition matrix $P = (p_{ij})_{(i,j) \in V^2}$ given by

$$p_{ij} = \begin{cases} \frac{1}{\deg(i)} & \text{if } (i,j) \in E \\ 0 & \text{if } (i,j) \notin E \end{cases}$$

where $\deg(i)$ is the degree of node i.

Let P^t the tth power of P, whose entries are $p_t(i,j)$, $(i,j) \in V^2$.

Since G is connected, if it is not bipartite, the Markov Chain has only one acyclic ergodic class of states, then $\lim_{t \to \infty} P^t$ exists and is a matrix Q with identical rows $\pi = (\pi_i, i \in V)$, i.e. $\forall(i,j) \in V \times V, \lim_{t \to \infty} p_t(i,j) = \pi_i$. π is the stationary distribution and can be computed such that $\pi = \pi.P$. Note that, in the particular case of random walks, the stationnary distribution satisfies

$$\pi_i = \frac{\deg(i)}{2|E|} \tag{1}$$

Some characteristic values are useful in the context of distributed computing. The mean time to reach vertex j (state j), starting from the vertex i (state i) which may be regarded as the conditional expectation of the random number of transitions before entering j for the first time when starting from i, is called hitting time and denoted h_{ij}. In particular, we have $h_{ii} = 1/\pi_i$. We often use the quantity $\max\{h_{ij}/j \in V\}$, which is an upper bound for a random walk starting at i to hit a fixed, but unknown vertex for example, when the average time to look for an information owned by a unknown vertex is required. $h_{ij} + h_{ji}$ called the commute time, is the expected number of steps for a random walks starting at vertex i to reach vertex j for the first time and reach i again. It can be viewed as the average time to fetch back to i an information owned by the vertex j. The expected time for a random walk starting at i to visit all the vertices of the graph is called the cover time denoted by C_i. Let $C = \max\{C_i/i \in V\}$. C_i will be the average time needed by i to build a spanning tree thanks to the algorithm described above. C will be an upper bound of the average time for an unknown vertex to build a spanning tree thanks to the algorithm described above. Bounds on cover time can be found [10, 9, 14]. In [5, 3] authors present an automatically way to compute such notions or nearby notions for any arbitrary graphs.

3 Self-stabilizing Distributed Random Tree Construction

3.1 The Basic Algorithm

In order to compute local spanning tree on each site, we use a random token circulation. More precisely, a token moves through the network with a random walk policy. The token collects identities of each site thus its contents can be viewed as the history of the tokens' moves [11]. Such a token is called circulating word [13].

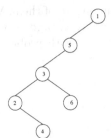

Let $w = 153236324$ the word constructed by the random moves of the token. Site 1 computes the following tree

Fig. 1. Tree construction rooted at site 1

Each time the token meets a site i, a random tree rooted on i is locally computed by i, using topological informations stored in the circulating word (see Algorithm 1).

Algorithm 1 Local Tree Construction

Procedure: Construct_tree_from_token(token)
$Tree = \phi$
for $k = 0$ to $size(token) - 1$ **do**
  if $token[k] \notin Tree$ **then**
    if $Tree = \phi$ **then**
      $Tree \longleftarrow token[k]$
    else
      $Add\_tree((token[k], token[k-1], Tree))$
      /* $Add\_tree(occ, parent, tree)$ this function add node occ in the tree $Tree$ as son of the node $parent$ */
    end if
  end if
end for

In a finite time all nodes have been visited, so the word in the token contains the identities of all sites. A site who receives such a token, can computes a random spanning tree over the network.

3.2   Token Size Reduction

The main drawback of this method is that the token size grows infinitely as the token size is equal to the number of moves of the circulating word. Solutions are presented to reduce the token size without loss of informations by deleting unnecessary informations in the circulating word. Thus the token size is bounded by $2n - 1$ where n is the number of sites in the network.

The reducing technique uses the notion of constructive occurrence.

Definition 1. An occurrence is said tree-constructive if it permits to add a new node either as leaf in the computed spanning tree, or as the father of a new leaf in the spanning tree.

We observe that the tree construction is based on tree constructive occurrences. If we remove the inner and last elements of the token if they are not tree constructive, the topological informations in the token is identical to the case without any reduction. Such results has been discussed in details in [11]. We call **inner cut** this reduction.

Algorithm 2 Token size reduction

Procedure : Inner_cut(Token T)
$Visited \longleftarrow \{\}$
for $k = 0$ to $k = size(T) - 1$ **do**
    if $k \neq size(T) - 1$ **then**
        if $T[k] \in Visited$ and $T[k+1] \in Visited$ **then**
            $Remove(T[k])$
        end if
    else
        if $T[k] \in Visited$ **then**
            $Remove(T[k])$
        end if
    end if
    $Visited \longleftarrow Visited \cup T[k]$
end for
return T;

Example: The word $W = 1532365324321$ is reduced to $inner\_cut(W) = 15323624$

The maximal size of the token does not depend on results on random walks. The longest possible token is composed by a succession of occurences of new nodes and occurrences of parent of new nodes. So the longuest token has a size of $2n - 1$, where n is the number of nodes of the networks.

3.3   Token Consistency

Let denote by T the token, and $T[k]$ the kth occurrence of T. We consider the token as a sequence of identities of visited sites. In order to define token consistency notion, we introduce the following definition.

Definition 2. Two occurrences (a, b) in the token are said linked iff for any node visited by the token,a is father of b in the local tree construction.

As all non tree constructive occurrences are removed, we have

Property 1. Two successive occurrences $(T[k], T[k + 1])$ are linked iff the value of $T[k + 1]$ does not appear in the k previous occurrences.

Thus, we define token consistency:

Definition 3. A token T is consistent if linked occurences in the token correspond to neighbors in the graph.

Transient failures and topological changes such as link crash can produce inconsistent token. Each time a site receives the token, it can check token consistency through definition 3 by a local test procedure, following by the inner cut procedure.

Algorithm 3 Internal test on site p

Procedure : internal_test(token)

for $k = 1$ to $k = size(token) - 1$ **do**
  if $(token[k] == p) \wedge (linked(token[k], token[k+1]))$ **then**
    if $token[k+1] \notin Neigh(p)$ **then**
      $token \longleftarrow Left(token, k)$
    end if
  end if
end for
$inner\_cut(token)$
$return(token)$

- $Left(token, k)$ return the word $token[0], ..., token[k]$.
- $linked(occ1, occ2)$ return true if $occ1$ and $occ2$ are linked in the token.
- $inner\_cut(token)$ apply the inner cut on the token.

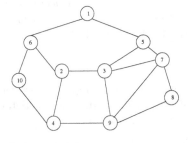

Example: internal test The token value is $(2, 4, 10, 6, 1)$. Next token move, we have $(3, 2, 4, 8, 6, 1)$. Clearly, the token is corrupted. By property 1, $(4, 8)$ are supposed to be linked. But since, site $8 \notin Neigh_4$, next time the token visits site 4, the token will be cleaned and we obtain $[prefix], 3, 2, 4$ as token value where $[prefix]$ is a tested inner cut sequence of sites visited before entering site 4.

Fig. 2. Internal test

3.4   The Main Algorithm

Token could be lost. We use timeout to create new tokens. When two or more tokens are present on a same site, they will merge to one, without loosing informations. Previous procedures are include in order to insure token consistency and token bound size.

Algorithm 4 Algorithm on site p

[**Upon a received message** ($Token$)]

$add(p, Token)$
$internal\_test(Token)$
$A \longleftarrow Construct\_tree\_from\_token(Token)$
if $Messagequeue\_not\_empty()$ **then**
  for Each Token T in the message queue **do**
    $add(p, T)$
    $internal\_test(T)$
    for k = 0 to size(T)-1 **do**
      if $T[k] \notin A$ **then**
        $add\_tree(T[k], T[k-1], A)$
      end if
    end for
    $delete\_token\_from\_Messagequeue(T)$
  end for
end if
$Token \longleftarrow Constuct\_token\_from\_tree(A)$
$local\_tree \longleftarrow A$
Send $Token$ to i chosen uniformly at random in $N(p)$
Rearm the timer

[**Upon a release of timer**]

$token \longleftarrow Construct\_token\_from\_tree(local\_tree)$
Send $token$ to i chosen uniformly at random in $N(p)$
Rearm the timer

This algorithm use the following functions:

- $add(p, token)$ add p in the circulating word contained in the token
- $internal\_test(token)$ view in section 3.3
- $Construct\_token\_from\_tree(local\_tree)$ creates the circulating word from tree $local\_tree$. (see algorithm 5)

Example: tokens collision Let consider now the case where we have 2 tokens on the system with respective values $T1 = (2, 4, 10, 6, 1, 9, 3)$ and $T2 = (7, 9, 8, 7, 5)$. Next moves, $T1$ enters site 3 before $T2$. The tokens merge on site 3 with $T1 = (3, 2, 4, 10, 6, 1, 9, 3) = (3, 2, 4, 10, 6, 1, 9)$ after an internal test (and inner cut) and $T2 = (3, 7, 9, 8, 7, 5)$. Tree constructed is given in figure 3, and by the algorithm, the result is a single token with value $T = (3, 2, 4, 10, 6, 1, 9, 8, 7, 5)$.

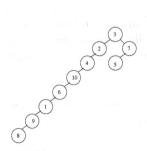

Fig. 3. Token collision

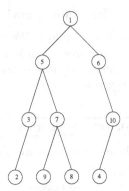

Fig. 4. Tree creation

Example: token creation Let A be a local tree contained in the site 1 (see figure 4). The word is constructed by visiting the tree with a DFS traversal and adding only constructive occurences. We obtain $Construct\_token\_from\_tree(A) = (1, 5, 3, 2, 5, 7, 9, 7, 8, 1, 6, 10, 4)$ from algorithm 5.

Algorithm 5 Constructing token from tree

Constructing token from tree (Tree)
Visit the tree by a DFS Traversal
tmp is a the variable used to keep the identity of the father of new constructive occurrence

$tmp \longleftarrow \phi$
for each node visited **do**
  if $current\_node \notin token$ **then**
    $token \longleftarrow token + tmp + id$
    $tmp \longleftarrow \phi$
  else
    $tmp \longleftarrow id(current\_node)$
  end if
end for
return $token$

---

4   Correctness Proof

In this section, we prove closure and convergence properties of the algorithm presented in previous section.

In order to define the notion of legitimate configurations, we specify the following predicate $\mathcal{PL}$

Definition 4. There is exactly one consistent token in the system.

Starting from any configuration, any execution of the algorithm satisfies the properties of the random local spanning tree construction problem. $\mathcal{PL}$ is a legitimate predicate and the closure property is shown. In order to demonstrate the convergence property, we show that starting from any initial configuration, a legitimate configuration is reached in finite time. Random walks ensure that the circulating word eventually visits each site infinitely often.

Closure

Lemma 1. Starting from any configuration satisfying $\mathcal{PL}$, no new token can be created.

Proof. We assume that timeout is an upper bound for a random walk starting at i to hit a fixed but unknown vertex. Then in any site, a token can be created only in case of configurations where there is no token in the system.

Lemma 2. Each site is visited in finite time by a complete and consistent token.

Proof. After one cover time, all sites have been visited by the token. The token is then complete and obviously consistent. After one more cover time, again, all sites has been visited by the complete and consistent token.

The following theorem states closure and correctness of the algorithm.

Theorem 1. Starting from any configuration satisfying $\mathcal{PL}$, each site eventually computes a random local spanning tree.

Proof. By lemma 1, no token creation is possible. This ensures closure property. By lemma 2, each site has been visited by a complete and consistent token. Then from these collected informations and the procedure $Construct\_tree\_from\_token$, each site computes a local spanning tree.

Convergence

Lemma 3. Starting from any initial configuration, the system eventually reaches a configuration where there is exactly one token with probability 1.

Proof. Two cases have to be distinguished.

Case 1 If there is no token, then by a timeout (cf. Algorithm 4), one or several tokens are created. Each token stores a word created from local informations where the token is created.

Case 2 Several tokens occur in the system. We know that in finite time, tokens will collide and merge to one with probability 1 (cf. [12, 15]). During that time, no new tokens could occur by the same reason lemma 1. Then the system eventually reaches a configuration with exactly one token.

From here, we consider that there is exactly one token in the system

Lemma 4. The token eventually becomes consistent

Proof. Each time the token visits a site, the algorithm executes an internal test procedure (cf. section 3.3) which - if necessary - corrects the token contents . After one cover time, all sites has been visited by the token. Then the token is surely consistent.

By lemma 3 and lemma 4 and theorem 1

Theorem 2. Algorithm 4 is self-stabilizing.

References

[1] R. Aleliunas, R. Karp, R. Lipton, L. Lovasz, and C. Rackoff. Random walks, universal traversal sequences and the complexity of maze problems. In *20th Annual Symposium on Foundations of Computer Science*, pages 218–223, 1979. 233

[2] H. Baala, O. Flauzac, J. Gaber, M. Bui, and T. El-Ghazawi. A self-stabilizing distributed algorithm for spanning tree construction in wireless ad-hoc network. *Journal of Parallel and Distributed Computing*, 63(1):97–104, 2003. 232

[3] T. Bernard, A. Bui, M. Bui, and D. Sohier. A new method to automatically compute processing times for random walks based distributed algorithm. In *ISPDC 03, Int. Symp. on Parallel and Distributed Computing.* pages 31–37. IEEE CS Press, 2003. 233

[4] A. Broder. Generating random spanning trees. pages 442–447. FOCS89 Proceedings of the 29st annual IEEE Symposium on foundation of computer sciences, 1989. 232

[5] A. Bui, M. Bui, and D. Sohier. Randomly distributed tasks in bounded time. In *I2CS*, LNCS 2877, pages 36–47. Springer Verlag, 2003. 233

[6] M. Bui, S. K. Das, A. K. Datta, and D. T. Nguyen. Randomized mobile agent based routing in wireless networks. *International Journal of Foundations of Computer Science*, 12(3):365–384, 2001. 232

[7] E. W. Dijkstra. Self stabilizing systems in spite of distributed control. *Communications of the ACM*, 17(11):643–644, 1974. 231, 232

[8] S. Dolev. *Self-Stabilization*. MIT Press, 2000. 232

[9] U. Feige. A tight lower bound for the cover time of random walks on graphs. *Random structures and algorithms*, 6(4):433–438, 1995. 233

[10] U. Feige. A tight upper bound for the cover time of random walks on graphs. *Random structures and algorithms*, 6(1):51–54, 1995. 233

[11] O. Flauzac. Random circulating word information management for tree construction and shortest path routing tables computation. In *On Principle Of DIstributed Systems*, pages 17–32. Studia Informatica Universalis, 2001. 232, 233, 235

[12] A. Israeli and M. Jalfon. Token management schemes and random walks yield self-stabilizing mutual exclusion. In *9th ACM symposium on Principles of distributed computing*, pages 119–131, 1990. 232, 239

[13] I. Lavallée. *Algorithmique parallèle et distribuée.* Hermès, 1990. 233

[14] L. Lovász. Random walks on graphs: A survey. In T. Szőnyi ed. D. Miklós, V. T. Sós, editor, *Combinatorics: Paul Erdos is Eighty (vol. 2)*, pages 353–398. János Bolyai Mathematical Society, 1993. 233

[15] P. Tetali and P. Winkler. On a random walk problem arising in self-stabilizing token management. In *10th ACM symposium on Principles of distributed computing*, pages 273–280, 1991. 239

A New On-Line Scheduling Algorithm for Distributed Real-Time System

Mourad Hakem and Franck Butelle

LIPN-CNRS UMR 7030, Université Paris-Nord, France

Abstract. In this paper we present a new on-line algorithm for servicing hard aperiodic tasks on a distributed real-time system. Many distributed scheduling algorithms have been proposed to schedule task with deadlines constraints. These algorithms consider the surplus information about other sites as the basis measure to transfer tasks when tasks deadlines cannot be met locally or when local load is high. We show that it is more appropriate for scheduling algorithms to take into account the distances between sites in addition to the surplus information to avoid potential deadline misses. Key features of our algorithm are 1) it includes the problem of the all-pairs shortest paths computation into account. 2) it uses a new policy for the management of the surpluses broadcasted periodically (when nodes in the system inform each other about their state) to minimize the overheads of exchanging information.

1 Introduction

Real-Time systems are those where the correctness of the system depends not only on the logical correctness of computed results but also on the time they were produced. Examples of this type of real-time systems include flight control systems, space shuttle avionics, robotics and multimedia. Loosely coupled, distributed real-time systems are prevalent and natural candidates for real-time application due to their high performance and reliability. These applications contain tasks which are inherently distributed and have deadlines constraints that must be met, scheduling these tasks to meet their timing constraints is one major problem that comes to mind and the most widely researched topic within real-time systems. This is due to the belief that the basic problem in real-time systems is to make sure that tasks meet their deadlines. Most previous researches in the area on scheduling tasks with hard deadlines constraints are restricted to multiprocessing systems and hence are inappropriate for distributed systems. In addition, the solutions devised by these researches assume that all tasks and their characteristics are known in advance and hence are designed for static scheduling.

This study differs from previous works since we take into account distances as well as surplus information for the target site's choice. Surplus information is composed of idle time in a schedule and indicates a site's ability to satisfy an incoming task deadline.

F. F. Ramos, H. Unger, V. Larios (Eds.): ISSADS 2004, LNCS 3061, pp. 241–251, 2004.
© Springer-Verlag Berlin Heidelberg 2004

In this paper we present a new dynamic scheduling algorithm for a hard real-time system (see section 3). The algorithm requires the presence of one scheduler per site. These schedulers interact in order to determine where a newly arrived task could be scheduled. Each site in the network run a scheduler independently of the other sites and tasks may arrive at any site. Each site in the system is associated with a (possibly null) set of periodic tasks which are guaranteed to execute on that site. Since a periodic task is known to represent regularly occurring tasks (the deadline of a periodic task is the beginning of the next period), it has to be determined at system initialization time, whether there is enough processing power to execute a given set of periodic tasks. We assume that the characteristics of periodic tasks are known in advance. In addition to periodic tasks, aperiodic tasks may arrive at any site at any time in the system. We attempt to guarantee these tasks dynamically without jeopardizing the schedulability of the previous guaranteed tasks.

The remainder of the paper is organized as follows: section 2 outlines some of the important works reported in real-time scheduling area, section 3 defines the system model and assumptions adopted in this paper. In section 4 we describe the modules of information and decision of the bidder as well as the all-pairs shortest paths algorithm. The scheduler's structure on a site is presented in section 5, section 6 discusses distributed scheduling. Finally, an example is fully described in section 7 and section 8 summarizes our work.

2   Related Work

For a distributed, multiprocessor environment, scheduling is an NP-hard problem [1]. The loosely coupled nature of distributed systems makes the problem even harder. Clearly then, heuristics have to be designed in order to reduce the scheduling costs.

In the design of distributed computer systems, the scheduling problem is an important one. However, most related works on scheduling tasks with real-time constraints are restricted to the use of surplus information, from some other sites in the network, to determine a good site to send task to [2, 3, 4, 5]. Krithi Ramamritham, John A. Stankovic and Wei Zhao [6] describes a set of heuristics to schedule tasks that have deadlines and resources requirements in a distributed system. They differ from this paper in the way a site treats a task that cannot be guaranteed locally.

1. The random scheduling algorithm: the task is sent to a randomly selected site.
2. The focused addressing algorithm: the task is sent to a site that is estimated to have sufficient surplus to complete the task before its deadline.
3. The bidding algorithm: the task is sent to a site based on the bids received for this task from sites in the system.
4. The flexible (mixed) algorithm: the task is sent to a site based on a technique that combines bidding and focused addressing.

In [7], a flexible heuristic that combines focused addressing and bidding is also proposed for scheduling mutually independent tasks in distributed hard real-time system. Using that heuristic, if a site cannot be found via focused addressing, the bidding scheme is invoked (in fact, the bidding scheme is invoked while communication with the focused site is in progress). Their goal is to schedule tasks such that maximum number of tasks can be guaranteed to complete before their deadline. This approach of only using the surplus information from other sites is insufficient to maximize the number of tasks accepted in the system. We believe that the identification of a target site should be based not only on the surplus processing power on its processor, but also on the availability of a shortest path from the sender to that receiver. And for this reason, in our heuristic, we use both types of information: Surplus and distance, this is the context in which we have been studying the problem of scheduling in loosely distributed systems.

3   System Model and Assumptions

The typical architecture in a loosely coupled distributed system consists of N sites interconnected via a communication network. The network will be seen has a graph $G = (V, E)$ where V ($|V| = N$) is the set of vertices and E ($|E| = m$) is the set of edges. No specific communication protocol is assumed here.

The system workload is composed of groups of periodic and aperiodic tasks which are independent of each other. Aperiodic task is one that occurs one time in the system at an unpredictable time. Each aperiodic task is characterized by an uplet (A_i, L_i, C_i, D_i), where A_i is the arrival time of the task, L_i is the earliest possible time at which its execution may begin (start time), C_i is the computation time necessary to complete the task, and D_i is the deadline by which it must complete its execution. The characteristics of an aperiodic task is not known a priori, they become known when the task arrives. Such a task can be scheduled any time after its arrival. A periodic task can be described by the pair (C_i, P_i), where C_i is the required execution time each period P_i. The characteristics of all periodic tasks are known a priori. Their initial assignment to sites is assumed known and their execution must be ensured.

Since the purpose of the paper is to evaluate the performance of the non-local components of a distributed scheduling system, we would solely use "Earliest Deadline First" (EDF) as our local scheduling policy [8, 9]. This choice is justified by the need to have maximum flexibility in the scheduling. The guarantee function has already been studied in [7] and will not be repeated here.

Unlike previous work in the area of real-time distributed scheduling, the system model involved in this study includes the problem of the all-pairs shortest paths computation which is based on the following assumptions:

- Our framework is distributed computing. So, the graph we work on is the underlying graph of the network. Of course, this graph must be connected. We will use both the graph terminology (nodes/edges) and the corresponding network terminology (sites or processes/communication links).

- The communication channels are faithful, lossless and order-preserving. The processes are faultless.
- All processes have distinct identities (IDs).
- Each process must distinguish between its ports, but has no a priori knowledge of its neighbors' IDs.
- Of course, each site also knows the weights of its adjacent edges. However, edges' weights do not satisfy the triangular inequality.
- A non-empty subset of sites of V, called initiators, simultaneously start the algorithm. In other words, an external event (such as a user's request, for example), impels the initiators to trigger the algorithm. Others (non-initiating) sites "wake up" upon receipt of a first message.

4   The Bidder's Modules

4.1   Information Module (Site Surplus Manager)

This module deals with the management of the surpluses broadcasted periodically by the sites and to answer to a request for bids. Surplus information is the sum of the idle times in a schedule and indicates a site's ability to satisfy an incoming task deadline. The module that we propose computes its surplus between the current and the near future activities of the site surplus manager (see Algo. 4.1 illustrated by figure 1). We scan only a part of the local schedule which is defined by the window $[t, t+window\_size]$ ($window\_size$ is a parameter of the system).

Algorithm 4.1 Surplus_computation(Min_time, Max_time)

$surplus \leftarrow Max\_time - Min\_time$;
$window \leftarrow [Min\_time, Max\_time]$;
if a task T is still in computation **then**
   $surplus \leftarrow surplus - (Min\_time - L_T)$
end if
for each task i s.t. $L_i \in window$ **do**
  if $D_i \leq Max\_time$ **then**
    $surplus \leftarrow Surplus - C_i$;
  else
    if $L_i < Max\_time$ **then**
      $surplus \leftarrow surplus - (Max\_time - L_i)$; **exit** ; (*ignore tasks outside window*)
    end if
  end if
end for

Each site evaluates its surplus and sends it to a selected subset of sites in the network. The selection is based on the proximity of the sites. The subset is computed as follows: first sort the sites according to their distances ds_i, in ascending order. Then, according to this sorted site list, the site selects only the

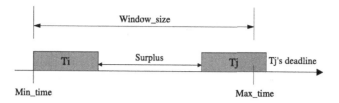

Fig. 1. surplus computation

first v sites to send information on its own current site surplus. The value of v is computed such that the ds_i of the v sites are lower than DS, a tunable parameter of the system. The above strategy minimizes the overheads of exchanging surplus information.

With the reception of the surplus, the site having the unguaranteed task can estimate if a site transmitting surplus is qualified for the guarantee of the refused task (see section 6.1).

The surplus is also computed to respond to a request for bids: it uses the remote task parameters (Arrival Time on the remote site: A_i, Deadline: D_i) to compute its surplus compared to a window equal to $[A_i + ds_j, D_i]$.

4.2   Decision Module

We propose in this section heuristics for the choice of a site when a task is not guaranteed locally. In a completely distributed system (loosely coupled), a major handicap is the geographical distribution of the sites which introduces an over-cost of communication due to information exchange and tasks transfers. Consequently the transfer policy of the tasks should not be too expensive in communications. Its obvious that the target site choice must be based not only on the surplus processing power on its processor, but also on the distance from the sender to that receiver (the communication delay must be not greater than $D_i - Ci - current\_time$). And, for that reason, in our heuristic, we use both types of information: surplus and distance (in terms of time) at the time of a possible migration.

Note that, ideally, if we have a way to know the exact surplus of every site at every time, the condition to send a task to site j is: $surplus_j(current\_time + ds_j, D_i) \geq C_i$. Of course we just have an approximation of the surplus of the others sites: the surplus that is sent periodically and the surplus explicitly computed when bids requests are sent.

4.3   All-Pairs Shortest Paths Computation

To compute the All-pairs shortest paths, we use the algorithm proposed by Butelle and Lavault [10]. This algorithms needs $O(nm)$ messages and $O(n)$ units of time. Any other all-pairs shortest paths algorithm or routing algorithm can be used here (for example to deal with dyynamic graphs) but this one has been choosen for its efficiency.

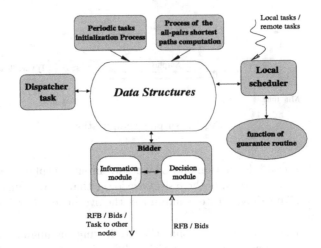

Fig. 2. The various processes that make up the scheduler on a site

This algorithm is (shortly) described from the viewpoint of site I, whose ID is id_I as follows:

It is organized in phases after the first initialization step done on "wake-up" (see the discussion around the initiators in the assumptions' paragraph). This step starts initializing sets and variables (id_I is the selected ID): the distance to id_I is set to 0, while all others distances are set to ∞, and the set UpdatedNodes is set to $\emptyset$. Next, every phase of the algorithm consists of three steps:

- Step 1. Send the selected site's ID and its distance to site I, to all neighbors.
- Step 2. Wait for reception of the same number of messages sent in step 1. Upon message receipt, update distance tables. If an estimated distance to a site changes, add this site to the set UpdatedNodes When the awaited number of messages is received, step 3 can begin.
- Step 3. Choose a site from the set UpdatedNodes with the smallest distance to I and go to step 1. If no such site exists then use the latest selected site.

5   Scheduling Scheme Overview

Each site in the distributed system has a scheduler. Each scheduler contains 5 processes to manage scheduling plus a guarantee routine which is invoked to determine if there is enough surplus processing power to execute a newly arriving task before its deadline (see Figure 2).

1. The local scheduler who receives the aperiodic tasks and decides if the new task can be guaranteed at this site by calling upon the function of guarantee routine. If the new task cannot be guaranteed locally, then new task is either rejected or is handled over to the bidder.

2. The dispatcher who determines which of the guaranteed periodic and aperi-odic is to be executed next.

3. The Bidder on a site is responsible for determining where a task that cannot be locally guaranteed should be sent. It does this either in response to an external request, or on request of the local scheduler.

4. Periodic tasks initialization process: it is executed just once, at system ini-tialization time before the guarantee function examines the newly arriving tasks. A set (possibly null) of periodic tasks exists at each site. Since a pe-riodic task is known to represent regularly occurring tasks with future start times, at system initialization it has to be determined if there is enough processing power to execute a given set of periodic tasks on a site. Let us define $L = LCM(P_1, P_2, \ldots, P_n)$, where LCM is the Least Common Multiple and P_i is the period of the ith task assigned to a site. The tasks have computation times $C_1, C_2, \ldots, C_n$. As Liu and Layland [11] have shown, the necessary condition for the periodic tasks in L to be guaranteed on that site is

$$\sum_{i=1}^{n} C_i * \frac{L}{P_i} \leq L$$

That is, the sum of the computation times of all periodic task instances that have to be executed within L is less than or equal to L.

5. The process of all-pairs shortest paths computation: it is executed just once at system start up.

6   Distributed Task Scheduling

When a task T, arrives at a site S_i, the local scheduler is invoked to try to guarantee the newly arrived task on the site. If the task can be guaranteed, it will be put into the schedule which contains all the guaranteed tasks on the site. Otherwise, the scheduler interacts with the schedulers of other sites in an attempt to find one, the nearest as possible (in terms of time) that has sufficient surplus to guarantee the task. This interaction is based on a scheme that combines focused addressing and bidding.

6.1   The Focused Addressing Scheme and Requesting for Bids

Determination of the suitability of a site for focused addressing is carried out in the following manner:

For $j = 1, 2, \ldots, n$ and $j \neq i$, the scheduler on site S_i estimates: $SD(T, j) = Surplus_j - ds_j$
where $Surplus_j$ = Surplus information available from previous messages issued by site S_j and ds_j = communication delay (smallest distance) between S_i and S_j.

Site S_i sorts other sites according to their $SD(T, j)$, in descending order. The first k sites are selected to participate in focused addressing and bidding. k is the number of sites of identity j such that the following formula holds:

$$SD[T, j] * (D - A) > FASDP * C$$

$FASDP$ is the Focused Addressing Surplus-Distance Parameter. This is a tunable parameter of the system. A is the arrival time, C is the computation time and D is the task's deadline.

If $k > 0$ then the task that is not locally guaranteed is immediately sent to the site with highest SD and this selected site is referred to "focused site". In addition to sending the task to the focused site, site S_i sends in parallel, a request-for-bid (RFB) message to the remaining $k-1$ sites (to handle the case where the focused nod cannot guarantee the task) with an indication that bids should be returned to the designated focused site. If $k = 0$, the site broadcasts an RFB message to all others. In that case, the scheme degrades to the bidding scheme...

6.2   Bidding Scheme

If focused addressing fails to schedule a task, the site broadcasts the request-for-bid (RFB) to all sites in the system with its own address. The main functions of the bidder on a site are the following: - Sending out RFB, - Responding to RFB, - Evaluating RFB, and - Responding to task awards.

When a site receives the RFB message, it computes a bid, indicating the possibility that the task can be guaranteed on that site. Next, it sends the bid to the focused site if there is one, otherwise to the original site who issued the request-for-bid. When a task reaches a focused site, it first invokes the local scheduler to try to guarantee the task, if it succeeds, all the bids for the task will be ignored. If it fails, the task will be sent to the site responding with the highest $Bid/Distance$ ratio, let's call it $best\_bd$. In case there is no focused site, the original site will receive the bids for the task and will send the task to $best\_bd$. If the focused site cannot guarantee the task and if no such bid is found, the task is rejected.

7   Example

To show the efficiency of our algorithm, we present an example on a loosely coopled system having six sites as shown in figure 3. On each site there is one and only one periodic task of 10 time units period. On this example, sites S_1, S_2,... , S_6 must carry out periodic tasks $T_1(\tau, 10)$, $T_2(2, 10)$, $T_3(6, 10)$, $T_4(2, 10)$, $T_5(3, 10)$, $T_6(8, 10)$ respectively. τ is the computation time of task T_1, note that all tasks are of period 10.

Let us consider an aperiodic task $R_1(0, 2, 10)$, which arrives on site S1. Now we study the behavior of the system according to the two parameters:ds and τ already defined.

If $\tau = 2$ then S_1 receives the task R_1 at time 0. The task is guaranteed and scheduled, without any interaction with other sites (see figure 4).

The chronograms reveal, on the same axis, all the tasks being carried out on the same site. T_1 and R_1, are carried out on S_1: T_1 is scheduled in the interval $[0, 2]$, R_1 is then scheduled to start at time 2 and finish at time 4.

If $\tau = 9$ then S_1 receives R_1 at time 0. S_1 is unable to guarantee the newly arrived task R_1. Thus it attempts through Focused addressing to find another

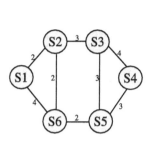

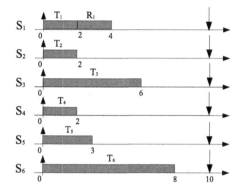

Fig. 3. the network

Fig. 4. scheduling produced with $\tau = 2$

site by checking its table of surpluses, it determines that S_2 has more surplus than S_3 and S_5 and it is nearer than S_4. The task is immediately sent to S_2 and at the same time, S_1 sends a request-for-bid message to S_3, S_4 and S_5 (S_6 is judged overloaded) with an indication that bids should be returned to S_2 (see figure 5).

At time $t = 2$, S_2 receives R_1. S_2 guarantees this task and all the bids for the task will be ignored.

Critical case: If $\tau = 9$ and another aperiodic task appears on S_2: $R_2(1, 7, 10)$ (see fig.6) then S_1 behaves as in the preceding case but, when S_2 receives R_2 at time $t = 1$, it guarantees it and inserts it in the list of the guaranteed tasks.

At $t = 2$, S_2 receives R_1 but it fails to guarantee it. It waits for bids returned in response to RFBs sent by S_1. The evaluation of the received bids is started after their reception. The site S_3 itself decides to not respond to an RFB, because it consider itself that it does not have sufficient surplus. Therefore, S_2 will receive only the bids of S_4 and S_5.

Two cases are to be considered at the time of decision for the target site choice of task R_1:

- Case 1: If we take only the surplus information as the basis mesure to tranfer tasks then R_1 is sent to S_4 that is estimated to have the highest surplus processing time. (*surplus $S_4 = 8 > $ surplus $S_5 = 7$*)
  At time $t = $ *current_time* $+ ds(S_2, S_3) + ds(S_3, S_4) = 2 + 3 + 4 = 9$, S_4 receives the task R_1, it cannot guarantee it, the task is rejected (see fig. 6).
- Case 2: But, if we take into account the distances between sites in addition to the surplus information, we show the following : For each Bidder, S_2 estimates $bid\_ds(S_i)$; $bid\_ds(S_4) = bid(S_4) - ds(S_2, S_4) = bid(S_4) - ds(S_2, S_3) - ds(S_3, S_4) = 8 - 3 - 4 = 1$
  $bid\_ds(S_5) = bid(S_5) - ds(S_2, S_5) = bid(S_4) - ds(S_2, S_6) - ds(S_6, S_4) = 7 - 2 - 2 = 3$

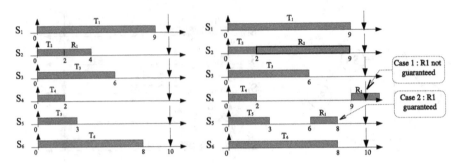

Fig. 5. scheduling with $\tau = 9$ and $R_1(0, 2, 10)$

Fig. 6. scheduling with $\tau = 9$, $R_1(0, 2, 10)$ and $R_2(1, 7, 10)$

R_1 will be sent to the site with highest bid_ds, therefore, to S_5. At time $t = current\_time + ds(S_2, S_6) + ds(S_6, S_5) = 2 + 2 + 2 = 6$, R_1 arrives on the site S_5, it is guaraneed and stored in the ready queue as shown in figure 6.

This example confirm the impact of distances on the number of guaranteed task. We conclude that our flexible policy reduces the number of deadline misses significantly. Simulations are under way to evaluate the performances of our algorithm compared to [5, 6].

8   Conclusion

In this paper, we have presented a new algorithm of distributed scheduling. Our scheme is a dynamic one that tries to maximize the number of hard aperiodic tasks that are accepted for excution before their deadlines – in the presence of critical periodic tasks that must always meet their deadlines. A salient feature of our algorithm is that it uses both surplus information and smallest distances between sites for the target's site choice. To our knowledge, no previous algorithm have used the distance information. Examples studied shown significant reductions in the number of deadlines misses when compared to algorithms taking only surplus information into account. Our current research is attempting to encompass a similar study presented in this paper, for a distributed real-time system by taking into consideration precedence and ressource constraints.

References

[1] Graham, R. L., Lawler, E. L., Lenstra, J. K., Rinnooy Kan, A. H. G.: Optimization and approximation in deterministic sequencing and scheduling: A survey. Annals of Dis. Math. **5** (1979) 242
[2] Chang, H. Y., Livny, M.: Distributed scheduling under deadline constraints: a comparison of sender-initiated and receiver initiated approaches. In: Proc. IEEE Int. Conf. on Distr. Comp. Syst. (1986) 175–180 242

[3] Ramos Corchado, F. F.: A MultiAgent approach to dynamic request placement in the Global Information Systems. PhD thesis, Université de Technologie de Compiègne (1997) 242

[4] Shivaratri, N. G., Singhal, M.: A transfer policy for global scheduling algorithms to schedule tasks with deadline. In: Proc. IEEE Int. Conf. on Distr. Comp. Syst. (1991) 248–255 242

[5] Zhao, W., Ramamritham, K.: Distributed scheduling using bidding and focussed adressing. In: Proc. IEEE Real-time Systems Symposium. (1985) 103–111 242, 250

[6] Ramamritham, K., Stankovic, J. A., Zhao, W.: Distributed schedulings of tasks with deadlines and resource requirements. In: Proc. IEEE trans. on Computers. Volume 38. (1989) 1110–1123 242, 250

[7] Stankovic, J. A., Krithivasan Ramamritham, S. C.: Evaluation of a flexible task scheduling algorithm for distributed hard real time systems. In: Proc. IEEE trans. on Computers. Volume C-34. (1985) 1130–143 243

[8] Chetto, H., Chetto, M.: Some results of the earliest deadline scheduling algorithm. In: Proc. IEEE trans. on Soft. Eng. Volume 15. (1989) 1261–1269 243

[9] Schwan, K., Zhou, H.: Dynamic scheduling of hard real-time tasks and hard real-time threads. In: Proc. IEEE Trans. on Softw. Eng. Volume 18. (1992) 736–747 243

[10] Butelle, F., Lavault, C.: Distributed algorithms for all-pairs shortest paths and minimum diameter spanning tree problems. In: Distributed Computing: OPODIS'98 (Proceedings of the 2nd Int. Conf. On Principles Of DIstributed Systems), Hermès (1999) 77–88 245

[11] Liu, C. L., Layland, J. W.: Scheduling algorithms for multiprogramming in a hard real-time environment. Journ. of the Assoc. for Comp. Machinery (1973) 46–61 247

Facing Combinatory Explosion in NAC Networks

Jérôme Leboeuf Pasquier

Departamento de Ingeniería de Proyectos
Centro Universitario de Ciencias Exactas e Ingeniería
Universidad de Guadalajara
J. Guadalupe Zuno 48, Los Belenes
Zapopan, Jalisco, México
jleboeuf@einstein.dip.udg.mx

Abstract. A previous paper introduced a model of architecture called Neuromorphic Autonomous Controller (NAC) conformed by interconnected modules, each one in charge of growing its own network of cells. The integration of all internal structures results from automatic mechanisms which, triggering elementary actions, leads to correlations learning between local states. Though concluding in the viability of this approach, aimed at performing autonomous training, adaptation and control, combinatory explosion was mentioned as the main challenge to face. Focused on reducing this side effect, this paper acquaints with some enhancements to the NAC model, including: improving internal module structure, generating an alternative representation and defining a more accurate cooperation between modules.

1 Introduction

The concept of artificial brain appeared more frequently in papers during the last decade [1]. Some approaches consider the participation of a large number of cells organized into adaptative structures thanks to soft-computing techniques like automata, neural networks, agents or genetic programming [2, 3, 4, 5]. Connecting and controlling these elemental computing units on Von Neumann architectures restricts the size of such systems, but the use of reconfigurable hardware like systolic array [6] greatly increases the potential of their implementations. On the other hand, robotics is considered by authors as an opportune field to test models abilities [7]. In particular, a self-learning legged robot offers a viable substantiation to evaluate the skills of an artificial brain, making use of control architectures to endow robots intelligent behavior [8]. This approach corresponds to the cognitive revolution introduced in artificial intelligence and robotics [9], referenced as neo-behaviorism; and more recently to a innovative field designated as epigenetic robotics, a concept first introduced in Psychology by Jean Piaget [10].

The overall goal of this project consists in designing a self-growing architecture providing an artificial brain able to control epigenetic robots. Our approach states that if the robot's design allows elementary acting and feedback sensing, both complementary and sufficient, then the NAC model can generate a structure able to control its environment and generate an effective behavior focused on tasks solving, in accordance with its sensing and acting capacities. So, our actual postulate stands

F. F. Ramos, H. Unger, V. Larios (Eds.): ISSADS 2004, LNCS 3061, pp. 252-260, 2004.

that a coherent behavior may result from the integration of elementary automatisms and, that even if such a system would not exhibit for example deductive abilities comparable to those of an expert system, it nevertheless could generate its own required basic concepts and show predictive attitudes. This paper only acquaints with some enhancements to the model aimed at enhancing the efficiency of the growing structures conforming the modules of the Acting Area; this includes improving internal module network, generating an alternative representation and defining a more accurate cooperation between those modules.

In a previous paper [11], an experiment aimed at controlling a very simple virtual robot concludes stating the prohibitive cost of the growth architecture: after ten hours of processing on a standard personal computer, the robot accomplished its first steps; but the NAC simulation implemented as the robot's brain creates over ten thousands connections between four thousand cells. Considered a huge amount of resources compared with the low complexity of the virtual robot, this result prevented further more elaborated trials and focused our work on improving the fitness of the growing structures.

2   Description of NAC Architecture

The NAC architecture is conformed by two strongly interactive areas, controlling respectively acting generation and sensing interpretation. The first one, in charge of generating a coherent global behavior, triggers the elementary signals transmitted to the actuators of the robot. This Acting Area takes permanently into account the feedback provided by its counterpart the Sensing Area which is in charge of elaborating a meaningful representation of the sensors stimuli. The term "meaningful" stands to qualify how discriminative and representative may be a combination of elementary stimuli. The Acting Area, the only one attended in the context of this paper, is organized in interconnected modules, each of which encapsulates a growing stochastic network of cells designed to memorize local correlations.

The internal structure of any new created module is free of any cell or connection but holds a set of mechanisms in charge of building, adapting and operating its proper and exclusive network. The basic process of an Acting Module (i.e. a module belonging to the Acting Area) consists in generating a sequence of signals attempting to reach a specific internal goal requested by a higher level as part of a global process. In the case of lowest level modules (in charge of acting), those triggered actions correspond to signals sent to actuators; in the case of other modules, they represent specific goals belonging to lower modules.

Initially, a finite number of Acting Modules, free of any internal structure, are assigned a respective set of actuators. Sending signals to these actuators eventually provokes state transitions; "eventually" only reflects the ability of the Sensing Area to detect them (depending on its stage of training and the capacity of its installed sensors). A state transition occurs each time a cell "fires" which allows propagation to prolong, pursuing the next predicted (optimal) transition; on the contrary a missing transition induces a network extension. Not only this learning process of novel correlations alters the network structure, as other adaptive mechanisms are involved in adjusting such correlations, mainly increasing or decreasing the connections weights according to the accuracy of the predictions. As our system is supposed to evolve in a non-deterministic universe, those weights play a stochastic role reflecting the probability (interpreted as convenience) of state transitions under specific actions triggering. To allow adaptation to the context, the values of these weights are actualized over time, in particular, in case of erroneous prediction, the actualization combines a short time but strong decay with a long time but dim one. The first correction, in contrary to the second one, pretends to deal with localized and exceptional disturbances. Construction and adaptation mechanisms allow dealing with context variations and handle perturbations due to noise while states definition and recognition, constitute a feedback information provided by the Sensing Area. Architecture design also includes an inhibition mechanism in charge of restricting internal propagation and avoiding activation of incompatible states.

3   A Time-Computing Expensive Mechanism

A specific mechanism, called retro-alimentation, plays a preponderant role in the network propagation, computing, each time a internal goal is requested and for each cell, the optimum path to the goal. Consequently, when propagation occurs in the network, any state reached during this process (being or not part of the optimum predicted sequence) instantaneously selects the appropriate transition to achieve its goal; in case no transition is available, a new one may be created. This powerful mechanism is, from far, the most expensive in term of processing time, and so represents the critical aspect when dealing with resources saving. Additionally, resources requirements raise exponentially with the size of the network: analysis shows that, in average, over ninety per cent of the whole process involves this specific mechanism.

So far, there is no evidence that this mechanism may be improved, so this study will focus on reducing the quantity of cells and connections required to extend the network structure.

4   Improving NAC Architecture

4.1 Improving Internal Module Structure

In the current implementation of NAC architecture, an action is triggered each time a cell fires, so each cell corresponds to a symbolic pair "state-action". The theoretical advantage of this representation was to engender more accurate sequences of states, taking into account the previous states involved in the propagation, e.g. the probability to reach state C being in B depends of B predecessor $\{A_1, A_2,..\}$. Consequently, the prediction associated to the transition from B to C depends of the global sequences $X*BC$ involving this particular transition, their respective valuations result from weights adaptation over time.

Nevertheless, there is no experimental evidence of the contribution of this representation to the enhancement of the global behavior. So, an alternative consists in using a more traditional representation, only associating a state to each cell (and not anymore a specific action). Therefore, the size of the network is reduced by a factor which tends to equal the number of involved actions. Experiments confirms this significant reduction of resources required by the architecture, considering both the allocated memory for the network storage and the processing time necessary to perform retro-alimentation. However, this alternative leads to redefine and reprogram all internal mechanisms of the network, as a consequence of integrating basic features like action, inhibition and retro-alimentation into the transitions.

Another enhancement, to reduce the demand of resources, consists to focus on creating a higher number of simplest modules, so each module develops a lighter structure. This is easily achieved as, until now, the global architecture (i.e. the interconnected modules) of the Acting Area, was manually designed. Furthermore, this consideration should constitute a more general policy when implementing an automatic sketching of the Acting Area: trying to integrate a higher number of modules while reducing the set of possible actions per module.

4.2 Generating a Second Order Representation

The previous adaptations may be cost effective but are still insufficient to avoid combinatory explosion. In practice, sometimes, the network grows at its maximum due to the high connectivity locally generated by the application it tries to control. A subclass of these applications, showing a continuous development over a subspace, includes, among others, robotic articulations. This last statement induces to conceive and implement a mechanism to shift from the primary discrete representation to a continuous one. Such a mechanism would both contribute, to induce a lighter representation and to enhance control over such subclass of applications.

The first step consists in uncovering the possible regularity of the input space, such an analysis is currently performed each time a cell is created: if the number of cells is fairly close to the maximum number of states then the shape of the network is analyzed to detect any potential grid configuration.

For example: given a set of elementary actions $\{\pm\partial x, \pm\partial y\}$ in two dimensions (x, y) and a specific continuous function f to mimic, the system should generate its approximation Af:

$$Af : [x_o, x_0 + N.\partial x] \times [y_o, y_0 + M.\partial y] \to IR$$

where N and M state for the maximum number of repeated elementary actions.

Lets S_i $0 < i < L$ be the cell i of a given module, when $L \approx N.M$ then the new mechanism tries to corroborate the following rule:

$$\forall i, j \mid S_i \xrightarrow{\pm\partial x/\pm\partial y} S_j \Rightarrow S_j \xrightarrow{-(\pm\partial x/\pm\partial y)} S_i$$

which could be interpreted as: when from any state i an elementary action a leads to a new state j then applying the complementary action $-a$ should lead to the original state i.

A second step consists in trying to apply a lineal approximation taking advantage of the regularity of the grid. First, the grid is divided in sub-grids, then on each dimension of this sub-grid the coefficients of a lineal approximation are calculated and finally, a combination of these approximations gives the equation of a tangent sub-space. If the highest value of all the errors, obtained comparing the real (experimented) and the approximate values over each sub-space, exceeds a percentage of the difference between the maximum and the minimum values of the approximated function over its input space, then we repeat the procedure using smaller sub-grids.

For example:

$$[x_o, x_0 + N.\partial x] \times [y_o, y_0 + M.\partial y]$$

$$= \bigcup_{h,k} [x_0 + h.\Delta x, x_0 + (h+1).\Delta x] \times [y_0 + k.\Delta y, y_0 + (k+1).\Delta y]$$

For each discrete pair *(x, y)*

$$(x, y) \in [x_0 + h.\Delta x, x_0 + (h+1)\Delta x] \times [y_0 + k.\Delta y, y_0 + (k+1)\Delta y]$$

We first calculate the approximation on *x*

$$Af_{\bar{y},h}(x) \quad x \in [x_0 + h.\Delta x, x_0 + (h+1)\Delta x]$$

And then its linear approximation on this sub-grid

$$a_{y,h}.x + b_{y,h}$$

Then combining this equation with its counterpart obtained from $Af_{\bar{x},k}(y)$

$$a_{x,k}.y + b_{x,k}$$

engenders the equation of a local plan

$$a_{y,h}.x + a_{x,k}.y + b_{x,y,k,h}$$

Initially

$$h = 0, \quad k = 0, \quad \Delta x = N.\partial x, \quad \Delta y = M.\partial y$$

then *h* and *k* are independently incremented until, at least, one local approximation error exceeds the previously computed maximum.

The three coefficients $(a_{x,k}, a_{y,h}, b_{x,y,k,h})$ allow to define, what we call, "second order" cells which, as a substitute of the previous discrete "first order" ones, represent a local and continuous approximation of an underlying function. A graphic illustration of this approximation is given by figure 1 and corresponds to a module in charge of controlling the height of a robotic leg counting two articulations.

Considering the worst case when the error cannot be decreased under its threshold, the smallest sub-grid is conformed by the four points situated at each corner of the sub-space:

$$[x_i, x_i + \partial x] \times [y_j, y_j + \partial y]$$

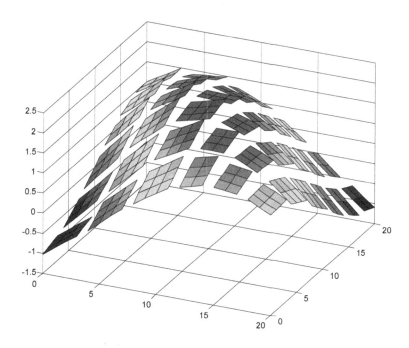

Fig. 1. Graphic representation of a module in charge of controlling a robotic leg

Nevertheless, replacing first order cells by second order ones still faces a great challenge as these new structures must comply with the mechanisms previously implemented. In practice, adaptation is no more preserved so, in case of multiple errors, the alternative consists in converting the actual network back to a first order one and, after an adaptation period, trying to evolve it again. On the other hand, to preserve compliance with object oriented programming paradigm, both class of cells inherit from an abstract one and moreover, the class corresponding to "module" maintains generic methods in charge of dealing indifferently with first or second order cells. In particular, propagation inside cells was previously a basic process, but it requires now a specific mechanism as cells hold at least one dimension. The actual implementation considers the association of internal shifts with its subsequent action, firstly applying an elementary and uniform cost for any of them, and secondly considering that any goal now corresponds to a precise internal location.

Table 1. Comparative values of computing time and memory allocation over 10 000 goals

	First Order Network				Second Order Network			
Precision	20	40	60	80	20	40	60	80
Memory Allocation (Kb.)	117	445	1014	1799	10	37	90	166
Computing Time (Sec.)	15	84	257	470	2	7	15	34

To evaluate the enhancement obtained through representation shifting, a series of 10 000 goals were submitted to a first and a second order grown networks in charge of controlling an articulation. A specific parameter, "precision", characterizes the resolution of the controlled system; in this particular case the number of steps for the servo to rotate 180 degrees. An increased precision constrains the network to generate more cells to match the corresponding performance. A simulation, of approximately 8000 lines of C++ code, was run on a 1000 MHz Pentium III computer with 512 Mb ram. The results, presented on table 1, show the high efficiency of the second order representation: memory allocation is reduced by a factor twelve and computing time reduction variation increases exponentially. However, this performances must be tempered considering that the second order network does not realize any kind of adaptation over time. On the other hand, few modules present the required regularity to allow representation shifting, but anyway this mechanism offers a critical improvement to the architecture, in particular to deal with articulations control.

The intent of using different sizes sub-grids looked, a priori, to be a reliable alternative to generate a network with a still lower number of cells as the error of approximation generally varies from one subgrid to another. But, as a side effect, this organization would contribute to double or triple the connectivity inside the network, increasing greatly the demand of computing time, in particular to accomplish retro-alimentation. For this reason, this alternative has been rejected.

On the other hand, a second order module appears to be a potential alternative tool to achieve basic real time automatic regulation. In fact, the computed three-dimensional surface may well represent the behavior of a particular plant the module is in charge to control. After an adequate learning period, the network is able by construction to reach any goal-state from the actual one. So, repeatedly giving the same goal to the module should be sufficient to counteract the effects of external perturbations and stabilize the state of a plant; thus leading to automatic regulation. Real time processing seems also achievable as the retro-alimentation mechanism is required only when submitting a new goal to the module.

4.3 Defining a More Accurate Connectivity between Modules

Enhancing memory allocation is a prior preoccupation to develop a reasonable simulation, able to manage a high number of modules. Both previous proposals contributes to this purpose, reducing the size of internal networks. The first one by a factor which tends to equal the number of involved actions; the second one by a factor proportional to the size of the sub-grid. Let (n, p) be the size of such a sub-grid and N the number of first order cells, shifting representation requires $N / n.p$ second order cells. Even considering that storing those cells require more memory than for the previous ones, the improvement is obvious but still insufficient considering the problem we have to face.

Each module which does not produce signals to monitor actuators, generate actions corresponding to goals for a specific set of lower modules. So the current module integrates a sequence of sub-goals, each one entrusted to its corresponding module when triggered. The basic strategy consists in reducing as much as possible this set of goals. To exemplify this affirmation, consider its opposite when each state of lower modules is considered as a potential goal. This would conduce to reproduce all local sequences of states into upper level modules, generating a completely redundant, useless and costly representation; thus recursively leading to the worst possible case of combinatory explosion.

The first mechanism to reduce the set of goals consists in dividing the range of original values into smaller subsets; each subset computes its own representative used later as a potential goal for an upper level. This conduces to a lost of precision quite similar to the one originated by using a smaller range of values for sensors and actuators.

A second and more subtle mechanism involves the Sensing Area whose feedback should provide meaningful states rather than precise ones. To illustrate this, consider a high level goal meaning something like "steady position", no matter what exact position the cell reaches while the sensing area judges it as satisfying: i.e. for example obtaining a similar pressure under each foot without mattering legs position. The integration of the Sensing Area to the whole simulation is still pending but early experiments shows the feasibility of integrating sets of stimuli by means of growing neural networks. Any combination of stimuli is received by the Sensing Area, discriminated and integrated to allow their classification into relevant states. For example, the "steady position" is conformed by a fuzzy set of stimuli and cannot be associated with precise values. The conformation of such sets and their particular relevance results from an emerging gradual process which should involve both areas. At this time, all experiments on Acting and Sensing Areas have been conduced independently and so, the feasibility of an unified process has not been established.

5   Conclusion

In conclusion, improving internal module structure and generating alternative representations constitute functional enhancements to the model. Both contributions alleviate computing time and memory requirements, but are still insufficient to face combinatory explosion. The answer to this problem resides in defining a more accurate connectivity between modules; which means creating smaller sets of more meaningful goals, ensuring a better integration of sequences from lower modules to upper ones.

Therefore, next step of this research will focus on fully integrating Acting and Sensing Areas into a single simulation to evaluate the ability of this growing architecture to face combinatory explosion while controlling a complex robot. The main difficulty concerning this integration consists in growing simultaneously two dissimilar network architectures which mutually contribute in evolving their respective structures.

Regardless of the initial problem (combinatory explosion), this study exhibits the feasibility of using a second order network to achieve real time regulation. Furthermore, this method presents the advantage of automatically building the controller while interacting with the plant (if technically possible). No previous description, like fuzzy rules or p.i.d. equations for example, would be required. A more complete study, offering an additional topic of research, will be designed to determine more precisely the advantages and limitations of this approach.

References

[1]   Cardon, A.: Conscience Artificielle et Systèmes Adaptatifs, Eyrolles (eds.) (1999) 284p.

[2]   Kondo, T., Ishiguro, A., Tokura, S., Uchikawa, Eggenberger, P.: Realization of Robust Controllers in Evolutionary Robotics: a Dynamically-Rearranging Neural Network Approach in Congress on Evolutionary Computation, IEE (eds) New Jersey (1999) 366-373

[3]   Balakrishnan, K., Honavar, V.: Experiments in Evolutionary Robotics in Advances in Evolutionary Synthesis of Neural Systems, Patel, M., Honavar, V. (Eds), Cambridge, MA MIT Press (2001)

[4]   Kamio, S., Mitsuhashi, H. and Iba, H.: Integration of Genetic Programming and Reinforcement Learning for Real Robots in Genetic and Evolutionary Computation Vol. 2723 Springer-Verlag Berlin (2003) 470-482

[5]   Wolff, K., Peter Nordin, P.: Physically Realistic Simulators and Autonomous Humanoid Robots as Platforms for Evolution of Biped Walking Behavior using Genetic Programming in Proceedings of the 6th World Multiconference on Systemics, Cybernetics and Informatics Vol. VI, Callaos Pisarchik Ueda (eds) (2002) 81-86

[6]   Korkin, M.: Reconfigurable Hardware Systolic Array for Real-Time Compartmental Modelling of Large-Scale Artificial Nervous Systems in Zhang, D., Sankar, K.P. (eds.): Neural Networks and Systolic Array Design, World Scientific (2002)

[7]   Kawato M.: Robotics as a Tool for Neuroscience: Cerebellar Internal Models for Robotics and Cognition, Proc. 9th International Symposium of Robotics Research (ISRR99), (2000) 321-328

[8]   Mataric M.J.: Behavior Based Robotics as a Tool for Synthesis of Artificial Behavior and Analysis of Natural Behavior in Trends in Cognitive Science Vol.2 No.3, (1998) 82-87

[9]   Brooks, R.A., Intelligence Without Representation, Artificial Intelligence N.47 (1991) 139-159

[10]   Zlatev, J. and Balkenius, C.: Why "Epigenetic Robotics"?, Introduction to the Proceedings of the First International Workshop on Epigenetic Robotics, Sweden (2001)

[11]   Leboeuf, J.: A Self-Developing Neural Network Designed for Discrete Event System Autonomous Control in Mastorakis, N. (eds.): Advances in Systems Engineering, Signal Processing and Communications, Wseas Press (2002) 30-34

Multiple Correspondences and Log-linear Adjustment in E-commerce

María Beatriz Bernábe Loranca[1] and Luis Antonio Olsina Santos[2]

[1]Cuerpo Académico de Ingeniería de Software – Aplicaciones Estadísticas.
Facultad de Ciencias de la Computación, BUAP.
Calle 14 sur y Avenida San Claudio, Colonia San Manuel, Puebla, México.
bety@cs.buap.mx
Fax 015 222 2295500 ext. 7225
[2]GIDIS, Departamento de Informática, UNLPam
Calle 9 y 110, (6360) General Pico, La Pampa, Argentina.
olsinal@ing.unlpam.edu.ar

Abstract. When an exploratory data analysis is performed where more than two qualitative variables are present, the application of univariate, bivariate and multivariate statistical techniques allows to successfully describe the dataset. Particularly, the single correspondence technique gives important correlation and dimensionality reduction results, which helps when giving an objective interpretation of the data. In this paper the technique known as factor analysis of multiple correspondences is used, which is a generalization of the single correspondence technique used to corroborate results. The log-linear adjustment is used too, with the purpose of continuing with the Principal Components and Cluster Analyses [3]. The binary variables under study are the result of the e-commerce sites' evaluation process for the quality attributes of the "Functionality" feature [8, 9]. These data is concentrated in a binary table of 49 sites and 17 attributes [3, 8]. (See table A.1 in the appendix for the list of variables).

1 Introduction

While the marked differences between physical and electronic commerce are evident, it is also known that many common features can be abstracted and incorporated when building a Web application for the *virtual* mode of commerce [7]. Therefore, we must resort to several tools and strategies for the development and evaluation of a software product of this magnitude. Specifically, and considering a general audience, it seems appropriate to ask, Which features and attributes must be taken into account at the design and evaluation stages of an e-commerce site or application in order to obtain a quality product with the potential to influence traffic and sales?, How to decide which evaluation process is adequate? Which strategy must be followed in the data collection and organization for the evaluation?, and ultimately, Which statistical techniques must be applied in order to effectively interpret the datasets stemming from the evaluation?

A starting point for this task comes from an Argentinean e-commerce sites quality study [8], where an evaluation was performed for directly measurable *functionality*

F. F. Ramos, H. Unger, V. Larios (Eds.): ISSADS 2004, LNCS 3061, pp. 261–273, 2004.
© Springer-Verlag Berlin Heidelberg 2004

attributes. Such attributes belong to the *Product Information, Purchase Features, Client Customization, Promotion Policies* and *Searching Mechanisms* sub-features; all of them grouped under the *Functionality* feature. The attributes and sub-features form the quality requirements for an audience called "General visitor".

Accordingly, this study's main objective consists on continuing the statistical analysis of the binary data obtained by the former survey. During such survey, seventeen attributes grouped in the sub-features already mentioned were observed from a sample of forty nine sites (in [10], about ninety attributes were considered for evaluation).

The experimental studies that are performed with a large number of attributes –i.e. explaining independent variables, follow data analysis methods and techniques that range from data description and summary up to exploratory analysis to identify potential relations among variables, or analysis to classify and categorize the objects under study.

In this paper multivariate statistical techniques were applied, in a way that allows to keep describing completely the binary data table; its dimensionality is also reduced and a classification of quality attributes is given, this time from a multiple factor point of view. Previously, an analysis on datasets was conducted using the Principal Components, Cluster and Single Correspondence Factor Analyses [3] techniques. Now, a Multiple Correspondence Factor Analysis is applied, and the established hypotheses of relationships and/or categorization of sites and variables are tested with a well-suited approach for this type of problems, called Log-linear adjustment. During this multivariate process the importance, relationships, and categorization of the qualitative attributes mentioned earlier are confirmed, among other aspects. Eventually, this leads to conclusions being drawn about the relevance of the sub-features involved, but now from a perspective that enriches the results produced by the used statistical technique: i.e., the log-linear adjustment.

Regarding the number of evaluated sites the field study required a sample of 49 e-commerce sites from the most diverse categories. The sample was drawn from 100 e-commerce Argentinean sites [8]. The sites were selected randomly with the use of a random value table. In addition, an evaluation of 17 attributes referring to five categories of the *Functionality* feature in the e-commerce domain was used. Table A.1 of appendix A shows the listing.

Finally, a binary data criterion was adopted for the assessment, i.e., it is *available* (1) or *not available* (0). This should be interpreted as "satisfies completely the elementary quality requirement" (100%) or "does not satisfy the elementary quality requirement at all" (0%).

The rest of this article proceeds as follows. In the next two sections the multiple correspondence factor analysis and the log-linear adjustment over data from e-commerce sites are discussed. Finally, concluding remarks are presented.

2   Multiple Correspondences Factoring

To begin the study we'll return to the first idea about the relation between qualitative variables from the e-commerce table (see Table 1), considering the p correlation coefficient.

Table 1. Correlation coefficients among variables

Variables			CC	P
IP-IMA vs	IP- DES		.63	.000001
CC-ICAN	vs	IP-IMA	-.30	.032999
CC-CAR	vs	MB-RES	.49	.000321
CC-CAR	vs	PC-CUEN	.43	.001904
CC-CAR	vs	CC-TRANS	.46	.000827
CC-CAR	vs	CC-V-OFF	-.46	.000869
CC-CAR	vs	MB-GLOB	.29	.044327
CC-CAR	vs	CC-V-ON	.54	.000073
CC-V-OFF	vs	CC-V-ON	-.34	.017172
CC-V-OFF	vs	CC-IEC	.29	.044566
CC-IEC vs	CC-TRANS		.29	.041356
CC-IEC vs	CC-IP		.70	.000000
MB-RES	vs	PC-CUEN	.35	.013890
MB-RES	vs	CC-TRANS	.30	.035447

It is wroth mentioning that this *correlational* number does not always implies *causality*. Moreover, *p* emerges from assuming the Null Hypothesis to be true

Table 1 contains the values for CC (Correlation Coefficients). They highlight the important relationship between the Shopping Features, which are correlated between them and also with some others. The attribute "shopping cart" has a high positive correlation coefficient with another five attributes, while its correlation coefficient is negative with the attribute "off-line sales". On the other hand, the largest correlation coefficient appears between two attributes from the shopping features: payment information and shipping and cost information, which means that the more one appears, the more the other appears too. The same occurs with the "product information" attributes concerning basic description and product image. The full names of the variables that appear in the table can be found in Table A.1 of Appendix A.

Even after performing a single correspondence study with the binary table, it is necessary to corroborate with another complementary techniques the results produced about the important classification and relationship between sites and attributes.

The multiple correspondence analysis [1, 4, 5] allows to study the relationship between the modes of all the qualitative features involved.

As a factor method, just like the principal components and single correspondence analyses, it is necessary to diagonalize certain matrix in order to obtain the factors. In this case such matrix is the product of the transposed complete disjunctive matrix (in our case, the table of site attributes) by itself, lets denote it with B. B has to be pre-multiplied by a diagonal matrix (D) which consists of the diagonal elements of B and zeros elsewhere and finally divided by the number of features or qualitative variables (Q).

Table 2. Eigenvalues by dimension

	Singular Values	Eigen- Values	Perc. of Inertia	Cumulatv Percent	Chi Squares
1	.414	.171	17.14	17.1	227.2
2	.354	.125	12.54	29.7	166.2
3	.349	.122	12.15	41.8	161.1
4	.321	.103	10.33	52.2	136.9
5	.272	.074	7.39	59.6	98.0
6	.259	.067	6.70	66.2	88.8
7	.242	.059	5.86	72.1	77.6
8	.230	.053	5.31	77.4	70.3
9	.203	.041	4.12	81.5	54.6
10	.198	.039	3.91	85.4	51.9
11	.181	.033	3.26	88.7	43.2
12	.175	.031	3.07	91.8	40.7
13	.163	.027	2.66	94.4	35.2
14	.156	.024	2.42	96.9	32.1
15	.118	.014	1.38	98.2	18.3
16	.100	.010	1.00	99.2	13.3
17	.087	.008	.76	100.0	10.1

The B table (Table A.2, appendix A) is known as *Burt Table* and is nothing more than a symmetric matrix formed by Q^2 blocks. The diagonal's blocks are diagonal tables that cross a variable with itself, the diagonal elements being the effective ones of each mode. The blocks outside the diagonal are the contingency tables obtained by crossing the features pair-wise and whose elements are the frequencies of association for the two corresponding modes. The Burt Table shows the values for mass, quality, inertia and cosine which makes possible the interpretation in three dimensions of the relationship between the variables under study [6].

The same concepts from simple correspondence are used in order to interpret the multiple correspondence analysis. The eigenvalues table (Table 2) shows that when we select three dimensions almost 42% of the phenomenon under study is explained. The first dimension explains 17.14% of the phenomenon's variance, the second explains 12.54% and the third 12.15%.

From the analysis of table A.2 (Appendix A) and the corresponding charts, the following facts stand out:

For the first dimension

If the attribute Shopping Cart is not present in a web-site, neither will be the Basic product description, On-line sales, Restricted search mechanism, nor Secure Transaction attributes. (Fig. 1)

When the attribute *Shopping Cart* is present, sites will also feature the *On-line sales, Secure transaction* and *Restricted search* features. (Fig. 1)

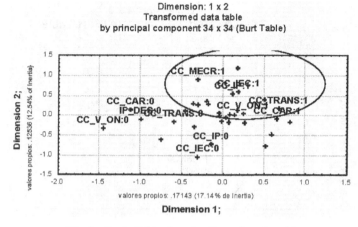

Fig. 1. Burt's Table chart for dimensions 1 and 2

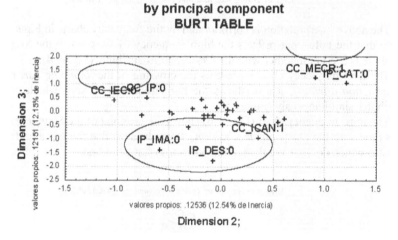

Fig. 2. Burt's Table chart for dimensions 2 and 3

For the second dimension

If sites have the *Shipping and costs information*, they generally have the *Payment information* and vice-versa (Fig. 2)

For the third dimension

Sites that do not feature product information attributes (*Basic description* and *Product image*) have *Purchase cancellation information.*

Absence of the *Product information by catalog* attribute is related to the presence of *Quick buy Mechanism* (see Figure 3)

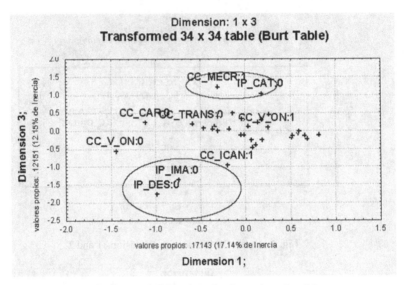

Fig. 3. Burt's Table chart for dimensions 1 and 3

The above interpretation is corroborated by the frequency charts in Fig.s 4 to 7. Note that the tallest bar reflects the high frequency of sites where the *Shopping cart* attribute is present together with the *On-line sales* attribute. (Figure 4).

The next frequency chart represents the crossing of the *Shopping cart* and *Secure Transaction attribute*, it also shows the high frequency of sites which feature both attributes simultaneously (Figure 5).

The third frequency chart (Figure 6) shows the crossing of the *Shopping cart* again, this time with the *Quick buy mechanism*. It can be seen that there is a high frequency of sites which do not have the second when they have the first.

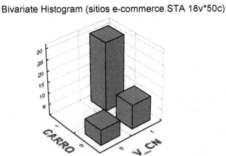

Fig. 4. Shopping cart and on-line sales

Bivariate Histogram (sitios e-commerce.STA 18v*50c)

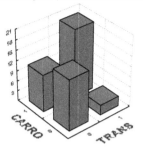

Fig. 5. Shopping cart and secure transaction

Bivariate Histogram (sitios e-commerce.STA 18v*50c)

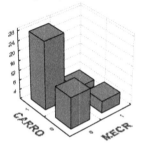

Fig. 6. Shopping cart and quick buy mechanism

Bivariate Histogram (sitios e-commerce.STA 18v*50c)

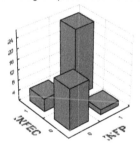

Fig. 7. Shipping & costs and payment information

Finally, the fourth and last frequency chart shows the high frequency of web-sites that simultaneously have the *Shipping and costs information* and *Payment information*. (See Figure 7)

The different statistical approaches used so far have brought to light the extraordinary importance the "Shopping Features" attributes have, independently of the other (also important) attributes such as "Product Information", essential for any e-commerce site and the "Promotion Policies".

Under the assumption that some of the attributes considered among the "Shopping Features" group are highly related and that these relationships have to be cleared up, we proceed to perform the confirmatory study of this hypothesis.

3   Log-linear Adjustment

Given that many of the "Shopping Features" attributes appear as important attributes in the web-site quality study, we decided to adjust some log-linear model that allowed us to point out relationships among these attributes. In this sense there is the inconvenience of having only 49 web-sites, while the number of shopping features is 8 and the cross-tabulations can't be analyzed since numerical problems of different kind appear.

After exploring different tables it was possible to pick the following one, which also presents important attributes, according to the exploratory studies formerly explained:

CC-TRANS (Secure Transaction), CC-CAR (Shopping Cart), CC-IP (Payment Information), CC-ICAN (Cancel Purchase Information), CC- MECR (Quick buy Mechanism) .

The model with all the second-order interactions achieves a good adjustment, since the Pearson's χ^2 statistic has 11.07 with 16 degrees of freedom, with a value of 0.8048 for p. The cross-tabulations of two entries and the corresponding "odds" ratios are shown in Table 3.

As it is known, the Odds ratio (likelihood ratio) in the two-entry tables, that we'll denote by θ, may take the following values:

$\theta = 1$ When the variables are independent

$1 < \theta$ When sites from row 1 are *more likely* to fall into column 1 than sites from row 2.

$0 < \theta < 1$ When sites from row 1 are *less likely* to fall into column 1 than sites from row 2.

From the values calculated in the table the next relationships arise:

Web-sites that do not have shopping carts are 27.27 times more likely to not having secure transactions compared to the ones that do.

The web-sites that do not have quick buy mechanism are 0.28 times less likely to not having shopping carts compared to the ones that do have quick buy mechanism.

Web-sites without quick buy mechanism are 0.32 less likely to have secure transactions than the ones that have it.

Web-sites without payment information are 1.87 (i. e. almost twice) more likely to not having secure transactions compared to the ones that have payment information.

Table 3. Cross-tabulations of attributes

CC- TRANS

CC-CAR	0	1	Total
0	15	3	18
1	11	20	31
Total	26	23	49

Odds ratio = 27.27

CC- TRANS

CC-IP	0	1	Total
0	13	8	21
1	13	15	28
Total	26	23	49

Odds ratio = 1.87

CC- TRANS

CC-ICAN	0	1	Total
0	23	20	43
1	3	3	6
Total	26	23	49

Odds ratio = 1.15

CC- TRANS

CC-MERC	0	1	Total
0	20	21	41
1	6	2	8
Total	26	23	49

Odds ratio = 0.32

CC- CAR

CC-IP	0	1	Total
0	8	13	21
1	10	18	28
Total	18	31	49

Odds ratio = 1.11

CC- CAR

CC-ICAN	0	1	Total
0	16	27	43
1	2	4	6
Total	18	31	49

Odds ratio = 1.18

CC- CAR

CC-MERC	0	1	Total
0	13	28	41
1	5	3	8
Total	18	31	49

Odds ratio = 0.28

CC- IP

CC-ICAN	0	1	Total
0	20	23	43
1	1	5	6
Total	21	28	49

Odds ratio = 4.35

CC- IP

CC-MECR	0	1	Total
0	17	24	41
1	4	4	8
Total	21	28	49

Odds ratio = 0.71

CC- ICAN

CC-MECR	0	1	Total
0	36	5	41
1	7	1	8
Total	43	6	49

Odds ratio = 1.028

4   Conclusions

After an exhaustive analysis of the dataset for the 49 web-sites, the following conclusions were drawn:

All selected attributes for the quality study of the "functionality" aspect of web-sites are relevant and even though, logically, the "Product Information" attributes should be considered essential and are therefore available in a high proportion of the sites, we consider that the "Shopping Features" attributes stand out because of their importance in these sites' quality. Such attributes are:

On-line sales, Secure transaction, Shopping cart, Payment information, Purchase Cancellation information and Quick buy mechanisms. The relationships between these attributes have been described in prior analyses [2, 3, 9].

The "Promotion Policies" attributes follow in order of importance.

Particularly, and returning to the log-linear adjustment results, we can state that those web-sites that feature shopping carts should consider having secure transactions.

On the other hand, the e-commerce sites without quick buy mechanism are unlikely to lack shopping carts. That is, even though the probability ratios obtained by the log-linear adjustments are low for this pair of variables, it is necessary to pay special attention to them when an e-commerce site is being designed/built. In other words, it is not completely necessary to include a shopping cart if a quick buy mechanism is present, but it is highly advisable to have both. This conclusion stems from the fact that the probability of finding an e-commerce site without both of these attributes is low, but not zero.

It is unusual not to pair quick buy mechanisms with secure transactions. The probability of finding a site which lacks both attributes is low. Given this, we recommend that when building an e-commerce site and including a quick buy mechanism, there must be a secure transaction mechanism.

If a web-site does not have cancellation information then it is more than four times more likely to also lack payment information than having it. This means that there is a four times higher probability of finding sites without both attributes than finding a site that does not have the attributes mentioned in conclusions 2 and 3.

The payment information attributes can not be exclusive.

To put into practice these recommendations of pairing some attributes with others requires a redesign of one of the sites with the observed restriction, and then a comparison of the "new and improved" with the original, which implies an expensive marketing study. As attractive as it sounds, the cost is not only a function of the research work associated, but also of the high economic and time investment.

A competitive alternative for predicting results from the above recommendations is to use a data mining approach, which may give good results for economic models, but the data involved has to "have a history". For this reason, the binary table we have is not of much help and we should consider another data collecting process, adequate for the data mining approach.

At first look it could be said that certain quality attributes are obvious, but without backing it objectively. Even tough different methods exists for evaluating usability of websites [11], and other methods and techniques to analyze data and make predictions, a comprehensive study has yet to be made to study site's behavior and client satisfaction. There is a great complexity involved in combining different mechanisms to know the exact state of e-commerce websites. For example, the evaluation activity should have been adopted in practice to such a degree as to guarantee the quality of a website the moment it enters the market. This rarely occurs though.

Leaving aside the strategies currently used by companies to ensure quality and predict potential sales, it is not only useful to have a quality model that reflects the features and attributes necessary to guarantee the quality of an e-commerce website, but it also allows to follow the behavior of sites that comply with a subset of such features. In this way, this work starts an investigation line for e-commerce from several angles.

References

[1]   Anderson, T.W, 1984, "An Introduction to Multivariate Statistical Analysis", 2nd Edition,. Wiley.
[2]   Bernábe L., B.; 2003, "Evaluación Estadística de Datos Cualitativos en Comercio Electrónico", Tesis Master, Universidad Iberoamericana -l Golfo Centro, Puebla, México.
[3]   Bernábe L., B, Olsina, L, 2003 "Análisis Factorial de Correspondencias Simples en el procesamiento de datos cualitativos sobre funcionalidad en comercio electrónico", Novena Conferencia de Ingeniería Eléctrica 2003, CINVESTAV-IPN.
[4]   4. Chatfield, C.; Collins, A.J., 1991, "Introduction to Multivariate Analysis", Ed. Chapman & Hall.
[5]   Dillon, W.R. & Goldstein, M., 1984, "Multivariate Analysis: Methods and Applications", Wiley, New York.
[6]   Dixon,W.J , 1990, "BMDP Statistical Software Manual", Vol I, II., Dixon,W.J Eds, University of California Press, Berkeley, California.
[7]   Kalakota, R.; Whisnton, A.B.,1997, "Electronic Commerce: A Manager's Guide", Addison-Wesley.
[8]   Lafuente, G.H.; Oliveto, J.; Olsina, L.; 2000, "Requerimientos de Calidad en Sitios de E-commerce" Proceed. JUCSE 00, Nuevas Tendencias en Ingeniería de Software, Universidad Católica de Santiago del Estero, Arg., ISBN 950-31-0045-3.
[9]   Loranca, M.B. & Olsina, L.; 2003, "Técnicas Estadísticas para el Análisis de la Calidad de Sitios Web ", 6o Workshop Iberoamericano de Ingeniería de Requisitos y Ambientes Software (IDEAS 2003), Asunción Paraguay.
[10]   Olsina, L.; Lafuente, G.J.; Rossi, G.; 2000, "E-commerce Site Evaluation: a Case Study", Lecture Notes in Computer Science 1875, Proc. 1st International Conference on Electronic Commerce and Web Technology (ECWeb 2000) , Springer-Verlag, London-Greenwich, UK, pp. 239-252.
[11]   Ruíz Shulcloper. J., Alba, E. y Lazo Cortés, M. "Reconocimiento de Patrones", (ediciones I, II, II y IV). México, D.F. (1994). Diplomado de titulación. Benemérita Universidad Autónoma de Puebla.

Appendix A

Table A.1 Functionality and Content-oriented E-Commerce Attributes and Variables

1		Product Information	
	1.1	Basic Product Description	IP-DES
	1.2	Product Image	IP-IMA
	1.3	Catalog	IP-CAT
2		Shopping Features	
	2.1	On-line Sales	CC-V-ON
	2.2	Off-line Sales	CC-V-OFF
	2.3	Secure Transaction	CC-TRANS
	2.4	Shopping Cart	CC-CAR
	2.5	Shipping and Cost Information	CC-IEC
	2.6	Payment Information	CC-IP
	2.7	Purchase Cancellation Information	CC-ICAN
	2.8	Quick Buy Mechanism	CC-MERC
3		Client Customization	
	3.1	Subscription	PC-SUS
	3-2	Customized Account	PC-CUEN
4		Promotion Policies	
	4.1	Promotion at Sale	PP-PROV
	4.2	Promotion by prizes	PP-PROVR
5		Searching Mechanisms	
	5.1	Global	MB-GLO
	5.2	Restricted	MB-RES

Table. A.2 Column coordinates and inertia contributions (Burt Table).

	Row Num	Coo D1	Coo D2	Coor D3	Mass	Quality	Rel Inertia	Iner D1	Cos² D1	Iner D2	Cos² D2	Inert D3	Cos² D3
IP_DES:0	1	-.99	-.09	-1.76	.007	.570	.052	.04	.13	.000	.000	.180	.430
IP_DES:1	2	.14	.01	.25	.052	.570	.007	.006	.137	.000	.001	.026	.430
IP_IMA:0	3	-.76	-.60	-1.36	.011	.625	.048	.036	.129	.031	.080	.165	.416
IP_IMA:1	4	.17	.13	.31	.048	.625	.011	.008	.129	.007	.080	.037	.416
IP_CAT:0	5	.181	.20	1.05	.006	.293	.053	.001	.004	.069	.165	.054	.125
IP_CAT:1	6	-.02	-.14	-.12	.053	.293	.006	.000	.004	.008	.165	.006	.125
CCVON:0	7	-1.45	-.32	-.55	.008	.418	.050	.103	.350	.007	.017	.021	.051
CCVON:1	8	.24	.05	.09	.050	.418	.008	.017	.350	.001	.017	.004	.051
CCVOFF:0	9	.50	.41	-.18	.024	.312	.035	.036	.175	.032	.116	.006	.022
CCVOFF:1	10	-.35	-.28	.12	.035	.312	.024	.024	.175	.022	.116	.004	.022
CTRA.:0	11	-.60	-.15	.19	.031	.473	.028	.065	.406	.006	.027	.009	.041
CTRA.:1	12	.68	.17	-.22	.028	.473	.031	.074	.406	.007	.027	.011	.041
CCCAR:0	13	-1.12	.15	.24	.022	.779	.037	.159	.734	.004	.012	.010	.033
CCCAR:1	14	.65	-.08	-.14	.037	.779	.022	.092	.734	.002	.012	.006	.033
CC_IEC:0	15	-.31	-1.04	.42	.022	.782	.037	.012	.056	.185	.623	.031	.102
CC_IEC:1	16	.18	.60	-.24	.037	.782	.022	.007	.056	.107	.623	.018	.102
CC_IP:0	17	-.15	-.72	.51	.025	.603	.034	.003	.016	.105	.392	.054	.196
CC_IP:1	18	.11	.54	-.38	.034	.603	.025	.002	.016	.079	.392	.041	.196
CCICA:0	19	.03	-.05	.13	.052	.151	.007	.000	.006	.001	.018	.008	.127
CCICA:1	20	-.21	.36	-.95	.007	.151	.052	.002	.006	.007	.018	.054	.127
CCME:0	21	.06	-.18	-.24	.049	.474	.010	.001	.019	.012	.159	.023	.296
CCME:1	22	-.31	.90	1.23	.010	.474	.049	.006	.019	.062	.159	.120	.296
PCSUS:0	23	-.18	.28	.05	.043	.315	.016	.008	.093	.027	.216	.001	.006
PCSUS:1	24	.51	-.77	-.13	.016	.315	.043	.024	.093	.074	.216	.002	.006
PCCUE:0	25	-.37	.31	.04	.036	.363	.023	.028	.212	.027	.147	.001	.003
PCCUE:1	26	.58	-.48	-.07	.023	.363	.036	.045	.212	.042	.147	.001	.003
PPPRV:0	27	-.05	-.01	.35	.034	.164	.025	.001	.003	.000	.000	.033	.161
PPPRV:1	28	.07	.01	-.46	.025	.164	.034	.001	.003	.000	.000	.044	.161
PPPPR:0	29	-.06	.04	-.10	.048	.071	.011	.001	.015	.001	.009	.004	.048
PPPPR:1	30	.25	-.20	.46	.011	.071	.048	.004	.015	.003	.009	.019	.048
MBGO:0	31	-.31	.27	.00	.038	.317	.020	.022	.184	.022	.133	.000	.000
MBGO:1	32	.59	-.50	-.01	.020	.317	.038	.041	.184	.041	.133	.000	.000
MBRE:0	33	-.47	.10	.07	.037	.401	.022	.047	.376	.003	.017	.001	.008
MBRS:1	34	.80	-.17	-.12	.022	.401	.037	.082	.376	.005	.017	.002	.008

A Distributed Digital Text Accessing
and Acquisition System

Adolfo Guzmán Arenas and Victor-Polo de Gyves

SoftwarePro International*
a.guzman@acm.org

Abstract. BiblioDigital ® is a network of reservoirs (R) of text documents. Each document exists *primarily* in one R, with possible duplicates in other Rs. Each R sits in its own server. Each document in indexed in three ways: * by themes (vocabulary controlled by that R's librarian); * by *each word* in the document, * by the *concepts* which the document covers (using Clasitex ®). Each R contains the *global index* (of all Rs), so that each R can provide the following services: * browsing by themes; * by concepts; * by words; * by metadata; * by Boolean combination of above. Also, BiblioDigital * allows subscription to a personal News Services: through a user interest profile; * BiblioDigital combs the Web for documents that could fall in the themes or topics contained in its indices, and indexes them, thus enriching its knowledge content.

Keywords: Digital library, distributed, concept classification, crawler

1 Introduction

BiblioDigital, a distributed collection of reservoirs (R) containing full text documents is described. The system is already implemented and some small examples are given.

1.1 Executive Summary

In addition to what the summary explains, other important features of BiblioDigital®:

- A reader can, through *any* R, have access to *all* its documents;
- A *librarian* (owner of an R) registers *authors;* readers (users) do not need to register; documents are primarily free and without encription;
- It allows document *versions,* auxiliary documents (tests, software...);
- Subsumes (absorbs full texts, and/or just indexes them) documents sitting in foreign libraries, thus allowing its full exploitation;
- It uses meta data (example: Dublin Core), if this option is on;
- Multimedia documents can be indexed, if they contain a text description;
- It handles documents in popular formats (plain text, PDF, Word, Excel...);

---

* BiblioDigital ® is property of SoftwarePro International. Adolfo Guzman is a researcher at CIC-IPN.

F. F. Ramos, H. Unger, V. Larios (Eds.): ISSADS 2004, LNCS 3061, pp. 274-283, 2004.

- Allows each librarian to have his own taxonomy of themes, and also uses its own global ontology of concepts imposed by Clasitex ®);
- Each R has a *cache* of frequent documents.

Features of a (yet to exist) second version of BiblioDigital®:

- Fault tolerance; damaged document correction;
- Servers can "get in" or "get out" of the mesh of Rs, *a la* peer-to-peer, without a root node (to be explained below);
- The global index will be distributed when too large for a single server.

1.2 Comparison to Previous Work

The field of digital libraries has made much progress; an early but still influential collection of articles is [1].

Most of the features of BiblioDigital can be found in other systems; it is the unique mixture of them, coming from the experience of the builders and some users in effective uses of text documents, that make BiblioDigital unique. Another unique feature of BiblioDigital is its use of Clasitex ® [3] to classify a document in the themes it talks about.

Single-server (not distributed) digital libraries are useful; in Mexico, Phronesis [2] is popular.

Federated libraries, or federated search, is handled often [4] by converting an initial user query in semantically equivalent queries expressed in other dialects, that "the other" libraries can answer directly. BiblioDigital does not use this approach, instead, it " milks" each document of a foreign library (§2.8) and indexes it, keeping the document in its original library.

To keep a replica of the global index (§3.2) in each R is a simplification of the peer-to-peer protocol, which we felt too complex to be of use now. In attention to the growth of the global index, tables are kept in R to migrate later to a more advanced distribution of the index, in which each server has only part of the total global index.

The mail service of personalized information (§2.4) according to a user profile is hardly new, but its use in digital libraries is somewhat of a novelty. Another novelty in digital libraries seem to be the *collections* introduced in §2.5.

Advanced search services (§2.7) can be found in some systems, like Amazon's book store; in previous experiences, we have found them quite useful, so that their implementation is coming (§3.5).

The handling of video files in BiblioDigital is possible, but due to limits in bandwidth, is not sponsored. Instead, the architecture in [5] is more appropriate this purpose.

2 Description

BiblioDigital® is a confederation of independent similar libraries, linked by a global index.

A node of BiblioDigital®, to be called R (reservoir) is a physical place (a computer) where text and image electronic documents are stored in an organized way, to be provided to users, which can access them through any computer connected to Internet.

The manager of an R is its *librarian*: he registers *authors*, *collections* and their *editors*; he defines the taxonomy of themes in that R. *Readers* need not be registered in order to use BiblioDigital.

Rs form a tree: each R (except the root, called *Adam*) has a parent R. Each document and each collection sits in (*belongs to*) exactly on a R. Each R lies in a PC (a *server* of BiblioDigital) with enough disk, no-break, antivirus... See figure 1.

A reader, connected to any R, can access all documents in BiblioDigital, not only those of the R to which he is connected.

An author can (a) add new documents to the R to which he belongs; (b) update his documents; (c) add supplemental documents to (primary) documents previously entered into R. An editor of a collection can add (links to) documents to it, and update its *status*. Adding copyrighted material by an author can be illegal or punishable; a warning is posted at the upload window.

2.1 Access to a Document

By Theme. The thematic structure or taxonomy of an R is defined by its librarian. Each author classifies his document into one or more of those predefined themes (controlled vocabulary), including the theme "others."

By Concept. The structure (ontology) of concepts is given by the system, which [automatically] classifies (using Clasitex ®) the document in the concepts covered by it.

By the Words and Special Phrases ("In God we trust") in it. The structure is an alphabetical list; classification is automatic (by the system).

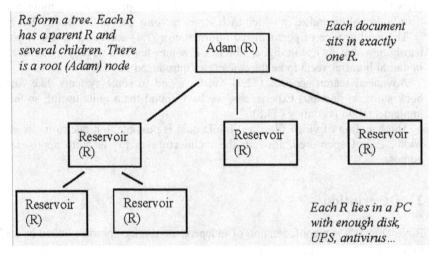

Fig. 1. BiblioDigital is a tree of physical reservoirs (R) holding electronic documents. Rs share a global index that is updated every night

Bivariate Histogram (sitios e-commerce.STA 18v*50c)

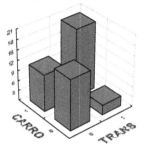

Fig. 5. Shopping cart and secure transaction

Bivariate Histogram (sitios e-commerce.STA 18v*50c)

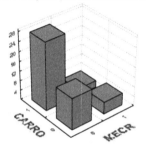

Fig. 6. Shopping cart and quick buy mechanism

Bivariate Histogram (sitios e-commerce.STA 18v*50c)

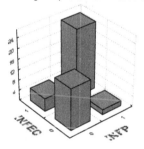

Fig. 7. Shipping & costs and payment information

Finally, the fourth and last frequency chart shows the high frequency of web-sites that simultaneously have the *Shipping and costs information* and *Payment information.* (See Figure 7)

The different statistical approaches used so far have brought to light the extraordinary importance the "Shopping Features" attributes have, independently of the other (also important) attributes such as "Product Information", essential for any e-commerce site and the "Promotion Policies".

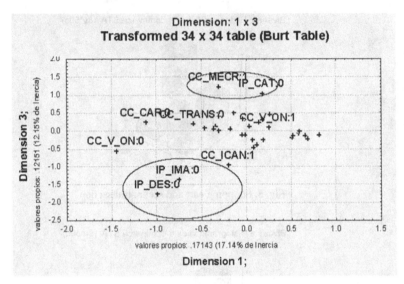

Fig. 3. Burt's Table chart for dimensions 1 and 3

The above interpretation is corroborated by the frequency charts in Fig.s 4 to 7.
Note that the tallest bar reflects the high frequency of sites where the *Shopping cart* attribute is present together with the *On-line sales* attribute. (Figure 4).

The next frequency chart represents the crossing of the *Shopping cart* and *Secure Transaction attribute*, it also shows the high frequency of sites which feature both attributes simultaneously (Figure 5).

The third frequency chart (Figure 6) shows the crossing of the *Shopping cart* again, this time with the *Quick buy mechanism*. It can be seen that there is a high frequency of sites which do not have the second when they have the first.

Fig. 4. Shopping cart and on-line sales

instance) may trigger the transitions; thus, *collections* are a hook for workflow software. A document can belong to 0, 1 or more collections.

2.6 More on a Document

A document (called now the main document.) can have: (a) versions; (b) associated or auxiliary documents: exercises, slides, solutions, additional examples, software…

Metadata. Each document has a small table (metadata) describing it: autor, date, language… which the author fills, with some fields pre-filled by R. Currently, we use Dublin Core.

2.7 Advanced Search or Markov Search

These are based on the dynamics of the reader, as he jumps from a set of documents to the next, or from document to document. Examples. "I offer you documents similar (in concepts content) to those you have been reading." "I offer you documents that other readers with your same dynamic reading path have been reading." "70% of readers that read document A and then B also read document C; here is C." "Give me all the documents read last month by Carlos Fuentes." "Or by the Engineers Association." "And about the NAFTA agreement."

Some of these searches, although technically possible, are not available since they go against the privacy of readers.

2.8 Access to other Existing Digital Libraries

Documents in existing digital libraries can be indexed and served (shown) by Biblio-Digital:

- if they possess metadata, by the items in such metadata;
- In any event, by concepts and by word content;
- If they have a summary, it will be used by BiblioDigital.

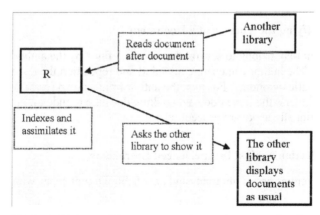

Fig. 4. From BiblioDigital it is possible to access and serve documents in other existing digital libraries, if these provide the two APIs shown

Each document can be shown to the user by calling the original software (that is, calling the *other* digital library). The foreing documents are kept at their original site; BiblioDigital does not acquire (import) their full text. See figure 4. It is also possible to import those documents in full text, duplicating them.

2.9 Cache of Recent Documents

Automatically, BiblioDigital keeps in the disk of the local server R a cache area with the recent documents most used by readers logged in that R. This area is updated automatically. This increases access speed to those documents.

2.10 Modifying the Taxonomies

Changes to the taxonomy of themes defined by a librarian for his R are infrequently allowed. To add new themes (nodes) initially empty is no problem, except that some documents belonging to the parent (of the new node) now belong more appropriately to the new node (the new son). So, these documents must be "moved down" by the author from the father to the new son. This provokes additional work for the authors, which they will tolerate if infrequent.

In general, repositioning the documents from an outgoing (old) part of the thematic taxonomy to the incoming (new) corresponding part, is done by the librarian as follows:

1. The old part of R (with all its documents) is brought down ("erased.")
2. The new part of R (new part of the taxonomy) is brought up ("created"), initially empty.
3. Each author takes his documents deleted in (1) and adds them to (some of) the new nodes of (2),

Notice that no changes are needed to the concept taxonomy. With respect to the Full word index, the librarian can introduce more "stop words;" that is, words that should not be indexed.

2.11 Modifying the Themes of a Document

A document may belong to several themes, as defined by the author at upload ("entering") time. The author can change his mind and reposition the document in the nodes of the thematic taxonomy. For this, the author brings down (erases) his document and brings up (enters) the same document, taking due care to index it in the new themes. It is an intentionally awkward procedure.

2.12 Protection against Inexperienced Librarians

Some frequent errors of librarians and how BiblioDigital copes with them:

Frequent Changes to the Thematic Taxonomy. They will not be possible, since this is an intentionally painful procedure. Cf. §2.10.

To Register an Excessive Number of Authors. This may be allowed up to disk capacity, or there could be limits imposed by BiblioDigital (none at present).

Badly Constructed Taxonomies, where the grandfather is brother of the grandson. There are guides, some of them accessible inside BiblioDigital, about how to construct good (solid, sound) taxonomies. If the librarian produces a bad taxonomy, it is his responsibility. BiblioDigital makes no further checking or advising.

2.13 Protection against Inexperienced Authors

Some frequent errors of authors and how BiblioDigital copes with them:
  Controllable by the librarian:

- An author uploads pornographic or irrelevant documents (music, pictures). This can be tolerated or prohibited by the librarian.
- An author enters too many texts. The librarian can set a limit in number of documents, or in megabytes.
- An author assigns the wrong themes to his document. Fixable by the author.

An author assigns to a document of him themes that do not exist in the thematic taxonomy. This is impossible, since the themes are selected from a menu. The only "new" theme is the theme "others." Also, an author can request from his librarian the addition of a new theme to the thematic taxonomy of their R.

2.14 Several Authors Write a Document

This is simple in BiblioDigital:

- The librarian defines one of the authors as the editor of a (new) collection.
- An author writes his parts and sends them to that collection in R. He also sends comments and criticisms to the other parts,
- The editor accepts, rejects or modifies parts and criticisms.
- When finished, the editor erases the collection and creates (enters) the document as a new document. Or the final form of the document is kept in the collection.

3   Handling Foreign Documents

No matter how many documents can sit in all Rs, there always be more documents *outside* (in the Web). To tap these foreign riches, BiblioDigital reads and indexes (by concepts, and by words) the documents "outside BiblioDigital."

For this, librarians provide a set of sites (URLs) where there exist indexable documents. BiblioDigital divides this set into subsets, one for each R. The crawler of each R will search Web pages in each subset for suitable documents, to be added to that R (the document is not imported into R, but is kept in its original site).

To avoid work duplication (an spider or crawler accesses node NSF, and another spider is doing the same), there is a procedure where these crawlers share and synchronize themselves for time to time, avoiding overlap in search.

3.1 Other Documents: Audio, Images

They can be indexed, as long as they have metadata or a written (text) description or introduction. Only certain kinds of formats can be stored in BiblioDigital: (TXT, HTML, XML, PDF, PS, DOC, MPG).

3.2 High Performance

More than 100 queries/second (with 5 servers)

- The themes, concepts and words *are already indexed.*
- Each R has the total index and *all* summaries of every document (of all Rs).
- Normally, a user connects to an R of themes intesting to him:
  - A physician connect to the medical R;
  - This diminishes traffic between Rs;
- Automatic caching of frequently read documents; a cache for each R;
- I can order a query the night before.

3.3 Module to Manage Taxonomies

BiblioDigital comes with an editor for the librarian to arm and maintain his taxonomy: update, add and delete nodes. Every change to a taxonomy already in site (active, with documents) will affect the indices and introduce re-indexing, much of this of manual nature. It also comes with a manual of "good manners to form a taxonomy."
    Recommendation: think and test a taxonomy before enabling it.

3.4 Mail from Readers, to Authors, Editors...

BiblioDigital allows a reader to send a document to a friends. There is also communication with the autor, librarian and editor of a collection. Also, a reader can add small comments to an article that he has read. An author, editor or librarian can add in BiblioDigital a pointer to his Web page.

3.5 Status

Version 1 is running since January 2004, it is a development of the authors for SoftwarePro International. More information at: a.guzman@acm.org Version 1 also handles audio files, as well as it monitors the principal news in (electronic) newspapers of national coverage. Version 2 will have the features of §§2.7-2.9

References

[1]   Computer, Vol. **32,** number Two. Feb. 1999. Digital Libraries. IEEE Computer Society.

[2]   David A. Garza-Salazar, Juan C. Lavariega, Martha Sordia-Salinas. Information Retrieval and Administration of Distributed Documents in Internet. The Phronesis Digital Library Project, in *Knowledge Based Information Retrieval and Filtering from Internet*, Kluwer Academic Publishers, Boston, MA. 2003.

[3]   Guzman, A. Finding the main themes in a Spanish document. (1998) *Journal Expert Systems with Applications,* Vol. **14,** No. 1/2, 139-148, Jan./Feb Phronesis.

[4]   Bruce Schatz, William Mischo *et al.* Federated search of scientific literature. In [1], pages 51-59.

[5]   Howard. D. Watclar, Michael G. Christel *et al.* Lessons learned from building a terabyte digital video library. In [1], pages 66-73.

Author Index

Álvarez, Juan Salvador Gómez .. 67
Angelotti, Elaini Simoni 54, 91
Arenas, Adolfo Guzman 1, 274
Ávila, Bráulio C. 137
Azevedo, Hilton de 54

Balet, Olivier 19
Beccue, Barbara 42
Bernard, Thibault 231
Buenabad, Jorge 219
Bui, Alain 231
Butelle, Franck 241

Calsavara, Alcides 31, 145
Carrillo, Victor Hugo Zaldivar .. 67
Carvalho, Deborah 54
Castro, Miguel 219

Delot, Thierry 125
Drira, Khalil 158, 197
Duthen, Yves 19

Enembreck, Fabrício 137
Espinosa, José Martin Molina ..158

Fanchon, Jean 158
Filho, Juarez da Costa Cesar 31
Flauzac, Olivier 231

Goddard, John 219
Gyves, Victor-Polo de 274

Hakem, Mourad 241
Hasegawa, Fabiano M. 137
Hernandez, Ivan Romero 78

Jamont, Jean-Paul 105
Jessel, Jean-Pierre 9

Koning, Jean-Luc 78

Lechner, Ulrike 170
Loranca,
  María Beatriz Bernábe 261
Luga, Hervé 19

Martínez, Alma 219
Mishra, Mayank 207
Moo-Mena, Francisco 197

Noda, Agnaldo K. 31

Occello, Michel 105
Ocegueda, Francisco 118

Pasquier, Jérôme Leboeuf 252
Pulido, Luis Jose 9

Ramos, Félix 118
Ramos, Milton 54
Rodríguez, Gerardo Chavarín ...67
Rodriguez, Nancy 9
Román, Graciela 219

Sakaryan, German 170
Sánchez, Roberto 118
Sanchez, Stéphane 19
Santos, Emerson L. dos 137
Santos, Luis Antonio Olsina ...261
Scalabrin, Edson 54, 91
Schmidt, Glauco 145

Thilliez, Marie 125

Unger, Herwig 170, 186

Vila, Joaquin 42

Wulff, Markus 186

Lecture Notes in Computer Science

For information about Vols. 1–3028

please contact your bookseller or Springer-Verlag

Vol. 3139: F. Iida, R. Pfeifer, L. Steels, Y. Kuniyoshi (Eds.), Embodied Artificial Intelligence. IX, 331 pages. 2004. (Subseries LNAI).

Vol. 3133: A.D. Pimentel, S. Vassiliadis (Eds.), Computer Systems, Architectures, Modeling, and Simulation. XIII, 562 pages. 2004.

Vol. 3125: D. Kozen (Ed.), Mathematics of Program Construction. X, 401 pages. 2004.

Vol. 3123: A. Belz, R. Evans, P. Piwek (Eds.), Generating Language. X, 219 pages. 2004. (Subseries LNAI).

Vol. 3120: J. Shawe-Taylor, Y. Singer (Eds.), Learning Theory. X, 648 pages. 2004. (Subseries LNAI).

Vol. 3118: K. Miesenberger, J. Klaus, W. Zagler, D. Burger (Eds.), Computer Helping People with Special Needs. XXIII, 1191 pages. 2004.

Vol. 3116: C. Rattray, S. Maharaj, C. Shankland (Eds.), Algebraic Methodology and Software Technology. XI, 569 pages. 2004.

Vol. 3114: R. Alur, D.A. Peled (Eds.), Computer Aided Verification. XII, 536 pages. 2004.

Vol. 3113: J. Karhumäki, H. Maurer, G. Paun, G. Rozenberg (Eds.), Theory Is Forever. X, 283 pages. 2004.

Vol. 3112: H. Williams, L. MacKinnon (Eds.), New Horizons in Information Management. XII, 265 pages. 2004.

Vol. 3111: T. Hagerup, J. Katajainen (Eds.), Algorithm Theory - SWAT 2004. XI, 506 pages. 2004.

Vol. 3110: A. Juels (Ed.), Financial Cryptography. XI, 281 pages. 2004.

Vol. 3109: S.C. Sahinalp, S. Muthukrishnan, U. Dogrusoz (Eds.), Combinatorial Pattern Matching. XII, 486 pages. 2004.

Vol. 3108: H. Wang, J. Pieprzyk, V. Varadharajan (Eds.), Information Security and Privacy. XII, 494 pages. 2004.

Vol. 3107: J. Bosch, C. Krueger (Eds.), Software Reuse: Methods, Techniques and Tools. XI, 339 pages. 2004.

Vol. 3105: S. Göbel, U. Spierling, A. Hoffmann, I. Iurgel, O. Schneider, J. Dechau, A. Feix (Eds.), Technologies for Interactive Digital Storytelling and Entertainment. XVI, 304 pages. 2004.

Vol. 3104: R. Kralovic, O. Sykora (Eds.), Structural Information and Communication Complexity. X, 303 pages. 2004.

Vol. 3103: K. Deb (Ed.), Genetic and Evolutionary Computation - GECCO 2004. XLIX, 1439 pages. 2004.

Vol. 3102: K. Deb (Ed.), Genetic and Evolutionary Computation - GECCO 2004. L, 1445 pages. 2004.

Vol. 3101: M. Masoodian, S. Jones, B. Rogers (Eds.), Computer Human Interaction. XIV, 694 pages. 2004.

Vol. 3100: J.F. Peters, A. Skowron, J.W. Grzymała-Busse, B. Kostek, R.W. Świniarski, M.S. Szczuka (Eds.), Transactions on Rough Sets I. X, 405 pages. 2004.

Vol. 3099: J. Cortadella, W. Reisig (Eds.), Applications and Theory of Petri Nets 2004. XI, 505 pages. 2004.

Vol. 3098: J. Desel, W. Reisig, G. Rozenberg (Eds.), Lectures on Concurrency and Petri Nets. VIII, 849 pages. 2004.

Vol. 3097: D. Basin, M. Rusinowitch (Eds.), Automated Reasoning. XII, 493 pages. 2004. (Subseries LNAI).

Vol. 3096: G. Melnik, H. Holz (Eds.), Advances in Learning Software Organizations. X, 173 pages. 2004.

Vol. 3094: A. Nürnberger, M. Detyniecki (Eds.), Adaptive Multimedia Retrieval. VIII, 229 pages. 2004.

Vol. 3093: S.K. Katsikas, S. Gritzalis, J. Lopez (Eds.), Public Key Infrastructure. XIII, 380 pages. 2004.

Vol. 3092: J. Eckstein, H. Baumeister (Eds.), Extreme Programming and Agile Processes in Software Engineering. XVI, 358 pages. 2004.

Vol. 3091: V. van Oostrom (Ed.), Rewriting Techniques and Applications. X, 313 pages. 2004.

Vol. 3089: M. Jakobsson, M. Yung, J. Zhou (Eds.), Applied Cryptography and Network Security. XIV, 510 pages. 2004.

Vol. 3086: M. Odersky (Ed.), ECOOP 2004 - Object-Oriented Programming. XIII, 611 pages. 2004.

Vol. 3085: S. Berardi, M. Coppo, F. Damiani (Eds.), Types for Proofs and Programs. X, 409 pages. 2004.

Vol. 3084: A. Persson, J. Stirna (Eds.), Advanced Information Systems Engineering. XIV, 596 pages. 2004.

Vol. 3083: W. Emmerich, A.L. Wolf (Eds.), Component Deployment. X, 249 pages. 2004.

Vol. 3080: J. Desel, B. Pernici, M. Weske (Eds.), Business Process Management. X, 307 pages. 2004.

Vol. 3079: Z. Mammeri, P. Lorenz (Eds.), High Speed Networks and Multimedia Communications. XVIII, 1103 pages. 2004.

Vol. 3078: S. Cotin, D.N. Metaxas (Eds.), Medical Simulation. XVI, 296 pages. 2004.

Vol. 3077: F. Roli, J. Kittler, T. Windeatt (Eds.), Multiple Classifier Systems. XII, 386 pages. 2004.

Vol. 3076: D. Buell (Ed.), Algorithmic Number Theory. XI, 451 pages. 2004.

Vol. 3074: B. Kuijpers, P. Revesz (Eds.), Constraint Databases and Applications. XII, 181 pages. 2004.

Vol. 3073: H. Chen, R. Moore, D.D. Zeng, J. Leavitt (Eds.), Intelligence and Security Informatics. XV, 536 pages. 2004.

Vol. 3072: D. Zhang, A.K. Jain (Eds.), Biometric Authentication. XVII, 800 pages. 2004.

Vol. 3071: A. Omicini, P. Petta, J. Pitt (Eds.), Engineering Societies in the Agents World. XIII, 409 pages. 2004. (Subseries LNAI).

Vol. 3070: L. Rutkowski, J. Siekmann, R. Tadeusiewicz, L.A. Zadeh (Eds.), Artificial Intelligence and Soft Computing - ICAISC 2004. XXV, 1208 pages. 2004. (Subseries LNAI).

Vol. 3068: E. André, L. Dybkjær, W. Minker, P. Heisterkamp (Eds.), Affective Dialogue Systems. XII, 324 pages. 2004. (Subseries LNAI).

Vol. 3067: M. Dastani, J. Dix, A. El Fallah-Seghrouchni (Eds.), Programming Multi-Agent Systems. X, 221 pages. 2004. (Subseries LNAI).

Vol. 3066: S. Tsumoto, R. Słowiński, J. Komorowski, J.W. Grzymała-Busse (Eds.), Rough Sets and Current Trends in Computing. XX, 853 pages. 2004. (Subseries LNAI).

Vol. 3065: A. Lomuscio, D. Nute (Eds.), Deontic Logic in Computer Science. X, 275 pages. 2004. (Subseries LNAI).

Vol. 3064: D. Bienstock, G. Nemhauser (Eds.), Integer Programming and Combinatorial Optimization. XI, 445 pages. 2004.

Vol. 3063: A. Llamosí, A. Strohmeier (Eds.), Reliable Software Technologies - Ada-Europe 2004. XIII, 333 pages. 2004.

Vol. 3062: J.L. Pfaltz, M. Nagl, B. Böhlen (Eds.), Applications of Graph Transformations with Industrial Relevance. XV, 500 pages. 2004.

Vol. 3061: F.F. Ramos, H. Unger, V. Larios (Eds.), Advanced Distributed Systems. VIII, 285 pages. 2004.

Vol. 3060: A.Y. Tawfik, S.D. Goodwin (Eds.), Advances in Artificial Intelligence. XIII, 582 pages. 2004. (Subseries LNAI).

Vol. 3059: C.C. Ribeiro, S.L. Martins (Eds.), Experimental and Efficient Algorithms. X, 586 pages. 2004.

Vol. 3058: N. Sebe, M.S. Lew, T.S. Huang (Eds.), Computer Vision in Human-Computer Interaction. X, 233 pages. 2004.

Vol. 3057: B. Jayaraman (Ed.), Practical Aspects of Declarative Languages. VIII, 255 pages. 2004.

Vol. 3056: H. Dai, R. Srikant, C. Zhang (Eds.), Advances in Knowledge Discovery and Data Mining. XIX, 713 pages. 2004. (Subseries LNAI).

Vol. 3055: H. Christiansen, M.-S. Hacid, T. Andreasen, H.L. Larsen (Eds.), Flexible Query Answering Systems. X, 500 pages. 2004. (Subseries LNAI).

Vol. 3054: I. Crnkovic, J.A. Stafford, H.W. Schmidt, K. Wallnau (Eds.), Component-Based Software Engineering. XI, 311 pages. 2004.

Vol. 3053: C. Bussler, J. Davies, D. Fensel, R. Studer (Eds.), The Semantic Web: Research and Applications. XIII, 490 pages. 2004.

Vol. 3052: W. Zimmermann, B. Thalheim (Eds.), Abstract State Machines 2004. Advances in Theory and Practice. XII, 235 pages. 2004.

Vol. 3051: R. Berghammer, B. Möller, G. Struth (Eds.), Relational and Kleene-Algebraic Methods in Computer Science. X, 279 pages. 2004.

Vol. 3050: J. Domingo-Ferrer, V. Torra (Eds.), Privacy in Statistical Databases. IX, 367 pages. 2004.

Vol. 3049: M. Bruynooghe, K.-K. Lau (Eds.), Program Development in Computational Logic. VIII, 539 pages. 2004.

Vol. 3047: F. Oquendo, B. Warboys, R. Morrison (Eds.), Software Architecture. X, 279 pages. 2004.

Vol. 3046: A. Laganà, M.L. Gavrilova, V. Kumar, Y. Mun, C.K. Tan, O. Gervasi (Eds.), Computational Science and Its Applications – ICCSA 2004. LIII, 1016 pages. 2004.

Vol. 3045: A. Laganà, M.L. Gavrilova, V. Kumar, Y. Mun, C.K. Tan, O. Gervasi (Eds.), Computational Science and Its Applications – ICCSA 2004. LIII, 1040 pages. 2004.

Vol. 3044: A. Laganà, M.L. Gavrilova, V. Kumar, Y. Mun, C.K. Tan, O. Gervasi (Eds.), Computational Science and Its Applications – ICCSA 2004. LIII, 1140 pages. 2004.

Vol. 3043: A. Laganà, M.L. Gavrilova, V. Kumar, Y. Mun, C.K. Tan, O. Gervasi (Eds.), Computational Science and Its Applications – ICCSA 2004. LIII, 1180 pages. 2004.

Vol. 3042: N. Mitrou, K. Kontovasilis, G.N. Rouskas, I. Iliadis, L. Merakos (Eds.), NETWORKING 2004, Networking Technologies, Services, and Protocols; Performance of Computer and Communication Networks; Mobile and Wireless Communications. XXXIII, 1519 pages. 2004.

Vol. 3040: R. Conejo, M. Urretavizcaya, J.-L. Pérez-de-la-Cruz (Eds.), Current Topics in Artificial Intelligence. XIV, 689 pages. 2004. (Subseries LNAI).

Vol. 3039: M. Bubak, G.D.v. Albada, P.M. Sloot, J.J. Dongarra (Eds.), Computational Science - ICCS 2004. LXVI, 1271 pages. 2004.

Vol. 3038: M. Bubak, G.D.v. Albada, P.M. Sloot, J.J. Dongarra (Eds.), Computational Science - ICCS 2004. LXVI, 1311 pages. 2004.

Vol. 3037: M. Bubak, G.D.v. Albada, P.M. Sloot, J.J. Dongarra (Eds.), Computational Science - ICCS 2004. LXVI, 745 pages. 2004.

Vol. 3036: M. Bubak, G.D.v. Albada, P.M. Sloot, J.J. Dongarra (Eds.), Computational Science - ICCS 2004. LXVI, 713 pages. 2004.

Vol. 3035: M.A. Wimmer (Ed.), Knowledge Management in Electronic Government. XII, 326 pages. 2004. (Subseries LNAI).

Vol. 3034: J. Favela, E. Menasalvas, E. Chávez (Eds.), Advances in Web Intelligence. XIII, 227 pages. 2004. (Subseries LNAI).

Vol. 3033: M. Li, X.-H. Sun, Q. Deng, J. Ni (Eds.), Grid and Cooperative Computing. XXXVIII, 1076 pages. 2004.

Vol. 3032: M. Li, X.-H. Sun, Q. Deng, J. Ni (Eds.), Grid and Cooperative Computing. XXXVII, 1112 pages. 2004.

Vol. 3031: A. Butz, A. Krüger, P. Olivier (Eds.), Smart Graphics. X, 165 pages. 2004.

Vol. 3030: P. Giorgini, B. Henderson-Sellers, M. Winikoff (Eds.), Agent-Oriented Information Systems. XIV, 207 pages. 2004. (Subseries LNAI).

Vol. 3029: B. Orchard, C. Yang, M. Ali (Eds.), Innovations in Applied Artificial Intelligence. XXI, 1272 pages. 2004. (Subseries LNAI).